FREE GERMANY

*The National Committee and the*
*League of German Officers*

# FREE GERMANY

## The National Committee and the League of German Officers

*By* BODO SCHEURIG

*Translated from the German by*
HERBERT ARNOLD

WESLEYAN UNIVERSITY PRESS
*Middletown, Connecticut*

*To my father
and to the memory
of my mother*

# Contents

FREE GERMANY
*The National Committee and the*
*League of German Officers*

## Preface

WHEREAS those resistance groups that dared to become active against Hitler within Reich or Wehrmacht have found sympathetic treatment, the Free Germany movement has for the most part remained taboo. Even today it still arouses a defensive, passionate reaction that makes it impossible to write a sober treatment of it anywhere, be it in daily newspapers, magazines, or books. Even in trials, German courts have refused to accord the National Committee for a Free Germany and the League of German Officers the same recognition that is given to the resistance of July 20. The causes for these attitudes are only too comprehensible. Was not what one could celebrate as patriotic action in one case base betrayal in the other? Did not what was intended to save Germany from the worst in the former case betoken dishonorable aid of the enemy in the latter?

The time seemed riped for picking up these hotly debated questions without prejudice or resentment. The present book—a history of the Free Germany movement in the Soviet Union—is such an attempt. It is the result of years of research and is intended to present results which should be judged on their own merits, but which are also intended to stimulate an objective discussion.

Books on contemporary history are often open to the accusation that they are written without sufficient distance from their subject matter. Such accusers fail to see that temporal distance is no guarantee of objectivity. Such accusation is, therefore, basically, justified only if the historian has worked from insufficient source material.

I have not had access to material from Soviet archives. Personal communications of Communist witnesses could not be used either: their partiality would have grossly distorted many of the interrelationships between events. However, the mass of the material used in both Germany and the United States allowed the reconstruction of a basic outline; the communications of former members of the committee and the officers' union, now living in the West, began to round out the picture gathered from the documents. With the increasing number of communications from witnesses, the necessity of putting them into shape without delay increased. For the fresher the memories of the participants, the greater the chances for a study of the Free Germany movement seemed to be.

Some parts of the book are, however, still in need of emendation. I want to call upon all those witnesses who have until now refused to participate or who have remained unknown to help complete my researches through providing additional oral evidence and material. I shall, of course, include only such material (as I have done in the past) as relates to the National Committee and the League of German Officers in the Soviet Union. To treat irrelevant postwar developments or the Free Germany movement in other countries would be hardly meaningful and certainly premature. Their history is still shrouded in mystery and darkness, thus making necessary the deliberate limitation in subject matter of this study.

My thanks are due, finally, to all those who have courageously supported my labors. I would like to mention especially W. v. Seydlitz, H. Abel, A. Bredt, H. Graf v. Einsiedel, H. Gerlach, J. v. Puttkamer, W. Frhr. v. Senfft-Pilsach, and the late Theodor Plievier. The Library of Congress and the Hoover Library at Stanford gave valuable assistance. I am indebted to both those libraries, which magnanimously provided a considerable number of documents. A special word of thanks is finally due to my former teachers, Professors Herzfeld and Hofer. Without their understanding and sympathy the present book would probably never have come into being.

BODO SCHEURIG

*Berlin, Fall 1959*

## Preface to the Second Edition

FOR THIS second revised and expanded edition all the new material has been used that accumulated since the first edition was published and that relates to the subject matter of this book. Additional documents, publications, and statements have broadened the source base of this study. For all this I have to thank, once more, many people, including those who do not wish to be named as witnesses.

The criticism with which the first edition of my study was met in the Soviet Occupied Zone has caused me once more to ask a number of questions of some witnesses living in East Berlin and in East Germany. I did not receive any fruitful reply, although two of those witnesses had come forth as reviewers. Those who did answer merely substantiated my findings. None of them, unfortunately, was prepared to permit the use of his name in connection with his statement.

In substance the study remained unchanged, although some mistakes were corrected and additions made that had become necessary. The criticisms which had been voiced amid the general approval necessitated only a few changes in the basic conception of the book.

BODO SCHEURIG

Berlin, January 1961

## CHAPTER ONE

## Stalingrad

THE STORY of the Free Germany movement, an unusual organization behind Soviet barbed wire, started in a dark moment. Its inception is contained in the tragedy of the Sixth Army, which met its end at Stalingrad after a horrifying struggle.[1] Here in the pocket at the great bend of the Volga, within an exceptional human and military situation, there developed an attitude which was to break down all barriers set up by the military code of honor.

A revolution must have occurred within the German army if its soldiers denied in spirit and action the oath they had sworn to their head of state and Commander in Chief. Whatever it was, therefore, that had dared to question the foundations of an army that had been protected by a spirit of traditionalism deserves our attention especially with regard to its motivation. This kind of attention becomes especially pressing in our age of ideologies: its battles have a tendency to discard all ties together with moral values. Historical analysis must, therefore, treat the phenomenon of resistance first of all. There also remains the question of all those forces which attempted to re-establish the threatened order of state and society.

Events of revolutionary importance normally reveal their significance only to the retrospective eye. Thus to contemporaries the second summer of the Russian campaign held no hint of unusual future developments. When the Sixth Army was once again committed to battle in May of 1942, it differed from the other units of the German Army only by its reputation of outstanding bravery.[2]

Always fighting at the front lines, the Sixth Army had had a decisive part in the victory over Belgium and France.[3] In Russia, too, this army fought with distinction as part of Army Group South since June 22, 1941; its bravery was rewarded—after several crises—by the great victories of the battles of encirclement at Uman and Kiev. Victories of such scale created, not surprisingly (how could it be otherwise?), unbounded faith in their Supreme Commander. His image was so dazzling that the soldiers even came through the fateful Winter of 1941–1942 without any serious doubts about his abilities. It is therefore not surprising that the Sixth Army proceeded to storm ahead once more with unbroken spirit immediately after the brilliant defensive victory at Kharkov.

This time it had the order first to break through the enemy's front, together with the other units of Army Group B, and then to conquer the area between the Donetz and Don rivers.[4] Again it must have appeared as if leadership and soldiers of the Sixth Army had operated with exceptional luck. Severely shaken by the counterattack at Kharkov, the Russians put up only a little resistance while constantly retreating.[5] Even though these maneuvers were initially kept from a decisive outflanking movement or an encirclement, the army nevertheless was able to achieve a significant success at the Don by the middle of August 1942. It was here that the Russians stood to give battle before crossing the river at Kalach. The result was the annihilation of two Russian armies, which as a fighting force were almost equivalent to that of two German army corps.[6] Although the fighting in the steppes had been unusually fierce, the attack on Stalingrad, now ordered by Hitler, gave rise to the hope that the city on the Volga would also fall soon.[7]

This hope turned out to be false. After securing its flanks, the attacking Sixth Army was successful on the whole in throwing the bulk of the enemy back to the Volga and closing in on Stalingrad itself from the west, north, and south.[8] But the eastern bank of the mighty river remained firmly in Russian hands, and the attacking German divisions ran into a doggedly fierce resistance. What had initially begun as a swiftly progressing operation aimed at a decisive victory turned into an increasingly costly struggle for every yard of ground, for every house, and finally for every stone.[9]

This situation did not change significantly even after the concentrated attack on the center of the city in the first half of September. It is true that the southern part of Stalingrad fell and so did the center of town after a breakthrough.[10] But the troops, called on to fight beyond their powers for some time now, lacked the strength for additional offensive thrusts which could have decided the issue. More serious still: whereas the Russian defenders were reinforced during the ensuing hard fighting, the German divisions began to dwindle alarmingly.[11]

The alarming numbers of German casualties, which stood in no relation to the operational goals, the costly experiences of the winter battle of Moscow of 1941–1942—all those factors should have suggested a circumspect defense of Stalingrad in October 1942, especially in view of the over-all military situation. The German troops may have retained their unbroken spirit in the faith that it was here that essential decisions were to be won.[12] They may have turned back every Russian counteroffensive with very effective artillery support—as they did at the northern front barrier, which formed the continuation of the Don Army's right wing.[13] Nothing, however, could conceal their general exhaustion, which kept increasing because the OKH (General Headquarters) had not provided any reserves worth mentioning for the Sixth Army for a long time.[14] In addition, there was the exceptional massing of seven Russian armies at the Stalingrad front,[15] indicating a Soviet counteroffensive; that above all should have prohibited any further German attacks. The preparations for such a countermove had been diagnosed beyond any doubt in the northwest and the southeast, on both wings of the Sixth Army.[16]

Hitler was deaf to all warning indications; as far as he was concerned, the Red Army was too exhausted to launch any further attacks. He ordered the continuation of the offensive.[17] This disquieting order was a mockery of the forces that were to launch the attack. The Sixth Army did indeed receive a few weakened combat-engineer battalions via airlift. But the Sixth Army's High Command had to gather its reserves essentially out of its own battle-weary divisions. They had to be withdrawn gradually from other parts of the front before they could be deployed for the attack against the fortified and difficult northern sector of Stalingrad.[18]

The offensive operations went accordingly. They did not succeed in conquering the Russian-held parts of the city in one decisive thrust. Instead, the insufficiently renewed divisions were thrown into the attack separately and successively, each time allowing the Russian defenders to concentrate their numerical superiority on a narrow field of attack. After successfully storming the tractor factory and the gun factory, the strength of the decimated German troops finally gave out.[19]

With all this, the situation had essentially reached the stage which allowed the Soviets to attempt an encircling counteroffensive. In the late fall of 1942 the situation on all fronts practically demanded such a move. The Sixth Army had considerably exposed itself and had become locked with the enemy without any hope of a decisive success, all on the basis of an order from the highest quarters, which indicated growing irresponsibility. The Sixth Army held a point from which extremely overstretched and highly vulnerable flanks extended backwards; a fact which in itself held considerable danger. It might trigger unpredictable consequences unless the allied armies stationed in the critical sections of the front were properly armed for combat.[20] We cannot here enumerate in detail all the elements which had created this dangerous situation. Suffice it to say that now the error of judgment which had made the German leadership send their inadequate forces without sufficient flanking cover against both Stalingrad and the Caucasus took its toll.[21]

Thus came about what a megalomaniacal leadership had refused to acknowledge despite continuous warnings and worried criticism from the ranks of the Sixth Army. On November 19, 1942, the troops of the Russian Don front under Rokossovsky attacked from the beachhead of Kremenskaya, supported by the Stalingrad front of Yeremenko which battered the German lines south of the hotly contested city.[22] The thin lines of the Roumanian Armies dissolved under their massive impact. Isolated resistance here and there managed to slow down the Russian breakthrough without, however, being able to stop it. On November 22 the two Russian spearheads met at Kalach—the Sixth Army was cut off from its communications area.[23]

Although Hitler had ordered General Paulus to go into Stalingrad and to await further orders[24] before the encirclement was actually completed, the situation now required a bold decision. The Sixth Army was encircled and gravely endangered. A catastrophe of enormous scale was unavoidable, unless the German Supreme Command drew the inexorable conclusions from this situation without regard to losing face.

Paulus and his chief of staff did everything in their power to convince their Supreme Command of the seriousness of the situation. They knew that their army, which in fact amounted to two armies, containing as it did five corps staffs and twenty-two combat divisions, must not be allowed to freeze into immobility.[25] They had to fight their way back to a substantially reduced front line and to regain the all-important freedom of operation by renewing contact with the German lines that had been pushed back. The demands of strategy and tactics could only further highlight the situation of the directly threatened Sixth Army. Most of its commanders were of the opinion that a sufficient air supply of the encircled mass of troops was out of the question and any further delay therefore senseless. The possibility of forming an inner front within the pocket seemed nonexistent. Everything strongly suggested a liberating action. The breakthrough, which offered the best chance of quick success in the southwest, could not be delayed. It had to be pushed with all urgency as the way out of a situation fraught with overwhelming dangers.

It was, therefore, with full justification that Paulus asked for freedom of decision in a teletype message on November 22.[26] The situation had deteriorated so seriously since November 19 that a breakthrough was even more urgently suggested. Regarding his appraisal of the situation, Paulus also knew himself to be in full accord with his commanding generals, who had given their support to his radio message to Hitler either in person or via telephone.[27]

How much the expectations of the generals reflected also those of the soldiers was shown by the reactions and the attitude of the troops.[28] They had certainly been hit very hard, especially where they had had to bear the brunt of the Russian attacks. In some places their retreat had taken place under strong pressure. Morale and faith, however, had not been shaken. The soldiers followed their commanders in the faith that they would pry open the ring which had closed around them.

Paulus' radio message must have caused Hitler some awkward moments. Obsessed by the idea of holding Stalingrad at any price, the thought of withdrawal or of even an evasive action was unbearable for him.[29] Up to now the German soldier had always had to cling to his positions; he could never be allowed to leave the field to the enemy here in front of the city named after the Russian dictator. But Zeitzler, the new chief of staff, fought the battle of his life and gradually began to make headway with his opinion that it would be criminal to leave the Sixth Army in its deadly encirclement.[30] It was impossible to relieve the Sixth Army. If left encircled and immobile, it was condemned to death and starvation. The scales began to be weighted in favor of the Sixth Army; it received the communication to prepare the breakthrough. At this moment a fateful intervention took place. In the morning of November 24, Göring communicated through his chief of staff that the Air Force (Luftwaffe) could take over the task of supplying the encircled divisions. That decided the issue. For now Hitler seemed to have all the cards that enabled him to hold on to the chimera of an unconditional defense of Stalingrad.

It remained a decision the irresponsibility of which bordered on the criminal. Certainly, the voice of the "Reichsmarschall" carried some weight. Göring could be expected to know the potential of his air force and, therefore, to judge correctly whether it was sufficient to supply the Sixth Army with a daily minimum of 500 tons.[31] Yet did not the significance and scope of that decision, once taken, suggest a testing of its premises by the man who ultimately must bear the responsibility for it? Would not an objective testing of all factors have pointed to the conclusion that Göring's promises were meaningless? And would this not have suggested the necessity of an immediate breakthrough of the Sixth Army?

Nobody in Stalingrad had any idea what had happened at Hitler's headquarters. All the more violent was the shock when Hitler's radio message tied the twenty-two cut-off divisions to their positions with the remark that everything would be done "to supply them appropriately and to liberate them."[32] Paulus, who had every reason to believe that he had given a circumspect report of the situation, received the new order with resignation.[33] Other commanders seemed paralyzed by this order; not, however, Einigeln, the commanding general of the 51st Corps, who opposed the order to stand and fight. In a brilliant analysis General of the Artillery von Seydlitz, on the basis of his experiences in the Demyansk pocket, stressed the impossibility of getting adequate supplies by air.[34] He pointed out that the enemy knew the situation and would attack if only because the liberation units had been pushed far back and would only be able to attack again after time-consuming redeployment. Therefore, before they could be of any use to the Sixth Army, the latter would have used up its ammunition in its ordered "hedgehog position" and would thus have become defenseless. This, by itself, showed how essential a breakthrough was, and without delay. In this decisive hour nothing should keep the army's leadership from doing what reason and experience demanded of them. Going even further: "If the OKH does not immediately countermand its order to dig into our present positions, there arises for our conscience and before the army and the German people the *overruling* duty to assume the operational freedom denied to us by the present order and to make use of the still existing possibility of preventing the catastrophe by an attack of our own."[35] In words which plainly reflect the consciousness of a challenging exceptional situation, Seydlitz did not leave any doubt that the total annihilation of 200,000 fighting men was at stake. Only an immediate thrust through the enemy lines might save them.[36] Seydlitz's assessment of the situation, drawn up by his chief of staff but which the general bore responsibility for, was meant to stimulate and provoke action. To put pressure on Army Headquarters, the 51st Corps began to shorten its front, which seemed all the more expedient as everyone expected the order for the breakthrough attempt.[37]

Yet Paulus' decision was to be different: he decided in favor of the obedience Hitler had demanded of him.[38] Friedrich Paulus was no rebellious soldier possessing the will power or the toughness to get his way against all obstacles. Used only twice as a field commander in a brilliant career, he showed his mettle—apart from

personal bravery—especially as an educated officer of the General
Staff who strove for the right kind of decision with a high sense
of duty and great operational abilities. These characteristics occasionally gave less scrupulous persons palpable ascendancy over
him. No less typical were the scruples which paralyzed rather than
spurred bold action in the position of a field commander. Paulus
must have suffered under the Führer's orders both as soldier and
as a man, and his documented resignation testifies to the fact that
he suffered. For the military specialist the situation was still problematic: the army remained exposed to all kinds of dangers and
dependent upon a dubious aerial supply line. Seydlitz's assessment,
which had impressively summarized what the army had been unable to push through despite the concurring opinions of its commanding generals, must have reawakened nagging doubts.

Paulus, however, the commander in chief of an army, sworn to
obedience, was incapable of resistance to Hitler's orders, not merely
because of the chaos which would have been the consequence of
general disobedience. The man who was commanding more than
270,000 soldiers rarely had had any knowledge of the over-all strategic situation. Frequently, he had been informed only about his own
section of the front. This limiting state of affairs had made an independent decision difficult enough; but it must have been the
insistent reminders of Manstein and the OKH to think of the ad-
jacent units in the Caucasus which finally tied Paulus' hands. The
supreme command had ordered a holding of the Volga front as the
basis of its plan of operations. It had promised sufficient air support
and imminent relief by the Fourth Panzer Army, whose attack was
to turn the developing crisis into a victory. Those were the sober
tactical arguments which were to override all objections. The commander in chief of the Sixth Army was convinced that he and his
divisions had no right to assume that risks and sacrifices were
demanded of them without compelling reasons and dire necessity.

Paulus' decision could be based only—if at all—on this set of
considerations. Once taken, this decision demanded, in the situation the Sixth Army found itself in, unconditional perseverance
based on good faith because no other values could serve as inner
support. This obedience, ordered and rendered, also increased the

responsibilities of the Supreme Commander immeasurably. It was Hitler's decision that had brought this army to its present straits; it was, therefore, incumbent upon him to liberate it.[39]

So much for the attitudes of the leading soldiers who were plagued by doubts, worries, and bitterness. And how about the rank and file? They, too, had at first been gripped by a paralyzing fear when the order for the breakthrough had been refused after it had been promised, the order which had seemed to hold the greatest hope of meeting the crisis-laden situation.[40] But the soldier in combat normally is not given to considering strategic, let alone political, aspects for any length of time. The matter-of-fact obedience with which he dynamited or dug his foxholes at the edges of the pocket even here had its roots in the unquestioning faith in the Supreme Commander. This remained the uncontested premise without which any sacrifice would have become senseless. And new hopes had been raised, too. The fast-spreading news that Manstein would relieve the encircled divisions strengthened the fighters at Stalingrad and their battle lines.[41] The Sixth Army's conduct of operations, however, found itself under considerable pressure from the start. Not only did the finally completed formation of the defensive positions, which Hitler had laid down at his theoretical remove in such senseless fashion that many sections could only be held at the price of an exorbitant struggle, prove oppressive.[42] From the very beginning, developments also made it clear that it was out of the question to supply twenty-two divisions adequately by air. Despite the devoted efforts of the air force the daily average tonnage reaching Stalingrad was at best 80–120 tons.[43] Under these conditions it is not surprising that the strength of the troops deteriorated rapidly. By December of 1942 hunger and cold had already inflicted terrifying losses.[44]

The relief operation also ran into unexpected difficulties and looked increasingly bleak. Ever since Field Marshal von Manstein had succeeded to the command of the newly formed Army Group Don, the Russian counteroffensive on both sides of Stalingrad had also threatened Army Group A in the Caucasus with encirclement. After their defeats on the Don and in the southern steppes, the Italian and Roumanian armies—who had been left without heavy weapons until the very end, despite their entreaties—had pulled back so hastily that the Soviet attacks had gained territory at an alarming rate.[45] Once more, quickly gathered forces managed to set up a thin front at the lower Chir which denied the enemy possession of the all-important air bases for Stalingrad and the fatal breakthrough to Rostov. But it would only be a matter of time now before the failure of all German operations would be revealed.

Despite all that, Operation "Winter Gale" was risked after a troublesome gathering of a relieving army southwest of Stalingrad; it was risked in the knowledge that the pressured Sixth Army simply had to receive support. This knowledge also inspired the attacking troops. After they had formed themselves for the attack on December 12,[46] the impetus of the attack carried them closer and closer to the pocket, thanks to a flexible leadership. But even here delays and crises slowed down the advance. While the situation on the left wing of the army group grew increasingly menacing, the enemy continuously threw new troops from the encircling armies into battle to prevent contact between the relief divisions and the Sixth Army. The race between life and death had now reached its critical stage. This caused Manstein's request that Paulus be ordered to attempt a breakthrough towards the southwest.[47] Hitler, however, refused, despite the fact that the relief forces could not count on any additional reserves! Instead, he asked the commander in chief of these forces whether Stalingrad might not still be held once contact had been established.[48]

Strategical dilettantism on this scale could only compel Manstein on his part to inform the leadership of the Sixth Army of the general situation.[49] General Paulus was informed by an envoy that it had become doubtful, because of the critical situation on the left wing of Army Group Don, whether the relief forces would be able to reach the encirclement perimeter. They kept on running into additional Soviet forces. This did, on the other hand, increase the chances for a successful breakthrough of the Sixth Army. If it started the attack now, the enemy would find himself in a position which would certainly make it impossible for him to prevent the breakthrough of the encircled army. Of course, it had to reckon with the fact that now the divisions of the Sixth Army would have to cover a greater distance than before by continuous fighting. But this seemed to offer their only chance because in the opinion of the army group the insufficient supply by air would remain insufficient in the future. This ruled out any clinging to Stalingrad; it even made it look irresponsible.

Paulus seriously and thoroughly weighed these considerations. His chief of staff, Major General Schmidt, however, rejected them as a "catastrophic solution" (*Katastrophenlösung*). No operational arguments were able to shake his opinion. Thus the stronger personality won out over the more lucidly reasoning head: following Schmidt, General Paulus finally declared also that a breakthrough of the army was impossible.[50] This reaction betrayed a vacillating army command. Did not the very expression "catastrophic solution," occasioned by the weakened and largely immobile Sixth Army, reflect the actual situation? Indeed, Hitler's order for the unconditional defense of Stalingrad had hardly been necessary to highlight the results of his art of military leadership. It now became all the more disastrous as his decisions could become effective without amelioration or correction.

Disappointing as Manstein's contact with Paulus had been—unfortunately undertaken only through a staff officer—the former was nevertheless not yet discouraged. All it took, surely, to move the Sixth Army to a decision it did not yet want to take was a better starting position. On December 19 it seemed as if the decisive moment had come. Once again the relief divisions had successfully managed to advance fighting: hardly thirty miles separated them from the southern perimeter of the pocket.[51] But this was as far as they would get.

Even where the army group succeeded, with the help of a momentary stability on its left wing, to hold the positions reached for a while, it was clear that now the Soviets' resistance could be broken only by a simultaneous attack from inside the encirclement. Manstein, therefore, sent an urgent wire to the Supreme Command asking it to order the encircled divisions to break through now.[52] Hitler left the message unanswered—apparently under the insane delusion that he still had lots of time. Thus the army group on its own responsibility ordered the Sixth Army to prepare the breakthrough.

Paulus, however, was unable to overcome his reservations, just as any other commander would have had to mobilize his whole

abilities for bold decision to attack the Russian ring of encirclement. Manstein never authorized the breakthrough with the pre-
arranged code word "Thunderclap," let alone ordered it; thus Hitler's order to hold on to Stalingrad at any cost still stood.[53] It was
now the enormity of the risks above all else that throttled any liberating decision. Tied down at all points in the pocket and almost
immobilized, Paulus did not see any hope if it meant crossing
thirty miles. It was not only the weakened divisions and the serious
doubts that the forces intended for the breakthrough could be
withdrawn from their front sectors at all. Graver still was the
danger, inherent in a premature breakthrough undertaken against
express orders, that the army would bog down in the steppes, thus
signing its own death warrant. The issue was decided when
Paulus radioed that he had gasoline for only about twenty miles.[54]
Hitler, who had his own liaison officer inside the pocket and who
didn't want to withdraw from Stalingrad, felt justified. He forbade
the Sixth Army to move.[55]

With this the last chance for relief was lost. Although Manstein
left the relief forces in their dangerous positions for a few more
days, a growing crisis on the left wing of the army group forced
him to call off the operation on December 25.[56] What had so far
been prevented at great cost had now become reality: the enemy
had broken through the armies of Germany's allies and had also
pushed the German units into the maelstrom of retreat. If he
pushed on any farther, the fate of the entire southern wing of the
German front in Russia (Eastern Front) would be sealed. The
Sixth Army had ceased to be Manstein's chief problem. One by one
the relief divisions, pressed on several sides by violent Russian
onslaughts, fell back far beyond their original positions.

That General Paulus did not find his way towards the liberating decision for a breakthrough testifies to a personality more
doubting than daring, for whom revolt was out of the question.
If one were to judge the battle of Stalingrad solely from a military
point of view, this soldier above all others would have to bear considerable responsibility for its bitter end. As far as the psychological
developments are concerned, however, it remains decisive that,
tied to his immediate task by highest orders, he had acted with
the kind of obedience which the Supreme Commander had de-

manded from the beginning. Thus everything that from now on forms the palpable beginnings of the catastrophe must be laid at the door of Hitler himself. From this point of view, future events would reveal the dictator's personality and motives.

Events up to now had already revealed enough to destroy any illusions that the leaders of the Sixth Army may have had. The relief divisions had pulled back hastily and seemed unable to find any sort of foothold.[57] Air supply was hardly worth mentioning. Unless hundreds of planes could land inside the pocket every day, the fighting power of the army would be worn out only too soon. And even if they succeeded, against all expectations, in supplying the encircled divisions adequately, nobody could avoid the nagging question of whether relief might not come too late anyway. Thus General von Seydlitz's assessment of November had become reality in all its implications;[58] the operational timetable had been set up without regard to logistics. The contradictions between the two condemned the army to death.

Paulus and some members of his staff tried to cover up their resignation to the depressing situation by hectic activity. Now, Paulus' chief of staff quickly came to the fore, taking the place of his chief, who may have already guessed the whole scope of his misguided trust. It was Major General Schmidt in particular who mobilized the last defensive forces.[59] Since the army could hardly count on being liberated any more, it at least had to make a last stand and tie down enemy forces. Thus *Festungsbataillone* (special defensive units) were formed out of reserve units and units that had become partly dispersed or useless.[60] Their name was a mockery of their actual fighting strength, which remained negligible if only because the army's supply situation had not improved in the least.

As far as outward appearance was concerned, however, the name gave the illusion of confidence that had no basis in actual fact. Hitler himself contributed to and underscored this somber state of affairs. Addressing the commander in chief of the Sixth Army at the beginning of the year in a personal message that was neither passed down nor mentioned, he hailed the endurance of the Sixth Army as one of the most glorious feats in the annals of German military history.[61] Did not this expression, which had a depressing rather than an elevating effect, already presage the catastrophe of the twenty-two encircled divisions in a dubious apotheosis? On the whole, that is the way it was taken.[62]

None of the painful thoughts or feelings of the leadership, which suppressed its own rebelliousness, were allowed to filter through to the rank and file.[63] For months called upon to do the impossible, the army merely had to form the special defensive battalions. But it was mostly the rank and file that was hardest hit by the development of the fateful events. In a state of enormous tension, the troops feverishly awaited the breakthrough.[64] They had already seen the flares with which the advance columns of the approaching relief divisions communicated with each other.[65] But then the sound of the liberators' guns faded away without their being ordered to attack the encircling enemy ring, although they had been on the alert for the attack. This incomprehensible passivity resulted in a numbing paralysis. It gave rise to doubts, questions, and finally fear. But the soldier also sought refuge in promising slogans and in his faith, which convinced him that neither Hitler nor anyone else would ever sacrifice a whole army.[66] Thus the troops kept on hoping for Manstein, and they were once more convinced that they would soon be liberated when Hitler solemnly vowed in a New Year's message that the Sixth Army could rely on him one hundred per cent.[67]

Pronouncements of this sort managed to rekindle the encircled divisions' will to resist. They could now be justified by pointing out that the encouraging order of the day was designed to spur the Sixth Army to do everything possible to relieve the German southern wing, which was now fighting for survival.[68] None of that, however, could obscure the fact that Hitler's irresponsible promises were not backed by any real chance or by reality. Thus lies rewarded trust at a time when the superhuman efforts of the encircled army should have demanded the same sense of responsibility from its Supreme Command that it demonstrated by its continued fighting. Unjustified expectations and hopes had been raised. Would anything be able to temper the psychological bitterness if an already predictable negative outcome proved that everything that had been the only way to rationalize all the suffering was only a sorry deception? Here stands revealed the insufferable consciencelessness of Hitler, who thought he could demand anything from his soldiers.

But once more it appeared that the numbing inexorability of mass slaughter might be stopped. At the beginning of January 1943 the Soviets presented Paulus, who had meanwhile been promoted to Colonel General, with an ultimatum: pointing to the desperate situation of the Sixth Army, it demanded capitulation.[69]

The Russian offer could hardly overstate the German situation. When it was handed to Paulus in his command bunker, the encircled army was able to continue fighting only in a very limited sense—if at all.[70] Severe losses had taken a bloody toll among the troops. The survivors were weakened by hunger and barely withstood the bitter cold and the unbearable hardships.[71] The number of wounded had increased alarmingly; worse still, the protracted fighting in the pocket had made it increasingly impossible to care for them in any humane way. This negative balance sheet could be made only more terrible. And not only the troops had suffered alarming losses. Since the air supply had remained unsatisfactory, there were also shortages in fuel and ammunition.[72] Thus further successful resistance would become impossible if the army had to stave off another Russian offensive. The image of Soviet POW camps may have remained terrible despite all the assurances which the representative of the headquarters of the Red Army's Command had given;[73] but Paulus was open to the arguments of his opponents to such a degree that he now asked for a free hand, just in case.[74]

Hitler once more denied it: "Every additional day that the Sixth Army can hold out helps the entire front and ties down Russian divisions."[75] Even though this telegram no longer mentioned relief, it tied the encircled divisions to a task that Paulus thought they were obligated to fulfill. The Sixth Army rejected the Soviet ultimatum.[76]

The result was the Russian offensive of January 10, 1943. When the Soviet divisions attacked the northwestern, western, and southern fronts of the pocket after two hours of preparatory barrages from five thousand guns,[77] the hopelessly outnumbered German forces had to give way. The agony of the Sixth Army had reached its climax. The pocket, which had been thirty miles long and twenty-five miles wide when the offensive began, shriveled up. Desperate resistance might still hold off some of the attacking Russian units, which could afford to operate cautiously for a while;[78] once the western and northern segments of the circle had been smashed and the all-important air base of Pitomnik had been captured on January 16, all organized resistance had ceased to exist.[79]

The stage had darkened forever and nothing would brighten it again. With concentrated forces the Russian attack had brought about the end of the encircled army. Everywhere the remnants of the German divisions flooded back into the burnt-out ruins of Stalingrad, except those that had been completely routed.[80] Disorder and panic began to spread. Even in those areas where fighting continued, it was only out of a numbing acceptance of death and suffering. Many thousands had been killed in action. Thousands continued to die daily. In addition there were the innumerable victims of cold, hunger, and, last but not least, of untended wounds. By the middle of January there were 50,000 who continued to vegetate in unspeakable misery.[81] The slaughter could not be heightened any more, yet it kept bringing forth regulations and orders that could only have been inspired by desperation and insanity, totally unrelated to the soldiers' world.[82] Lines of defense were laid down that the enemy, swiftly following through, had long since taken; units and matériel that existed only on the maps of staff officers were reshuffled. And behind it all there remained in force for every trench and every foxhole the chimera of the order "To the last bullet," an order which the leaders and such troops as had again managed to survive disregarded the very moment the enemy proved to be superior. Certainly, there still occurred astonishing acts of individual valor in which an unreal faith and a sense of duty, pushed to its ultimate limits, shone for the last time. Apart from these, the limits of human endurance had, however, been so obviously surpassed that the now hopeless situation within the pocket called only for a delivering decision.

Together with the incomprehensible visions of an apocalyptic collapse, Stalingrad had also revealed the problematic nature of military obedience to its fullest inescapable extent. Defeats could be coped with in the soldiers' minds as long as they were inflicted by an enemy who simply proved himself superior in the cold strug-

gle of opposing forces. But here all the conditions had been eliminated under which a fight could have been fought with dignity.
Here an army struggled in a position whose hopelessness was surpassed only by the inhumanity of the order to defend it at any
price. If this fanatical task already presupposed a state of mind
that contradicted all traditional notions, then the eventual coming
of the catastrophe must further expose a conscienceless and fum-
bling leadership. It was now in the neighborhood of death the re-
vealer that it uncovered its amorality; it was cursed times without
number.[83]

Could these painful reactions leave the state and its ideology,
as represented by the National Socialist leadership, completely
untouched? Impossible, if only because Hitler had never tired of
insisting that Germany and National Socialism were one and the
same. Thus the battle of Stalingrad became an important test case;
the catastrophe that was finally decreed for the Sixth Army revealed the state to be incomparably violent and demonic.[84] It
forced many soldiers to the shocking recognition that this state
worshiped only the Leviathan of soulless power, a power which
seemed to have no feeling for the rape of human life or dignity.
Even where this profound experience did not bring about the
recognition that the National Socialist system had to go, at least
the numb sensation that one was the victim of serious mistakes and
misleading ideas became the dominant feeling.[85]

Did these insights provide a way out? The leading soldiers
could, of course, reaffirm their oath by unconditionally placing
orders above all else, thus standing by an attitude and using it, as
it were, to exonerate themselves. But to what avail? The fact that
Hitler had shamefully shirked his moral responsibilities toward his
troops and his people changed this attitude into something grotesque and irresponsible.[86]

Having to experience Stalingrad had, from the beginning, been
monstrous to the high-ranking commanders. But the greatest bitterness lay in the collapse of the world of those who had been brought
up to live their military code of behavior with devotion.[87] And the
unprecedented collapse became daily more apparent. Indeed, the
more painfully the fighting was drawn out, the more obvious it
became. For the dissolution of all standards had a thousand faces.

It was reflected in the visible and nameless situations of the struggle and it found its climax in the desolate last-ditch fighting of those who had nothing left for which they could willingly die.

Above even these chaotic pictures there might still be a shred of belief here and there that Hitler could not possibly allow a whole army to die miserably;[88] all thinking soldiers realized now that the Sixth Army was going to its death with its hopes dashed and its faith betrayed. They were now forced to accept the idea that it was no longer possible to obey—although obedience must be the basis of every army if lack of independence and of conscience are not to triumph as unsoldierly virtues.[89]

The inner turmoil into which events had plunged both the officers and men of the encircled divisions must have particularly troubled Paulus. Despite this, he and his chief of staff still did everything they could to ask, through their envoys, for any help that might still be available.[90] Captain Behr pointed out the true situation inside the pocket, first at Manstein's headquarters and later at Hitler's. But what good could his blunt language do? And what use were the orders to the combat-engineer commander Colonel Selle, when he was flown out of the pocket, to do everything in his power to see to it that the leadership of the Wehrmacht be put back on a realistic basis again?[91] All these adjurations remained pointless because the preconditions for their success no longer existed. On the one hand, the troops that might have freed the encircled and dying divisions were fighting far from Stalingrad to prevent their own encirclement. On the other hand, the Luftwaffe—tied down in all theaters of the war—had found it impossible to fly in even one-third of the required minimum daily supplies ever since the beginning of the encirclement. Now, with the loss of the air bases inside the pocket, regular supplies were to cease altogether. This fact could not be changed by appointing Field Marshal Milch as the Führer's special plenipotentiary for the aerial supply of Stalingrad.[92] If anything, the appointment underscored the dire facts.

Thus for the last time the leadership of the Sixth Army bestirred itself to some sort of decision. Colonel General Paulus invited all available commanders to a conference, hoping that they would approve his sending Hitler a radio message in which he planned to request that senseless resistance be ended.[93] The drama was drawing to a close. Any military objective for which the Sixth Army might have been asked to continue fighting had become illusory because its fighting ability was exhausted.[94] Since the Soviet attack of January 10, 1943, the encircled divisions had been unable to tie down any large portion of the enemy's fighting strength.[95] This was testified to by the fact, even apart from the considerably reduced pocket, that the Russian units, which must have known about the Sixth Army's order not to break out, could be sure of their victory in any case. Everywhere the Russians could dictate the course of events and it was only because they now, quite rightly, avoided pointless risks that they had not swiftly smashed the encircled divisions, despite their deep penetrations. Inside the pocket the hardships and death that visited all divisions were frightening. The troops, which had long since ceased to look anything like soldiers, had neither food nor ammunition. The air bases of Pitomnik and Gumrak had been captured; all discipline had apparently disintegrated when the last German planes left. A unified command structure had ceased to exist. The army could prevent neither dissolution nor defeat by deciding to continue fighting in the fields of rubble that were Stalingrad. The wire that Paulus sent to Hitler on January 20 once more depicted the scenes of horror inside the pocket. It now also requested immediate permission to capitulate in order to save human lives.[96]

No one whose sense of empathy had not completely disappeared could now have refused the Sixth Army its last request. Especially since its resistance had exceeded the wildest expectations and had been upheld by its faith in a relief operation—a faith that had been rekindled again and again. Even Manstein now recommended capitulation—Manstein who had always demanded that the Sixth Army stand and fight for the sake of his own hard-pressed army group.[97] Paulus' request was, nevertheless, based on erroneous assumptions. He apparently wanted to reaffirm his obedience. His previous experiences should have made clear to him, however, the impossibility of asking Hitler, of all people, for permission to capitulate. On the contrary: the inexorable outcome at Stalingrad suggested that an independent decision to end the enormous death toll would have to be made, because permission to surrender could have only theoretical significance as far as both ethical and military points of view were concerned.

This realization was amply justified by Hitler's negative answer, which reached Colonel General Paulus during the night of January 20–21, an answer which also showed an abnormal, even cynical, lack of conscience. Incapable of visualizing the atrocity of the fighting in the pocket despite forceful descriptions, Hitler again ordered resistance to the last bullet.[98] Once again the now meaningless explanation that enemy troops had to be tied down was used to mask his deep-seated aversion to seeing an army of the Third Reich surrender to the enemy.

Hitler's answer unleashed the deep resentment of the senior officers inside the pocket.[99] This resentment, however, did not prevent either Paulus or his chief of staff from continuing to obey Hitler's directives unconditionally. The resigned commander in chief had failed to take advantage of the only chances to save his army in November and December 1942. On both occasions he had bowed to higher orders for powerful reasons. Now his desperate and slavish obedience to Hitler's orders violated any military code of conduct. Perhaps this insistence on an order designed to save the whole southern front from the fate of the Sixth Army had spurred the divisions dying of hunger and cold to renewed resistance in a few places. But reality, which permitted only the question of how things would end, was more powerful. It left open only one possibility—of permitting the dissolution of all values to grow to insufferable proportions.

The final phase inside the pocket of Stalingrad revealed with numbing inexorability that without a firmly based moral and political sense of responsibility the soldier and his world were condemned to die a miserable death. The order was to fight to the last ditch.[100] On the basis of this order the leadership of the army acted ruthlessly, except where total exhaustion or complete chaos made it impossible. Special "mopping-up units" (*Aufgreifkommandos*) rounded up soldiers who had lost their units and were caught with a few ounces of bread in their pockets; special courts-martial tried to shore up a cracking discipline with numerous death sentences.[101] Last lines of defense were improvised, and even the sick and wounded were ordered to man them. Instead of heavy weapons, slogans were supposed to help in the defense against an enemy who could deploy himself, regroup, and attack without interference. Where isolated battalions or regiments ceased to fight, either because they were exhausted or overwhelmed by the Soviet troops, other defenders were ordered to shoot at their own comrades. Heitz, a corps commander, topped even this order by an order of the day in which every passage contained the lapidary phrase "Anyone who . . . will be shot."[102] Unofficially the Army High Command attempted to define certain rules of honorable conduct. According to them it was equally honorable to attempt a breakthrough, to kill oneself with one's own weapon, or to become a prisoner of war.[103] Chaos was complete. As the battle slowly died down, one saw inflexible military conduct side by side with desperate suicide, hoping against hope, and hate-filled curses for Hitler.[104]

Paulus did nothing. Fits of independent activity were primarily directed against any plan that meant to end the madness of fighting. Thus on January 25 General von Seydlitz believed that he would be able to persuade the Sixth Army's commander in chief to capitulate in an orderly fashion.[105] When Paulus rejected this demand, the general told him that he would now act on his own responsibility. He ordered his division to use up its ammunition and then to stop fighting—with the result that he was relieved of his command and his arrest was contemplated.[106]

Before it came to that, however, the enemy enforced what the German leaders had been unable to decide upon despite their better knowledge. During the night of January 27, 1943, Soviet attacking columns smashed the western front of the Stalingrad pocket.[107] Massive and concentrated artillery preparation of devastating force opened the way for a spearhead of tanks which split the Sixth Army in two, forming a northern and southern pocket. The final surge of resistance seemed to demonstrate the kind of heroism that Hitler wanted in order to be able to strike a note of provocative pathos in both press and radio. It also served as background for numerous decorations and promotions and, finally, for Göring's Leonidas speech, which expressed the incompetent leaders' gratitude to the army they had betrayed.[108] In Stalingrad this whole revolting spectacle was met with the contempt that it deserved.[109]

For in the shrunken pockets which lay under continuous Russian fire, suffering and death had once more reached such a pitch that no justification for it could be sufficient. It was also a unique event in world history: those soldiers who had not starved to death or been killed in action listened to their own funeral oration.

On January 31 the fate of Army Group South was finally sealed in the rubble of Stalingrad. Colonel General Paulus capitulated after having been promoted to Field Marshal at the last minute.[110] Although he swore in his messages that the Sixth Army would obey faithfully and devoutly to the bitter end, he did not himself seek the kind of death that Hitler wanted him to and hoped to inspire him to by the quick promotion.[111] On the contrary, instead of ordering his army to discontinue further resistance, Paulus himself surrendered, together with his staff and the guards that had been stationed in Red Square.[112] The surrender took place without formalities. The bitter death that had been ordered so irresponsibly at the end hit only the front-line soldiers. Their leaders, who had first obeyed and then simply acted without dignity, had chosen an undignified exit; by making a mockery of the kind of conduct they had so often demanded, they lost face.

This finale was so incomprehensible that it had the effect of a last judgment of the soldiers' own code of conduct; it struck the troops with lethal force.[113] Their belief and trust had so often been called upon in an unparalleled situation that it seemed incredible that it should all have gone for naught. When the Russians reached the last bunkers and trenches, the surviving German soldiers fell prey to profound bitterness. Until now the sense of duty, pushed to its extreme limits, had upheld them. Now, after it was unscrupulously abused, the only possible psychological attitude was to negate everything that yesterday had seemed inviolable.

Two days after the southern pocket capitulated, the northern pocket followed suit. On February 2, 1943, after violent artillery barrages, the Russian tanks rolled toward the tractor factory occupied by cut-off divisional remnants without encountering return fire.[114] All strength to resist had been exhausted. Colonel General Strecker, who had obeyed Hitler's orders to stand and fight to the very end, stopped the senseless bloodshed at the insistence of his commanders.[115]

The Battle of Stalingrad was over. Twenty-two divisions together with considerable portions of the entire German field artillery and of the Army Pioneers had died a miserable death.[116] Far
more than 100,000 soldiers out of approximately 270,000 had been
killed.[117] More than 90,000 now became Russian prisoners of war,
freezing and almost starved to death.

Every major defeat demoralizes the vanquished and reduces
his substance. But to the survivors what had happened in the
pocket of Stalingrad did not seem at all comparable to one of those
setbacks that occur in all wars and that testify to the fickle fortunes
of war.[118] The result of this military event was much more depressing and catastrophic. It not only revealed an unexampled violation
of the moral base of all human and military qualities; it also tore
the mask from the face of a political order for which men had
fought at Stalingrad—whether they had done so consciously or not.

Like all true soldiers, the officers and men of the Sixth Army had
their roots in obedience. Obedience had shaped the essence of their
world; it was something to live by in the self-evident conviction
that there was good faith on both sides. Out of this spirit of obedience were born authority, excellence, and a sense of duty, not to
mention bravery and strength under stress. Hitler, and with him the
Supreme Command, had abused these virtues to an incredible degree. They had ordered a whole army to allow itself to be encircled and, after the attempt to relieve it—questionable from the
start—had failed, had ordered it senselessly destroyed. The decision was irresponsible because it put an irrelevance—prestige—
above unavoidable operational necessity. The result of the decision
stamped it as criminal. By giving orders to stand and fight until the
end, the leaders denied, on the one hand, that the human and
military conditions for fighting on in Stalingrad had long since
ceased to exist. They showed, on the other hand, a cynical contempt for humanity by making, until the end, unrealistic and
ultimately mendacious promises to troops fighting under untold
hardships. In principle this had become more or less apparent to
every responsible and intelligent soldier of the Sixth Army ever
since the encirclement began. Even when they did not manifest
their opposition by protesting, they had to struggle against their
own nagging doubts, often, indeed, even against sentiments of

open rebellion. With their upbringing and breeding, however, they could not believe that the Supreme Command would deny its moral responsibility, without which no true profession of arms seemed conceivable, even under the conditions of catastrophic collapse. They therefore continued to obey. As a result, the order to obey to the bitter end raised Hitler's irresponsibility to abnormal heights. The force of events undermined all concepts of honor and obedience, since unquestioning loyalty had been rewarded by shameless betrayal. The soldiers of Stalingrad were not only deprived of a military way to react; as the battle raged on until all bonds were dissolved and only men without any ties and in profound despair were left, even an honorable soldier's death had become impossible. The soldier was chosen merely to destroy his world and himself completely, with satanic inevitability. Following the highest orders, he eliminated, as it were, himself.

This development was unique and overwhelming. Wherever more than a numb resignation prevailed, searching questions as to its causes perforce arose. Many survivors of the Sixth Army began to ask such questions and to view the path that Germany had followed up to this point as politically and militarily wrong.[119] Their soberness also included the hard-won conviction that they could not believe that the sacrifices they had made in the pocket on the Volga were important for either their people or their country. It was fairly clear that Stalingrad reflected senseless and certainly avoidable mistakes of leadership. The annihilation, under orders, of numerous divisions revealed the face of a political power of terrifying amorality, and this vision was the decisive experience. This power had shown itself in all its naked self-centeredness; people caught a glimpse of its past and future potential. What was stirred up here ultimately permitted only two possible reactions: either to stay free of political entanglements after these ghastly events or to fight against the inhuman conduct of politics and war.

This conclusion should not surprise anyone; it is even less surprising when we consider that the deliberate condemning to death of more than a hundred thousand men had made a mockery of any moral code. There was no goal that could justify or demand such a sacrifice. Both military considerations and humane moral sensitivity were in agreement on this issue. That was already shown by the traditional ethics by which an intact German military establishment had rightly felt bound. It also became apparent that the loss of the Sixth Army was not compensated for by any gain that decisively influenced the course of the war and that might have provided the authority for a broader responsibility. The encircled divisions at Stalingrad had certainly tied down considerable enemy forces initially and had thus relieved the German southern wing, which was fighting for survival. But just as this task had above all thrown a searing spotlight on the amateurish strategy of Hitler, the ability of the Sixth Army to hold out, which became less and less important to the enemy, did not bring about a German victory in the southern sector of the Russian front. On the contrary; since the twenty-two divisions on the Volga were ultimately needed by the German leadership, it eventually took the unbroken genius of a Manstein to escape an even greater defeat.[120] As the last resistance died out in Stalingrad, the divisions of the German southern wing were themselves forced to fight against being encircled and annihilated as they were hotly pursued. This stamped the Battle of Stalingrad, which had precipitated this disastrous development, as a well-nigh crushing catastrophe. After the Sixth Army's fighting power was eliminated, it spelled additional, unforeseeable material, moral, and, therefore, also political losses. Didn't these losses reinforce the conviction that Stalingrad was a defeat of exceptional proportions? Even more: didn't they and their consequences reveal that the war had reached a turning point after which there would be no more victories for Germany?

Although later successes of German military art tended to obscure this realization, no triumph could eradicate the memory of the disaster on the banks of the Volga. To the survivors of the Sixth Army, Hitler and the Supreme Command had shown themselves in such a light as to condemn themselves, morally and politically. Their criminal attitude had to be judged not as an accident but as the expression of a law that had essential significance. All this, and the experience of seeing several thousands of German soldiers die, necessarily gave rise to the idea that Stalingrad presaged the collapse of National Socialism. It also awakened the firm belief that Hitler would inflict the fate of the Sixth Army on the entire German nation should the war prove lost, which now seemed a real possibility. How real such worrisome visions were is shown by General von Seydlitz's words, spoken while still inside the pocket: "Stalingrad is Berezina squared. Germany will be Stalingrad squared!"[121]

"For Germany, against Hitler" was the slogan that the same general had thought about earlier as an answer to the unparalleled challenge that lay in the events of Stalingrad.[122] His moral outrage could hardly have lessened now that the full extent of the enormity of the catastrophe had become apparent. The continuity of the military world, which had been smashed in Stalingrad, where every soldier had become ensnared in guilt, made deliberate rebellion imperative. And above all there was the intolerable idea that an irresponsible régime would continue to govern the affairs of the Reich.

Soviet imprisonment might well quickly kill off all the impulses born out of the bitter experience, bury the testimony of the survivors of this betrayed army. And their testimony was that hundreds of thousands had been sacrificed for highly questionable goals, and hence it was imperative to act against a ruinous régime before it could unscrupulously ruin the people and the nation. Deep down, however, this will to resist somehow continued to live. If an appropriate organizational form could be found, it might even be mobilized behind barbed wire, which until now had always spelled one kind of end to war. For what the German soldier, from field marshal to private, had been asked to endure at Stalingrad remained so exceptional that equally exceptional reactions could be expected of him.

## CHAPTER TWO

## The Founding of the National Committee and the League of German Officers

THE SOVIETS must have sensed something of the changed inner attitudes of the Sixth Army's survivors and must have decided to put it to future use. For even though they wallowed in the stupefying intoxication of victory that often follows an important triumph, they could hardly fail to recognize that the generals, officers, and soldiers of the Stalingrad pocket offered new possibilities for their propaganda. The impetus for their activities certainly did not come from the destruction of the Sixth Army, which remained pointless even where it had exacted an enormous toll of blood from the Russians. It was probably born out of the recognition that up to now all attempts to influence the Germans on the front lines had generally failed.

Propaganda that aimed at undermining the fighting power or even the unity of the German Wehrmacht had been used by the Soviets since the beginning of the war in the east.[1] As an essential part of a struggle that was interpreted also as a struggle of ideologies, propaganda had at first been in the hands of the 7th Section of the Red Army's Central Political Administration. But it was also carried on to an ever-increasing degree by German émigrés who had found political asylum in the Soviet Union in 1933 and later.

The position of Pieck, Ulbricht, Ackermann, Florin, Matern, and others was very strange indeed.[2] All of them being captive minds, sworn to their Marxist doctrines, they had not taken their defeat as leaders of the KPD (Communist Party of Germany) by Hitler as a warning to re-evaluate their views fundamentally. It seemed to them that history had taught the rest of the German people a lesson because of its unforgivable mistakes. This inflexible and self-righteous reaction must certainly have seemed inevitable to these convinced party bureaucrats, but it also nipped in the bud any movement toward fruitful activity. The Communist concept of truth protected them from all doubt and even prevented all important ideas from reaching their conscious minds. Criticism and self-criticism were, of course, demanded of them where imaginary or real deviations from the party line were concerned. But as it was part of toeing the party line to be incapable of an objective analysis of events—especially in the non-Soviet world—all the discussions remained meaningless and sterile.

There was no forum that could contradict the official ideal visions of political thinking which suppressed any kind of intellectual independence. The theory of the class struggle by which the émigrés had lived and continued to live on highest orders had become the touchstone of their loyalty and reliability. Therefore, they increasingly destroyed their own ability to keep up intellectually with the rapid development of events.

The longer the Russian exile lasted, the deeper became the chasm between the Communists and Germany. This alienation may have been inevitable; under Stalin's dictatorship it became ever more disastrous. Ruthless and absolutist as it was, it tried to eliminate any political influence not its own. The insane purges of the *Yezhovshehina* and the incredible German-Soviet Non-Aggression Pact were the events which finally broke the backs of the Communist émigrés.[3] If they were not snuffed out, then they were forced into decisions they were hardly able to cope with despite their inbred party discipline. Frightened about possibly becoming the victims of intellectual "errors," the surviving émigrés finally tended to hymn panegyrics of the Bolshevist state, which were as harmful as they were foolish. Thus the incongruency of ideal and reality grew to immeasurable dimensions in the merciless Russian exile.

For while in Moscow men like Pieck and Ulbricht held fast to their doctrines, once they had been accepted, as if criticism of them were unthinkable, an almost diametrically opposed development took place in Hitler's Germany. There *the class struggle* and *internationalism* had ceased to be formative concepts in politics, let alone concepts relevant for the future. It was the hour of national revival, and it had its own legitimate problems and was accepted by the majority.[4] Even if this position hid secret goals linked tragically with each other and intended to unmask National Socialism, good faith and upbringing first elevated National Socialism to the highest position. That was especially true for the brief span of peace after 1933, which witnessed the restrengthening of Germany. It was even true for the war, whose intoxicating initial successes seemed to promise security for a Reich that had grown in power and size.

It is hard to imagine motives more varied than the ones which here pushed or were pushed toward historical realization. The propaganda with which the Red Army and the Communist émigrés attempted to influence the advancing German troops manifested, therefore, a spirit of ghostly unreality.[5] It tried to convince the German soldiers of the international solidarity of all workers—something that ought to make it impossible for the Wehrmacht to bleed or die for the interests of capitalism. It called upon the soldiers to hate their officers and to desert the flags of slavery and culminated by praising the Soviet Union as the true fatherland of liberty for whose sake it was imperative to reject all oppression.[6] The tone and tenor of this propaganda was of the past and spoke to people who no longer existed. As soon as the obtrusive indoctrination ceased, other leaflets came fluttering down on the German lines; they wished to create the impression, rather forcedly, that Soviet POW camps were like paradise.[7] The incredible intellectual world of this propaganda, which was in any case belied by the experience of Russia; its unbearable pathos, which provoked revulsion by its wild exaggerations and insulting accusations; and, finally, the obvious mendacity of the assurances in the face of proved atrocities against German POWs—all of this condemned the agitation of the Soviets and the émigrés to ineffectuality. Even if its standards had been higher, it still would not have achieved any results worth mentioning. The German soldier who fought in the vastness of Russia in 1941–1942 certainly had not gone into the campaign fearlessly, even if he believed that Germany had been threatened. But on the whole he fought with a firm faith in his leadership, elated by the proud knowledge of victories already won, and convinced of the mission of the Reich, which to him had become the leading power in Europe.[8] The German soldier had as yet hardly been confronted with atrocities and persecutions. Even in the Soviet Union he took the exultation with which he was greeted in the beginning in many cities and villages of the Baltic States and the Ukraine as a happy sign and to have a genuine ring.

The shoddiness of the propaganda must have become obvious to some of the émigrés. This was especially brought about by experiences with the few deserters from the Wehrmacht. Despite this experience, however, any doubts they might have had were suppressed, and they merely tried, with increased pressure, to achieve among the POWs what they could not bring about *vis-à-vis* the German fighting soldier. Here, too, they met with catastrophically disappointing results.[9] Although they were successful in forming the first anti-fascist activist groups, the rate of conversions remained exceedingly small. Here in the POW camps the old slogans had the same sobering and frightening effect that they had had back at the front,[10] and the platitudes likewise were equally repellent. No serious discussion of the situation was attempted in the camps because the prejudices of the Russians and the émigrés made it too dangerous. Every debate would have shown only that the POWs continued to believe faithfully in the German cause. Whoever wanted to make any progress against such attitudes had to employ methods quite different from those of propagandist hard sell.[11]

Behind barbed wire unaccustomed corruption was added to all this. Not only were many repelled by the regrettable practice of visibly terrorizing or putting pressure on those unwilling to be converted, but other prisoners were forced into icy rejection when they saw the converts rewarded with higher rations.[12] Russian practices as revealed here were especially out of place in the POW camps. First, conversions rewarded by ostentatious perquisites remained contemptible and incredible to the German mentality. Second, the desolate camps, difficult conditions of work, and gnawing hunger had long ago rendered the German prisoners indifferent. Incapable of positive or negative reactions, they generally supported any "resolution" the Russians suggested in the hope of escaping yet another ideological indoctrination campaign. As a rule, this is how the Communist recruiters scored their first propaganda "successes."

Walter Ulbricht was second to the infamous Commissar Wagner[13] as an exponent of these psychologically unsound campaigns. On October 8, 1941, he had staged a compulsory meeting at Camp 27. He succeeded in getting 158 prisoners to sign a prepared manifesto.[14] The overdone Marxist terminology, which drew a turgid picture of the fighting in the Soviet Union, could attract only NCOs and privates. There were not very many German officers who had been taken prisoner before the catastrophe of Stalingrad whose names alone might have influenced the prisoners; in any case, they would not have succumbed to propaganda, assuming that their names would have been of interest to the Russians and émigrés in 1941–1942.[15]

It certainly took intellectual independence to refuse to allow one's thoughts and reflections to be infected by the general lethargy in the camps. Thus the officers' group founded by Captain Ernst Hadermann in May 1942 clearly divorced itself from those anti-fascists whom Wagner and Ulbricht thought they had won over.[16] Dr. Hadermann, a college professor from Kassel, had been captured by the Russians early in 1941 as commander of an artillery unit. A humanist, he had always openly opposed National Socialism. The events of 1941 had convinced Hadermann that Germany could no longer win the war—especially under a Hitler. Under his leadership, Hadermann thought, even a tolerable peace seemed to have become more than uncertain. He was farsighted enough to recognize that the often discussed Communist danger was a real problem. But just as he felt himself increasingly justified by events, he also believed that German and Russian interests were identical, at least for the time being. Hadermann's ideas did not come out of either torture or blackmail. He was a man of acknowledged personal integrity and his ideas were the insights of a man who was used to thinking and acting independently. It speaks well for the Russians that they appreciated these circumstances and permitted him an unusual demonstration with his leaflet "How Can We End the War? The Honest Word of a German Captain."[17] The manifesto demonstrated his profound concern about the entire situation. It was an impressive settling of accounts with National Socialism, whose war and political objectives demonstrated its arrogance. He was quite obviously serious when he implored the German people and the Wehrmacht to end a fight which threatened to destroy Germany. Hadermann's analysis of a nation enchained by Hitler showed an astonishing objectivity; it clearly and believably showed that all Hadermann wanted was a Reich of liberty and of spiritual dignity. It probably took a good deal of soul-searching on the part of the Russians to allow Hadermann so much freedom of expression. But it made it possible for him to write with a tone that was completely different from the wooden phraseology of the usual propaganda; and this was indeed significant.

But Hadermann was no more successful than the émigrés; he failed and was boycotted.[18] Even the manifestos and leaflets with which he and the émigrés had tried to influence the troops in the Stalingrad pocket had no effect. Hope for relief, fear of being taken prisoner by the Russians, and finally Ulbricht's dogmatic propaganda ensured that any appeal to the entrapped defenders at Stalingrad would be ineffectual.[19]

The total failure of all their efforts had become obvious and forced the Russians to try a different propaganda approach. At first it was uncertain what form it would take, but it was inevitable that changes would have to be made. The defeat of the Sixth Army at Stalingrad provided the appropriate opening. More than 2,000 officers had fallen into Soviet hands, together with 91,000 German soldiers. To Moscow these officers represented a massive concentration of German intelligentsia. If an improved type of propaganda was to be employed through them, then certain elements at least had to be quickly won over with different methods from those that the Antifa (Anti-Fascist United Front) had hitherto used. It may be wrong in this context to imply that there was a clearly conceived Russian plan. In any case, the Russians certainly considered the 2,000 officers an asset that they were determined to utilize.

This is shown by the circumspection the Russians observed after their triumph.[20] Field Marshal Paulus, twenty generals, and a considerable number of other officers were not subjected to the usual hardships of POW camps. The victors spared them the encounter with a reality that might have destroyed any openness of mind that they had. The excruciating death marches were replaced by a special train which transported them to Krasnogorsk near Moscow under fairly humane conditions.[21] The psychological effect of this train ride was immense and revealed itself fully only much later; for while this treatment produced incredulous surprise among the top echelons of the Sixth Army, the enlisted men who survived were driven into an attitude of bitter resistance by the thousands of deaths accompanying their march into the drab forced labor camps.[22]

The special train had protected the high officers from all hardships. Now, tolerable quarters were cause for further surprise.[23] The bulk of the 2,000 officers found itself quartered in isolated officers' camps at Oranky, Yelabuga, and Susdal. Some of the camps were deliberately set up as so-called model camps. They had facilities for sports(!) and decent libraries; and, in June 1943, the officers were put on a special recuperation diet in order to restore them to health.[24] All commissioned officers were also relieved of any kind of work inside and outside the camps; this measure held until May 1945.[25] All in all, from the Soviet point of view, this treatment seemed to provide the most favorable conditions for winning over a considerable part of the captured officers for later attempts to influence both the German front lines and the home front.

Although months had passed since the capitulation at Stalingrad, the Russians were still interested in exploiting the battle on the Volga propagandistically. This interest led to the growing conviction that the organizing of a National Committee would best meet the needs of the hour. It is impossible to pin down exactly when the Russians finally made up their minds on this point. The only thing that seems certain is that the suggestion came from the highest quarters—possibly from Stalin himself—and that it spurred the émigrés to feverish activity.[26]

It began in June 1943 with several well-aimed "resolutions."[27] In the camps for enlisted men resolutions were passed and "National Fighting Committees" formed. At numerous guided meetings, which even now could not arouse more than a minority of the POWs, common action in an anti-fascist united front was demanded. A declaration from Camp 27 stressed that the endangered German people would no longer stand for any delay.[28] Many forces were already active. But all the patriotic forces at home and at the front were waiting for the single force that would unite all these energies in the struggle against fascism. This single force could be only a National Committee for a Free Germany, and it was imperative to form it now.

Every single resolution clearly reflected the guidelines to which the émigrés and anti-fascists had pledged themselves. Point by point, the new program came into being; fragments of traditional ideology were subordinated to nationalist slogans intended to arouse patriotic sentiments. This gave the propaganda the touch of a new spirit despite its confusion. Even so, the recruitment campaigns in the enlisted men's camps were much the same as the earlier unsuccessful ones. Here, apparently, it was still thought to be sufficient if the proposed resolutions, which were barely discussed at all, were approved by acclamation.[29]

It should have been obvious that such tactics would be self-defeating in the officers' camps. But the biases of émigrés and anti-fascists prevented them from seeing this obvious point.[30] Thus the main tactic employed was the mass meeting with its apparently inevitable tendency toward untenable simplifications that throttled whatever openness of mind and goodwill might have existed.[31] The attempts to win over sufficiently large groups of Stalingrad officers so that their numbers would count failed in Susdal, Yelabuga, Oranky—indeed, in all the officers' camps—because of unconvincing arguments and the fear that Communists would get control of the groups. Even where intelligent discussions about Stalingrad did begin, they got no further than the small groups already in existence that henceforth would form the germinal units of the National Committee. Émigrés and soldiers remained unable —especially in the rough-and-tumble atmosphere of public meetings—to overcome their mutual distrust. Largely incapable of giving up time-honored ideas and sentiments, the two camps became intransigent to the point of incompatibility.

There were at least a number of men with minds of their own who took a personal stand and who began to appear alongside the frequently discredited émigrés and anti-fascists.[32] They did not seek the acclamation of mass rallies, but aimed rather at personal contacts. They tried to work without threats or insinuations. They were first of all interested in establishing contact with officers who were expected to be capable of independent and critical thought. The representatives of this infinitely superior method of recruitment were the Soviet professors Arnold and Janzen, to whom the cultivated émigrés Johannes R. Becher, Friedrich Wolf, and Alfred Kurella were attached with increasingly important functions.[33]

The choice of these émigrés, which most dramatically illustrates the turning point of Russian agitation, could hardly have been more fortunate.[34] In Wolf, Becher, and Kurella the officers met often slandered Bolshevism in a shape which they had thought impossible because of their own backgrounds and the propaganda they had been subjected to. The dramatist Wolf and the lyrical poet Becher had proved themselves with notable artistic achievements, which also made them capable of fellow feeling, while the polyglot Kurella represented a mind open to the world. He even seemed to believe sincerely in a Communist humanism although he came from the propertied middle class. Arnold, Janzen, and these émigrés, who had not hitherto played any major role, no longer reiterated Marxist clichés. They simply addressed themselves to patriotic sentiments and, therefore, to feelings that needed no ideological dressing and that might even have become confused precisely by such clichés. This radical change of direction did not, of course, eliminate the inbred or given attitudes of the Communist representatives. The officers even discovered that Arnold and Janzen worked together closely with the Communist Party and that they taught Communist cadres at the Antifa School at Krasnogorsk.[35] All of that, however, did not prevent the selected émigrés and politruks (political functionaries) from accepting the mentality of the officers as a donnée and so adopting themselves in discussions that were almost "bourgeois" in character.

The recruitment method based on personal contacts ruled out aimless activity. It meant deliberately choosing among the officers, if only because knowledge, rank, and function had developed differences of awareness. Thus Colonel Steidle, a regimental commander and a staunch Bavarian Catholic, was approached, as were Lieutenant Colonel Bredt, a long-time member of the Stahlhelm (a paramilitary political organization of German soldiers that flourished under the Weimar Republic), Captain Fleischer, an eminent economics expert, and a number of intelligence and administrative officers of the Wehrmacht.[36] These attempts were now also supported by Dr. Hadermann, whose objectivity guaranteed a high level of discussion.[37]

The attitudes of the officers approached were strikingly similar.[38] They had been shaped by the profound experiences in the Battle of Stalingrad. They were now far removed from the battle between Don and Volga; but nothing could lessen its depressing catastrophic quality. On the contrary, anyone who knew how to interpret the course of the war must have felt himself justified and even surpassed in his dire predictions. According to these officers, the National Socialist leadership should long ago have been condemned by morally responsible Germans. It was the darkening military and political prospects that increasingly threatened Germany's immediate future that most frightened these observers. There was still room, of course, for differing opinions about Germany's chances in the war, and opinions did indeed differ about it. Thus Field Marshal Paulus and some of the generals were convinced that a stalemate was still feasible.[39] After the experience of Stalingrad, this conviction could not, however, dispel the considerable doubt that Hitler was the right man to make a stalemate possible. What the group of the disenchanted felt on this issue once again reflected the feelings that had already moved them in the pocket on the banks of the Volga.

It was at this point that the *apparatchiks* and émigrés saw their opening. In every one of their talks they stressed that Germany could no longer win the war against the Soviet Union after the defeat at Stalingrad.[40] It was true that Germany had not yet lost the war although there could be no doubt that the Grand Alliance would one day defeat the Reich because of its vastly superior material potential. In view of this situation, which nobody with any foresight could contest, was it not, properly understood, the duty of every German patriot to try to avoid the total collapse of his own country? Could not this collapse be avoided if one stood up against the man who had shown that the lives of hundreds of thousands meant nothing to him and who, therefore, would not hesitate in the least to annihilate Germany altogether if his plans were to fail? These arguments really hit the most sensitive spot of the survivors of Stalingrad, who were, after all, dominated by the

conviction that the catastrophe on the Volga represented the prologue to the catastrophe of Germany.

The question of Communism and of making propaganda from
the country of the enemy continued, however, to be disturbing.[41]
Even if most of the arguments advanced suggested that now was
the time to become active on the other side of the lines—and after
Stalingrad it would not do to succumb to resignation behind barbed
wire—there remained a difference between merely considering
resistance and actually practicing it inside the enemy's camp.

The complexity of the situation, which must have been overwhelming for officers who had grown up believing in the ideas of
loyalty and obedience, was fully acknowledged by the other side.
Arnold and Janzen stressed again and again that it was not at all
important that the planned National Committee be a Communist
central agency.[42] What was needed now was the free and equal
union of all Germans who understood that the fight against Hitler
was a patriotic necessity. And it would be a necessity later on as
well. For whatever the outcome of the war, it was unthinkable that
Germany could be rebuilt without the help of all her people.

But even the officers approached and wooed in this manner
were unable to make up their minds.[43] Decisions of that magnitude
took time to ripen, but time was the last thing the Soviets were
willing to grant at this moment. Hence, initial preparations for the
National Committee were undertaken without the officers.

On July 10, 1943, an appeal for a "National Committee for a
Free Germany" appeared in the news organ *Das freie Wort*, the
first newspaper for German POWs in the Soviet Union.[44] The appeal was signed by a founding committee. It presented a sober
picture of the situation at the front and called on all German
officers and soldiers then in POW camps in the Soviet Union to
join the fight against Hitler. The composition of the committee
impressively demonstrated the failure to penetrate the ranks of
the officers; besides Pieck, Ulbricht, Weinert, Becher, Hans Mahle,
and two privates, only two officers—Captain Hadermann and
Second Lieutenant Bernt von Kügelgen—appeared as members.[45]

In the beginning of July the émigrés were ordered to attend a
meeting at Moscow designed to speed up work among the POWs.
Speaking for the Communist Party of the Soviet Union, Manuilsky

conveyed to them Stalin's desire that all anti-fascist Germans should unite in a National Committee.[46] The details of the meeting, during which specific guidelines were doubtless presented, are obscure. The only thing certain is that the émigrés present suggested that the colors black, red, and gold (of the German Revolution of 1848) be adopted as their emblem, and the suggestion was emphatically rejected. In a keynote speech, Manuilsky explained that such a flag would be too reminiscent of the impotent Weimar Republic and would, therefore, hardly serve to arouse any special sympathies among the imprisoned officers and soldiers.[47] Thus the colors black, white, and red (Nationalist German) were imposed upon the National Committee.

Manuilsky had shown that a new party line would prevail: everywhere the class-warfare syndrome was to give way to the idea of the nation. This forced the émigrés into a position which was tantamount to a complete break with their own pasts. The dissolution of the Comintern in May 1943 had, as it were, paved the way.[48] This step had even been approved for the German section by Pieck and Florin. But if the abolition of the Comintern had already shaken the émigrés, it was nothing compared to the bitterness of the decreed partnership with *Schwarz-Weiss-Rot* (the hated Hohenzollern and Nazi colors), for here their self-abnegation reached its apex.

This development can be understood only in the light of Russian *raison d'état*, as Stalin had stressed it for some time. It was the Soviet Union that was in danger, and it was the Soviet Union which mattered to the exclusion of everything else. If the Soviet Union wanted to gain relief or free itself completely from enemy pressure, then Moscow could not pass up the help of forces which it had originally slandered, particularly if Moscow could provide convincing goals for them. This might turn out to be merely a bit of tactical maneuvering until a change in the political situation suggested a return to traditional ideas, but the Soviet change of procedure might equally well be of considerable duration.

The meager delegations which assembled in Camp 27 during the first days of July to found the National Committee can hardly be said to have represented the bulk of the German POWs.[49] Among them the members of the activist group, which had already formed before the Battle of Stalingrad, were in a majority. They also represented that intellectual bondage that had put off so many soldiers in the camps. Some officers had even been whisked off to Krasnogorsk swiftly and forcibly. Thus Majors Homann, Hetz, and Stösslein were present, and the staff officers' group in the future National Committee, Colonel Steidle and Lieutenant Colonel Bredt. Captain Fleischer was finally delegated to Camp 27 in the same way, to participate in the drafting of the manifesto.[50]

This manifesto, the program of the National Committee, caused violent debates, and its fate seemed to be rather dubious at first. There are no extant sources which reflect the controversies in detail, and the historian can only examine the text that was voted on during the founding day of the National Committee. At first two drafts stood opposed to each other: Ulbricht had drawn up one, and the group of staff officers, reinforced by Fleischer, had independently drawn up a different one.[51] The two parties could reach no common ground. Ulbricht thought that the nationalistic phrases of the soldiers went too far, while the soldiers found his ideology, handled without any inspiration, unbearable.[52] The discussion went around in circles for hours in the cellar of the Antifa School at Krasnogorsk. Finally Arnold intervened. Rejecting both drafts, he managed to push through a Russian version. In it the officers' point of view found some expression, while it mutilated Ulbricht's formulations almost beyond recognition. With this manifesto the agile Russians publicly acknowledged the national idea as important.[53]

With the controversy over the manifesto, the preparatory work for the constituent assembly was completed. It could now meet on July 12 and 13, 1943, in the house of the local Soviet at Krasnogorsk, to pronounce officially what had already been worked out and decided upon.[54] For those who had come from the desolation of various prison camps the scene had an unreal quality about it. Numerous émigrés and Russian representatives had arrived, besides selected POWs. Most prominent in the assembly were, however, the newspaper and film people, who were directed in exemplary fashion from the President's chair.[55] Now all discussions ended; only the arguments of unconditional determination triumphed. Thus a heavy round of speeches and resolutions was reeled off amidst many acclamations. Perhaps the order of the agenda was a concession to the needs of the moment. But it also revealed at this early date those pseudo-democratic characteristics whose questionable nature increased in the future commensurate with the dwindling influence of non-Communist groups.

On the first day, Major Hetz opened the session with the request that the founding committee be endorsed as the presiding board of the National Committee.[56] It was to include Hetz himself, Major Stösslein, Captain Dr. Hadermann, Pfc. Zippel, and Private Emendörfer; the émigrés were represented by Wilhelm Pieck and Erich Weinert. The suggestion was accepted unanimously, and the presiding officers could take their seats at once in front of an imposing banner proclaiming a free and independent Germany in black, white, and red colors.[57]

The speeches that were now given from the rostrum sought to make the intentions of the National Committee clear from several angles. Not every performance was a hit. There were, nevertheless, a number of convincing speakers among those who addressed the assembly. Filled with a passionate desire to act, they succeeded in arousing their listeners with lucid ideas. The addresses of Weinert, Pieck, and Hadermann were the high points of the first day.[58]

Hadermann justified his participation with a profound discussion charging National Socialism with betrayal of the best traditions of the German mind.[59] Pieck and Weinert, on the other hand, attempted to define the tasks of the National Committee.[60] Both their speeches had in common an occasional lapse into agitation. But both of them also gave precedence to a nationalist conception at the cost of all Marxist arguments, thus reflecting visibly what the Soviets wanted to see emphatically stressed by all the émigrés. If this fact already became apparent in the general propaganda slogans, it became even more evident in Pieck's address. If we disregard a certain personal slant on a number of questions, we can see him hinting at future goals which radically contradict Communist thinking not only in the economic field.[61]

All of this opened the way for emphases in the discussion of political and military events which would have been unthinkable before. Thus Erich Weinert, in a speech of fundamental importance, finally omitted any arbitrary, schematized view which would have interpreted everything the war had brought about as a non-sensical blunder.[62] By emphasizing that the national idea in recent German history was justifiable, he seemed to overcome the obstacles which might have separated him from the assembled POWs. It is true that even Weinert's speech did not always get through to the historically relevant essentials. But how could he discard the bias of the émigrés at the drop of a hat? Thus he overstated or dis-torted occasionally whenever he attempted to establish the National Committee as the necessary outcome of historical developments. While the speech thus showed its dependence on the spirit of the hour, its national tenor nevertheless frequently impressed and con-vinced the listeners, for it is this tenor which enabled him to paint an unusually accurate picture of many "German conditions." Only on the basis of this picture could Weinert afford to characterize the German campaigns in Poland, France, and the Soviet Union as "ordinary wars of aggression," as wars which were so despicable because they were waged only to serve a régime of demonstrable criminality.[63]

It now became possible to appeal convincingly to the predica-ment of those "who only followed the call of their patriotic con-sciences." Had the defeats since Stalingrad not made it apparent to them that Hitler followed a path which, given his mentality, could only lead into the abyss?

To Weinert the answer to this question was self-evident. He did not hesitate to paint the actions that would have to be taken against the National Socialist régime in glowing colors. And he showed once more that he knew how to differentiate intelligently. "I realize that it is not easy to throw overboard old ideas that one has got used to. But we are faced with the decisive hour in the history of our nation, and at such a time bowing to such hesitations means becoming involuntary accomplices in the greatest crime against our own and other peoples."[64]

To underline this thesis from the vantage point of the situation on the fighting lines, Hans Frankenfeld took the floor after Weinert. Just taken prisoner by the Russians,[65] Frankenfeld, a first lieutenant and leader of a company, had lived through the destruction of the German Panzer divisions in Operation "Citadel" near Kursk. Angry and showing his astonishment, he described the unusual German expenditure of forces, going on to demonstrate all the more force-fully, using the example of the bloody failure of this offensive—the last German offensive in the east—that a decisive military victory could no longer be expected. This address, imbued with the embittering experiences of the front-line soldier, reminded the assembly once again of the recent horrors of Stalingrad. Yet they now had to come to believe that the catastrophe at the Volga was not an isolated event but the prologue to a whole series of fateful events.

It cannot be established how it was that Frankenfeld arrived at Krasnogorsk in time to make a speech at the founding assembly of the National Committee. In any case, it is not important. What is important is the strong impression his graphic and moving report made even on those who were psychologically undecided.[66] After this it was not too difficult to achieve unanimous consent for the election of Weinert as president, Major Hetz and Lieutenant Count Einsiedel as first and second vice-presidents respectively, an election which took place on the evening of July 13, using this list of candidates.[67] The same consent was achieved for the manifesto.

This manifesto, addressed to the Wehrmacht and the German people, is the first public pronouncement of the newly constituted National Committee for a Free Germany.[68] Intended as both propaganda leaflet and program, its propaganda and its goals contradict one another. For the future is supposed to be realized along a path without any strictures, quite apart from the fact that the vision of the future is choked with slogans. It is here that the traces of Communist influence become most apparent. Here one also finds the salient point of the manifesto, for the assessment of the situation suggested, and the necessary mode of fighting demanded, action at any price. This proclamation, therefore, impresses mostly by its confessional spirit, which manages to gloss over the essential questions for the time being.

The hour of the founding of the National Committee was dark indeed: Germany had long ceased to be on the road to victory. The manifesto could therefore most readily substantiate its thesis that the events demanded immediate action by pointing to the existing situation;[69] thus we read: "The defeats of the last seven months are without parallel in German history: Stalingrad, the

Don, the Caucasus, Libya, Tunisia. Hitler alone bears the responsibility for these defeats. He still stands at the head of the Wehrmacht and the Reich. The German armies are deployed far from their homeland, thinly spread over thousands of miles of front lines, dependent on allies whose fighting power and reliability have been questionable from the start, at the mercy of the powerful strikes of a coalition which grows more powerful each week. The armies of Great Britain and the United States are knocking at the doors of Europe. Soon Germany will be forced to fight on all fronts simultaneously. The weakened German Wehrmacht, surrounded ever more closely by vastly superior enemies, cannot and will not withstand this pressure in the long run. The day of reckoning is near!

"At home Germany herself has now become a theater of war. Cities, industrial centers, and shipyards are being destroyed more and more. Our mothers, wives, and children are losing home and hearth. The free farmers are without rights. Total mobilization ruins tradesmen and craftsmen and deprives the working people of their last strength and health.

"For years Hitler has prepared this war of aggression without consulting the will of the people. Hitler has isolated Germany politically. He has irresponsibly challenged the three greatest powers on earth and has united them in the unconditional fight against the Hitler régime. He has turned Europe into an enemy of the German people and has stained the people's honor. He is therefore responsible for the hate which surrounds Germany today.

"No external enemy has ever brought Germany's fortune as low as has Hitler."

All these facts seemed to prove sufficiently that Germany had lost the war. The manifesto could therefore declare with justice that the fighting could merely be prolonged at the price of terrifying sacrifices and hardships which would mean the end of the German nation.

"But Germany must not die! The life and death of our country are being decided now.

"If the German people continue to allow themselves to be led to their doom without resistance or a will of their own, they will not only become weaker and more helpless with every day of the war but also guiltier, because then Hitler will be brought down only by the weapons of the coalition. That would mean the end of our freedom as a nation and as a state; it would mean the partitioning of our Fatherland. And we could then accuse nobody but ourselves.

"If the German people, however, were to take heart in time and demonstrate by their actions that they want to be a free people and that they are determined to rid Germany of Hitler, they will win for themselves the right to decide about their future and to be heard in the world. This is the only way to rescue the existence of freedom and the honor of the German nation."

There seemed to be no need to offer additional proof in the manifesto that under the present conditions, the German people needed above all an immediate peace treaty. Hitler, however, not only seemed unworthy of any negotiations; the experiences of Stalingrad had led to the conviction that no one would be able to conclude a peace with him. The only thing left was to proclaim the pressing need to form a new government. The statement that only such a government would be truly national and supported by the confidence of the people may have sounded too self-righteous; there remained, however, the recognition that only a non-National Socialist cabinet held out the best hope for the desired peace.

"Such a government must be strong and have the necessary powers to render harmless the enemies of the people, Hitler and his supporters and minions, to eliminate ruthlessly terror and corruption, to establish firm law and order and to represent Germany honorably in external affairs. It can be born only out of the fight for freedom of all sections of society, based on the activist cadres (*Kampfgruppen*) which united to overthrow Hitler. Those forces in the Army which remain loyal to the people and to the nation have a decisive role to play in this.

"Such a government has to stop the war immediately, pull back the German troops to the frontiers of the Reich, and initiate peace talks, giving up all occupied territories. This way it will achieve peace and lead Germany back into the community of equal nations. It alone will create the possibility for the German people of expressing their national will freely and in peace and of shaping Germany's destiny as a sovereign nation."

Looking at the military suggestions for the new German government, one can catch at least a glimmer of a program. But it was insufficient, for the fight against Hitler necessitated, apart from renouncing all conquests, at least some political goals as well.

In its context, it was certainly not the task of the manifesto to develop the picture of a complete new order. The war had unleashed forces which could render questionable tomorrow what looked inviolable today. But it had to formulate at least some general conceptions. These the proclamation did summarize under the heading "Free Germany!" It enjoined:

A strong democratic state, which has nothing in common with the weakness of the Weimar régime, a democracy which will ruthlessly suppress any attempt of a revival of the conspiracy against the liberties and rights of the people and the peace of Europe.

Complete elimination of all laws which are based on the discrimination against peoples and races, of all institutions of the Hitler régime which are dishonorable for our people; declaring null and void all tyrannical laws of the Hitler period which are directed against freedom and the dignity of man.

Restoration and expansion of political rights and the social achievements of all workers, freedom of speech, press, assembly, conscience, and religion.

A free economy, free commerce and trade. Securing the right to work and all legally acquired property, restitution to its owners of all property that has been robbed, confiscation of the assets of all warmongers and all war-profiteers, exchange of goods with other countries as a sound basis for secure national wealth.

Immediate liberation and compensation for all victims of the Hitler régime.

Just and unsparing judgment of all war criminals, all leaders, wire-pullers, and supporters who led Germany into ruin, guilt, and shame. Amnesty, however, for all those supporters of Hitler who in time renounce Hitler through their actions and who join the movement for a free Germany.

Then the manifesto addressed its appeal for resistance to all sections of society. It did not try to present a well-balanced argument evaluating the concrete conditions for a *coup d'état*. In a final peroration it wanted only to strengthen the will to action at any price. It turned once more to the German officers and soldiers on all fronts who, possessing weapons, were to keep them to make their way to their homeland and to peace under the leadership of brave and responsible chieftains. The men and women in Germany were assigned the task of forming guerrilla groups and of refusing to follow Hitler.

"The fight for a free Germany requires bravery, the will to act, and determination. Bravery above all. Time is of the essence. Quick action is necessary. Anyone who continues to support Hitler out of fear, pusillanimity, or blind obedience acts as a coward and will help bring Germany to catastrophe. Anyone, however, who sets the needs of the Nation above the 'Führer's' orders and who risks his life and honor for his people, acts bravely and will help save the country from utter shame."

The Russians seem to have expected an unqualified success from the manifesto, if only because the document contained, from their point of view, concessions that could hardly be bettered.[70] This belief was certainly well-founded, if one compared the manifesto with the appeals that had been used since 1941 to convince the German soldier of the senselessness of his actions. But this point of view was and had to be deceptive. Just as good intentions can not immediately redeem a bad reputation, so the first proclamations of the National Committee could not gloss over the fact that up to then Marxist propaganda had employed abominable lies and accusations. Its utterances about Junkers and capitalists, the Soviet paradise, and international solidarity were still so alive that the manifesto was necessarily met by marked skepticism. Thus no one at Yelabuga, Susdal, Oranky, or any of the other camps believed that the program of the National Committee offered a common platform or a common cause. Even though the analysis of Germany's situation struck many sympathetic chords in many of the soldiers of Stalingrad, the black-white-red surrounding the manifesto's text repelled more than attracted.[71] Weren't they used to frame incitement to subversion with a symbol that had been shamelessly abused? Weren't they merely diverting attention from the real forces that acted and made decisions behind the scenes and whose ideas could hardly be in keeping with these colors? Even a fleeting glance at the list of signatories to the manifesto seemed to corroborate these misgivings.[72] Aside from Ulbricht, Pieck, Weinert, Ackermann, and Florin, how much weight did the few names on the National Committee carry? Most had no influence, even those belonging to an important family or representing honest personal convictions, like the young second lieutenant of the Air Force, Count Einsiedel. The group of Reyher, Rücker, and Charisius carried no weight at all. It was especially burdened by the association of having forcefully represented the anti-fascist activist groups (Aktivs) whose brutal methods were still remembered and resented.[73] And how about majors Hetz, Homann, and Stösslein, whose names headed the list of thirty-eight signatures? They may have been reputable, like Hadermann and Fleischer, insofar as their former functions—Hetz and Stösslein had been engineers— had allowed them insights which were beyond the grasp of the extras in the cast of the assembly.[74] But could they disguise the fact that the generals of Stalingrad were missing at Krasnogorsk, those commanders, with Paulus at their head, whose names alone would have counted?

More or less consciously these questions influenced the bulk of the POWs. There remained the fundamental conviction that collaboration with the committee could not be risked as long as the leading officers remained on the sidelines.[75] This reaction, which reflected a distinct distrust of the Communists, was too unequivocal even to allow for any serious discussion. Thus the National Committee was mostly met by rejection and boycott in the camps. It would have scored a success if it had succeeded in winning five per cent of the German prisoners. And in any case the impression was very strong that many members were decisively motivated by something other than genuine idealism.[76]

The lack of independence among the committee's leading members had very deep roots; they were neither capable nor willing to search for the reasons behind their failures. On the one hand, their activities had not had time to prove themselves sufficiently; on the other hand, they would have been overtaxed in a situation that was complicated as it stood. It was fundamental, therefore, that no activity could be expected of them that would have gone beyond the framework of the organization. But resignation did nothing to further Russian intentions. Now that they had started out on an unusual venture with their manifesto, they wanted to go all the way and with success. Basically the Russians seem to have been most surprised that up to that point their wooing of the officers had failed. They had offered relative comfort: it had been interpreted as weakness and had caused the officers to dig in behind their soldierly code.[77] They had brought in Becher, Wolf, and Kurella; but even these émigrés had not overcome the officers' refusal to be won. It was clearly a poor showing. Individual talks had met with some open-mindedness. There were also a few officers who were impressed by the masterful handling of some discussions. Prejudices had been shaken, and occasionally it had become apparent that the individuals contacted might be moved to action at a later date.

Every opinion of the Stalingrad officers was carefully considered by the Soviets.[78] But if they surveyed the scene without blinkers, they could not fail to notice the failure of the National Committee's recruitment attempts. The influence of the officers' corps had become painfully obvious. The Russians were therefore forced to acknowledge that it was not at all a matter of indifference whether a large group of the captured officers could be spurred to propagandistic collaboration or whether they continued to stay aloof. Moscow had already offered considerable concessions; the facts of the situation now demanded that a determined effort be made to go even further. But where was Moscow to start? How was a new movement to be launched?

Those officers who had remained at Krasnogorsk and who had more or less voluntarily observed the constituent assembly of the Committee offered an opening.[79] These officers, all of them prisoners of the Stalingrad pocket, harbored no doubts about the present situation and the ultimate outcome of the war. They were also convinced, however, that the Communists' preponderance in the National Committee would prevent any major success among the soldiers.[80] Not that they opposed the Committee's political or military analyses! On these grounds the manifesto seemed to them to be objective on all counts and allowed for no objections. What did motivate them to deliberate rejection, however, was the propagandistic element with which, in their opinion, the Committee called for an unorganized subversion. It was this program which the officers rejected as inappropriate; it could never provide sufficient grounds for freeing them from their oath of allegiance.[81]

Fundamentally, the attitudes of the officers were disparate enough to keep them in a constant state of unrest. For there remained a contradiction, which had to be resolved sometime, between the recognition that Hitler's war was lost and the feeling that it was impossible to stand up against the destroyer of Germany within the Committee while one was a prisoner of war. Despite all the criticism against the National Committee there existed a willingness that needed only a concession regarding the way the propaganda was to employed.

Gradually the Russians grasped the possibilities that could open up if they met the officers on the propaganda concept. But it was not in their style to exploit a situation which had ripened by itself. They had to create it with a certain dash! Even as the discussions among the officers got under way, they suggested that a so-called initiating group be formed.[82] It was not to complement the National Committee, but was to found an independently functioning league of officers. Again it was Professor Arnold who met every wish, now as Russian agent, and who expressly declared that the initiating group was to develop exclusively according to its own ideas. Satisfied that yet another organization of German POWs was beginning to develop, he supported all recruitment drives among the officers. He also enthusiastically endorsed the key idea that the top echelons of the army had to be approached, for it was they and not subversion at the lower ranks that would bring about a change.[83]

This unexpected support for ideas that had as yet barely been formulated gave an impetus to the initiating group that soon led it to well-considered resolutions. This whole new development was underscored by the fact that a Colonel Stern now joined Arnold. The presence of the former showed that from now on the political administration of the Red Army would take an active interest in the league of officers that was about to be formed.[84]

Who then were the German officers who represented the quickly expanding initiating group? Its founder was Lieutenant Colonel Alfred Bredt, commander of the supply troops of the Sixth Army's XI Corps.[85] Bredt had been a leading member of the Pan-German Federation (*Alldeutscher Verband*) and of the *Stahlhelm*. Politically astute and active, he took Stalingrad to be a corroboration of his belief that, sooner or later, Hitler spelled Germany's doom. This conviction, which he did nothing to hide, compelled him to attend the constituent assembly of the National Committee as an observer. It also allowed the Soviets to keep in touch with him, and it gradually led, via a give-and-take of criticisms and concessions, to a binding understanding.[86] Bredt's age lent him respect and authority; he was followed by Lieutenant Colonel Bechly, majors Egbert von Frankenberg und Proschlitz, Lewerenz, and Büchler, Captain Domaschk, who had won the Knight's Cross, first lieutenants von Kirschhofer and Trenkmann, and Second Lieutenant Dr. Greifenhagen.[87] Colonel van Hooven, commander of the Sixth Army's Signal Corps, Judge Advocate von Knobelsdorff-Brenkenhoff, and First Lieutenant Gerlach were won over later.[88]

Von Frankenberg, Lewerenz, Domaschk, and von Knobelsdorff-Brenkenhoff had served as regulars in the army and the Air Force. The others had been reactivated or taken from the army's reservists.[89] Almost every one of them belonged to a different social class; they came from the nobility and from the upper and the lower bourgeoisie, and they reflected all the strengths and weaknesses of those social groups. Their occupational backgrounds were no less varied. Dr. Greifenhagen was an archeologist, Gerlach a college teacher, Büchler an exporter, von Kirschhofer a landowner, and Trenkmann a civil servant in the army's experimental station at Peenemünde. These officers were certainly motivated by widely differing political ideas. Their intelligence and functions had also led to differing insights. But Stalingrad had given them a common ground on which they could begin to communicate. A shattering experience had forced a decision. It was also strong enough to control even unusual motivations.[90]

The initiating group's recruitment campaign reached its high point when Colonel Luitpold Steidle joined the group.[91] Like Bredt, Steidle—who was an experienced regimental commander and had been decorated with the Knight's Cross—had been unable to bring himself to sign the National Committee manifesto. Although he could hardly be regarded as a National Socialist, having been close to political Catholicism (*Katholische Aktion*), he, too, had probably been put off by the obvious Communist manipulation of the organization of the German POWs. Now, however, new conditions seemed to prevail, and not only for Steidle. Where Russion concessions had not yet overcome basic reservations, the argument of the group around Bredt began to convince them that the influence of the left wing would be weakened to the same degree as they were able to push through a conception of their own. Steidle joined the initiating group late in the game. But when he did so, at the end of July, he did it with such verve, powerful personality that he was, that he soon began to play a leading role.[92]

Even before the initiating group left Zone I of Krasnogorsk Camp on August 16, 1943, to move to Lunyovo near Moscow, together with the National Committee, it had sent some delegations as recruiters into various officers' camps.[93] Yelabuga, Oranky, and Susdal had up to now stood out in their unanimous rejection of all anti-fascist propaganda attempts. The National Committee's attempt to elicit any response worth mentioning in the camps had failed everywhere because of the all too obvious leanings of its membership.[94] Once again it had been shown that the prisoners rejected any movement which could not lay creditable claim to a certain independence.

It corresponded to the essence and the goals of the future officers' league in that it kept a noticeable distance from all the methods of recruitment used earlier.[95] When the delegations of the initiating group appeared in the camps, therefore, their reasonable appeals attracted genuine attention. At Yelabuga, for instance, Major Schulze and First Lieutenant Trenkmann not only managed to present the new line impressively;[96] by pointing out the intention of offering the leadership of the officers' league to several generals they also convinced many officers who had attended their meetings. They were successful in all the camps; everywhere they managed to form noteworthy activist groups. At once their members were sent out to help christen the League of German Officers at Lunyovo.

The prospect of being complemented or even pressured by a distinctly "rightist"-oriented wing doubtless filled the National Committee with unconcealed misgivings, at first.[97] Even later there remained a certain coolness because of ideological *idées fixes*. But it was not always the barely concealed Russian pressure which forced the prominent members of the committee into collaboration with officers and generals. Weinert and some other émigrés had harbored doubts ever since Stalingrad whether their image of the German soldier still corresponded at all with reality.[98] Now they were able to correct their prejudices and errors with the help of concrete reality. The Communist section began to utilize this chance insofar as it was open-minded; it saw the common front as a necessity which, at first, it followed sincerely.

In the meantime the initiating group and several camp delegations had assembled at Lunyovo to prepare the work of the officers' union through general discussions. It is quite certain that some officers still had not reached a definitive decision at this time. Thus it became the task of the higher echelons to clarify unresolved problems. Now it was mostly Steidle—apart from the group around Bredt—who presented the most convincing arguments.[99]

In a fundamental discussion about the founding of the officers' union he argued that the destruction of the Sixth Army at Stalingrad represented a grave loss, considering the limited German potential. Now, with the defeat which the armed forces had just suffered in the twin battles of Byelgorod and Orel, the initiative had definitively shifted to the Red Army. If these costly reversals had already signaled danger, they turned into catastrophe because of Hitler's incompetent and irresponsible strategy. In the Stalingrad pocket it resulted in the collapse of a set of values thought sacred. In the light of these considerations there could not be any doubt as to future developments. Already lost, the war would go on with the continuing senseless attrition of German forces that had become so typical of the obstinacy of their Supreme Commander. There was no longer any hope that the leadership responsible for it would accept the consequences, militarily or politically. Hitler was incapable of any ethical reasoning and he was leading a *total war* in which *anything* was permissible and legal and where even ethical norms had ceased to count.

From this Steidle reached most impressive conclusions. Against an enemy like Hitler, only those could hope to win who were prepared for *total resistance*, that is, a resistance without reservations. Questions of their oath of allegiance, of international law, or of collaboration with the enemy were considerations which should not stand in the way of such a total conflict any more than personal or family considerations. Hitler spelled Germany's doom; all the greater, therefore, the responsibility for unconditional action, as only intrepid action presented a chance to stop a process whose consequences must be disastrous.

With these arguments Steidle had once more brought into view the full weight of the decision with which every one of the officers had had to struggle in a tough personal conflict before he was prepared to join in the work of the officers' union. He had also spoken for all of them when he confessed that it had only been his love for his country that had caused him to take the unusual step of open rebellion. Without it, the burden accepted by the members of the League of German Officers would have been unbearable. They even felt that any possible opportunism would be irrelevant in view of the dangers they incurred by their open resistance. Not only the members of their families but also their own return to Germany had been put on the line. They had to expect the vilest derision of the National Socialists, as well as the cutting contempt of the front-line soldiers whom they still felt very close to.

One thing, however, had become clear: since Stalingrad they knew more than the rest of the German people. They feared that the whole nation would suffer an intellectual and moral collapse similar to the one that they had experienced on the banks of the Volga, and they wanted to ward it off before the fighting was carried out in the rubble of the last German cities and villages. Thus they were prepared to turn to the leadership of the armed forces. They had to depose Hitler and pave the way for a compromise peace that still might be obtained and that alone could save Germany.

The seriousness of all these ideas was powerful enough to give the initiating group and the delegations a sense of genuine importance.[100] It removed all misgivings about details and created the determination necessary for successful action. But even the most determined attitude could not hide the fact that the officers' union must remain only a torso until they succeeded in winning at least a few generals. For they could hope to be listened to on the other side of the lines only if popular men decided to identify themselves with what had become their program.

This conviction was not shared by the initiating group alone. It was above all held by the Russians, who now raised the question, through Arnold, as to which of the generals could be approached.[101] The assembled officers agreed from the start that any undue optimism was out of place. Thus they thought that Field Marshal Paulus had to be ruled out as he could not be expected to act differently now than he had done at Stalingrad.[102] The same was true, only more so, with regard to his influential Chief of Staff. Active and self-assured, Lieutenant General Schmidt had demonstrated his pro-Hitler attitude at Susdal more than ever before.[103] But even if Paulus and Schmidt had to be ruled out, that certainly did not mean that none of the other commanders could be counted on. But who could be approached seriously? Within the initiating group Bechly and Greifenhagen suggested Major General Dr. Korfes; Domaschk and Gerlach proposed Major General Lattmann.[104] In contrast to Korfes, whose critical attitude toward National Socialism was known to his division, Lattmann was considered a general with National Socialist leanings. It was thought, however, that he could be counted on after the common experience of Stalingrad.[105] The most convincing suggestion—besides those of others who wanted to invite generals von Drebber and Deboi—was Bredt's. He suggested that they should try above all to win General von Seydlitz.[106]

Walther von Seydlitz-Kurzbach, General of the Artillery, had been commanding general of the Sixth Army's 51st Corps at Stalingrad.[107] Noble, warmhearted, modest, and with a high sense of duty, he had been decorated with the Oak Leaves to the Knight's Cross as early as January 1942 for the exceptional military exploits of his 12th Infantry Division, The Mecklenburg Division. Also linked to his name was the liberation of the encircled divisions at Demyansk. As an officer of the old school, Seydlitz was not used to thinking politically or to drawing political conclusions. He seemed to be the embodiment of the typical professional soldier. But as a leader of troops he not only possessed a strong sense of ethical norms, he also found it unbearable to see anyone act against well-founded judgment. It was, therefore, in the military field that

Hitler's true nature became apparent to the general. Hitler's methods of military leadership had already galled Seydlitz at Demyansk. At Stalingrad he had finally come out against the order to stand and be encircled with a courageous evaluation of the situation meant to spur Paulus to independent action. This manly opposition of the general had quickly made the rounds among the troops and had once again added to his high reputation among them. If there was one officer bearing the generals' red insignia who gave cause for optimism, it was Walther von Seydlitz.

Whether the Russians distrusted such optimism or whether they figured on a better chance by presenting the generals with a *fait accompli* is uncertain. In either case, they extended their invitation somewhat peculiarly, to say the least. Toward the end of August, Seydlitz, Korfes, and Lattmann were ordered to board a train.[108] Even hours after they had arrived at Lunyovo, they still did not know exactly where they were. But soon their uncertainty was to be removed.

Next day a meeting took place on the sports field of the Lunyovo camp.[109] Although the elation of the assembly and an impassioned speech by Steidle did not leave the generals unmoved, they raised some objections. After Seydlitz refused to appear in the company of deserters—an act aimed at Private Gold and Pfc. Zippel[110]— the generals summarized their refusal in a few counterarguments. On the one hand, they argued, no action from the enemy's camp could ever be countenanced; on the other hand, they had to refuse to act as cats' paws for any Bolshevist aims, since nobody knew whether the Communists had any interest in honest collaboration.[111]

The inner determination of the initiating group and the delegations was demonstrated by a quick rebuttal of these arguments, which they felt to be objections that merely reflected uncertainty. But all their answers remained without effect. It appeared that Korfes had raised only a few objections and that the question of the oath of allegiance was a stumbling block only with Lattmann. But the impression prevailed that the generals could not be counted on.[112]

It was all the more surprising, therefore, when on the morning after, Seydlitz, Korfes, and Lattmann declared, without any further discussion, that they were willing to join the League of German Officers.[113] What had happened?

On the evening of the very day that it appeared that the attempted recruitment had failed, the Russians intervened. Convinced that the most far-reaching concessions had now become necessary, they had delegated General Melnikov of the NKVD to Seydlitz, Lattmann, and Korfes.[114] And Melnikov overcame the generals' resistance. In a long night session behind closed doors he offered several concessions in the name of the Soviet Government.[115] If the officers' union were successful in getting the leadership of the armed forces to act against Hitler and thus end the war before it had to be fought on German soil, Moscow would use its influence to ensure a Reich with the frontiers of 1937, including Austria. Under these conditions Moscow would, of course, also support the retention by Germany of its armed forces. The only condition for this support would be a liberal, democratic government, linked with Russia by pacts of friendship.

Those were the offers that changed the generals' minds. After a sleepless night during which they struggled with their consciences, independently of one another, they decided to collaborate with the Russians. Each of them must have been convinced that if they managed to save the Reich without Hitler's conquests they would be scoring a great success. After Melnikov's assurances, how could they fail in their duty of working to bring to an end a war that they were convinced had already been lost and whose continuance only meant reducing Germany's chances? Now that a basis seemed to exist for their work, Seydlitz, Korfes, and Lattmann no longer refused the call of the moment. Whatever thoughts Melnikov's intervention had started churning in them, by next morning they had become a decision.

It seemed prudent to put the results of the night session on paper. But here the generals met with haughty refusal.[116] In a sober reply Melnikov pointed out that the officers' union had first to create the conditions without which no discussion about binding undertakings was possible with the Soviet Government.

One might, at this point, accuse the generals of a lack of political astuteness, but this kind of criticism would be superficial. Seydlitz, Korfes, and Lattmann negotiated, after all, in a situation which excluded any binding undertaking. Thus the procedure and the outcome of the negotiations testified to the unequal strength of the two parties and not that the Russians had intended from the start to trick the generals, as an unhistorical point of view might imply. The one thing that the generals had to have was the assurance that timely propagandistic successes would not be cancelled out politically. This assurance was given, and it fulfilled its purpose. That it would be valid only as long as the German side still held some trump cards merely expressed the unwritten rules of the free play of political power. Viewed from this standpoint, Melnikov's qualification "before the war had to be fought on German soil" expressed, on the contrary, an honesty which could only develop on the basis of unflinching realism. This realism is also documented in the succession of Russian public figures that came and went at Lunyovo. During the first year the intelligent and heavy-set Melnikov took the spotlight.[117] His supporting cast was Lieutenant General Petrov and, as interpreters, Colonel Stern and the Georgian Georgadze. Starting in the fall of 1944, the sinister figure of Kobulov, a general in the NKVD, dominated the scene. Kobulov acted more officiously and seemed bound by highest orders when he found it impossible to remember the activities of his predecessor.

Melnikov's assurances made the generals believe that their arguments had become irrefutable. Would it not be possible now to start their own propaganda work in an inspiring fashion? Indeed, were they not now in a position to approach even Paulus and the other generals of Stalingrad, who still remained aloof in their isolation? These considerations seemed understandable in their situation and compelling enough to ask the Russians for permission, which was quickly granted. In the first week of September Seydlitz, Korfes, Lattmann, and two other officers returned to Voykovo. They wanted to get complete, unanimous support for the officers' union through urgent appeals to their comrades of Stalingrad.[118]

But the generals who entered Camp 48 with high expectations were cruelly disappointed. They neither achieved any successes nor were they able to overcome the boycott which was the final answer to all their efforts.[119] The delegation had immediately decided on holding tumultuous assemblies instead of convincing one or the other of the commanders in individual and quietly objective conversations. Thus argument and counterargument clashed in the not too serene discussions. Thus bitterness developed, amid mutual accusations of treason, which could not be kept in check even by self-evident ideas.[120]

There is no question that this tactical move was inept. Seydlitz, Korfes, and Lattmann had not rehearsed their propaganda approach, and the sentiments of the generals whom they now approached still needed clarification—which the trio, caught up in their own emotions, considered as solved. The mistake was all the more disastrous, for a feeling that Russian approaches should be rejected had developed at Voykovo, and at that time, this feeling was so strong that even the most outstanding personality of the resistance movement would have been ostracized.

There had been sufficient time for this feeling to coalesce. Ever since the generals had been transported to Voykovo, after a brief stay in the camps at Krasnogorsk and Susdal, they had been a world unto themselves.[121] Not forced to make any decisions, indeed almost forgotten, they had been moved, as their physical conditions gradually improved, by the experience of Stalingrad and by the concern with the effect that this catastrophe would have on the over-all position of Germany in the war. The generals of Stalingrad did not doubt that the sacrifice of the Sixth Army reflected irresponsible decisions. But they also agreed that the Sixth Army had had a job to do. The encircled divisions had to fight to the end if the southern sector of the German eastern front had been threatened. Certainly, this order reflected the catastrophic situation of all German operational plans; but the order to stand and fight at any price did at least have some goal. Retrospectively it was accepted, if only because the death of thousands in those January days of 1943 would otherwise have become unbearable.

Hitler as commander in chief had at least sobered up the generals to the point that they regarded as doubtful a victory over the Soviet Union by itself. The losses of the German armed forces and of their allies as a consequence of Stalingrad spoke for themselves and dampened any optimism. Most of the generals were unable to see their way to a political judgment about the total context of the war, although Hitler the statesman had already evoked pitiless criticism while they were trapped in the pocket. Convinced that the fight could no longer be won and that future operations would be conducted according to the experiences of Stalingrad, they nevertheless sought escape in the hope for a general stalemate. They hoped that Germany would successfully repel the invasion in the West and stiffen the front lines after which "a desire to open negotiations would have to come about." They also believed that it would be possible to have a rapprochement with the Western powers, an assumption which seemed to be supported by the failure of the Second Front to materialize.

Thus, above all, the illusions about the phenomenon of Adolf Hitler separated the generals of Stalingrad from the Free Germany movement. In June 1943 Pieck had certainly managed to tell Field Marshal Paulus in the camp at Susdal that there was no way out of the war for the politician Hitler, who had broken treaty after treaty.[122] He had talked of the constant warnings of his party against National Socialist rule and of the duty of every German patriot to join the planned National Committee. But if this conversation led the former commander in chief of the Sixth Army to political reflection, it did nothing of the sort for the rest of the generals.

Seydlitz and his delegation therefore met with the most violent resistance. True, their arguments were no longer unfamiliar to Paulus. Seydlitz could even go beyond Pieck by pointing to the fact that the military situation had grown considerably worse and that therefore the chances of a tolerable peace for Germany were increasingly endangered.[123] But to the generals the unanimity of the German people and the armed forces seemed absolutely essential, especially in view of these considerations, and they further saw any public appearances behind barbed wire simply as contemptible subversion of front lines and home front. Here the comparison with World War I, when the German High Command had attempted to dictate its peace to Russia with the help of subversive measures, was frightening. There was also the paralyzing fear of being accused of a stab in the back, an accusation they were unwilling to saddle themselves with, all the more so as any activities of prisoners of war contravened all international regulations.

All these factors condemned the recruitment attempts to failure.

The Free Germany movement was sharply rejected by the generals of Stalingrad; they turned their backs on their colleagues who had decided upon political activity amid unrelenting defamations. True, Seydlitz managed to arrange a talk with Paulus after the unfortunate general meeting, a talk whose objectivity corresponded to the Field Marshal's personality.[124] Much later Paulus was even able to lift the collective condemnation of the generals in the officers' union and to leave political decisions up to the consciences of the individual general. But at first the Field Marshal himself also refused to participate, arguing that the over-all situation could be neither observed nor judged from behind barbed wire.[125]

All this left the League of German Officers a fragmented affair for the time being. In complete isolation again since the Fall of 1943, the generals stood aloof at Voykovo, either as bitter opponents of or keeping a critical distance from the League. Even though there remained the hope at Lunyovo that the future would convince them, the present results remained depressing enough. What possibilities might have opened up had Paulus, the widely known commander of the Sixth Army, been ready at this time to join in collaboration, a collaboration in which everything could be wrong tomorrow that made sense today.

These considerations had a depressing effect and continued to weigh heavily. Now increased devotion had to make up for the failure to win over any converts.

It was on September 11 and 12, 1943, that the founding ceremony of the League of German Officers finally took place in the House at Lunyovo.[126] Once again the scene was festive. Once again movie cameras and microphones were present and hundreds of people were assembled, together with delegations from five officers' camps. But this time the field-gray of the soldiers seemed to push the civilian appearance of the National Committee into the background. The atmosphere of the hour was, therefore, imbued with the distinct feeling that the officers had come together freely in their own cause. Thus the atmosphere which filled those two September days was in no way reminiscent of the atmosphere of agitated public meetings. It was dominated rather by a profound seriousness and the determination that had been created by compelling ideas and enthusiastic leaders.[127]

The speeches that presented in summary form the reasons for

the officers' union and what was to guide it in the future were equally serious and exhortatory. If one looks at them closely, they reveal a complete lack of the agitator's tone. The speeches neither groped for justification by the party nor were their individual arguments presented sentimentally. But although the officers' temperament in itself seemed to rule out the inciting phrase, the speakers succeeded all the better by their sober conclusions in convincing their listeners of the necessity to act decisively.

The prepared speeches easily filled the sessions of both days.[128] The first day was reserved for declarations of principle, while the practical working plans were offered on the second day.

Colonel Hans Günther van Hooven's basic paper was the climax of September 11.[129] Hooven developed a comprehensive view of the situation. Observing that this particular meeting of POW officers that sought to bring about an immediate end to the war was probably unique in history, he continued by pointing out the common interests of the German and the Russian people. These interests alone were already a strong argument for an early armistice. But they also comprised politically and economically strong guarantees that "an honorable peace, which would secure the basic rights of the nations and eliminate the possibility of future wars," would be achieved.[130]

In his description of the land operations, Hooven candidly admitted that the German armed forces had achieved noteworthy successes. He did not deny that the victories over Poland and France had been inspiring. But had not the space conquered grown to abnormal dimensions with every triumph? And did not the unexpected campaign against the Soviet Union finally bring about a great change of public opinion in Germany?

At this point Hooven broadened his analysis by introducing psychological and political elements. In an impressive general survey he not only threw light on the German offensives of 1941 and 1942, but he also weighed the undeniable military successes of the Red Army and the situation of Germany's allies so objectively that the position of the Reich in Europe began to take on very depressing features.[131] This survey did, indeed, attribute certain insights to the German people which most certainly could not be so calmly implied in view of National Socialist propaganda. But after describing the capitulation of Italy, the failure of German submarine and aerial warfare, and territorial losses in the East, Hooven comes to extremely bitter conclusions. For in addition to everything else the diminishing forces of the Reich also had to fight against a coalition whose enormous potential had already taken a horrible toll in the bombing offensives of the Allies.

"As a general," Hooven argued, "Hitler has lost this war militarily. He usurped the leadership of the war after Field Marshal von Brauchitsch left his office. The failure of the winter campaign of 1941 to 1942 without winter equipment, the adventure of the offensive against Stalingrad and the Caucasus, the loss of Africa, are the results of his desultoriness and his lack of expertise.

"As a statesman, Hitler has lost this war politically. He has united the most powerful states of the world in a coalition against Germany and, by the measures taken by him and his régime, has brought about a situation in which our soldiers face not only weapons of war but the powerful weapon of the deep hatred of the enemy's people. Today his handiwork, the Axis system of alliances, has collapsed.

"As a leader of the economy, Hitler has taken into account only 'Blitzkrieg' and 'Blitzsieg' [lightning wars and lightning victories]. Space and time, whose effects he meant to use for himself despite all experience, have turned against us as they had done in World War I."[132]

Thus, Hooven continued, total war had become totally hopeless. The armed forces, however, still represented a power factor. They would still be able, in the case of a withdrawal to Germany's frontiers, to guarantee the internal order of the Reich, which would collapse without the solidarity of the army.

Hitler neither could end the fight nor did he want to. Germany, therefore, was left with only the choice of either continuing the war under this leader until it was totally destroyed or overthrowing him and forming a new, strong, national government of the people which could bring peace. To choose the way of peace, however, was now an inexorable duty. The officers' union was working toward this end, and their activities were based on Marshal Stalin's statement of November 6, 1942, in which he declared that democratic liberties, equality of nations, and the inviolability of their territories were his goals.[133]

"Stalingrad was the flaming signal of the catastrophe threatening our people. The Sixth Army, the army of Stalingrad, has been pronounced dead. Today, the officially dead arise to issue a last-minute appeal for introspection and for the rescue of the Fatherland. And no one has a greater right to do this than we do.

"Long live free, independent, and peaceful Germany!"[134]

Colonel Steidle and Major General Lattmann took the floor after Hans Günther van Hooven.[135] With sound, forceful arguments, Steidle had already paved the way for the officers' union to such an extent that now all that was left for him to do was to reinforce Hooven in a second programmatic survey. It was now Lattmann's task to focus his speech on the disturbing question of the oath of allegiance. With its dignified determination it impressively reflected the traces of his own personal conflict over this issue.[136]

> . . . We have taken our oath on the person of Adolf Hitler; there are no two ways about that. And we have done so with a solemn vow given in the face of God. We must therefore consider the question seriously, very seriously: May we break that vow? Are there reasons by which we may justify such a step before our own consciences, before our God, and—although this does not seem as important to me—before the world? Let us leave out of consideration the questions which are based on the fact that some individuals did not take the oath of their own free will, that there are examples in history which make the breaking of an oath appear retrospectively as a great, saving deed. A deeply felt Christian conception may even deduce the right to undo the tie of an oath from the commandant according to which the Christian is to obey God rather than man. But the ethical concept of loyalty ultimately depends on the relationship between the leader and his men, whose loyalty the leader has secured by the oath. At Stalingrad truly loyal generals and officers have told their men openly and honestly what the situation was. Let me recall the order of a commanding general long before the end of the fighting; it said: 'The Führer has ordered us to fight to the end. God be with you, men!' Such generals and officers have demanded of themselves and their soldiers the fulfillment of their oath of loyalty even to the ultimate test in a situation where death had indeed lost its sting

compared to the psychic and physical horrors around them.

Recognition of the need to sue for peace must have gone very far if personalities such as these can only be prevented from acting by invoking their oath of loyalty. Were one to take this fidelity to its logical conclusion, one would be forced to conclude: The oath of loyalty must remain inviolate even if Germany perishes! This ultimate conclusion offers the justification to regard any further allegiance to the oath as unethical. Since we are of the opinion that any further continuance of the fighting will bring about the destruction of our people, we regard the oath, sworn to Adolf Hitler in person under different conditions, as null and void. He could think up plans which were to make him 'the Greatest of all Germans' because he knew that our oath would bind us to him. It was for this idea that the precious blood of our fellow soldiers was sacrificed and not for Germany! Was that not an abuse of our loyalty, the pressing of a claim which he dared presuppose, counting on our ethical interpretation of the words of an oath?

We never took that oath to make him or ourselves the 'Masters of Europe'! We swore by God to be wholly loyal when the time came to prove ourselves in a fight for Germany. But he to whom we vowed that loyalty turned this oath into a lie. We therefore regard ourselves all the more responsible to our people. And it is out of this inner responsibility that we take the right to act, out of which we feel compelled to act. . . .[137]

During all the speeches General von Seydlitz sat apart listening. But now he rose to accept the chairmanship of the founding assembly offered by Bredt, and he did so with the intention of lending the weight of his name to the speeches of van Hooven, Steidle, and Lattmann.[138] The general could hardly surpass the speakers that preceded him. But he, too, forcefully underscored the notion that the only attitude that was truly honorable was one that developed from a sense of responsibility toward one's own people. He also emphasized once more Stalin's important statement. Relying on the good faith of this declaration, the officers' union was prepared to act. "By accepting the office of chairman, I also recognize these goals and tasks as my own."[139]

This left only the required election of the top positions in the

League of German Officers on the agenda for the first day. Here lists of candidates had again been prepared as they had at the founding of the National Committee. The candidates were: General von Seydlitz as President, Lieutenant General Edler von Daniels and colonels van Hooven and Steidle as vice-presidents. Most of the other candidates for the directorate, with the exception of major generals Korfes and Lattmann, came from the initiating group which was expanded by five more officers.[140] Finally the officers' union had the task of proposing some delegates for the main officers' camps, among them Captain Markgraf, bearer of the Knight's Cross.[141]

The election of the leaders, the board, and the camp delegates was unanimous,[142] although Daniels had not been nominated by the officers' union and had only arrived at Lunyovo on September 10.[143] Seydlitz had simultaneously put two documents before the assembly which ninety-five officers approved either by acclamation or by their signatures.[144] These documents—an appeal to German generals and officers, to the German people and armed forces, and a survey of the tasks and goals of the officers' union—represented a concise summary of everything that had been presented at the founding assembly up to then.[145] The former was intended as a propaganda leaflet and was persuasive in its nationalist tenor. The latter clarified the guidelines which the League of German Officers intended to follow in its work.

Under the existing conditions it was to be expected that the émigrés present would work for a merger of the officers' union with the National Committee. The generals, too, were strongly given to the idea that all differences had to give way to a united front which would comprise all forces in the prison camps that were willing to cooperate.[146] Before any fusion, however, the question of a propaganda slogan had to be solved. Ever since the League of German Officers had first begun to take shape, it had taken an unequivocal stand on this question by demanding that efforts be made to influence the High Command and that subversive moves be refrained from. On this issue the two camps differed. Here a binding concession on the part of the Committee was necessary if that unity was to be realized which had become so necessary for successful action. The National Committee actually did come around to the view of the officers' union. The Soviets had already approved the propaganda line of the officers. Now Pieck, Ulbricht, and Weinert also agreed to the new tactical line in a personal conference with Seydlitz.[147] Although this semi-official agreement caused violent debates within the Committee as it had been constituted up to then during the first common plenary session, it was nevertheless pushed through and observed by the Committee as long as the agreement remained binding to the House at Lunyovo.[148] With this the officers' union had scored a decisive victory which enabled it to take a conciliatory stand in turn. Convinced that its ideas were sound, it thought that permitting the Committee to continue its attempts to influence the rank and file was a harmless concession.[149]

The second day of the founding assembly affirmed what the conversation between Seydlitz and the émigrés had prepared. True, Greifenhagen and Bechly emphatically re-emphasized the principles of the officers' union during the discussion of the propaganda.[150] But they were also so mindful of the necessity for a common base that Major Hetz could finally request that he and all the officers of the National Committee be admitted into the League of German Officers.[151] Seydlitz complied with the request; the fusion of the officers' union with the committee had begun.

It would be incorrect to assert that this development was welcomed by all the officers.[152] Did not the committee have a considerable superiority already, even as things stood? Could the officers' union ever hope to challenge this superiority? But just as it could not remain indifferent to the necessity of concerted action, it could not deny the generals' argument that their own influence could only be secured in an expanded National Committee.[153] No one missed the point that the émigrés living in Moscow were in a better position than the officers. But neither could anyone deny that in an expanded presidium no decision could be taken without the officers' union. And now the Committee itself seemed to offer the greatest chance for this influence. After the League of German Officers had been founded and merged with the National Committee, the doubting officers unconditionally joined the other officers. Filled by the euphoria of the moment, they not only declared with some emotion that both sides could learn from each other; by emphasizing the common national goal they also created an atmosphere in which especially the officers began to foster far-reaching hopes.[154]

The plenary session held by the National Committee on September 14, 1943, approved the addition of the League of German Officers by accepting eighteen of its members into the Committee.[155] After these mutual exchanges of members the pyramid of leadership looked like this: Erich Weinert was president and Seydlitz, Daniels, Hetz, Einsiedel, and Emendörfer figured as vice-presidents. A new manifesto seemed superfluous after the agreement on a propaganda line. Thus the new members of the National Committee signed on their part the guidelines which they had already basically agreed to before the founding of the officers' union.[156]

With this fusion completed the Free Germany movement had taken on the outlines which it was to retain until November 2, 1945. That leaves the questions: what were the Soviets' intentions regarding the committee and the officers' union? What are the most significant historical aspects of these two organizations?

It is impossible to answer these important questions conclusively. Documents which would conclusively reflect the Russian goals are not available and are not likely to become available in the near future. They would almost certainly reflect the political vacillations of the Soviets, and it would hardly be in their interest to provide knowledge of that. Perhaps the Free Germany organization, groping experiment that it was, has only found its way into a few documents anyway. But although there are considerable difficulties in reaching an accurate analysis, a few insights can, nevertheless, be gathered from a look at Soviet foreign policy between 1941 and 1943.

Ever since Hitler had attacked the Soviet Union in June 1941, the Kremlin had tried to expand its military cooperation with Great Britain and the United States to include political agreements that would determine its future weight as a major power. On this issue Russia's ambitions were based on the conviction that a guarantee of those territories which Russia had acquired under the Hitler-Stalin Pact was the necessary precondition for any binding agreement.[157] In refusing this demand despite continued Soviet pressure, Great Britain and the United States followed the Atlantic Charter which they had proclaimed.[158] The American Secretary of

State, Cordell Hull, felt that he had to reject any idea of a change of frontiers during the war "for reasons of principle and practicality," although Churchill had been willing to compromise with regard to the Baltic states in May 1942.[159] The Russian attempt to secure Western approval for their acquisition of the "old" Soviet territories carved out of the territorial expanse of Eastern Europe had thus failed for the time being.

This reversal, which the Russians put down to the influence of the Polish government in exile,[160] had already filled Russian leaders with considerable misgivings. The failure of a second front to materialize, however, increased their doubts enormously. A second front had been demanded so often that failure to open it was bound to produce bitterness, especially as the Red Army was still bearing the brunt of fighting the German Army. The victory of Stalingrad certainly had brought some relief in the East. Now Stalin could assume that he had escaped the catastrophe which seemed to threaten during the summer of 1942. But the general picture still looked critical for the Kremlin by the middle of 1943. The Soviet Union had neither managed to push through the recognition of its territorial demands nor had the Western Powers provided any palpable military relief despite their aid programs.[161] As the Russians saw it, the Allied landing in North Africa was obviously designed to distract attention from the second front, while the tacitly approved Polish plan of an Eastern European Federation seemed to be another *cordon sanitaire*,[162] for the Soviets maintained that the Allied landing could only bring appreciable relief if it were undertaken on the mainland of Europe. Perhaps this point of view all too cavalierly ignored the difficulties of an invasion of France at that time. Stalin learned to appreciate these difficulties only at the Conference in Teheran.[163] But in the given situation nothing could overcome Moscow's suspicion that the Soviet Union was to be isolated and taken advantage of.

This was the situation—and measured by Russian standards it was a disagreeable one—that probably caused Stalin to cast about for fruitful alternatives. If he could not reach the kind of agreement with the Western Powers which alone would justify the Soviets' heavy toll of blood, he had to try to play the German card once more. It was at this point that the National Committee and

the officers' union came in as the highest trump cards! Prepared by
the dissolution of the Comintern,[164] which complemented Stalin's
oft-repeated statement that the German people were not identical
with Hitler,[165] both organizations represented the most astute step
the hard-pressed Russians could have taken at that time. The
political situation in which the Free Germany movement made its
appearance can be judged in various ways and for equally good
reasons. But it is certain that the Committee and the officers' union
offered the Kremlin a momentary possibility which the previous
set of circumstances had not presented to it.

Under these aspects the intentions toward the Western Powers
are clear. The National Committee and the League of German
Officers were basically intended to demonstrate the disquieting
fact of a German-Soviet collaboration, intended to disturb Great
Britain and the United States and to make them more pliable to
the Russian demands. This speculation could hardly fail to produce
results in the long run. No matter how often Moscow might protest
that the only point of the Free Germany movement was to bring
the war to a victorious end, London and Washington had reasons
for apprehension until broad agreements with Stalin had rendered
the organization pointless. For it was only too easy for this collaboration to grow into an understanding.

The goals which an agile Kremlin tried to achieve with its
German partners seem hardly less obvious. Here, too, the Kremlin
worked toward openings that were supposed to lead the Soviet
Union out of its isolation. According to the initial concept of the
committee and the officers' union, their propaganda was to be
directed at rolling back the German front with the aim of reducing
the military pressure of the Wehrmacht. This consideration was
completely valid because the hard fighting against the German
eastern armies more than justified any relief measures. But the
crux of the Russians' deliberations will have to be sought in the
realm of politics. As there was reason to believe that the Free
Germany movement suggested that the Soviet Union was showing
its goodwill toward a newly oriented Reich, so it had the main
task of strengthening the forces of resistance in Germany, of any
groups that could be assumed to be prepared to bring about
Hitler's fall in view of the impossibility of a German victory and

the still considerable strength of the German position. Should such a coup d'état, by any of these groups, be successful, there was the possibility that Lunyovo could significantly help in bringing about direct contacts between them and the Kremlin. Were a coup to fail and should the propaganda also remain without response, then the Soviets could at least set up the cadres for rebuilding Germany within the Free Germany organization.

Whichever of these possibilities would come to fruition, by establishing the National Committee and the League of German Officers in the fall of 1943, Moscow had taken an initiative which had to be successful one way or the other. As an undeniable by-product of their initiative, the impression now existed that Communists had united with forces which they were fighting before.

But are not the Russian intentions and goals hinted at above contradicted by the fact that the Kremlin had extended peace-feelers toward Germany ever since 1942?[166] Did not the Kremlin's continued endeavors to interest the government of the Reich in talks expressly contradict the slogans of the National Committee? Is this a case of deliberate effrontery *vis-à-vis* the National Committee or was Soviet politics simply employing its proved duplicity once again?

It appears that the talks for which the Russian go-between Edgar Clauss met Dr. Peter Kleist in Stockholm in December 1942 and in June and September 1943 were merely additional evidence of the attempt to finish the costly conflict by a German-Soviet rapprochement. Historians have, in fact, viewed these contacts as concrete steps toward just such a goal.[167] Insofar as it has been demonstrated that the Russians intended to blackmail the Western Powers with these Stockholm talks—which Kleist himself has called mysterious[168]—one will definitely have to agree.[169] But the greatest caution should be employed before assuming a real Soviet-German agreement. There are too many factors which make such an agreement improbable. Was an understanding still possible after the Reich had attacked Russia and devastated large parts of that country? Could this psychologically deeply disturbing fact simply be eliminated? Would it not have remained powerful so long as Hitler, the man who had instigated the surprise attack on the Soviet Union, remained at the head of the Reich? Ribbentrop was only too accurate when, considering the Russian feelers, he concluded that one could not keep on oscillating between an anti-Soviet stance, a pact with the Soviets, and then a campaign in the East.[170] And finally: could Hitler have politically survived a separate peace with Russia? Germans would have taken it to mean that the Russian adventure had failed.

These questions are debatable, for it is clear that Hitler's brusque and indignant refusal to permit any further contacts shows that he believed that he still held some powerful cards.[171] Once again it became obvious that with his abnormal state of mind he could choose only between victory and destruction. It is hardly credible that this trait had been overlooked by the cold realism of the Russians. Even if one assumed that they would have been willing to accept the continuing existence of Hitler, their hint that Ribbentrop and Rosenberg would have to be relieved of their posts and a more favorable climate created by this step before any real negotiations could get under way was clear enough.[172]

Thus the series of meetings in Stockholm comes down to one more instance of the general attempt to make the Western Powers reconsider Russian desires by threatening a Soviet-German rapprochement. This interpretation should also eliminate any serious contradiction to the political line of which the National Committee and the League were to remain the most characteristic examples. Basically the talks between Clauss and Kleist simply suggest the possibilities a Germany without Hitler might perhaps have used until early 1944.[173]

On the other hand: what were the chances of the Free Germany movement after its founding?

If one eliminates the absurd argument that its purpose had always been to staff the future government of Germany, then there remained the hope that it would stir up internal German opposition with its propaganda so that Hitler would be eliminated and thus an end brought to the fighting, which had become pointless. The sooner they brought about a successful coup d'état, the more tangible would be a peace that would preserve the substance of the German people. As yet the Allied Powers had made no binding agreements to divide Germany or to eliminate it as an entity.[174] Still very much alive was the well-founded expectation that sufficient weight could be achieved by a timely change of the German situation so that it would be possible to discuss the conditions of peace for Germany. Of course, very little time remained in which these expectations could still be fostered. For by October 1943 at the Conference of Foreign Ministers in Moscow the Allies were already at the fork in the road that was to lead to Teheran and that would render illusory the highest hopes of the committee and the officers' union. But no one can deny the potential that existed during those fall months of 1943. It rested not merely on the relatively intact strength of Germany but also on the desperate need of the Russians, who had to withstand it. If one wanted to, one could point to the similarities between the utterances with which Clauss surprised the Germans at Stockholm and those of Melnikov at Lunyovo.[175]

If, however, the intended coup were only partially successful and Hitler were still in a position to continue the war and undercut any arrangement with the USSR, then at least the war would have to be shortened on separate fronts. Such a development might bring on a sense of tragic depression, might call up the vision of the war's end leaving behind it a broken and divided Germany: none of which, now that the nation at war was going towards its doom under Hitler, could eliminate the need to save whatever could still be saved from the shambles of bankruptcy and agony.

Thus the National Committee and the League of German Officers not only offered a chance to the Soviets. The political developments which were supposed to be influenced by the Free Germany movement had to show which of the two sides would be able to put its ideas into practice in the end.

## CHAPTER THREE

## Allied and German Reactions

THE SOVIET UNION was to triumph this time: the reactions of the Allies fully justified the founding of the National Committee for a Free Germany and the League of German Officers. The statements of London and Washington not only showed distinct traces of fear and shock; their briefness also betrayed a promising helplessness which seemed to bring Stalin a good deal closer to the fulfillment of his wishes.

The Soviets had not officially informed the Western Powers of what was afoot, although the various stages of the development of the Free Germany organization had been reflected in the pages of the POW newspaper *Das freie Wort*.[1] The surprise was therefore complete. While Roosevelt, Hopkins, and Hull refused to comment on the National Committee and the League,[2] Eden declared before the British House of Commons that His Majesty's Government had neither been informed about the founding of the committee nor had they any intention of founding any similar movement themselves.[3]

The embarrassed reactions were based on an agreement reached some time before that Germany could end the war only by unconditional surrender. This understanding meant that there could be no German centers of resistance with political power, and it was mainly intended to free the Soviet Union of its fear that the Western Powers would come to a unilateral separate peace with Hitler. The Allied shock was all the greater because it was the Russian partner to the agreement who refused to honor its terms, which had in principle been laid down by London and Washington. Did not the existence of the Free Germany organization suggest that Moscow, contrary to the common goals, was working toward a separate arrangement with the enemy they were still fighting? Did this not open up disturbing vistas of the future and unity of the coalition which had been formed to win the war and set the world to rights?

Any misgivings of this kind were not voiced. The smooth official statements glossed over them in order not to increase the disquiet. The press, however, raised a hue and cry only after it had got over the paralyzing effect of the initial surprise. But as sober reflection returned, the first comments appeared.

An examination of them may reveal what the statesmen in London and Washington kept silent about. It is true that the *New York Herald Tribune*[4] felt reassured by the "impeccably democratic-capitalist" program of the National Committee; the paper concluded that Communism no longer was an export article after this manifestation of Soviet foreign policy. It is true that the *New York Times*,[5] following Stalin's well-known saying that Hitler was not the German people, viewed the Committee as a move in the war of nerves with the purpose of convincing Germany of the senselessness of its resistance. But the dangers of the Russian step were obvious. Thus a feeling of uncertainty prevailed in the daily press. Reflecting this, the *New York Times* conjured up the specter of a separate peace in another issue and confessed with some trepidation that nothing created problems quite as difficult as the manifesto of the so-called National Committee.[6] Meanwhile the *New Statesman and Nation* surmised two things; either the founding of the Free Germany movement at Krasnogorsk signified an independent Russian action or it called for an intensive collaboration between the Allies.[7] This last reaction not only highlighted the faulty coordination of the Allies' goals; one could also read it as a reminder that it was time to seriously consider those Russian demands that Great Britain and the United States had overlooked up to then.

These Anglo-American comments showed a breadth of vision that contrasted favorably with later reports.[8] The Swiss press, too, tried to judge the bewildering events soberly. Even the *Neue Züricher Zeitung* reflected in its columns the general astonishment about the founding of the National Committee.[9] But it added to this reaction by the insight that this collaboration between Communists and officers, which conflicted with the theory of class warfare, was no accident. The *Basler Nachrichten* emphasized this fact even more forcefully and ironically.[10] It wrote: "Magnanimous man that Stalin is, he has permitted the German Committee to issue a program which is anything but Bolshevist. It is only on the personnel side that the thing begins to smell of Communism."

Here, too, in accord with press reactions in Britain and the United States, the argument that weighed most heavily was that the Free Germany movement would cause grave misgivings. On the one hand, it put into question all the principles valid up to then; the Soviet Union's maneuver also remained, on the other hand, highly misleading, because it divided the Allies instead of uniting them.[11]

Did the Axis Powers sense the propaganda possibilities that this issue offered despite the fact that a considerable number of German soldiers had renounced Hitler? Did they grasp their chance?

Rome spoke of the disunited nations with great satisfaction.[12] Tokyo emphatically proclaimed that *Pravda's* report about the National Committee had hit Washington's political circles like a bombshell.[13]

Berlin, however, remained silent. Here, too, official instructions had to be given before the German public could be informed. Goebbels' private diary provides impressive evidence how difficult it was in this case. There is no lack of abuse heaped on Seydlitz and Count Einsiedel,[14] but the fact that the National Committee was very detrimental to German interests could hardly be denied even amidst accusations of political tactlessness.[15] Despite all this, Schmidt, chief spokesman of the Minister of Propaganda on foreign affairs, issued a first official version at a press conference on July 27, 1943.[16] It stated blandly that Stalin just had established a "Soviet-Germany" at Moscow, which, after the liquidation of the Comintern, had to be viewed as a "purely political maneuver."

For some time the German government seemed to believe that this simplistic "explanation" had solved the problem of the Free Germany organization; the laconic official version was supposed to suffice. But would it still convince anyone if the activities of the National Committee and the League really entered the lists against the leadership of the Reich?

During the final stages of the fighting at Stalingrad, Hitler, with the special sensibilities he possessed for propaganda effects, had already guessed what might happen after a capitulation. Although he did feel responsible for the destruction of the Sixth Army, according to Manstein's evidence,[17] he had not merely heaped abuse on the generals for having chosen Russian imprisonment instead of going heroically to their deaths.[18] Deriding this decision in the presence of his chief of staff, Zeitzler, he also foresaw future moves. "Now the heroism of so many soldiers will be blotted out by one single weak personality—and that man [Paulus] will do it. You just have to imagine it: he'll come into Moscow and then imagine that rat cage [*i.e.*, the Lubyanka prison]! He'll sign anything there. He will make confessions, appeals. You shall see it—they [the generals] shall go the path of weakness all the way down, to the lowest depths.[19] He [Paulus] will soon speak on the radio, you'll see. That Seydlitz and that Schmidt will talk on the radio. They'll lock them up in the rats' nest and two days later they'll have them so broken down that they'll talk immediately."[20]

The repulsive nature of this necrologue, the self-righteousness of which is obviously intended to preclude any attack of remorse, represents, however, only Hitler's first reaction. He continued to follow the fortunes of the National Committee and the League for the rest of the war with special interest, while later his predictable hatred of them continued to burn with undiminished flame. Even though they were to lose in importance because of the lack of success of their propaganda, Hitler remained only too ready to use them for his own purposes from time to time. Thus in the winter of 1944 he triumphantly declared at a briefing session at his headquarters that the Russians had assured the Americans that they had not entered into any binding agreements with the Free Germany movement. This was proof that "those people" had simply been misused and had received neither promises nor assurances.[21] Hitler nevertheless was also plagued by fear and distrust. When the German fortunes of war declined toward their ultimate nadir he attributed possibilities to the National Committee and the League that they had long ceased to possess. In January 1945, he accused the Fourth Army's commander, Hossbach, of complicity with the "Seydlitz officers" after hearing of his independent decision to withdraw from Eastern Prussia.[22] When Colonel General Rendulic took over Army Group North, Hitler conveyed to him his fear that if Königsberg was lost, the Seydlitz group might proclaim a revolutionary government in that old city of the Prussian kings.[23] Not to miss a macabre climax even here, Hitler finally opined during a conversation with Göring and Jodl that they might use the National Committee and the League as a scarecrow against the Western Powers.[24] Possessed by the idea that a Bolshevist Germany must scare the Western Powers, he intended to play reports into the hands of London and Washington according to which "200,000 Germans, led by their officers and drunk with Communism, would march into the Reich." This unrealistic notion characterizes the personal reactions which the National Committee and the League evoked in Hitler. But all those more or less absurd utterances within the inner circle could not free Hitler from the necessity of coming out with an official statement on the collective action of German POWs in the Soviet Union. Both the soldiers at the front and the people at home had to be "enlightened."

It is impossible to determine whether all of the measures directed against the Free Germany organization emanated from Hitler himself. Wherever they may have originated, he can only have approved of their harshness and relentlessness.

German countermeasures took two forms. One took the form of practical decisions, the other, propaganda guidelines which tried to refute the arguments of the committee or the officers' union that filtered across on the air or via the Eastern Front lines.

On the practical side extremely tough orders were issued; they demanded the court-martial of all those who were known to be active collaborators and who had fallen into German hands again.[25] Here the only possible sentence was death. Members of the National Committee and the League who had returned of their own free will, however, were to be concentrated in a special camp and there interrogated thoroughly. Even if it turned out that these officers and soldiers had obviously been forced to join, the army was not to use them on the Eastern Front any more because of their political unreliability.[26]

No official statement had been issued up to that time, although all these measures indicate that National Socialist leadership did not doubt in the least the existence of the Free Germany organization. Hitler started to hit back only after the committee and the officers' union had tried to influence the divisions trapped at Cherkassy. The Supreme Court-Martial of the Reich was ordered to open proceedings against Walther von Seydlitz-Kurzbach. It reached its verdict at Dresden on April 26, 1944.[27] The Court sentenced the general *in absentia* to death for military and high treason; it pronounced him unfit to serve in the armed forces and revoked his rank; his property was confiscated and he lost all civil rights for the rest of his life. All relatives of members of the committee or the officers' union were placed under the lurking surveillance of the Gestapo. Later on, wives were told that they could ease their position by getting a divorce. But after July 20, 1944, all "kith and kin" were held responsible and interned in prisons and concentration camps.[28] This decree even extended to distant relatives and children. In some cases entire families suffered together. But the younger children of General von Seydlitz were isolated by the State. Under a false name they found themselves put into the custody of a boarding school at Bad Sachsa. It was the same place in which the children and grandchildren of Stauffenberg, Tresckow, and Goerdeler were put under surveillance.[29]

Repressive and provocative as these measures were, they were nevertheless unable to eliminate the activities of the National Committee and the League. Thus the guidelines which had been drawn up in the meantime relating to the whole "Free Germany" affair gained considerably in importance.

From the start the same information was to be valid for both the Nazi Party and the armed forces. One can nevertheless distinguish two phases in the development of its content; it was only later that the two arguments became mixed and remained unchanged until the end of the war.[30]

During the first phase the National Socialist régime pretended to incredulity. By presenting individual names of the Free Germany organization as forgeries, it intended to rob the slogans of the National Committee of their effectiveness from the start. German leadership was definite: a collaboration of German soldiers with the Soviets remained inconceivable to the German troops. They therefore asserted in this case that the formation of the committee and the officers' union had been brought about only by torture, hunger, and drugs—by means, in short, which made any genuine decision impossible. This version had a good deal of probability to recommend it. It corresponded to the picture of Soviet Russia that German propaganda had drawn, that had become generally accepted, and that had killed off many critical voices.

Even as the names of members of the committee and the officers' union became increasingly known through the front and the radio, the German side still clung to its version of enforced treason. For a long time it kept discovering "especially crass falsehoods" in the illustrated loose-leaf newspaper *Free Germany*. It stopped denying the activities of once leading soldiers but still could not endure seeing their often poorly reproduced photographs. But now—during the second phase—the propaganda which Lunyovo dared to distribute in the shape of the manifesto and other appeals had to be met by a counteroffensive.

This "counteroffensive" took a strictly polemical form and gathered its greatest strength from the perspective of the friend-foe relationship which had become traumatic in the East. Consequently, the knowledge of the ruthlessness of Bolshevism was used to the hilt, and it was insinuated that having any truck with Bolshevism only meant furthering its cause.[31] This argument defined the stand which the party and the armed forces had to take toward the Free Germany movement. Individual personal stories of "the organization of traitors" were intended to undercut still more the words emanating from Moscow. That these portraits dealt mainly with "fanatical Communists and Jews" was self-evident, if only because they were best suited to evoke or stir up anew emotions of repulsion.[32]

In the polemic against the goals of the National Committee any hint of self-criticism that might have given the appearance that the manifesto contained legitimate arguments was avoided. The committee's thesis that the coalition of Germany's enemies was growing daily was called an "assertion unsubstantiated by anything" in the "Bulletin of the High Command of the Armed Forces."[33] Its intention to establish a strong, democratic state was brushed aside with the remark that in view of the rape of the Baltic states that could only refer to democracy "as we do not define it." But that was not all. Presupposing unconditional faith in the supreme leader, the High Command countered the appeal that Hitler step down with the argument that such a move would be equivalent to deliberate suicide. "For who is to take the Führer's place? A 'genuinely German Government' perhaps!? —as the appeal says. To call a government of shanghaied men and traitors German, true and strong, is more than ridiculous. How could any government be strong that was born out of chaos? In 1918 they also promised us paradise on earth and they gave us hunger. What would a free, independent, and peaceful Germany look like? It would only be the shabby transitional stage to a Soviet Republic. For if the Red Army were permitted to march unopposed to the frontiers of Germany, Messrs. Weinert and Pieck would see to it that nothing would ever come of their free Germany."[34] The sentences might have been half-baked propaganda, but by evoking memories of 1918 they touched the soldiers' nerve spot. It was an appeal to prejudices that were too deep-seated to make anyone challenge the empty phrases of the High Command.

Thus the glorification of fighting and of doing one's duty at any price once more remained all that was left. With the troops this apotheosis fell on fertile ground and found support, especially after July 20, when the men of the Resistance were accused of having worked together with the Free Germany organization.[35]

The harshness of all this counterpropaganda also corresponded to the stand of the Wehrmacht's High Command, which had sharply denied the existence and goals of both the committee and the officers' union ever since they had first made their appearance.[36] It remained sympathetic, up to a point, to the exceptional bitterness which must have filled the generals, officers, and soldiers of Stalingrad when they saw themselves left to their destruction. It was the virulence of the so-called "encirclement-psychosis" which partially explained how a National Committee could have come into existence in Moscow at all.[37] But could that justify the public apostasy to the extent documented by the Free Germany organization? Could it become the basis of a position that supported the enemy, with the doubtful intention of subverting the German front lines? To the High Command the answers to these questions were self-evident.

Hitler, nevertheless, decided that a special gesture of his field marshals was in order. On March 19, 1944, Field Marshal von Rundstedt, in the presence of commanders from all parts of the armed forces, handed Adolf Hitler a document in which the military leaders not only swore unconditional loyalty and obedience;[38] by contemptuously turning their backs on Seydlitz, they also agreed tacitly with his contumacious death sentence and his dishonorable discharge.[39] Although Hitler could hardly have been in doubt about what this circle thought of the National Committee for a Free Germany, he nevertheless chose to handle the declaration as an ultimatum: any refusal to sign would have been tantamount to demonstrating sympathy for the National Committee and the League of German Officers. Thus General von Seydlitz, accused by a hate-filled megalomaniac of having deserted his hard-pressed troops, finally saw himself ostracized by the field marshals of the armed forces also.

It is quite remarkable that those generals who were captured in the summer of 1944 and who signed various appeals were neither mentioned nor, like Seydlitz, dishonorably discharged from the army.[40] Quite clearly the intention was to strike out at the Free Germany movement only in the person of the one Stalingrad general whose name, apart from that of Paulus,[41] was best known to the fighting troops.

Now finally the official radio stations of the Reich, the *Völkischer Beobachter*, and the journal *Front und Heimat* picked up the field marshals' declaration and held forth with their own observations on the Committee about which they had been silent up to then.[42] This, however, produced no new arguments. On the contrary, the unbridled hate campaign of *Front und Heimat* on the lines of "Not National Committee—Soviet Committee!" managed to fall far below the previous level of National Socialist counterpropaganda.[43]

These journalistic comments represented only a part of German reaction to the Free Germany movement, and their crass propaganda had only a partial influence on a blinded public. But even diplomatic circles, normally more adaptable in their ideas and combinations, tended in the same direction on this issue.[44] In both cases the dominating impression was that the National Committee was an all-too obvious maneuver. In both cases the opinion was that the German officers and soldiers had condemned themselves to false hopes if they actually collaborated with the Soviets. Remarkable as such a harmony of views must have been, it could not keep the group of experienced Eastern experts from according considerable importance to the Free Germany organization.[45] They were generally of the opinion that the committee and the officers' union had the primary task of undermining the morale of Germany's Eastern Front. But they were also convinced that these organizations could alter their goals if conditions changed.[46]

The émigrés in the West, too, showed differing reactions. It is true that the National Committee received enthusiastic congratulatory telegrams from Switzerland, England, and Mexico.[47] It is also true that Thomas Mann sent a message of unconditional approval. All these manifestations expressed deep satisfaction that the National Committee had been founded and showed a surge of optimism and a determination to step up the efforts to get rid of National Socialism. But there was also one discordant note among all the panegyrics; it came from London and originated with the German Social Democrats (SPD).

They certainly did not condemn resistance to the Hitler régime, but they nevertheless expressed important reservations about the National Committee for a Free Germany. This negative reaction related not only to the people on the Committee. It was directed mainly against some of the goals in the manifesto that seemed unacceptable to the Social Democrats. In a letter to Dr. Kuczinsky, who had issued an appeal for the founding of a Free Germany movement in Great Britain, Wilhelm Sander thus declared emphatically and programatically: "The German Social Democrats will not participate in any common front that includes generals of the Nazi Army that has brought shame and contempt upon the name of Germany. We furthermore reject the arguments concerning legally acquired personal property. We are well aware of the probability that our fight for a Socialist Germany may not lead to success in the near future. But we do not consider it the task of German political émigrés to express the demands of capitalistic society."[48]

Such thoughts had shaped the Social Democrats too profoundly to allow them to change. Whatever Sander might have omitted in his reasoning in September 1943, Erich Ollenhauer hastened to add in January 1945. In answer to an article by Wilhelm Koenen, he once more clearly delineated the limits of agreement between Social Democrats and the Committee. Once more he stressed the fact that the Free Germany organization in the Soviet Union did not provide an appropriate platform for political collaboration. The colors black-white-red furthermore gave rise to the criticism that they confused rather than clarified the lines of the democratic front.[49] The tone of Ollenhauer's voice became cutting when he once more refused any alliance between the generals and officers and the SPD. "The truly national interest of a future Germany demands not the united front of all 'Free Germans' but an unequivocal and uncompromising fighting position and the continued willingness of all German democrats to fight against German nationalism. Even those *Junkers* who today, as German officers, are crying 'Down with Hitler' have to be thrown out of their social position of power. The framework of a genuine community of action would have to be much more narrowly conceived than that of the National Committee, but it would only reflect reality."[50]

Did this not express the very sentiments that, deep down, had probably never left the Communists who belonged to the committee? Did not these sentences unmask the cramped, unnatural character that marked the alliance within the Free Germany organization? Anyone surveying the whole development in all its stages might get the impression that here we have a prophetic foreshadowing of all that would later be ruthlessly revealed. But essentially these utterances of the Social Democrats represent no more than one reaction and that not even a good one, considering the promising insights which moved the non-socialists within the Resistance. For the paramount question remained whether or not the National Committee and the League of German Officers would be successful with their concept of propaganda. First, it remained to be seen if they would contribute to that change without which a new Germany could never flourish.

## The Organization, Front and Camp Propaganda of the National Committee and the League of German Officers

AFTER THE NATIONAL COMMITTEE merged with the League of German Officers in September 1943, the delegations present had been sent out charged with the task of winning additional members in the camps. The League's activities remained limited to the four officers' camps, Yelabuga, Oranky, Susdal, and Camp 150, while in the enlisted men's camps only a Free Germany movement, which was directed by the National Committee,[1] was to exist in the future. Lunyovo had strictly divided the work in both cases. The representatives for the officers' camps were nominated by the board of the League of German Officers, while Ulbricht picked the National Committee's representatives in the enlisted men's camps. There was no exchange of experiences; the two spheres of influence were sharply defined and mutually respected.[2]

At Lunyovo, too, the impression was maintained that the Free Germany movement comprised two organizations. Weinert, Hetz, and Einsiedel represented the twenty-five members of the National Committee. Seydlitz, Daniels, and van Hooven were placed at the head of the board of the officers' union, which included nineteen officers in all.[3] Both bodies had been elected by the delegations and were charged with taking up propaganda work in their name.

Although this organizational structure reflected the existence of two entities side by side, the mutual exchange of members had already suggested a merger. Now, after the election to the vice-presidency of generals Seydlitz and Edler von Daniels, it was actually carried out. In principle forty members (later a certain number of free corresponding members without a vote were added to this number) represented the National Committee at Lunyovo acting as its plenary and highest executive body.[4] According to the statutes that had been prepared, a plenary session had to meet on all important occasions, and at least once a month, to take a stand on topical issues and to decide upon necessary measures by simple majority vote.[5] This presupposed at least a relatively firm operational framework which was provided by an Executive Committee (*Geschäftsführender Ausschuss*).[6] The National Committee members on this executive organ were the president and first vice-president as first and second chairmen and the two chief editors responsible for newspaper and radio. It further included another ten members who were elected in equal numbers by the National Committee and the League. This important committee had the task of putting into practice the decisions reached by the National Committee as a whole, of preparing the agenda of the plenary sessions, and of reporting on the activities of the previous sessions. Independent of these powers, the Executive Committee had considerable additional powers. The plenary sessions had to vote on basic questions that arose between sessions, but the Executive Committee could express its opinion immediately on any important question of politics or propaganda and could hand down binding guidelines to all the working bodies of the movement.[7] It also had the mandate to keep in contact not only with the representatives at the front and in the camps and with Soviet administrative bodies, but also to form a so-called Operational Section (*Operative Abteilung*) in addition to groups of experts for economic, socio-political, and cultural affairs. The members of the Operational Section came out of the Executive Committee which thus tried to delegate some of its work and to remain more flexible.[8]

Given his mentality, it was predictable that Ulbricht would plan, direct, and push by concerted action the reports of the National Committee's left wing in the various working groups.[9] He often tried hard to find out ahead of time what the officers' union had deliberated on and what they were trying to get through. Quite frequently one had to expect Communist attempts to outflank the "right wing." The practice instituted by the board of the League of German Officers, in which none of the old National Committee officers held a seat, of conferring independently once a week and receiving reports became, therefore, all the more important.[10] Here the Communist side had managed to secure the services of First Lieutenant von Kirschhofer, who suddenly left after an Austrian National Committee was founded.[11] But the internal cohesion of the League was helped because its members in committees and editorial offices remained responsible to and received directions from the board of the League of German Officers.

At Lunyovo, the National Committee and the officers' union were housed in a building which had once been a recreation center for Russian railroad employees.[12] The two-storied, flat-roofed building of rough brick was situated near the Moscow-Leningrad road, directly on the banks of the Klyasma River, in surroundings not without a certain charm. A steep bank led down to the small river. There was a playing field behind the house. But the superficially pleasant panorama also had its darker touches. The guards and patrols had orders to keep out of the sight of anyone in the house. The absence of watchtowers, otherwise a fixture of normal POW Camps, also gave the impression of unusual freedom of movement. But cleverly placed stockades topped with barbed wire stifled this impression of freedom even though a relatively large space had been kept open for moving around freely. The impression of a camp remained, therefore, even here, and it contrasted unpleasantly with the purposes for which the whole National Committee had been formed. All attempts to change the situation failed because of the repeatedly stressed security considerations of the Soviets.[13] They seemed, in view of German surprise operations, not to be so far-fetched that the Russian attitude should be taken to be simply a thinly disguised maneuver.

It seems that other problems, too, at first served to mitigate the feeling that they were in a POW camp—which the well-arranged barbed wire obstacles simply had to foster. Although General von Seydlitz was given a simple private room and all the other living quarters housed no more than four inmates, the food at Lunyovo was at first below the level of many other camps.[14] It was only after massive protests forced the Soviets to remove the corrupt Russian administration of the mess hall that the rations gradually moved up to the level of the generals' camp. But even so, it still was bread, soup, and kasha. The dreary monotony of the food was marked and kept alive the fear of insufficient nourishment even at Lunyovo.[15]

The Russian guards, on the other hand, reflected the importance of the House.[16] In addition to Colonel Schostin, the camp commandant, generally known to be kind-hearted, there were a female doctor and three or four administrative officers. Even at Lunyovo, however, they were outnumbered by a strong NKVD detachment; it comprised more than ten officers and occupied half of the first floor of the House, which was reserved for the Russians. But they remained in the background until the moderate elements of the House had lost all their influence.

But only one part of the Free Germany movement was in Lunyovo. The other part worked and lived in Moscow, about twenty miles away. Here civilians ruled supreme. Here the executive powers were in the hands of the émigrés who came to Lunyovo by bus from time to time to discuss matters with the soldiers in the mess hall of the House of Lunyovo and to make decisions.[17] This helped dispel the feeling of isolation that must have weighed heavily on the National Committee's members in uniform, but it could not disguise the fact that the so-called Town Committee always had more leverage.[18]

This impression was created by the Russian support of the émigrés even on issues on which they ostensibly agreed with the officers' union. And it was reinforced even more by the inscrutable Muscovite machinery, where it was quite possible that something was approved and carried out which might well distort the German officers' intentions.[19]

Moscow was indeed the center of the organization, if only because it was the seat of the National Committee's president, and of the editorial offices of the newspaper and radio programs of the Free Germany movement. The National Committee was given one floor of an inconspicuous building near Arbat Square which Weinert, Ulbricht, and the editorial staffs moved into.[20] Together with them the Russian personnel chief Vorobiev, and Kozlov, liaison man to the CPSU (Communist Party of the Soviet Union), settled down there, both men who significantly enough kept pressure on the National Committee's work and who were painstakingly careful simply to fulfill their functions.[21] Officially, the National

Committee, which did most of its political work here, was named "USSR–Institute No. 99." This designation had to be used for all contacts with Soviet officials. All the Committee's members in Moscow had received identification cards, but they had been told not to name the National Committee as their employer.[22]

Weinert and Ulbricht had private rooms.[23] Their activities thus remained essentially unknown. If this situation seemed justifiable for the Committee's president—and Weinert went to Lunyovo regularly—it certainly opened up some less acceptable prospects in the case of Walter Ulbricht, who was rather cautious at first. For in his case drive, unscrupulousness, and an indefatigable ability for work combined in a special way. His narrowly conceived ideology always searched for the orthodox way, even in the exceptional situation of 1943, for paths which were often simply aimed at thwarting the soldiers' intentions.

The work of the newspaper's editors was much more open to public view. Rudolf Herrnstadt was the first editor in chief.[24] As a onetime correspondent of the *Berliner Tageblatt* in Warsaw, Herrnstadt combined an arrogant personality with a cold, overbearing intelligence. He always kept everyone at a distance and could barely conceal his loathing for everything German. This journalist, who liked to appear superior and elegant, ran the weekly four-page newspaper *Free Germany* with considerable independence. He provoked considerable conflict by his editing of many articles, and his coldness made it impossible for the editorial staff of the newspaper to form a happy working team.

It was Herrnstadt's colleague Alfred Kurella who tempered his negative influence.[25] During the recruitment of the officers, Kurella had already made an impression as a first-rate mind. Now this noted Russian translator of Asian lyrical poetry once again impressed one by his lack of dogmatism. It was, therefore, thanks to him and to the writer Willi Bredel, who was later editor in chief for a time, that the newspaper had an unusually liberal tone.[26] Thus the military analyses by Karl Maron, whose character had set many people at Lunyovo guessing, showed flexibility which got very close to the actual events. The economic, cultural, and political columns, too, mostly reflected a spirit of astonishing openness.[27] Not all of this, certainly, was merely a tactical maneuver, determined by the knowledge that it was momentarily opportune to withdraw ideologically in order to march forward later with Marxist slogans once more. These articles and appeals are rather a marked and precise reflection of the Russian point of view, which held that Moscow's interests at that time were identical with those of the generals and officers. Had it been otherwise, the soldiers could hardly have been moved to a collaboration for whose sake they held weekly working sessions at Lunyovo.[28] At these sessions they decided what articles to publish and established the general line that the contributors would follow. The suggestions and criticisms, the discussions and decisions that succeeded each other at Lunyovo did not, of course, alter the fact that the editorial office at Moscow still had the final word on the manuscripts, as was Herrnstadt's way. A general survey of the contributions of generals and officers, however, shows that overwhelmingly they found their way into print in the form in which they had been conceived.[29] One must note, on the other hand, that some collaborators, like generals von Daniels and Lenski, simply accepted and signed articles prepared at Moscow.[30] This type of collaboration, however, remained limited, as it could be imposed only on persons without intellectual independence or of expressed Communist leanings.

The news items which formed the base of the analyses and commentaries in the newspaper were provided by Radio Monitoring Service 205.[31] Known as the successor to the Comintern, this institute monitored German and Allied radio broadcasts. The picture of the outside world thus obtained remained, therefore, relatively accurate, although the young collaborator Wolfgang Leonhard's task was simply to collect all the news that seemed important to him for the newspaper *Free Germany*.[32]

When the National Committee's newspaper began to take an increasingly radical stand during 1945, this change reflected the change in the situation. After Germany's surrender, all ideological considerations for the officers' nationalist line ceased to be binding. It is therefore not surprising that the last editor in chief, the Communist lawyer Lothar Bolz, a narrow-minded, spineless character, once more provoked the same violent conflicts that Herrnstadt's absolutism had caused earlier.[33] It was the all too fitting closing of the circle. For after the National Committee had been dissolved, Bolz also took over the *News for German Prisoners of War in the Soviet Union,* a paper which completely gave up the anti-fascist united front for a rabid Marxism.[34]

The editorial staff of the radio station, like that of the newspaper, was composed of free and imprisoned members of the National Committee.[35] Anton Ackermann was the head of Radio "Free Germany."[36] He had been active at an early age in the youth movement of the Communist Party, and shortly before he was sent into the Spanish Civil War this exceptionally gifted thirty-year-old had been elected to the Central Committee and the Politburo of the KPD. This small, gaunt man had remained an independent thinker of high caliber, despite the fact that he was considered a reliable functionary. Open-minded and conciliatory, this brain of the radio editorial staff not only ruled with an easy hand; but, convinced that something was to be learned from the experiences of the generals and officers, his open-mindedness also guaranteed successful teamwork.

Insofar as émigrés and members of the town committee were responsible for them, the broadcasts were prepared at Moscow.[37] The generals, officers, and soldiers, on the other hand, wrote their contributions at Lunyovo. Every week, Hans Mahle of the editorial staff drove out to them to record speeches and appeals and then transfer them onto records.[38] His work was only rarely criticized. Wherever a speaker insisted that nothing be changed or cut, his wish was respected.[39] And all of this could be checked, too. The inmates of the House at Lunyovo had the constant use of a radio set and could thus check whether the broadcasts were put on the air distorted or unchanged.[40] This set also enabled the officers to receive German and foreign broadcasts without interference.

This freedom of action remained typical for quite some time. At first the Hungarian Communist Ernö Gerö proofread the manuscripts of the newspaper *Free Germany* and he did so sympathetically and with astonishing technical knowledge.[41] Special tolerance was also shown by the "Glav PURKKA" or Political Central Administration of the Red Army, whose Section 7 had to grant the permissions for the radio broadcasts.[42] Its chief, Colonel Braginsky, a loyal officer, would most certainly have refused to act on the basis of anything but directives given to him. Since these apparently

permitted considerable conciliatory latitude, his checks were, as a
rule, carried out without any objections. All this worked without
complications because Braginsky, a former university professor, had
the intellectual caliber to grasp the essentials very quickly and
thus shorten the censorship procedure considerably.[43] Whenever
the newspaper or radio did, however, raise problems, it was Braginsky's immediate superior, Colonel General Alexander Shcherbakov,
who had to make the decision; he was the representative of the
Politburo in charge of the National Committee and the officers'
union.[44]

In the summer of 1944 the Town Committee moved into a villa
in the center of Moscow, which it shared with the Polish Committee
of National Liberation. Even then the newspaper with its black-
white-red stripes continued to be printed at the Iskra Revoliutsii
printing house across the street from the National Committee's
first home.[45] The radio station, however, was situated in the Soviet
Union's first television studio, which had been set up in Shablovka
Street in a Moscow suburb in 1938–1939.[46] The soundproof speaker's booth from which they broadcast had been tuned in to German
wavelengths by special equipment. It guaranteed reasonable reception even when German stations tried to jam this sender. There
were no mechanisms that would have eliminated at this point what
had been approved earlier. There was, however, one operator in
the house who took the place of the monitoring service usually
obligatory for all other sections of Radio Moscow; his sole task was
to spot the occasional grammatical mistake and to correct it later.

The station was on the air starting July 18, 1943. Its signature
tune was the opening bars of the German song *"Der Gott, der Eisen
wachsen liess"* ("God, who made the iron to grow"); its announcers,
Wolfgang Leonhard and Fritz Heilmann. Both belonged to the
left wing of the émigrés and the Young Communists and they took
turns announcing. "Free Germany" was on the air four times daily
between 10:30 A.M and 11:45 P.M. Later seven broadcasts were
sent in the same span of time. Over the years its staff included almost all members that had made a name for themselves in the National Committee or the League of German Officers. Thus there
were no limitations on the topics to be treated. The commentaries of
those staff members working in the Town Committee's villa were

broadcast anonymously, as opposed to those of the soldiers, whose contributions went on the air with their full names. For this reason some of the émigrés remained largely behind the scenes, although their activities at the radio station carried special responsibility. Parallel to all this, they ran cultural broadcasts, mostly on Sundays, which challenged National Socialism with the philosophers and poets of German idealism. They were edited by the two émigrés Alfred Kurella and Fritz Erpenbeck, as well as Dr. Hadermann, who also was on the air as military commentator.[47]

The broadcasts normally followed one and the same pattern, news and commentaries, followed by a listing of the names of German POWs in the Soviet Union.[48] The newscasts were taken from Soviet, Western European, and American sources. Although their selection clearly showed a desire to make the situation of Germany unmistakably clear, they nevertheless revealed a degree of objectivity unimaginable under Russian conditions up to then. There was only one exception to this objectivity. It concerned the official communiqués of the Red Army, which were reproduced unchallenged. Their figures for booty and victories border on the fantastic, even where undeniable successes of the Red Army could be extolled. But here many commentaries made up for any damage that glib or tendentious newscasting might have caused. For it was easy enough for even a cautious commentator to make the impending catastrophe clear to the Wehrmacht and the German people.

Numerous officers, especially generals von Seydlitz, Dr. Korfes, and Lattmann, were the authors of strongly personal commentaries which cast a searching light on the agony of German arms that was to last several years.[49] They tried not to influence the common soldier directly but attempted to clarify the military situation by sober analysis. All their commentaries tried to prove that Germany could no longer win the war and that all further resistance to the Allies would only weaken the forces which were essential to a tolerable peace. This faith was never denied, and it lent an exceptional dignity to these commentaries. Even when the lines became stabilized for a time and gave rise to optimism, the speakers remained convinced that it was only a breathing space and could not alter the general course of the war. Unequal strength, the senseless attrition of men and materials, empty phrases, and Germany's increasingly frightening isolation—taken together they all lent a prophetic vision to those commentaries that appears even more impressive when viewed in retrospect. Korfes' polemical replies to the official military commentator on the German side, Lieutenant General Dittmar, have a special power.[50] They often left the conclusions up to the listener, but their clear logic was all the more convincing because of it. By eschewing malicious polemics, Korfes let the depressing reality speak for itself.

The reading of the names of those who had been taken prisoner by the Russians normally came at the end of the broadcasts.[51] It was not merely intended to take in the other side subconsciously. It was chiefly a humane act, since the government of the Reich had refused, to the great and bitter disappointment of the officers and soldiers of Stalingrad, to accept any communications from German POWs in the Soviet Union.[52]

To start with, the newspaper and radio were more an outgrowth of the existence of the committee and the League than a guarantee for the form of their activities. If both organizations at Lunyovo intended to move from thought to action, they had to influence the German side with a clear-cut slogan. Decisive successes could be achieved only here, if they could be achieved at all. It was here, too, that it must become apparent which forces determined and supported the Free Germany movement. This gave propaganda a central importance, which it retained to the end.

Many recruitment drives had shown that it was on precisely this question that various groups diverged from the start. Ever since it first published its manifesto in July 1943, the National Committee had been solely animated by the idea that the end of the war could be brought about only by mobilizing all forces.[53] The German people and the armed forces were called upon to turn against the National Socialist régime and to put an end to the fighting. The overriding conviction that Hitler had to be overthrown required no nuances. The aim was above all a broad base, and the revolutionary action demanded for Hitler's overthrow seemed totally unconcerned about the potential chaos, which was hardly a suitable goal of a revolution.

The officers in the National Committee were a hopeless minority. They could not have won out against the ideas referred to above even if they had taken a stand against them. Only after it was apparent that a new situation had developed with the founding of the League did the line that the initiating group, and later on the generals, had fought for begin to gain ground. All subversive activities yielded to a propaganda campaign that was directed above all at that leadership in the Army that could still act.[54] This concept was approved by the Soviets. Prior to the fusion of the officers' union and the National Committee, separate discussions with the émigrés were, however, needed before they subordinated themselves to the soldiers.

The first joint plenary session of September 24, 1943, where the differences of opinion once more clashed violently, made clear how strong the resistance to the new line still was.[55] When several members of the National Committee, who had not been privy to the agreement between Seydlitz and the émigrés, insisted on the old line, the League publicly charged that it was absurd. The officers argued that to continue in the old way would spell certain failure, because no propaganda aimed at the lower ranks could ever set in motion any decisive actions. Moreover, if the Wehrmacht were subverted, future order would be imperiled, for without the Wehrmacht any meaningful change of government would remain illusory. These arguments not only had in their favor an intimate knowledge of the German military, of which the men of Stalingrad had been a part; by tearing to shreds the propaganda employed up to then, they necessarily led toward the argument that it was above all the Wehrmacht leadership that had to be approached. The League believed that on this basis they could work with and encourage many existing feelings of opposition in the future. Besides, their position and power of command alone enabled them to act in a way that held out hope for the preservation of Germany, which was the common goal of the National Committee and the League of German Officers.

After the Russians and the émigrés both agreed with the League, the propaganda line was basically set. Any further agitated discussions would merely serve to clarify it. Thus the approach which all sides finally agreed on most decidedly reflected the point of view of the League of German Officers. The word "subversion" became taboo and was avoided. The Wehrmacht had to remain intact. This decision meant that there must be no appeals for anarchic actions. It was proposed instead to win over the top echelons of the German army. They were supposed to lead the German armed forces back to the frontiers of the Reich in an orderly fashion and thus give the signal for the overthrow of Hitler.

On the surface, it may look as if even this clearly defined conception had its drawbacks. Had not the officers approved the manifesto, and therefore its propaganda line, by their signatures?[56] Had they not agreed with the National Committee that the attempts to influence the bulk of the fighting soldiers should be continued?[57] Strictly speaking, this indicates an inconsistency that from the very beginning endangered their propaganda plans. But the officers were convinced that the manifesto was acceptable as long as the National Committee and the League of German Officers both adhered to the new tactics, just as they were convinced that by itself the manifesto would never effect a violent change of affairs.[58] Their concessions concerning propaganda directed at the lower ranks, however, showed hardly more than decorative good will. For left to themselves, the lower ranks could not act independently. If the Wehrmacht was to carry out an organized withdrawal to the Reich's frontiers, then the soldiers would always need the guiding hand of resolute superiors. That meant that the propaganda, whose influence could not be limited to the officers corps anyway, could ultimately only bear fruit in keeping with the intentions of the League. This propaganda had to awaken a sense of urgency in the troops and thus prepare the measures which were to be taken by the higher echelons exclusively.

But suppose a higher commander, addressed by name, chose to follow the appeals by a bold decision. Wouldn't that, in any case, help Russian interests? Wouldn't it mean tearing holes in the German lines, leaving fellow soldiers defenseless against an enemy who stood to reap all the advantages of such disorganization? To put it differently: could the propaganda approach of the National Committee and the League not be carried out except at the price of chaos after all?

It would be absurd to assume that the League of German Officers expected the chief of an army to remove his troops from the firing lines in order to fight against Hitler single-handedly.[59]

It is true that at this stage the officers' union was in no position to co-ordinate a potential conspiracy; but such co-ordination would itself have to be brought about just as surely by the troop commanders that had been won over. It would be their job to co-ordinate any decisions conspiratorially with men of the same persuasion and to ensure concerted action at a later date. Insofar as such a development could not have been an exclusively German affair, the establishment of contacts with Seydlitz, possible in many ways, would have suggested itself. A withdrawal of the German forces would certainly have been under discussion only after an effective organization had been formed and a cease-fire arranged with the Red Army for various sections of the front. Such an agreement, or even to assume that such was possible, may seem utopian today. But abuse of such an agreement for the sake of a partial military success would have immediately deprived the Soviets of any more far-reaching opportunity. The general situation in the fall of 1943 pointed toward a different interpretation. At that time, at least, Moscow's wooing of the National Committee and the League of German Officers aimed at more than just a breakthrough at the front. What was at stake then and what was discussed with some Russian generals in a detailed review of all eventualities was rather how to avoid fighting outside the Soviet Union. It was thus a goal that, in the view of the men at Lunyovo, was in the well-considered German interest and that therefore reflected an over-all conception acceptable to both sides.

No matter what might eventually be realized of all this, now was the time to start the new front-line propaganda. The situation seemed ripe. In the East the last German offensive, Operation "Citadel," had already been drowned in its own blood.[60] Ever since the German divisions had melted away pointlessly near Byelgorod and Orel they had been involved in a bitter defensive struggle which threatened in time to decimate them completely. The whole front had fallen back on the Dnieper River, but even now it remained more than doubtful whether the weakened eastern armies would be able to hold this unfortified line, considering Hitler's method of leadership. The questions about the future took on a particularly pressing urgency in Russia. In view of this situation it was beyond all doubt that salvation could be found only in a withdrawal which would bring about peace and overthrow Hitler, that fount of evil. So they went to work at Moscow and Lunyovo.

The structure and organization of work at the front had to be created, as it were, from scratch. Although some experiences were available from the period between 1941 and 1943, they were inadequate on the whole; in a changed situation new forces had to be taken into account. New problems of ever-expanding space also demanded attention. For contrary to the first years of the Russian campaign, when propaganda experiments had been possible only at the focal points of battles, all fronts could now be reached.[61]

Although the Executive Committee had the power to delegate representatives for the various parts of the front, it was the Town Committee—and above all Ulbricht—who ultimately decided upon their selection and competency.[62] All crucial directives came from him; all the information which the delegations sent back to him was first gathered in his hands. Not that he always kept it to himself! At that time there was such a strong desire to maintain the equality of both organizations at Lunyovo that most of the reports were communicated to the generals and officers. But the Town Committee retained the upper hand from the start even in cases where a number of delegations of the League had been sent to the front together with those of the National Committee.[63]

The representatives' area of activities extended from Lapland to the Black Sea.[64] Their numbers varied from time to time, but must have been quite considerable altogether. The exact number is unknown. Frequently the number of missions had to make up for the limited number of delegations. The delegations normally consisted of one main delegate (*Frontbevollmächtigte*) and several aides, who, sometimes in German uniforms and sometimes in Russian quilted uniforms, wore black–white–red armbands with the legend "Free Germany" around their left arms. The chief delegate acted as spokesman for the delegation *vis-à-vis* the Red Army, while the aides, often not recruited until reaching the front, had the job of supporting his work. But they were also frequently instructed in such detail that they could function independently as delegates or trustees within a division or army.[65]

Originally all the directives delimiting the delegations' work derived from the propaganda line of Lunyovo.[66] The tenor of the directives, however, did not exclude the possibility that, depending on the individual situation, the spoken propaganda contained arguments which above all reflected the personality of the individual delegate. Because of the changing situation at the front, this drawback had to be accepted, for it was impossible to direct every detail of the work at the front.

Far more serious was the unwillingness of the Red Army to tone down, let alone stop, its own propaganda.[67] It continued side by side with that of the National Committee, although it had long ago foundered completely with its appeal to the lowest instincts. The result was a propaganda mélange that inflicted serious damage on every mission and decreased its chances of success, which were not very good to start with. For the National Committee and the League of German Officers pushed the slogan "Orderly withdrawal to the frontiers of the Reich," while the insulting propaganda of the Division VII [of the Political Administration of the Red Army, in charge of propaganda to the *Wehrmacht*] continued its appeals to desert to the enemy, which it had used since 1941. Lunyovo never did get the Russians to give up their propaganda activities. Any success on this issue would have meant Moscow's giving up a facet of the war that it apparently regarded as essential. But this kind of multiple approach, which might prove politically fruitful from time to time, was to be a dead end in the given context, for it overtaxed one and the same object—in this case the German soldier.

All of this was exacerbated rather than ameliorated by Russian encroachments. True, the chief delegates at the front and their aides had received, among other things, papers which established their legitimacy and requested Soviet co-operation.[68] The co-operation, however, was far from uniform and reflected extremely varying sentiments. Understanding and help born out of an atmosphere of sober insight was counterbalanced more often than not by hate and ideological blinkers that hampered many a mission and distorted it beyond recognition.[69]

These highly dubious aspects were not the only ones of their kind. To activate and increase propaganda activities at the front, courses were established right behind the firing lines in which prisoners just captured were being "re-educated."[70] Even though these proselytes had taken a pledge, like the chief delegates at the front, "to fight with the National Committee for a Free Germany out of loyalty to the German nation,"[71] they were nevertheless used later for entirely different tasks. Innumerable courses and circles tried to peddle Marxist ideas leveled at the lowest common denominator and aimed once more at fostering the subversive practices rejected at Lunyovo.[72] The prisoners thus re-oriented were also trained unscrupulously as diversionary commandos (*Diversionstrupps*), and they saw action behind the German lines on several occasions. Such goings-on were all the more embarrassing as in this case certain elements operated under the motto "Free Germany" that were beyond the influence of either the National Committee or the League of German Officers. All the attempts that aimed at supervising those activities which had become known despite all precautions failed, as did all attempts to co-ordinate them with the propaganda goals of Lunyovo.[73] As organizational cells, the schools at the front remained under the exclusive supervision of Ulbricht. He also disposed of their trained cadres and he directed their missions with the unconcealed conviction that the general propaganda had to be supplemented by special actions concerning which the League of German Officers had allegedly not laid down any rules.[74] The myopia of this practice almost immediately became apparent. On the one hand, it bred a shifty opportunism which was quickly seen through by the German front line soldier. On the other hand, confusion of propaganda endeavors, which already resulted from the differing concepts of the National Committee and the Red Army, became even more catastrophic by the senseless independence of the re-education centers.

Wherever propaganda material reached the German front lines, it had been prepared at Lunyovo and printed in Moscow.[75] That was the case not only with the newspaper *Free Germany* and the illustrated front magazine of the National Committee but also with the propaganda leaflets which were issued centrally and which reflected most unequivocally the propaganda tactics decided upon. But frequently there were not enough copies of the material that had been prepared behind the Russian lines to saturate the extensive front lines. Thus additional Soviet printing shops at the front had to close the gap. They had to complement the materials issued and had to work out the topical leaflets which had been drawn up by the chief delegates at the individual sections of the front.

Newspapers, proclamations, and leaflets were either dropped by Russian airplanes or left in the German lines by patrols or prisoners of war that were sent back.[76] When these methods were impossible, whole packages of propaganda were catapulted in rocket fashion into the German lines. In addition, loudspeakers were employed in the trenches, and special mobile loudspeaker and radio car units were used.[77] The trench loudspeaker was handled by one man and was always used when there was any certainty that the nearby German front could be reached by it. If greater distances had to be overcome, the mobile loudspeaker and radio car unit, manned by several men, was brought up from behind the lines.

As a rule the broadcasts of the chief delegates, which were announced in advance, were opened by a trumpet signal. After that the front often fell silent and the voice of the announcer rang across the lines where firing had died down: "Attention! Attention! This is the voice of the National Committee for a Free Germany!"[78]

Propaganda could not follow one monotonous pattern; along the front, morale and circumstances differed too widely. One kind of appeal had to be chosen when German troops had been trapped in a well-nigh hopeless situation; a different one where the front lines faced each other in a tough, open struggle. The propaganda missions generally followed proved principles. First, some objective military matters were taken up. Sharply highlighted and pointedly arranged, they were presented as established reality, and over-worked conclusions were then linked to them. But was there any better way than dealing with the military situation first? It was sufficiently catastrophic to allow of its being cleverly linked with more or less obvious oversimplifications. The National Committee's propaganda, therefore, generally first broadcast the news that presented a dark view and was intended to influence both feeling and intellect. After that came the appeal itself: "German officers and soldiers! The fate of your nation lies in your hands. You must realize that Hitler leads Germany deeper and deeper into destruction every day of the war. Do not allow irresponsible adventurers to give you empty promises. The continuation of the war can no longer alter the fate of Hitler's régime; it will lead to the destruction of our fatherland. Fellow soldiers! You know the situation and you are asking yourself what the individual can do about it. Fellow soldiers, all you individuals make up an army of millions! You cannot win against the three greatest powers on earth. But you are an enormous power if you organize yourself against Germany's true enemy, against Hitler. Organize all front-line soldiers! Organize against Hitler, in all units and at all ranks of the armed forces! Against Hitler!"[79]

But such appeals could reach the soldier, if they reached him at all, only if he was told that every action could only mean the support of the great Free Germany movement, which had been started long ago and whose strength was its justification. For this reason the propaganda at the front did not shrink from the obvious lie that the organization of German soldiers here demanded had already become reality in many divisions and that it should not be impeded.[80] For the appeal of the hour followed this example: "Organize in small groups and fight for our platform. The elimination of Hitler by the army! Orderly withdrawal to the frontiers of the Reich! Immediate signing of a cease-fire! Sometimes one word, one apt criticism will open a fellow soldier's eyes. Work illegally until you have won your unit. From the individual to the group. From the group to the army unit. That is the way to prepare the uprising against Hitler. You can be sure to find a large enough number of determined men among the generals, who will act if they know that the fighting men are on their side. Every individual can and must act! Fellow soldiers! Onward for a free and peaceful Germany!"[81]

Sporadic as the National Committee's front-line work looked at first, it now sought to intensify propaganda with this version.[82] Several thousand copies of the manifesto were distributed; innumerable appeals and leaflets came fluttering down on the German lines. Day and night the voices of the loudspeakers echoed across the no-man's-land between the lines.

The troops—often appealed to directly—listened to it, sometimes quietly, sometimes firing in the direction where they suspected the propagandists to be.[83] Many a broadcast captured someone's attention and started him thinking. Many a leaflet was picked up, read, perhaps even handed on and discussed. But from the beginning there was no visible reaction that the National Committee and the League could point to as a significant success.[84]

With a soldier engaged in heavy fighting, propaganda falls on deaf ears.[85] During the hard, tiring struggle there exists only the law of war. The sole way to survive intact in the face of this law is to overcome the willingness to act on orders by re-examining one's philosophy of life. But wars of attrition take on a reality of their own. The soldier has to obey this reality for his whole being has been trained essentially to stand up in the face of a tough challenge. The overwhelming violence of the struggle in the East made any propaganda success difficult to achieve. But even apart from this, the troops showed no inclination to listen to the arguments of the Free Germany movement. The war itself brought about this attitude; only by tracing the development of the war can we therefore hope to understand it.

Ever since the German soldiers had again taken up arms in September 1939, their skepticism or sober good sense had increasingly been replaced by faith and confidence. It is true that their lightning victories were of that dubious nature that today makes their laurels look withered. But in the fighting, the sense of unity with which every army rewards its successful leader was awakened. Here all the triumphs seemed to be due to Hitler and the ideas of National Socialism which had overcome outdated political systems. The soldier was led to believe that he was fighting for a new Europe. If he accepted any part of his mission, it was the self-evident necessity to serve the Reich in its new role as the leading power. What had grown into an unexpected elation was threatened by extinction on June 22, 1941. The enormous expanses in which the German soldier now fought the Soviet enemy he had challenged, the threatening atmosphere rendered more threatening still by memories of Charles XII of Sweden and Napoleon—all this was enough to dampen any great expectations and to give rise to anxious thoughts. But brilliant victories in unprecedented open-field battles and battles of encirclement soon brought back the old feeling of superiority. The soldiers regained their faith in the luck of their own arms. They had such powerful psychological reserves that even the bitter reverses of the winter campaign of 1941–1942 were absorbed without ill effects. Hitler and his general staff, who had led them from triumph to triumph up to now, might have made a mistake. The front was fair enough to give them another chance.

There were other aspects too. In the summer of 1941 most German soldiers had believed that they had barely prevented a Russian attack on the Reich.[86] Brought up by successful propaganda to view Bolshevism as a powerful threat, the German soldier began to sense the contrast between Europe and Russia all the more as the fighting in the Soviet Union revealed the shocking reality of Communism. There was no way of understanding this kind of reality; it ought never to deface Germany and Europe. The really important factor was, however, the pitiless nature of the fighting itself; its reality rendered meaningless any questions of cause and effect. The soldier did not understand it and simply did his duty, a duty which would have been accepted even if unquestioning obedience had not existed, which in itself apparently undercut any revolutionary uprising of the German army.

The defeat at Stalingrad had made the forces of July 20 close ranks even more closely, for now the handwriting on the wall could no longer be ignored. Stalingrad had also made those soldiers who had suffered through the battle at the Volga with open eyes disavow their upbringing with revulsion. Otherwise the Free Germany movement, which had now declared war on the National Socialist régime, could never have come into being. But to the bulk of the men in uniform Stalingrad was not a bewildering trauma.[87] Their faith in their leaders remained intact even after the Wehrmacht had begun to retreat step by step, forced to switch from offensive to defensive.[88] It is true that the troops fought in the East amidst ever-increasing crises and sufferings. It is also true that here and there it had become apparent to them the crimes National Socialism had been guilty of in the Soviet Union. But just as the fighting men never questioned their own superiority over the enemy, they also remained psychologically unable to accept defeat. The German soldier had become ensnared in the fate of the Reich and the German people. He rarely held convictions which would have made him ready to sacrifice for the sake of a higher law.[89] Only too rare was the independence of thought that would have given

rise to doubts, especially in face of the Russian enemy. And wherever they did begin to stir, the possible consequences of Soviet
success outweighed any skepticism. Compared to those consequences the risks of victory seemed smaller by far. For behind the
enemy's triumph there stalked the horrors of unconditional surrender, which threatened to eradicate Germany and ultimately tied
its fate to Hitler.[90] The propaganda thesis of the Free Germany
movement that all further resistance was senseless could not even
become a temptation under these circumstances. If your only
alternative is annihilation, you will fight with unreasoning fervor.

One thing was basic: the common soldier did not regard the
war as lost by a long shot. Its results may have presented only a
dim vision of the future but the troops clung to their conviction
that the bitter struggle did have some meaningful goals. With their
traditional sense of decency they trusted their Supreme Commander; they thought him bound by his conscience and aware of
his responsibility toward the German people. This conviction arbitrarily subordinated a glorified Hitler to the laws which the Wehrmacht was willing to obey. The soldiers also felt obliged by the
commitment of their commanders who, again and again, provided
psychological strength to the troops. Eventually the soldiers' mis-
understandings on this point were to grow to enormous proportions. To escape the manifold pangs of conscience many commanders
took refuge behind their concern for the unbounded abuse of the
men at the front. But the lack of information about the general
situation remained the most effective means to lend an air of credibility to the continued demonstration of National Socialist confidence.

But even if this attitude had failed the soldiers, they would
still not have been prepared to give in to propaganda from the
enemy camp. It was the general assumption that anything coming
from the enemy lines could only serve to help him. The troops,
therefore, unmistakably and sharply rejected all Russian propaganda.[91] Overwhelmingly they despised the treason that they saw
reflected in the propaganda of the Free Germany movement. Most
of them turned their backs on Moscow's cheap trick of using the
colors black, white, and red, the nationalist emblem. Was it credible that those same Communists who had up to now only heaped

abuse upon them would now support these colors? Was one justified in assuming that any German generals, officers, or soldiers actually participated in the National Committee? For the most part
those questions were answered in the negative. The German army
in Russia was convinced that it was familiar with the methods by
which the Soviets broke every resistance. Wherever the appeals
and leaflets were not simply regarded as forgeries, it was eloquent
enough for the German soldier that a "free" Germany had to make
do without Paulus and many of the Stalingrad generals.

It was in keeping with the propaganda goals of the League of
German Officers that appeals and proclamations to the common
soldier did not become the primary means of propaganda. They
were to remain a concession to the National Committee, whose
task it was, within the context of front-line propaganda, to prepare
the army for the actions of their commanders. Thus everything
depended on those commanders. Therefore Seydlitz, among others,
wrote to Colonel General Model and Daniels to Field Marshal von
Manstein to persuade them to secede from Hitler.[92] These letters
are the first of many, and they represent the core of the League's
propaganda. Adapting themselves to the personalities of the recip-
ients, who frequently were personal acquaintances of the generals,
these letters stressed with varying arguments but always impressively the seriousness of the situation. Seydlitz and Daniels knew
that the German generals were open only to military reasoning.
They therefore tore apart the foolish belief that Germany still had
time on its side, that it could afford to give up territory, and that
it would be victorious in defense. They argued that the war was
going in favor of Germany's enemies, who could better and more
readily retrieve their losses than an already reeling Reich. With
sober conclusions they pointed out a situation which could only
become worse after the experience of Hitler's kind of "strategy."
For this hopeless and senseless fight could create only a desperate
future for Germany. For the sake of the Reich they demanded
both military *and* political responsibility of the generals approached. Thus Seydlitz wrote to Model: "You have to force Adolf
Hitler to step down! Leave the Russian soil and lead the German
Eastern Army back to the German frontier. By this decision you
shall create the political prerequisites for an honorable peace which

will allow the German people to retain the rights of a free nation."

United in their intention to save the existence of the Wehrmacht, Seydlitz and Daniels could hardly exaggerate in their letters. The question of the point of any further fighting had been raised long ago. Even if the generals were willing to overlook the political defects of the National Socialist régime, there still remained its ideology, personified in Hitler; it prevailed everywhere. Its cancerous growth was also shown in military affairs. Here too the diagnosis was one of deterioration. The field commanders and higher commanders were called upon to resist because the irresponsible dictator wielding supreme command had shown them more and more that in the final analysis it was the fighting soldiers, for whom the leading soldiers had so often claimed to be responsible, who would be destroyed.[93] The Battle of Stalingrad, in which mistaken considerations of prestige had sacrificed a whole army, was merely the first signal. It is true that the catastrophe at the Volga had been pushed to abnormal proportions by Hitler's obstruction of all necessary decisions. But it was only after this turning point of the war that it became apparent what he really was capable of. The obstinacy that did not permit him to think ahead operationally, let alone strategically, became complete, and pure will power was elevated to the level of magic.[94] Whether it was in the Donetz area or in the Dnieper bulge, Hitler could not be moved to make defensive concessions that could have husbanded the strength of the overtaxed troops. And all the time his well-trained generals had the right insights! Not only did their arguments adapt themselves to the ever-changing situation; they were also dictated by cogent, logical reasoning. Thus the generals continuously explained to Hitler that the choice during the defensive battles at the Don and Dnieper could lie only between losing both the coveted economic resources and the army by an inflexible defense and making up for momentary losses by a flexible conduct of the war. But they had always bowed to the order to hold those overextended lines without any reserves although they knew in advance that they would be smashed by the vastly superior Russian forces and that they would create increasingly disastrous crises. Even worse: what the magical trick of well-tried makeshifts could no longer guarantee, the so-called "fortresses" (*Feste Plätze*) were now supposed to do—with the result that additional valuable divisions bled to death pointlessly in these quickly outflanked fortified bases. Since the early fall of 1943 all operations according to priorities had thus ceased to exist. The period of open operations and the willingness to take risks was quickly nearing its end. It frequently became the primary task of the military leadership to deprive Hitler's intuitive decisions of their most deadly sting in nerve-wracking confrontations.

This chaotic situation was fraught with considerable problems. The morale of the troops seemed to be unshakable on the whole. But it was precisely their willingness, which went beyond anything the soldiers had already achieved, that shed a glaring light on the unsavory nature of this power of command. For were not all sacrifices meaningless if the flood of enemies continued to rise instead of gradually receding? Did not Hitler have to fall and give way to a new power in Germany—a power which would try to save Germany from a truly destructive holocaust and a total collapse by a timely compromise? People and Reich could survive only if they put an end to the fighting.

But the letters from the generals of the League remained unanswered despite all this. They were left with the dubious satisfaction of having accurately described a chaotic situation. Although the men of the resistance within the Reich had already sent fruitless appeals to the leaders of the German armies in the East, they never stopped to consider seriously the arguments coming from Lunyovo.[95] Not that they doubted that these were genuine documents or that they did not also sense the conflict between their orders and their consciences. The specific detail of the letters and leaflets did not leave much room for strong skepticism; it had also been apparent for some time that the general trend was downward. But was not the alternative a defensive struggle against a pitiless enemy, whom one viewed as the greatest danger of all? Under these circumstances their oath of loyalty counted all the more, as a *Putsch* would simply break up the front lines which separated the Red Army from Germany. And despite their conflict of views with Hitler, who fiercely fought against the foreseeable future, they remained convinced of their chance of a general stalemate.

They still felt powerful enough to enforce an arrangement with the Soviet Union after repelling the invasion in the West.

Thoughts and hopes of this type were questionable and astonishing, for day by day it became more apparent that Hitler's holding supreme command must in itself render any expectation impossible. Even as a statesman he was condemned to failure now. But even those German generals who did not accept the basic concepts of National Socialist ideology were held back from rising in rebellion above all by the Allied demand of unconditional surrender.[96] This alternative weighed heavily on all plans for a *Putsch* by raising the question of whether or not it would be effective. Compared to this alternative the continuation of a tough stand seemed the better choice, especially if there were a chance of limiting Hitler to the leadership of the state. In this way any open-minded attitude was smothered. The appeals to the higher demands of the hour remained without response. All the German generals' energies were reserved for their troops, all their contempt for the National Committee and the League. As the embodiment of high treason and treason against the state, they were ostracized by the generals too.[97]

Given these circumstances, it was easy for the dictator to influence the troops by instructions.[98] What he put before them in the communications of the Wehrmacht mentioned above did not have to be imposed upon the officers and soldiers; it seemed to voice their own feelings. Staff and propaganda officers never had to deal extensively with the National Committee or the League. There was nothing to suggest that they were or ever would be successful. The regulations to hand in enemy propaganda material were overwhelmingly followed without objection. Mountains of appeals, leaflets, and handouts were collected by the staff officers in charge of enemy intelligence. Frequently the material dropped on the various sections of the front was used to instruct the troops right on the spot. There was no need to issue a quickly written booklet for the soldiers. Both discipline and morale of the troops were so unquestionable that, apart from certain basic attitudes of resistance, even objective arguments constituted no danger.[99]

The camp propaganda of the National Committee and the

League could not make up for the lack of resounding success in the work at the front, for that was the decisive work. The Wehrmacht's leadership had to move against Hitler. It had to risk this change of attitude in recognition of the fact that he was neither able to finish the hopeless fighting nor willing to put an end to it. Hence propaganda activities had to seek out the other side. Only by convincing the other side could propaganda fulfill its most important function. Even a successful recruitment campaign in the camps would pale into insignificance compared to this task. The bulk of the POWs had, after all, ceased to play any part in events that mattered. Any intensive work at the front could best be helped by the generals of Stalingrad, who still remained standing on the sidelines with Paulus at their head. This applied even more, considering that the League of German Officers already included a considerable number of members. There were plenty of them to replenish numerous front delegations.[100]

There remained, of course, the unavoidable argument that the National Committee was under a moral obligation to care for the continuously increasing number of prisoners of war, whose existence was denied by their own government.[101] They were in need of intercession and protection, and it was for those reasons that it seemed necessary to become politically engaged in the camps also. But here only unrestricted activity was meaningful. Such activity, however, was not permitted. Lunyovo was not even allowed to have the machinery with which it could have controlled a large portion of the POW camps.[102]

The National Committee and the League nevertheless started broad recruitment drives. Their influence remained limited to the general vicinity of Moscow,[103] but the Soviets were soon gripped by the intoxication of numbers. There had to be propaganda everywhere. Even the most distant camp was supposed to form an activist group; everyone everywhere had to demonstrate his solidarity with the Free Germany organization, a solidarity which, for the most part, looked as questionable as it was misleading.[104]

For the stage had been dark from the start and looked less and less like brightening up as the surrender of Germany drew closer.[105] The top echelons of the National Committee and the League had, for the most part, been won over by decency, and an acceptance of Marxism had neither been expected nor demanded of them; but in the camps, the Soviets seemed incapable of this attitude from the start. There the most blatant methods of recruitment again dominated, without any thought of the consequences and with considerable distortions of the aims of Lunyovo. Once again the anti-fascist subalterns, who could not understand how the officers and soldiers in the camps could resist Communism although they might still have some reservations, triumphed. As a result the most atrocious blunders of camp propaganda were committed between 1943 and 1945. They proved all the more disastrous as the living conditions of the German POWs should have ruled out any propagandistic arrogance.

These considerations, perhaps obvious to rational thought, did not, however, play any role in a totalitarian ideology. For if the claim is accepted that it is always identical with the truth, then it must also be universally valid. Therefore, the Communist sections in the camps invariably viewed propaganda from the start as the use of force against "unbelievers."[106] The appearance of recruitment could not be totally avoided if the all-powerful teaching of Communism were to be spread at all. As long as the propaganda was unsuccessful, its objects continued to be viewed as enemies whose resistance had to be reckoned with. Ideologically the émigrés and *politruks* regarded the thousands of German POWs as one fascist bloc which had to be broken up at all costs. An unreal reorientation began therefore, fraught with lurking suspicion. Now, as before, somewhat convincing arguments followed fixed patterns which kept repeating themselves incessantly. It was always the same Marxism which was forced on the POWs in meetings and circles and which—in its Stalinist narrowness—permitted only mindless repetition. The exclusivity of its methods did not allow for any doubts. But frequently even this Marxism was replaced by a well-tested dialectic whose shakily overextended theory of historical development had long ago become the magic wand for turning black into white. All the usual reservations were gobbled up by the "closed system" of an ideology which stood or fell by its absolutism. In keeping with these ideas collaboration was interpreted as submission and even the most humble objections were branded as "fascist" bad faith. Under such conditions there could be no frank speaking, or even discussion that aimed only at clarification. For no genuine debate could take place without criticism. Anyone opening such a debate would have been accused of attacking the ideology, which was based on the prepotency of a leadership free of error and correction. The spiritual shroud, which had already covered the Soviet Union for decades, now also descended on the POW camps.

Not that the German prisoners, often with bitter war experiences behind them, had by any means all closed their minds.[107] In some cases they turned their backs on National Socialism even without experiencing the apocalyptic horrors of Stalingrad. Even more frequently they showed a sense of shame about the crimes that had become known, which could have been used as a starting point of conversion. But propaganda that above all threatened and slandered ruled out any serious discussions from the start. Instead, the prisoners' fear that talking about the experiences of the war could give rise to charges of "fascism" made them shy away from discussing the abyss they had barely survived. The recent past was glossed over with the help of abstruse pseudo-historical explanations. The first thing demanded of them was an acceptance of that kind of Marxism which was rejected in all the camps.[108]

This is not to deny that Marxist theory was capable of engaging some, especially if it was carefully expounded to the younger prisoners of war.[109] For although National Socialism had provided them with a few ideas, they frequently and quickly succumbed to the fascination of newness. But it was limited to a few exceptions among thousands, and their enthusiasm frequently ended in yet another tragedy. On the whole, Marxism's claim to absolute validity repelled even where it was correct in detail. Overwhelmingly the charge of "heresy" was met by unconcealed indifference and rejection.

The Communists and anti-fascists were hardly the men to change that situation. Enmeshed in their own world in which truth and lies, reality and fictions had become the absolute lie itself, they operated without intellectual or moral scruples.[110] They also haughtily dismissed the possibility that an active POW could reach opposition to Hitler outside their ideology. The chasm that had always separated the political activists from the bulk of the prisoners remained unalterably wide and deep. Thus the camps with their widely enforced in-group resentments continued to be dominated by a retreat into modes of thought which the war had basically long since shown to be dead ends. But those who would have been prepared to enter into an open discussion stood aside in an attitude of tragic silence. For them the option of collaborating with naked Bolshevism was out of the question.[111]

These reactions which now, of course, ostracized the National Committee and the officers' union could hardly come as a surprise, especially since hunger, corruption, and exploitation in the camps frequently increased the ideological pressures.[112] This chaotic reality and the many victims it took led many to form a completely negative opinion of Communism. The vastly superior living and working conditions of those prominent in the camps perforce isolated the *politruk* completely and made him incapable of entering into the state of mind of the other prisoners. Their material privileges might be rooted in the Soviet system of which the POW camps were a part; taken together with the widespread use of spying on each other, which destroyed self-respect as well as good faith, it could only result in catastrophe for the efforts at political propaganda. Because of all this, political activity met a wall of resentment, envy, and contempt. The recognition that the men talking, spying, and torturing were the opportunist servants of the Soviets became an unshakable certainty. The prisoners in the camps often enough knew only too well why these men had joined the activist groups which used the colors of the Free Germany organization. Torture and confinement had frequently broken their resistance; other times the decisive motives were hunger or the determination to escape the killing slave labor in factories, mines, quarries, or forests. Everyone knew the vulnerable spots. Whether it was the threat of having allegedly committed war crimes or that of having had a National Socialist past—after which return to Germany was possible only on condition of unquestioning political zeal —there was no means too degrading to employ to exert pressure, which robs any decision of genuine value.[113]

The extent of these experiences was too provoking to allow for any objectivity on the part of most of the prisoners of war, although here, too, any generalization would miss the point. The attitude of the *politruks* was by no means one of repulsive conformity, just as no camp was quite like any other.[114] Even the Soviet version of totalitarianism allowed for exceptions. They made it particularly apparent that it was up to the individual to what extent he was willing to give in to political pressures. There were false and genuine anti-fascists preaching, respectively, fanaticism and tolerance. There were the pressures on consciences and the attempts to ease the burden of those who threatened to collapse under the competitive conditions of forced labor. Much as all this might serve to show the lack of justification in the charge that death and suffering in the camps were the fault of the Committee and the League, the hollow-cheeked and tortured POW could hardly escape making a bitter generalization of this sort. The surface appearance of things obscured the fact that National Socialism itself might already have created these tensions and that its legacy demanded soul-searching discussion in any case.

As a result, the political activities in the camps produced rival groups incapable of coming to terms with each other.[115] Their mutual hatred grew to abnormal proportions and continued to smolder just beneath the surface. Later on, force of habit was to triumph and in the end the majority of the POWs endured the litany of propaganda with complete apathy. They apathetically approved resolutions which had been prepared beforehand and simply required unanimous acceptance. Continued resistance was rarely attempted, especially not by the common soldier. It seemed pointless and useless. Most of the POWs had reached this conclusion. Physical and psychological deprivation had killed off all active interest. Only the hope of surviving and returning home mattered to them, a hope which turned the Soviet imprisonment into a present without any value.[116] The political Stakhanovs no longer had a problem in meeting their political "quotas." Fantastic successes and figures found their way into the achievement reports of many camp delegates.[117] But even they could not turn into a triumph of propaganda what for the most part had its origins in pure opportunism.

Even this picture, however, is incomplete. Continued rebellion in the camps for the enlisted men was, on the whole, impossible, but among the imprisoned German officer corps the propaganda led to fierce resistance. Here it was above all the generally known isolation Block VI of the Kama camp at Yelabuga where the struggle between the parties had become totally unreasonable.

The myopia which classified anyone resisting as a fascist or, even worse, an incorrigible enemy of the Soviet Union, was the most frequent mistake. It led to concentrating in this stockade all those prisoners who already had the reputation of being especially dangerous before they even got there.[118] The experiences of these officers, who were joined by a few noncoms, were curiously alike. Clumsily wooed and frequently treated with condescension, they had proven unsusceptible to any propaganda; all the more so as the *politruks* had frequently demanded immediate decisions and rejected all counterarguments.[119] Thus, unsupported accusations had gradually forced these officers into a defensive attitude which became increasingly intransigent and which tended to provoke hate-filled attacks. As long as these individuals were isolated, this attitude had no recognizable influence. Within a group where all were of one mind, it perforce turned into a kind of obstinacy, countering every Russian action with a reaction. Yelabuga set an example. Successful hunger strikes and insubordination had created a sense of complete superiority in this camp. The inmates even risked barely concealed acts of sabotage and seemed prepared rather to go to extremes than to meet the Soviets halfway, with the Soviets reacting more and more angrily in the face of this insubordination.[120] Accusations, solitary confinement, and beatings were the rule of the day, but so were written treaties between the German highest-ranking officer in a particular block and the helpless Soviet camp commandant. They concerned camp discipline and boosted the prestige of the isolated community.

Any doubts or considerations which might have threatened their conscious solidarity were fended off by their ethos, which they had raised to the position of an absolute. In Yelabuga's Block VI the same friend-foe relationship, which had already ruled the fighters on the battlefields and which now rendered even the tamest political debate impossible, became once more apparent. The slogans of the National Committee and the League, which here were completely identified with Communism, were treated as taboo once and for all.[121] The officers were not bothered by the possibility that the Free Germany movement might have something to offer, that it might be worthwhile to consider, nor were they willing to regard their own unflinching strength as a fateful sign of cowardice. Unobeyed, the enemy, who was, as a Marxist, bound to dangerous theories, remained unchallenged. The officers and soldiers consoled themselves with the Communists' apparent personal shortcomings, which left all the essential questions untouched. The "foe" found himself either boycotted or expelled from the block.[122]

It is true that even within this consciously accepted isolation there were reservations about the idea and the leadership of National Socialism.[123] Many were considerably shaken in their faith and found it painful to think of Germany's future fate. But any conclusions from this recognition were now crowded out by the certainty that Bolshevism would administer "the *coup de grâce*" to Germany "as soon as it would be able to do so."[124] They also believed that they had to show good common sense and, as officers, be true Germans—whatever the consequences.[125] This led to a renewed and forced optimism, which had a magic appeal. Whoever, therefore, after July 20, 1944, believed any part of the news about the plot against Hitler was already thought guilty of high treason.[126] At night, they sang White Russian freedom songs which were answered beyond the walls of the isolation block by warning salvoes from the Russians.[127] Misguided energies ran wild, leading the officers ever further astray because of their defiance raised to grandiose proportions. . . .

At first the uncompromising fight of one ideology against another seemed to be without parallel, but Block VI at Yelabuga did not remain an isolated case. Similar resistance showed itself in other officers' camps, too.[128] For all too often the political activists threatened that only members of the Free Germany movement would be allowed to return to Germany. Too often those joining up were rewarded by special functions in the camps and by prerogatives which immediately destroyed all solidarity. There was also the deterring example of all those who accepted the National Committee and the League according to the changing fortunes of the war; the others replied with an abnormal belief in miracles. Germany's surrender later caused especially violent cases of moral breakdown among this group, but for the time being organized watchwords kept a steady opposition alive. The frightening intellectual submissiveness of many officers still guaranteed this position considerable effectiveness. It continued to force many to leave the Free Germany movement and thus to attract the particular hatred of the activists.[129] In the face of this exacerbated enmity, the meetings for atrocity trials and appeals for restitution could hardly flourish.[130] Wherever revulsion against unseemly self-accusations did not exist, there was at least the determination to take no step voluntarily. It was in the officers' camps especially that psychological mistakes had smothered willingness to think about the problems raised by these questions.

Although these realities appeared to eliminate effectively any genuine political conversions, they could not, of course, totally prevent the success of camp propaganda. Step by step, the recruitment, especially of the League of German Officers, gained ground in the Officers' Camps 150, Oranky, Susdal, and even in Yelabuga. Often the generals and officers of Lunyovo were faced with the bitter task of having to win back the confidence which Communist talks had destroyed.[131] But wherever its sober military and political commentaries predominated, it managed to convince, especially as the disaster of Hitler's leadership became apparent and as the situation at the front turned more and more gloomy. A distinct contrast to any forced decision of conscience was also marked wherever an honest appreciation of the trials of conscience—which concerned the question of the oath of loyalty and the fear of retribution against one's relatives in Germany—became apparent.[132] It is possible that even now many still joined out of a more or less conscious opportunism. There was no political recruitment which could have overcome the serious doubts and reservations growing out of the overwhelming realities of a Russian POW camp. But now there were also many officers who had been moved by the appeal that they should not just inactively watch a development that, under Hitler, was bound, in any event, to end with the destruction of the German people and the Reich.

Slowly the number of members grew, especially where it was possible to win influential, high-ranking officers.[133] Thus more than a thousand out of something under three thousand officers in Camp

150 joined the League of German Officers during the period extending from the end of 1943 to summer 1944.[134] Later, from the collapse of Army Group Center to the surrender in May 1945, these numbers continued to grow steadily. No exact and reliable information is available but apparently 30 per cent of all prisoners remained members of the League of German Officers.[135] The majority were older staff and reserve officers and civil servants. Professional officers of the lower ranks as well as the oldest members of this profession, however, could hardly be moved to join the officers' union.[136]

The National Committee's organization in the camps assumed different forms at various times. The Russians apparently did not want to commit themselves fully even though in principle the committee was responsible for the common soldiers while the officers' union remained in charge of the officers. On directives from Lunyovo, the structure that emerged in the experimental camp at Krasnogorsk, which was an exception by the final stage in 1945, was that there were two groups: one of the lower ranks with an activist cell of its own and one of the officers with an activist cell of its own. Heading both was a *troika*, consisting of a representative of the National Committee, who functioned as chairman and was in charge of determining and carrying out the political guidelines, an ombudsman of the lower ranks, and a representative of the League of German Officers.[137]

Camp propaganda had been intensified even more than the work at the front. During 1944 in particular, recruitment and political activities increased. After that, as the end of the war, which was being won by the enemy's arms alone, drew closer, they slackened off to the same degree.[138] One activist group after the other was formed. Without exception they bore the name "Free Germany" even if their connection, primarily to the Town Committee in Moscow, was limited to the situation reports of the camp delegates.[139] These reports had to be sent in from time to time and had to provide information on what had been undertaken and accomplished and on the resolutions adopted, as well as the general program. Whatever seemed useful in these reports was put before the House at Lunyovo, where they never, however, learned the exact number of POW camps in existence. The immediate activities of the House at Lunyovo which also included the regulation of economic questions were, however, always limited to a few camps only. With the exception of the irregular reports referred to above, anything that happened outside this area was screened from it.[140]

The Russians systematically prevented any contact with the realities of the Soviet Union. The members of the committee and the officers' union were deliberately kept from gaining any knowledge of the conditions in many of the camps. From time to time especially "reliable" persons were allowed to go to Moscow for recording sessions. But all applications for visitors' permits to communal farms, industrial plants, and distant camps were put off and never granted. Indeed, the House of Lunyovo was, therefore, sealed off from the outside world more completely than any other POW camp.

Any kind of help within its granted area of activity had to be all the more welcome because of this situation. Camp propagandists succeeded in convincing additional well-known prisoners, although it seemed that the arguments of the front propaganda could hardly be improved on. They could hardly hope to remove the irreconcilability between the contending groups of officers. Indeed, they frequently even fanned the hate between them.[141] But perhaps they could hope to overcome the reservations of those who had only looked to their superior officers for guidance or who had merely affected indifference. Events after July 20, 1944, proved that these hopes were justified. The appeals of Field Marshal Paulus and of numerous generals increased the political activities in the camps, and considerable success was scored.[142] The quickly distributed appeals of captured Catholic and Lutheran military chaplains also seemed to make some impression.

The activity of the German generals was no longer very surprising. To the thinking military man Germany's situation was clear enough. But the fact that the churchmen had given up their seclusion must have made people take note if only because as an independent group they completed the united front reaching all the way from Communists on the left to the conservatives on the right. They stepped forward in the name of their faith, to which they felt bound above all else.[143] Stalingrad had especially shocked the priests. They had shared in the fighting of their divisions to the bitter end, and they had witnessed human suffering which, in the end, with the miserable death of thousands, overwhelmed their powers. To the soldiers, the battle at the banks of the Volga was an incomprehensible military catastrophe. The clergymen saw its destructive force as a sign that "we literally live by the Ten Commandments and that we die if we disobey them."[144] It was impossible to tone down the tragedy. What at first merely seemed to be the ugly reality of war clearly became a crime after talks with high-ranking officers revealed the true practices of Hitler's leadership. His cynicism, which denied every divine bond, made the helpless and desolate deaths of countless German soldiers look even more cataclysmic. Considering Hitler's cynicism and the now-public crimes in the concentration camps and the occupied territories, the clergy, too, were willing to support Hitler's enemies and to bear witness that Germany was not identical with Hitler.[145]

The clergymen had no doubts about one thing: had there been an equitable public law in Germany their resistance would have been preposterous. But now both Christian denominations in the Reich were deprived of any legal means of opposition.[146] It had long since become apparent that National Socialist support of "positive Christianity" was only a cover-up for its own ideology. It was not prepared to give up totalitarian power; political faith would take the place of Christian faith. In memoranda and protests, both the Churches had long ago come out against lawlessness, the use of force, and the organized killings of the SA, SS, and Gestapo which disavowed law and order in the Germany of Adolf Hitler. But the Lutherans in particular were hardly cut out to be rebellious revolutionaries. It was an unchallenged tenet of faith in the struggles of this denomination that the individual and the Church of Jesus Christ could never rebel against the state if the state oppressed and persecuted the Church. But if an irresponsible government were to threaten with death and extinction not only the Church but the whole people and innumerable individuals—what then? Did not such circumstances indicate that the time had come for the Christian to stop the wheel of history, not for the sake of the Church, but for the sake of his fellow man?

Many clergymen had long since solved this profound problem for themselves.[147] When, however, a group of imprisoned clergy

met at Lunyovo, these pressing questions were again seriously discussed.[148] They considered the problem of the oath of loyalty,
taking the point of view that Hitler, on whom the oath had been
taken, had himself become disloyal, and they finally found that
even as Christians they could support the political goals of the
National Committee and the League. A timely cease-fire must
prevent the total collapse of Germany. From the start all the discussions were carried on in the knowledge that a true conflict of
duties existed. They wondered whether they would become guiltier
by keeping silent or by taking action.[149] Every clergyman knew that
the ultimate decision in favor of action constituted a revolutionary
act. This decision, which went far beyond the previous resistance
of the Churches in Germany, was based on the existence of a
perverted government whose modern all-encompassing power the
established categories could no longer deal with.

The thought that the many unknown crimes of National Socialism demanded that some Germans attempt to preserve a clean
shield of honor for their people before the world also encouraged
many to this rebellion.[150] They were depressed on the one hand by
the fear of the bitter retribution, which would become even more
terrible if they stood aside waiting and passive. On the other hand,
the limits of the obedience that the Christian owes to human government had here been reached.

The clergymen, too, also wanted to spare Germany a second
Stalingrad. Pro-Communist action was impossible for them for
reasons of faith.[151] That could hardly be surprising. The repeatedly
affirmed anti-Christian position of Bolshevism and of the German
émigrés could never be ignored. In a way, the ideologies seemed
sufficiently well-defined in this case. Ulbricht had stressed the
strictly tactical necessity of the common undertaking without minc-
ing words.[152] Forcefully Weinert coined the somewhat problematical statement that the Church could be guaranteed all its rights
only if it limited itself to matters spiritual.[153] The clergymen had
to warn the people of another fight between church and state (*Kirch-
enkampf*) at this point, on which their collaboration was endangered by many things. But as much as these dangers had to
be taken into account, what mattered was to prevent Bolshevist
omnipotence in a future Germany.[154] The unification of all men of

goodwill, of all those who realized that Hitler was Germany's most pressing evil, was still the main goal. It was Hitler who led Germany to destruction and who tied men to an oath which he had blasphemously called on God to witness.[155] The united front against Hitler was and had to be possible. How often had the experience of dictatorship in Germany done away with mutual prejudices? Had not personal encounters and trials shown that they were capable of fruitful collaboration and should remain so?[156] In the concentration camps and under the gallows there was room for Christians, conservatives, generals, Communists, and trade unionists. Now the fight for a new Germany had to spur them on even more toward a common undertaking.

Even these insights, however, alien as they were to the émigrés, could not shake the clergymen in their faith. They never stopped declaring unequivocally that they had not been converted to Communism.[157] They rejected any pseudo-Christianity. As soon as they began to reflect upon the fundamentals of their faith, even the religious Socialists seemed under great danger.[158] But even denominational principles did not justify obstinacy at any price. Thus the priests in the Free Germany movement believed without exception that they owed it to their principles to enter into serious discussion with Socialism in particular.[159]

Even the Russians began to realize which possibilities an anti-Christian emphasis would close off. They granted all kinds of freedom and tried hard to establish a temporary truce respecting differences of opinion and postponing potential conflicts for the time being.[160] Insofar as it was influenced by the Soviets' attempts to re-establish contacts with the pre-revolutionary past, this attitude was certainly genuine. As recently as 1942 Stalin had restored its traditional rights to the Orthodox Church of Russia.[161] This peace treaty between Party and Church was probably simply intended to unify all the spiritual forces of resistance in the Soviet Union challenged by Hitler. But in practice it had brought about changes which had to be taken into account if only because of the Russian Church.

Thus the Tenth Plenary Session of the National Committee, at which almost a hundred clergy were present and an impressive declaration of war on anti-Christian National Socialism was issued, created a "Study Committee for Ecclesiastical Questions" at Lunyovo.[162] On June 16, 1944, the plenary session, which had previously voted unanimously for a motion by Weinert on this point, approved (from among its membership) for the Catholics the military chaplains Kayser, Mohr, and Dr. Ludwig, and for the Protestants (Lutherans) the Military Chaplain Schröder, the Divisional Chaplain and High Consistory D. Krummacher, and the Reverend First Lieutenant Sönnichsen.[163] This cleared the way for far-reaching activities.

The emphasis of the work lay in the now almost unimpeded pastoral activities in the camps and in the activities of the Church Committee, which turned into a sort of parsonage for the National Committee and the League at Lunyovo.[164] From now on sermons complemented the programs of Radio "Free Germany" every Sunday. They were based solely on the Gospels and dealt with issues which the clergy would also have preached about at home in Germany.[165] Their thoughts and reflections continued to be directed toward the postwar period; they wanted to prepare the ground for ecclesiastical life as it would be under a German government that would include also Communists. Open discussions and memoranda showed émigrés and Soviets what they would have to expect from the Churches in the future. The clergymen always made clear that their concept of the "Freedom of Church and Faith" by no means coincided with the life of the Orthodox Church in Russia. They never tired of presenting clearly defined demands.[166] As far as they can be reconstructed, these demands called for a democratic government, the elimination of National Socialism, ending the persecution of the Church by the State, reestablishing denominational schools and the youth organizations of the Churches, freedom of religious instruction in the schools, and a Catholic and Protestant press.[167] Additional demands concerned the restoration of the organization and property of the *Innere Mission* (the Protestant charitable organization), the reopening of the theological seminaries (Bethel), and the maintenance of Faculties of Theology at the German universities. To lend additional weight to these demands, the conditions for and the forces of the resistance of the Churches in the Reich were presented also.[168] On the one hand, these surveys were intended to educate toward tolerance in the future and to represent the general outline of the Churches in all the multiplicity of their currents. On the other hand, by their acknowledgment of the other Christian denominations they had to set forth those tenets of faith which they would not be willing to give up in the future.

Because of its moral weight, the clergy could only strengthen the National Committee and the League when it joined them and issued its proclamations. This was all the more true as the military chaplains (*Wehrmachtsgeistliche*) made their appearance at a time when the Free Germany organization seemed to have become almost ineffective. It was furthermore quite important to be able to point to specific results in the camps of the German POWs. But even in the case of the clergy no one could claim any results other than those actually possible from insight and camp psychology. The missions directed toward the German front remained of primary importance. The front was all-important because the basic goals of the committee and the officers' union would remain illusory if it did not respond. Thus everything tended to point back to propaganda on the battlefields even as the House at Lunyovo continued to win additional members in the camps.

## CHAPTER FIVE

## From Teheran to Cherkassy

ALTHOUGH THE LEAGUE OF GERMAN OFFICERS believed that the slogan "Orderly withdrawal to the frontiers of the Reich" best met the needs of the hour, it had not so far achieved any noticeable results.[1] Even intensive propaganda could not disguise the fact that the German front responded with rejection and silence. At the same time, Hitler's irresponsible strategy became more and more apparent. The Wehrmacht's casualties mounted incredibly in a defensive struggle which already began to undermine faith in its leadership. Outwardly loyalty and obedience triumphed despite all, and the contrast between hopeful expectations and bitter reality grew enormous. Occasionally, to be sure, the Free Germany movement managed to raise and foster a few doubts; for the German army of millions hardly burned with an enthusiasm whose ardent flames would have satisfied the National Socialist dictators. The German soldier did his duty, without question, with dedication, convinced of the historical mission of the Reich. But he also fought with doubts in his heart and suffering in the knowledge that his was a cursed fight, guilt-ridden, in which he could not afford to tire for the sake of his country and his fellow soldiers. Such being the case, opposition could count on receiving attention and a hearing. This is why the propaganda of the committee and the officers' union attracted attention in individual cases.[2] But how rare were the independent thinkers and how meager the immediate results of appeals and entreaties! The field marshals and generals ignored the appeals of Seydlitz and others, while the troops at the front nowhere even tried to establish the cadres that the National Committee had suggested.[3] The dictates of war alone ruled su-

preme; all significant emotions fell under war's stern rule. Having
become a master of retreat, the German soldier braved even bleak
situations. Whenever he was outflanked or encircled, he was not
moved by any political impulse but exclusively by the will to break
through at any price. Unverifiable reports of German turncoats
present only a misleading picture of reality until one looks at the
actual figures.[4] Wherever the Russians succeeded in capturing new
prisoners of war, they had either been vanquished by the enemy's
superiority of numbers or by a military situation without any
alternative. Where they identified themselves with the Free Germany movement with the help of leaflets they had kept, they
normally did so somewhat too hastily with meaningless gestures of
opportunism. All of this might count for public consumption, but
it could not take the place of the organized activities of determined
conspirators that the National Committee and the League aimed
at. And the first-rate analyses of the communiqués of the Wehrmacht High Command by the National Committee also remained
without results.[5] These analyses had impressively torn to shreds
the mendacious arguments of Germany's leadership, but they did
not reach the troops, nor did they manage to change the troops'
unresponsiveness, which made all the propaganda ineffective. For
the battles raged on undiminished.

In the House at Lunyovo the lack of success at the front spread
incredulity, consternation, and paralyzing alarm.[6] Were not their
personal motives so convincing that they more or less had to sway
the Wehrmacht too? Had it not become obvious by now that
Stalingrad was merely the beginning of considerably larger losses
and reversals? What kind of faith was it which prevented the
fighting soldier from having the same insights that men of the National Committee had? Questions of this kind led them around in
circles and gradually caused a disturbing helplessness. They could
still fall back on the argument that the activities at the front had
to be continued much longer before they could evaluate the content and tactics of their propaganda. But the military commentaries
of Lattmann and Korfes had already shown in the fall of 1943 that
Germany's position had become increasingly hopeless by the successful counteroffensives of its powerful enemies.[7] Many hopes
became questionable, many an illusion was destroyed. They were

still inclined to stick to their old concept of propaganda, but even the most patient intentions could not prevent the conceptions of the committee from becoming more radical step by step.

Weinert and other émigrés had probably doubted from the start that any of the German army commanders would see his way to rebellion against Hitler. In September 1943 they had assented to the arguments of the League of German Officers, but during the first joint plenary session they had already questioned whether better paths should not be pursued towards a quick ending of the war, "considering the continued (!?) negative attitude of the commanding generals."[8] Now they increasingly felt justified in their never-concealed belief that a successful initiative could come only from the general mass of the people and the Wehrmacht. On October 31, 1943, the president of the National Committee therefore issued an appeal to the German soldiers. In a propaganda leaflet he declared that soon there would be no alternative to honorable surrender and capture.[9] For the commanding officers "have not acted in time. They have missed the best chance of saving you. They are responsible for the meaningless bleeding to death of thousands of you. . . ."

A significant appeal. It not only conceded that all propagandistic endeavors up to that time had ended in a fiasco. It also impatiently moved toward the new concept, which was to be once more linked with the kind of tactics that the committee had pursued before, immediately after its founding. But the situation did not yet appear to be ripe for a change in the front propaganda. The orderly withdrawal slogan of the League of German Officers was still valid. It was the task of the German troop commanders to oust Hitler by a *coup d'état*. At the time of the Teheran Conference the Town Committee was already busy discussing the future slogan, "Save yourself by joining the National Committee,"[10] while at the same time Seydlitz was still insisting to the delegations of the League of German Officers that any attempts at subversion of the Wehrmacht were to be avoided.[11]

Nevertheless, the spokesmen of the left wing won out within a short time. The propaganda failure at the front and the rapid implementation of the Allied policy enforced a change of the general concept and significance of the Free Germany organization.

In the reports of the delegations at the front, the House at Lunyovo first received an indication of the weaknesses which had burdened propaganda work in the various theaters of the war up to now. Two members of the committee, just back from the front, Count Einsiedel and Friedrich Wolf, claimed that they did not have a sufficient number of propaganda leaflets and that what they did have could not countervail that of the Red Army, the tenor of which was an unbearable burden.[12] This was a first hint of problems that were to become very serious indeed. But now Einsiedel and Wolf suggested going beyond the attempt to concert and coordinate the activities at the front. Without presenting in detail the controversial position of the delegates and their aides, they proceeded instead to present proposals which amounted to an outright propaganda appeal for desertion.

At the hotly contested Melitopol front, Einsiedel and Wolf had up to then worked according to the guidelines laid down at Lunyovo.[13] That was also true for those missions with which they had tried to establish cells of the Free Germany movement within the German troops. Continued assignments had, however, convinced them that the rebellion of one or even several commanding German generals could not be counted on. They argued, however, that this might render the argument for an orderly withdrawal to the Reich's frontiers absurd, since the present military situation ruled out any German passivity. According to them, the German troops had been fighting without reserves or rest for some time now. Defending overextended and nonsensical positions, they were continually asked to do the impossible, while they fought against an enemy to whom they were markedly inferior in numbers. And once more they were faced by a cold winter, which would bring them additional unforeseeable hardships and which would certainly heighten their sense of being lost in the limitless space of Russia. These circumstances alone suggested that their propaganda plan should be changed, but there were further considerations which seemed to make it even more imperative. Even if some unit decided to march back to the frontiers of the Reich without its officers, wouldn't they be overwhelmed right behind the front lines by the SS and the Military Police? In the case of trapped units, which Hitler's dilletantish strategy increasingly forced into useless pockets, the hitherto used approach had proved completely useless, for in such cases there were only two alternatives open to them: either to be destroyed or to save themselves by joining the cause of the National Committee.

With all their arguments, Einsiedel and Wolf, as well as the men of the committee, were intelligent enough not to forget what Soviet imprisonment meant.[14] They admitted that life behind the barbed wire was full of hardships, although they were hardly troubled by the scruples of the League of German Officers when they heard any talk of "subversion." It was especially during the time the bulk of the prisoners were collected in special camps that they would have to endure bitter hardships. But would not resistance to the end bring about even greater dangers? Encircled or outflanked units that continued to fight to the end as a rule fell into Soviet hands completely ragged, demoralized, and exhausted. If Stalingrad had taught them anything, it had been to avoid any chaotic collapse in the future. These arguments may have deliberately overlooked the state of mind of the German fighting soldier on the Eastern Front who was determined to fight on unconditionally just as the Sixth Army had once done on the banks of the Volga. But they were right in one respect: casualties among German prisoners would have been lighter if troops trapped in hopeless positions had more frequently surrendered earlier, while they still had some strength left.

On this issue, too, the ultimate goal again seemed to settle the argument. Hitler was waging a merciless war, the outcome of which could be nothing but total destruction if he was allowed to sacrifice irresponsibly people and Wehrmacht to his insane illusions without meeting the resistance of those who saw through all this; hence, what was now imperative was defiantly bringing about the cessation of war by *any* means available. This attempt might also destroy structures of order that a new government would have to be based on. But as long as the German dictator's will remained triumphant, the only way out was to save as many people as possible from the maelstrom of catastrophe.

Adjurations of this kind were especially directed at the officers' union, since it was the only organization from which reservations were expected. And it did indeed find itself incapable at first of giving in to the eloquently presented arguments of the committee.[15] Not that they were rejected out of hand or that open discussion was refused. Here, if anywhere, they watched the unfolding of military events with deep emotion. They saw that their worst fears were surpassed by the practices of the German leadership. Retreats were followed by defeats, but no countermove or change in German strategy became apparent. The path laid down by the closed minds of Hitler and his High Command led steeply downhill. In the East, the Wehrmacht had simply become an object that was being mercilessly crushed between the upper millstone of the Red Army and the nether millstone of a senseless power of command. Its demoralization continued apace and at best offered the chance to enter into the macabre race for the final dissolution of the German armed forces. Basically, this race had already been entered by the League of German Officers. General von Seydlitz had long addressed himself to all ranks in propaganda leaflets, in which he told them that the shortages of ammunition in various units was the start of the impending doom.[16] At the end of November 1943, when the 123rd Infantry Division was spotted on the island of Khortitz in the Dnieper, an unsuccessful attempt was made "to win over the entire unit to the cause of the National Committee."[17] But these attempts did not mean that the original basic propaganda line had been jettisoned,[18] for a general propaganda line directed at encouraging desertions remained intolerable to the generals and officers. It again raised the specter of chaos, which they had tried to avoid from the start. Once again it was recognized that a huge mass of prisoners of war would serve neither the cause of the National Committee nor that of Germany. Their own experiences taught them that earlier Wehrmacht propaganda, which had been effective, was false: Soviet barbed wire had lost its terror. The 85,000 out of 90,000 survivors after the surrender at Stalingrad who died of exhaustion and epidemic diseases were certainly the responsibility of the German leadership.[19] But this depressing state of affairs, which was of truly symptomatic importance, was hardly recognized within the Wehrmacht. And even if it had been known to every single German soldier, it would hardly have made Russian imprisonment any more attractive to him, for there were no guarantees that the promises made to all those who complied with the appeals to join the National Committee's cause would be kept. This led to a violent clash of opinions in the House at Lunyovo; a compromise was impossible and had to be postponed.

At the turn of the year 1943–1944, the results of the Teheran Conference provided the straw that broke the camel's back.[20] Although the actual course of events at the conference had remained hidden from the Free Germany organization,[21] detailed analyses now complemented the official communiqué. Thus *Izvestia* wrote, among other things, that now the Allies would only be satisfied with the occupation of all of Germany and the imprisonment of the Wehrmacht.[22] This decision, especially emphasized, had a sobering effect. If it was binding—and the authority of the Soviet government's organ could hardly be denied—then the previous base for the front propaganda had been knocked out from under it. The Grand Alliance could, of course, realize its decision. Indeed, if it wanted to defeat the Reich at any price, then the appeals of the National Committee to join its cause took on a new meaning. They now appeared to be not only logical, but outright necessary, if only as a formula and conception born out of desperation.

While the League of German Officers was still pondering the fundamentally changed situation, Major General Lattmann had already joined the ranks of the left wing of the committee.[23] This started an avalanche. Many years before, Lattmann had been a well-known training director at the Jüterbog Artillery School; now he was deeply shaken by the catastrophe of Stalingrad, in which he fought as commander of a panzer division.[24] Once a devout National Socialist, Lattmann had come to hate intensely the man whom he had worshipped before, because of the Sixth Army's destruction. His absolute determination to hurt Hitler and to free Germany from his criminal rule now swept along Seydlitz, Korfes, and the board of the League of German Officers. This led to the plenary session of January 5, 1944. Here, after another round of discussions, Weinert was able to proclaim officially that "the only possible demands were those calling for a cessation of hostilities and for joining the cause of the National Committee."[25]

The acceptance of this new concept was a considerable success for the left wing of the National Committee. It weighed heavily on the generals and officers at Lunyovo, although it was to be cheated out of success later on.[26] To them a cause that ultimately reflected the collapse of their world despite their strong resistance had collapsed. None of them wanted to subvert the Wehrmacht to which they had, in some cases, dedicated their whole lives. They all knew that the new propaganda line would exclude them from the community of their fellow officers forever, the same fellow officers whom they had hoped to win for the overthrow of Hitler without ensuing chaos. To give up this original goal for the sake of uncontrolled rebellion or desertion was for them a fateful involvement. For if all the dikes were similarly to break, then future reconstruction threatened to become impossible, since it could only get under way on the basis of inalienable values which had now been left behind. But would they now not have to double their efforts to save their people, to whom they primarily felt bound? Was it now fated that the resistance provoked by Hitler would become more and more absolute the deeper Hitler led Germany into catastrophe? They understood that basically their self-sacrifice was to atone for their previous mistakes. But they also began to realize that an irresponsible régime had freed them from all obligations. Thus they gradually came to affirm psychologically what continued to evoke painful feelings for a long time to come. What decided the issue was the concrete situation, which extinguished all hope for the compromise they had worked for up to then. Generals and officers did not doubt that the Allies were seriously determined to fight until the Reich was destroyed. Sooner or later their strength would overcome the already reeling Wehrmacht. But since Stalingrad, the generals and officers were also convinced that Hitler would continue the war until Germany was totally destroyed. Could they simply allow this apocalyptic prospect to run its course without trying to stop it by *any* means available? Was it not their duty to avert the blow?

"Save yourself by joining the cause of the National Committee" —under this slogan used at the front, the committee and the officers' union also took on a new dimension. Up to the end of 1943 they could still be regarded as organizations that held out the hope of a tolerable peace for Germany should they be successful. Now they became a resistance group that simply propagated a popular uprising against Hitler without any future guarantees. This change was so important that it deserves a closer look, as do the steps which led up to it. For the new propaganda concept may have accurately reflected the situation after the conference at Teheran, but none of the arguments that Weinert and Einsiedel advanced had fully clarified the background of the events on that eventful January 5, 1944.

The National Committee's suggestion that it had been Germany's leadership alone that had made hope for an acceptable compromise impossible was perfectly justified militarily. The leadership had continued to act unrealistically, although the belated offensive blow of Operation "Citadel" and its bloody failure in the summer of 1943 had already suggested that only a flexible defense afforded any chance against the Soviet enemy.[27] The results were not long in coming: the German central and southern fronts were forced back by reverses and Russian breakthroughs. Only after several months were the troops able to come to rest for a short time along the Dnieper line. But Hitler showed little inclination to accept a flexible defense no matter how much these battles seemed to call for an imaginative decision, which alone could have averted future disastrous losses. An inflexible defense, holding positions at any price according to highest orders, still ruled the day. This kind of stubbornness became all the more fatal as the impending invasion in the west suggested that a strong defensive position should be established in the east, although the Germans still tended to believe that they could throw back the invasion. Instead of leaving the Crimean Peninsula in orderly fashion, where a German-Roumanian army was tied down, instead of retrenching the vastly overextended front along the Nikolayev-Kiev line, which would have shortened the front by about 130 miles and which would at last have created a sufficient reserve—instead of all that, Hitler accepted the winter battles offered by the Russians along the existing front.[28] The result was once again a defense without any chance of success from the very beginning. Once again the front was smashed. North of Kiev an unpluggable operational gap had opened wide, while further north the Red Army broke through the German lines north and south of Leningrad, and Gomel was seized from the Army Group Center. The Dnieper line of defense had thus become unhinged; the wide river ceased to be an insurmountable obstacle to the attacking Russian armies. Their overwhelming superiority, which, like a Hydra, seemed to grow two new heads for every one cut off, carried them all the way to Zhitomir and Krivoi Rog.

Under this apparently irresistible onslaught Germany's political prestige declined while great numbers of its divisions were reduced to weak fighting units. But the art of leadership of the German commanders and the fighting ability of the soldiers still managed to deny the Soviets many victories.[29] Again and again the German front was ripped open and routed by powerful Russian offensives. But it always closed again and stood its ground once more. Discouraging crises were repeatedly overcome, pockets were broken out of, and the Soviet enemy was forced to pay a frightening blood toll in weeks-long battles. Wherever they managed to meet the enemy at a tolerable ratio of strength, experienced German troops even managed to win significant defensive victories. If these troops had always and not just on exceptional occasions been led intelligently, their military strength would not have been exhausted so readily. All of this, of course, could not obscure the fact that the Wehrmacht was bound to tire eventually in this unequal struggle. Germany's eastern armies were virtually fighting alone in that enormous theater of war, since Italy had dropped out as an ally and the help of Hungary, Roumania, and Finland could hardly relieve the pressure. They remained a military factor all the same, one which the Russians became increasingly aware of the closer the fighting came to the frontiers of the Reich.[30]

Thus one can hardly assert that the Wehrmacht had at that time already been eliminated as an instrument for a *coup d'état* of the forces of order. Up to this time even the disappointments of front propaganda could hardly justify the early switch of the propaganda line, for a bare three months were not enough time to evaluate its final effectiveness. That leaves the Teheran Conference as the major element. It alone can, indeed, explain the new tactics pushed through with such obvious haste. For on the political level, which the National Committee and the League ultimately depended upon, most German interests had long ago taken on an atmosphere of gloom.

This state of affairs had not been reached suddenly, but the

House of Lunyovo had contributed to its development. Teheran had not been the first Allied conference since the founding of the Free Germany organization. The foreign ministers of the Soviet Union and Great Britain, and the Secretary of State of the United States had already met at Moscow from October 19 to October 30, 1943,[31] in order to reduce their considerable differences and to change the ambivalent state in their relations as allies that had allowed the National Committee to come into being. This meeting of Molotov, Eden, and Hull was a promising overture for the Kremlin's aspirations; for the first time some of the previous "strangeness" of the coalition was lifted from it.[32] For one thing, Hull's plans to weaken Germany had delighted the Russians, who regarded this as a "minimal program."[33] Then there was also the declaration of Austria's future independence. This second step forced Lunyovo to state that the Austrian people themselves would have to decide about their future.[34] But now that the Allies strove jointly for Germany's surrender, its territorial shape had become uncertain. Thus no binding arrangements were reached at this time except on East Prussia, which was to become part of the new Poland.[35] The ideas on both sides were either too indistinct or too much opposed to each other; but the three Foreign Ministers at least parted on good terms. Their most serious misgivings seemed to have been eliminated and the mutual determination strengthened.[36] Now the Soviets issued reassuring statements concerning the National Committee and the League.[37] The Western Powers could now rest assured that they had dispelled the worst Russian fears about "their" separate peace with Hitler.

But the Moscow Agreement was only the first step toward the broader rapprochement with Great Britain and the United States that the Kremlin wanted. Important problems had remained unsettled. The second front so urgently demanded by the Russians, which would have relieved the pressures in the Eastern theater of the war, still had not materialized.[38] The Soviet Union had yet to overcome the isolation due to its problematical Western frontiers. The session of October 26 was only the latest demonstration of how difficult future negotiations on this issue would be. Here Eden had dared to propose a plan for an eastern European federation that, like a revamped "cordon sanitaire," could only be directed against the Soviet Union and that, therefore, had been sharply rejected by Molotov.[39]

Moscow, therefore, continued to extend its feelers toward Germany. In Stockholm their agent, Edgar Clauss, once more tried to establish contacts.[40] But the National Committee and the League of German Officers continued their work. The basic line with which Lunyovo tried to save both Wehrmacht and Reich was maintained, although Weinert warned the hesitating German army in his proclamation of October 31, 1943, in accordance with the results of the Foreign Ministers' Conference.[41] Front propaganda could still be given a new direction at this point. And Clauss's mysterious mission, in which he told Peter Kleist that Marshal Stalin was willing to give Hitler a last chance,[42] could only have been undertaken to exert strong pressure on the Western Powers. For how could Germany's dictator concede now, if ever, what he had already denied at the turn of the years 1942–1943 when he gave the order to ignore the Russian offers?[43] But the shadow of a potential Russo-German rapprochement continued to fall over London and Washington. It could hardly be doubted in those capitals that they had insufficiently met the requests of the Soviets, who until then had fought under the greatest pressure.

It would be going too far to assert that the Free Germany movement, as the visible manifestation of an invisibly sought Russo-German arrangement, had brought about the Teheran Conference. That decisive meeting of the Allies was, rather, born out of the dire necessity to come to an understanding about the continuation of the war and about a future peace.[44] Edgar Clauss, therefore, seems to have gone too far when he implied that the American "fortress" had been taken after the Soviets had turned on the heat with the committee and the officers' union.[45] But even if this highly suggestive thesis is rejected, it can hardly be doubted that the House at Lunyovo had acted as a catalyst and that it had fulfilled one of the tasks set for it by the Soviets. It had speeded up complete agreement between Moscow and the Western Powers up to the conference in the Iranian capital. The Soviet Union's goal in its diplomatic game with London and Washington had now been realized. Within the Grand Alliance Teheran not only brought forth the firm assurance of the second front so long requested;[46]

by accepting, even though not in writing, the Russian western frontiers of late fall 1939, Great Britain and the United States also conceded that Poland had to be compensated for its losses by large portions of Pomerania and Silesia, in addition to Eastern Prussia.[47] All of these far-reaching decisions of Roosevelt, Churchill, and Stalin had come about amidst serious discussions, which belong to the weird picture of that conference but need not be pursued here in detail. Suffice it to state that Germany had become an object of great power politics and that nearly all hope for an acceptable peace had been lost, for it was at this meeting that the carving up of the Reich was accepted in principle, a carving up which could hardly be done thoroughly enough as far as the Soviet chief of state was concerned.[48]

The Kremlin was fully justified in viewing the Teheran Conference as a great success. It had fulfilled some of Stalin's essential wishes and had certainly reduced his distrust of the other coalition powers. The military operations of the near future were now in harmony, and an alliance which once had been fraught with dangerous tensions had been cemented. But if it had become firmer than ever before, then any Russian attempt either to use the German side as a trump card or simply to threaten the Allies with supposed contacts had become pointless. Berlin was no longer in on the bidding at the sell-out of Teheran. In the end, Edgar Clauss therefore informed Kleist in Stockholm that Germany's hesitancy had lost her all chances in the east.[49] Now the National Committee and the League had to join the forces that were united by the unconditional intention to overthrow both Wehrmacht and Reich. This was clearly documented by the change of the propaganda line. The slogan of orderly withdrawal to the Reich's frontiers gave way to the formula "Save yourself by joining the cause of the National Committee"—to a concept, in short, that ultimately thought so little of a Germany still united that it agreed with the decision of the Allied Powers.

Did the Teheran Conference mean that the usefulness of the committee and the officers' union had ended? To the Soviets their usefulness had certainly been reduced considerably. But the Free Germany organization still had some value for them: on the one hand, its propaganda, which would reinforce that of the Red Army in the future, still had value, and, on the other hand, it was a cadre through which the political game in Germany could still be influenced. If the Wehrmacht undertook a *coup d'état* in 1944, then, through the generals of the League, Moscow could hope to have a direct wire to those forces that would then have to be dealt with. If the *Putsch* failed or was not even tried, there remained perhaps the opportunity to form within the National Committee some of the groups which could be used in a conquered Germany. Such thoughts had hardly been hinted at up to now. The indoctrination sessions at Lunyovo did not demand acceptance of Marxism; the officers had not even given a thought to attending the Antifa School with its brief instruction, undignified self-criticism, and subsequent oath of loyalty.[50] But in an ideologically oriented state the idea of forming cadres was bound to occur, especially since the continued fighting reduced the non-Marxist groups to total insignificance.

The Soviet triumph at Teheran reduced the influence of the National Committee and the League of German Officers; both were deprived of their most rewarding goals. That was the case even with those for whom the new propaganda line had not yet extinguished the hope that a successful conspiracy in the Reich could still save Germany and keep it more or less intact.[51] They now knew of the fierce determination of the Grand Alliance; they sensed the growing weakness of their own nation, and already had the depressing knowledge that it was too late. If they had known about the secrets of the latest Allied meeting, they would have been taken aback and perplexed even more.[52] But such knowledge could hardly have added to the tragedy of a situation which made any further propaganda impossible; for what was it supposed to achieve beyond the preliminaries of Germany's final collapse before the background of the now generally accepted demand for unconditional surrender? Now there was not even the slightest psychological starting point for recruitment. That left only the appeal to realization and understanding, the time for which had not yet arrived, since a beaten man will acknowledge defeat only after all hope has been extinguished.

Nevertheless, the decision to resist Hitler by any means still weighed heavily and painfully in the Free Germany movement.

In one way or another the German people would continue to exist, while an unchecked Hitler led them into total destruction, claiming command even over their consciences. Having been gripped by the chimaera of a martyrdom of self-destruction and thereby become a tool of the enemy, Hitler undermined the sapped strength of the German people morally and physically. If the Reich continued to fight even though beaten, then its losses could only increase a thousandfold. The moral irresponsibility which characterized all these earthshaking events had to be met by correspondingly unusual means. For both political and nationalist considerations, the guiding thought was that of people and Wehrmacht, and of the risk that both might be sacrificed by the National Committee's inactivity now that they had burned all bridges behind them.

The new propaganda line of the committee and the officers' union was soon to be put to the test. By the end of January 1944 a considerable number of German fighting units had become trapped in the area around Cherkassy.[53] Once again Hitler's myopia, his absurd notion of prestige, and his "concept" of fixed defense had combined to create a situation which spelled disaster to tens of thousands of German soldiers.[54] The events followed the pattern of Stalingrad and once more highlighted the type of leadership practiced at Rastenburg, a leadership which ruined the troops that gradually grew sensitive to the crises.

After the Red Army had pushed back the German front behind the Dnieper, two narrow strips of ground near the river, on both sides of Cherkassy, remained in German hands, ignored by the Russians. But soon great dangers were to threaten them. During the Christmas days of 1943 the 1st Ukrainian Front of General Nikolaí Vatutin had started an offensive in the northwest, west of the recaptured city of Kiev. Its massed attack had extended the northern flank of Army Group South to such an extent that it was practically begging for a Russian attack against the diameter of the overextended German pocket of the front. The powerful enemy had foiled all attempts to assail the Soviet armies from their flanks. Only with difficulty did an improvised German defense manage to halt the Russian forces, which had also turned southwards along the line Berdyichev–Byelaya Zerkov.

Although these battles threatened above all German Eighth Army units standing near Cherkassy, they still remained tied to their front sections. In the framework of the concept of digging in at any price they were supposed to retain contact with their neighbor, the First Panzer Army, whose divisions, spread as far forward as Nikopol, were supposed to cover the Donetz area. But on the Eighth Army's eastern front the tenacious attacks of the Second Ukrainian Front under General Koniev continued to gain territory. When Kirovograd fell to the Russians the German defense was threatened from the North and from the South.[55] By the end of January when the Soviets tried to break through the German defenses at several points in the area of Byelaya Zerkov, their aims concerning the Eighth Army could no longer be doubted. Now was the last chance to wrest it from the deadly grip of the Russians by a quick retreat to the southwest. But Hitler refused this opportunity, too, of a timely evasive action. Flexible movement was prohibited by a reference to the coal mines at Krivoy Rog, which the First Panzer Army would have had to give up if the Eighth Army pulled back. Now the Soviet spearheads could no longer be held back. On January 28, 1944, the Russian units attacking from the north and the east met near Svenygorodka in the rear of the Eighth Army. Two army corps were cut off: the 11th Army Corps of the Eighth Army and the 42nd Army Corps of the First Panzer Army.[56] Five German divisions had been trapped, among them the SS-Panzer Division "Viking," one corps detachment, and the SS-Volunteer-Brigade "Wallonien."

This time, at least, countermeasures were immediately initiated to prevent a repetition of Stalingrad. This time the trapped mass of troops was not to be squeezed to death. The German High Command therefore marshaled all available planes of the Luftwaffe to supply the pocket which was still relatively close to the German lines. The commanding general of Army Group South, Field Marshal von Manstein, furthermore, tried hard to free several large units which were to liberate the trapped forces and to overcome the dangerous situation.[57] At first the fighting force of seven, and later nine, Panzer divisions looked impressive on paper, but it faced the almost impossible task of overcoming five Soviet armies and one elite cavalry corps. But bottomless mire, local crises, and the usual lack of reserves permitted neither a concentration of the German forces nor their unified action.[58] Too late, disorganized, and in parts attacking in absurd directions, the few divisions soon got bogged down, after promising initial progress, against a tough and numerically superior enemy. In this fierce struggle, officers and soldiers had often taken risks that could be justified only if one boldly assumed crass Russian errors of judgment. Six miles from the edge of the pocket the strength of the combat group that had operated most sucessfully was exhausted. The two trapped German corps continued to be squeezed into a narrow area near Korsun; they had considerable losses and were exposed to incessant Soviet fire.[59]

At the end of January, even before the situation of the German corps had reached its critical state, Colonel General Alexander Shcherbakov and his interpreter Colonel Stern arrived at the dacha near Kunzevo, which the Russians had provided as a weekend retreat for Seydlitz near Lunyovo.[60] In the person of Shcherbakov, who headed the Political Administration of the Red Army as a member of the Soviet War Cabinet, the so-called Council of Five, one of the highest Russian representatives had, for the first time, gone to meet with the German general. This fact attests to the importance of the meeting.

Shcherbakov informed Seydlitz of the situation at Cherkassy and asked him whether he thought it possible that this pocket could and would be defended as obstinately as that of Stalingrad.[61] Referring to Hitler's strategy, the general answered in the affirmative. This led almost automatically to the question whether, considering the circumstances, he would be prepared to help by personal appeals, to urge the trapped units to stop fighting and to spare them the terrible fate which the Sixth Army had had to suffer at the banks of the Volga. Seydlitz once more agreed. The subsequent exchanges concerned the immediately impending trip to the front. And so a momentous conversation concluded.

Shcherbakov's visit set in motion the most far-reaching campaign of the National Committee and the League of German Officers. For the first time, a joint action was planned for one of the focal points of battle. For the first time, too, Ulbricht's influence, which up to then had played such a pernicious role in the front propaganda because of his string-pulling behind the scenes, had been bypassed.

The National Committee's organization within the 2nd Ukrainian Front provided the base for significant activities; Colonel Steidle and Major Büchler had served there as delegates for quite some time.[62] Both were therefore instructed by Seydlitz to prepare —over his signature—all measures which could lead to contacts with the two German corps and to their ceasing resistance. For his part, he addressed the trapped divisions over radio "Free Germany" in support of these measures.[63] The appeal presented the arguments contained in the guidelines that had meanwhile been forwarded to Steidle and Büchler. But they were now complemented by guarantees which Seydlitz had been empowered, with Russian consent, to offer to the two corps in the event of their surrender. They culminated in the promise of complete safety of the lives of all officers and men, of food, clothing, shelter, and their return home after the war; in short, in the promise of any means of easing the fate of imprisonment "by the Russian Army within the framework of the humanly possible." The only condition mentioned was that the units stay together with their officers.[64]

The events in the pocket at Korsun were approaching their climax while, after this appeal, Petrov, Seydlitz, Korfes, Hadermann, and Major Lewerenz were on their way toward General Koniev's front section in a railway carriage under antiaircraft cover in order to lend their weight to Steidle's and Büchler's endeavors.[65] To prevent further bloodshed, a Soviet bearer of a flag of truce accompanied by bugler and white flag appeared in front of the lines of the trapped German divisions on February 8.[66] He delivered an official ultimatum signed by Marshal Zhukov. The Russian staff colonel was received and accompanied back with strict observance of etiquette; but the two corps did not answer the ultimatum requesting them to surrender immediately. Everything was now up to the committee and the officers' union and their broad offensive action.

Since February 10, propaganda leaflets had come fluttering down by the thousands to the troops in the pocket.[67] Their tenor was always the same; they described the situation of the encircled and exhausted units and suggested that the only way to save themselves was by joining the cause of the National Committee. The leaflets, which often covered the trenches, were followed by personal appeals. As soon as Seydlitz had arrived at the front, an attempt was made to reach the communications centers in the pocket by radio.[68] They were given a code that was supposed to facilitate communications with the delegates of the committee. Then the imploring voice of the general of the former Sixth Army was heard on the air. Speaking from a farmhouse behind the Russian lines, he not only asked for a cessation of the senseless fighting;[69] but while repeating the Soviet guarantees several times, he also addressed the staff officers and the soldiers with obvious emotion, hoping to prevent another Stalingrad. Limited contacts were made with German front line units and several signal corps men answered "We hear you," but nothing palpable resulted from it.[70]

At the same time, near the command posts of officers whom Seydlitz and Korfes knew, Russian fighter planes dropped letters that the two generals had written.[71] Other written appeals were carried to the German lines by prisoners of war who were sent back.[72]

Most of the letters reached their destinations.[73] There could hardly be any doubt in the minds of the addressees about their authenticity. The commanders of the two unfortunate corps, generals Lieb and Stemmermann, especially could not harbor any such doubts.[74] All letters referred to facts and events that only Seydlitz and Korfes could have known. This also made it a certainty that the actions of the National Committee for a Free Germany, which many news reports had already reported on, were not simply a fiction of the Soviet enemy.[75] But what position were the generals to take concerning the content of the letters?

Lieb and Stemmermann were too experienced and professional to harbor any major illusions about the situation which they and their units faced.[76] The thrusts of the relief divisions had been unable to free the two corps, although radio messages about the attacks had been received and continued to come through. Indeed, the plight of the men in the pocket grew hourly because of marked shortages in food and ammunition. It was only due to successful counterattacks and regroupings that the Russian siege ring had not yet crushed the more than 50,000 German soldiers.[77] Should they succeed in grasping the outstretched hands of their fellow soldiers who had tried to come to their rescue with only a part of that number, or, better yet, should they break out of the pocket, much would have been gained.

The psychological pressure reflected the military situation. Leadership and troops had fought with all their might ever since Stalingrad. They had come through a whole year of the toughest battles of retreat without affording the Soviet offensives the crowning success of a collapse of the German army.[78] The German divisions on the southern front had been hit hard and in parts even decimated, but their spirit had neither been broken nor had they been routed. Unique as their achievement had been, they could hardly fail to notice that the battles at the Dnieper of the past fall and winter had almost used up their last reserves. Contrary to all their expectations, the struggle against insurmountable odds continued even on the far western banks of the river which they had mistakenly regarded as the *Ostwall* that would save them.[79] Once again lack of forces destroyed any possibility of deploying themselves in depth on the battlefield and of closing the wide gaps in their front lines by counterattacks of their own. Their sense of superiority began to wane. Even the most unexpected success failed to produce a spirit of victory. The orders from above were felt to be more and more absurd and incredible. A forced optimism and an absolute sense of duty frantically glossed over the supposedly greater insight of the "Führer" and the waning confidence in him. The struggle against enemy, climate, hardship, and Hitler's strategy went beyond human powers of endurance; the struggle seemed endless and it had become hell on earth. There existed, therefore, a certain disposition to accept the arguments of the Free Germany movement as valid. For everything had combined to make it hard, extremely hard, for the German soldier not to lose faith in himself and his situation.

But could the commanders, tied to the limited sections of the front that they could observe, judge the general situation correctly?[80] Were they not in danger of extending the conclusions they had drawn from their own positions to the total situation, about whose pros and cons they had been deliberately kept in the dark? Did their oath of allegiance lose its binding force as soon as their own cause seemed to fare badly? Question upon question. To some soldiers the enemy had already provided the answer by his declared war aim, unconditional surrender, which simply forced them to fight on. This also led to the belief that Hitler was the only person who could still save Germany from ending in chaos.

But all these somber thoughts were outweighed by the contempt which the "stab in the back" of the committee and the officers' union had unleashed.[81] Did they realize what they inflicted upon the troops by trying to influence them from behind the Russian lines? Did they know the results? And even if a commander were to pay attention to them, the order to surrender would be obeyed only after the last desperate steps had failed.[82] Every German soldier thought Russian imprisonment worse than death. Many were haunted by the image of their slain and mutilated fellow soldiers, who had fallen into Russian hands in the changing fortunes of battle and who had not been freed in time by a counterattack. In large part, the merciless nature of the fighting may have been forced upon both sides by the German political leadership with its inhuman measures, but the front-line soldier was convinced that in any case Soviet barbed wire spelled humiliation, hunger, sickness, and death. This thinking was so widespread among the troops that no commander would have dared to act against it.[83] It could not be changed by the National Committee for a Free Germany, either. Deep down, its existence only reinforced the determination to seek safety and deliverance by breaking through to the west.[84]

In view of this attitude of both officers and men, all appeals remained without result. Seydlitz's exhortations to think of Yorck's example[85] and of the lives of German soldiers were of no avail as long as the same soldiers would rather take on the greatest hardships rather than courageously trust him whose role they could not understand. All endeavors were pointless as long as they were convinced that they knew what would happen to them as Russian prisoners of war and as long as they therefore rejected all propaganda as repugnant and primitive.[86] But if this was the dominant attitude among the regular troops, then there could be no doubt of that of the SS units also trapped in the pocket. It is true that Korfes addressed a letter also to *Gruppenführer* (Lieutenant General) Gille in which the former tried to talk him and his men out of any fear of punishment for war crimes they might have committed.[87] But the letter was not only rather weak, it was also unable to remove even a particle of the hate which existed between the National Socialist elite units and the Red Army.

The action of the National Committee and the League of German Officers at the Korsun pocket thus ended in total failure. Instead of surrendering in orderly fashion, as had been hoped, the two German corps, in deep echelon formation and without any preparatory firing, broke out of the Russian ring, using only side-arms, in the night of February 16 to February 17, 1944.[88] After the troops had been concentrated under heavy losses, the attack, which was supposed to reach the advance units of the relief army soon, took the enemy by complete surprise. His initial reaction was weak. The second and third wave followed the advancing infantry according to plan; about 40,000 men surged westward. Freedom, the official password of the day, seemed near. But the positions in which they had expected their German fellow soldiers were held by the enemy.[89] Russian tanks, antitank guns, and artillery fired furiously into the charging troops. All order was smashed. Weapons and equipment were destroyed, wounded left behind; the bloody losses rose rapidly. With a final push, the shattered mass of soldiers rose desperately to escape the threatening annihilation. Only fragments of the divisions finally succeeded in breaking through. Almost frozen to death and hungry, without weapons and demoralized, about 20,000 to 25,000 survivors, no longer fit to fight, finally assembled in the reception area behind the German lines. Thousands of casualties, among them General Stemmermann, marked the path of the hastily escaping columns on the battlefield. At least 15,000 prisoners were added to matériel captured by the victors.[90]

Many of these soldiers had indeed surrendered, still in possession of propaganda leaflets; but they had become prisoners of war only because the military catastrophe had left them no chance to escape.[91] No one could put down these 15,000 as having been won by the success of the Free Germany organization and no front delegate felt like celebrating.[92]

A profound depression came over the committee and the officers' union.[93] Both had now failed in a mission which in the beginning had been accompanied by extraordinary hopes and ex-pectations. Could they still believe in their own front propaganda in the future if the troops themselves preferred to be massacred in a hopeless situation than to join the cause of the National Com-mittee? What were the thoughts and feelings of the German sol-dier? Perplexed, the committee men searched for the miraculous force which animated the German soldier to continue doing a duty that was demonstrably unreasonable. Dismayed, they began to sense that Germany's doom lay in the German soldier's obedience, a doom which they fought against alone and under exceptional circumstances.[94]

It is, indeed, hard to imagine two more diametrically opposed positions than those of the National Committee and the German army in the East. There existed among the former the firm con-viction that the war had been lost by the Reich and that it had to be ended immediately, even at the cost of unconditional surrender, that Hitler drove Wehrmacht and people toward total ruin, and that Russian imprisonment had to be regarded as a viable alter-native. But in the army there ruled the overwhelming certainty that the fight had to be fought on until the two inexorable enemies' will to destroy was played out, that only the "Führer" could prevent the defeat of Germany, and that Soviet barbed wire was no alter-native at all. Considering these factors, the National Committee and the League of German Officers tried to influence forces that were opposed to their aims and to their very existence. The enemies' struggle at the front, at any rate, followed its own laws; these laws followed the false star of destruction and thoughtlessness.

The questions to which the mission of Cherkassy had given rise were disquieting, but the conclusions reached at Lunyovo turned out to be completely beside the point. Now all deliberations were to take on an element of unreality. This became apparent during the first plenary session of the National Committee in February 1944. Here Erich Weinert declared that the new propaganda line failed to convince because the German soldier still cherished illu-sions about Hitler from which he first had to be liberated.[95] What Weinert here called illusion still represented, as a rule, the deter-mining reality for the divisions on the Eastern Front. How was he to shake them in their faith? By rational arguments? By answering this question in the affirmative, Weinert had already fallen prey to considerable self-deception, for as long as he continued to speak from the Russian side, whose reality put off the German soldiers and which was beyond his influence, all rational arguments remained without force or impact.

Even more foolish was the tendency to woo only the lower ranks of the Wehrmacht from now on. Perhaps some prisoners from the Korsun pocket had "admitted" with calculated opportunism that only their officers had prevented them from discontinuing their senseless fighting. But when Heinrich Homann picked up these dubious statements in an article, in order to attack the German army leaders, he only made matters worse.[96] For to encourage the troops to internal dissension by propaganda was the last thing appropriate to a member of the old group of majors in the committee. Slogans which suggested that now the common soldier counted above all else and that he should act even against his superiors when it became necessary had to go unheard at the German front lines.[97] Unless they were arguments of individuals, these slogans were bound to maneuver the Free Germany organization into defaming the German officers corps—a tactic that had already failed miserably when émigrés and politruks had tried it.

Perhaps miscalculations and accidents merely coincided, perhaps the officers' union was to be even further reduced in importance anyway—the failure of Cherkassy produced results which began to undermine and ultimately destroy the united front of Communists and soldiers.

The overture to this development was a statement by *Tass* which treated Polish-Soviet relations in such detail that its official character was obvious.[98] It commented, as it were, on Churchill's speeches in the House of Commons and eliminated all doubts that at Teheran the Kremlin had been promised the western borders as of late fall of 1939 and that Poland had been granted far-reaching compensation. Any uncertainties disappeared as to who would have to pay for this arrangement. Commentaries in the Russian press already spoke of large areas of Germany's eastern provinces, which up to that time had been regarded as inviolable in the National Committee. After the disaster at Korsun, the statement of the Soviet news agency—a statement which had obviously become opportune for the Russians—created considerable shock.[99] It was acknowledged that the last Allied conference allowed no further room for illusions anyway and that the deadline for Melnikov's past promises had apparently long since passed. It was now up to the equally surprised émigrés to jump into the breach with their agile ideology. They called the future borders between a socialist (!) Poland and Germany irrelevant, attacked outmoded nationalism, and stressed above all the interests of the Soviet Union, which was directing its own fate as the home of Communism.[100]

An abyss of horror had opened up. The only way to bridge the gulf would be for the League of German Officers to accept an ideological dogma that they in particular rejected. The revolutionary vistas that the left wing of the National Committee now hoped to conjure up would not appeal to the officers, especially not when the former tried to justify the annexation of German lands dialectically. Weinert's remark that he had always predicted a dire end if the Free Germany movement should fail to make a decisive achievement could therefore hardly calm the waters.[101] For even the most "popular" argument—that the Reich had lost its buffer zone in Pomerania, Silesia, and Eastern Prussia to the *raison d'état* of Poland[102]—presupposed intellectual dexterity of a kind still rejected by the generals and officers.

The *Tass* statement and the reactions of émigrés and *politruks* to it weighed heavily enough. But even more problematical than these events were the scandals associated with a misguided memorandum and the name of First Lieutenant Hans Huber.

The work of representatives and delegations at the front was mere waste motion. The fortunes of war decided what should have been achieved by the weapon of propaganda. Cherkassy had simply once again underscored that realization. But the structure and organization of the whole National Committee had to strike one as no less dubious. Chairmanship, committees, plenum, and other aspects had their origins in democratic principles formalistically applied; but the top echelons of the League of German Officers would have been hard pressed—as time passed on increasingly so—to name their areas of clear-cut responsibility.[103] There were no victories to be won on the battlefields. But the possibility that valuable energies could still be activated for the future had by no means been eliminated. Everything that had for some time been leading to a feeling of frustration now found its way into a memorandum during a meeting in von Seydlitz' weekend dacha.[104] The generals' blueprint suggested a tightening of the various areas of responsibility and the preparation of the committee and the officers' union for their tasks in Germany. They proposed a clear separation of political, military, economic, and cultural affairs.[105] With a deliberate concentration of forces they wanted to include in the Presidium only generals and former deputies of the Reichstag, *i.e.*, only Pieck and Ulbricht of the émigrés. This memorandum was intended only as a basis for discussion and did not labor under the delusion that it could still demand border guarantees for a future Germany. It deliberately avoided the whole problem, as it also suppressed existing ambitions to plead for a clearly defined shadow cabinet.[106]

Some of the proposals were quite sound, but they did not exclude interpretations which the generals felt were misleading. The memorandum was an attempt to secure a platform for future codetermination, without which all efforts would have been for naught. But this presupposed, basically, an entirely different distribution of power than the one existing in the Free Germany movement. Weinert, Pieck, and Ulbricht, therefore, most decidedly rejected the suggestions of the officers' union. They very cleverly pretended that the time had not yet come for a reorganization of the National Committee.[107]

The generals believed, nevertheless, that they could send their memorandum to the Russians through their regular official channels—only to fail painfully. The proposal with its independently presented ideas did indeed reach Melnikov through his deputy Colonel Schwetz. But Seydlitz was immediately requested to withdraw the memorandum and to apologize during one of the usual weekly sessions of the Executive Committee for his "violation of democratic principles."[108] The unpleasant apology turned out to be brief, but the general, and some others, had been taught a drastic lesson.

Melnikov's reaction can hardly be called surprising. No more guarantees were to be given to groups that would ultimately be eliminated anyway, as now seemed more and more certain. For a long time the war had favored the Communist section. What might have further induced the unusual sharpness on the part of the Soviet adviser to the committee may have been intimations which led him to expect a unique kind of sabotage coming from within the League of German Officers.

The man who would bring it off had already decided on his move some time ago. He was a man of superior and cynical intelligence, a former *SS-Obersturmbannführer* (Lieutenant Colonel) in the SD (*Sicherheitsdienst,* Security Police) who had been captured by the Russians while serving as a first lieutenant in an armored car unit: Doctor of Laws Hans Huber. The history of his machinations is involved and significant.[109] As early as Spring 1943 Huber had planned to create cells to obstruct the Antifa work of the Soviets. His plan did not remain theory; at Yelabuga he won over and indoctrinated several officers, among them Captain Stolz and Second Lieutenant Lohmann. Later they spread among several officers' camps, working along Huber's lines within the Free Germany movement.

In August 1943 Huber himself came to Lunyovo as a member of the Yelabuga camp delegation.[110] His attempts to be elected to the board of the League of German Officers failed, but at the insistence of Major General Korfes he was allowed at least to join the staff of professional correspondents of the House at Lunyovo. Avoiding any conspicuous activity, he prepared the ground for his subversive activities step by step. He pursued several goals. For one thing, Huber wanted to provide the Gestapo with information about the National Committee through coded messages in its newspapers and radio broadcasts; collaborators from the ranks of the front delegations were to help in this.[111] He also sought to exacerbate the differences between generals and émigrés and to undermine the committee and the officers' union from within. In the event these intentions failed, Huber had concocted an imaginative operation. In a fit of overambition he thought of having the House at Lunyovo raided by German paratroop units.[112]

Even here at Lunyovo palpable results were achieved, as they had been at Yelabuga. Later Huber not only admitted to having received acknowledgments for his messages from the German side;[113] he had also got his crony Captain Stolz an office in the presidium of the officers' union. His attempts to sound out officers on their political views and recruit additional officers had been successful at least in the case of Lieutenant General Rodenburg.[114] Commander of the 76th Infantry Division during the Battle of Stalingrad, Rodenburg found himself forcibly transferred to the National Committee's house in the spring of 1944. Later he was to give up his resistance against the committee and to appear in public with considerable success;[115] but there remains the incontestable fact that he participated in the drafting of the generals' unfortunate memorandum, and therefore the question arose as to whether or not he had suggested that document deliberately, considering his continued contact with Huber.[116]

Whatever may have been independent or joint action in this matter, the development and outcome of the affair turned out to Huber's complete satisfaction. He believed, nevertheless, that he had now passed the zenith of his possibilities at Lunyovo. Picked by Seydlitz for the next front delegation, he now planned his escape.[117]

Systematical as his planning had been, it was upset by a source of error that was bound to start flowing sometime and that exposed Huber. In April 1944, when a delegation of the officers' union started out for the front near Leningrad, comprising Major Bechler, Captain Stolz, and Second Lieutenant Dr. Wilimzig, Huber approached Wilimzig, thereby revealing his role.[118] Huber asked him to desert to the German lines when he reached the front and inform a Gestapo office, with which Huber claimed to be in contact, with the help of a password and a telephone number which Huber provided. Wilimzig played along with Huber's instructions but informed a fellow officer at Lunyovo before he left, leaving any further steps up to that officer. He himself reserved judgment at first, thinking that he had reason to doubt Huber's sanity in view of this seemingly fantastic information.

But the front delegation soon opened his eyes. Stolz revealed himself as Huber's confidant, and one who could be expected to follow his directives.[119] Now Wilimzig prevented the captain's desertion by sabotaging the whole delegation. Its mission was indeed canceled and Wilimzig was cashiered by the officers' union for "political unreliability."[120]

The state of innocence was not to last much longer in the

presidium of the League of German Officers. For at the same time
that Wilimzig reported Huber's machinations in Moscow, one of his
confidants at Lunyovo had, by chance, revealed himself to the
dentist Dr. Zimmermann, whom Huber had already sounded out.[121]
Although Huber's friend and Zimmermann at first hesitated, they
finally decided, under the influence of the news about the front
delegation, to impart their knowledge to the totally surprised Lattmann. It was the right moment. On the night of May 6, 1944, Huber
was waked up in bed by a Soviet officer and arrested.[122]

To prove the "vigilance" of the officers' union, Major General
Lattmann presented his notes at the NKVD investigations which
now began.[123] But to no avail. Even though Huber's machinations
had been the activities of one individual, they had prospered in
the circle around Seydlitz and compromised the League of German
Officers beyond repair.

The enormous credibility gap thus created showed itself not
only in a thorough "purge" of the presidium of the officers' union
at Lunyovo, from which Lieutenant Colonel Bechly and second
lieutenants Dr. Greifenhagen and Dr. Wieder were removed, all
of them men whose pronounced conservatism had long been a
thorn in the side of the committee's left wing.[124] It also manifested
itself in recalling all front delegations of the League of German
Officers, who were now without exception under the paralyzing
shadow of suspicion for sabotage. Slowly the candid tone that up to
now had characterized conversations among the officers—at least
at Lunyovo—began to die out. Ideological clichés and purely
Marxist formulations prospered more and more, and even the generals could no longer counteract their influence.[125]

What an outcome! Teheran had forced them into adopting front
propaganda that culminated in appeals to desert and that continued
to evoke a bitter taste even though it corresponded to the hopeless
situation of Germany. Cherkassy had seen its failure only to reveal
the incredible war aims of the Grand Alliance. They had also failed
in the attempt to create a basis for future work and to assure a
certain community of interest of all Free German forces whose
coexistence was now obviously dictated only by tactical considerations. And the final outcome had been a senseless intrigue. The
solidarity of the officers' union had been broken; purged and re-

duced in number, it found itself at the mercy of the largely unpredictable machinations of its radical elements.

Thus nothing seemed to be left at the beginning of the summer of 1944 except the hope for a *Putsch* in Germany itself, for a turn of events which alone could dip the scales a little in favor of sensible goals. But had not precisely this hope become untenable in the face of the military situation?

## CHAPTER SIX

## July 20, 1944, and the Free
## Germany Movement

ON JULY 20, 1944, the event for which almost all hope had been given up finally took place. On that day Colonel Claus Count von Stauffenberg attempted to assassinate Adolf Hitler at the Führer's Headquarters at Rastenburg and subsequently gave the signal for the uprising which was supposed to rescue Germany from its disastrous situation. This step finally initiated the kind of development that the National Committee and the League of German Officers had pressed for from the beginning. When the first news of the attempt reached Lunyovo, it stirred up great excitement and satisfaction.[1] In view of the event all the reverses and intrigues of the recent past were forgotten. Spontaneously both wings of the committee viewed the promising act as the beginning of a general reorientation of the German people and the Reich.

But nothing seems more revealing about the Free Germany movement than the fact that it was completely in the dark not only about what had happened but also about the men who had tried to bring about the revolution.[2] The goals and scope of resistance inside Germany was a closed book to the committee and the officers' union. As early as 1943 they had tried to approach by letter the men who, they surmised more than they actually knew, might plan a *coup d'état*.[3] But the genuine emotion of many an appeal turned out to be a useless expenditure of energy, since the letters of the captured generals and officers were never forwarded by the Soviets. Thus the only way open was that of turning directly to the German people with radio appeals. Seydlitz, Daniels, Einsiedel, and Emendörfer therefore implored the nation to take their stand courageously

behind Stauffenberg.[4] Even Weinert and Erpenbeck called on all
segments of society to follow the dictates of the hour without
reservations. "We do not know who they [the assassins] were. But
we welcome Stauffenberg's action and support it wholeheartedly."[5]

But the sweeping exhilaration that had characterized the first
hours soon gave way to bitter disappointment and resignation.[6] The
hope that the war was ending and therefore a new Germany beginning lasted barely two days; then press and radio revealed that the
assassination attempt had failed. Courts and gallows ruled in the
Reich instead of the desired new order; instead of an armistice,
acts of terror began to heat up a hopeless fight to the point of
excess. Hitler had survived once more. Again his magic had triumphed over conscience and reason, the magic that had become
an incomprehensible enigma to the committee and the officers'
union. Now Germany's dictator could bid farewell to all scruples
in order to bind the nation to himself and his agony with deadly
force.

At first, considerations like these were too depressing to allow
for anything except resignation at Lunyovo. Dignified and aloof,
Anton Ackermann delivered a funeral oration.[7] Although this open-
minded émigré deplored the failure of the men of July 20 to secure
a broad base among the army and the people for their uprising, he
nevertheless praised the courage of the conspirators in the Reich.
Ackermann refused to indulge in a cheap attack against men who
had been moved by ideals of their own. He lauded Stauffenberg's
act as an attempt which was to be regarded all the more highly as
it was unique.

This speech represented the swan song of the community of
interests which had united the committee and the officers' union in
the Free Germany movement. Trying to present a nonpartisan
interpretation of the *coup d'état*, the speech raised only some criticism against its tactics. These objections were, however, beside the
point, since the Beck-Goerdeler conspiracy and the stern necessities
of a military *Putsch* made impossible any "*levée en masse*."[8] But now
more extreme arguments took the field and revealed only too clearly
that Ackermann's speech had to be viewed as only academic speculation. The mask fell. Rudolf Herrnstadt confessed brutally that
July 20, undertaken by the ruling classes in Germany for the sake

of a capitalist democracy, had been the last obstacle in the path of Communism's progress in Europe.[9] From now on Russian advisers and guests of the House at Lunyovo made no bones about the fact that the Soviet Union no longer needed the National Committee to finally vanquish Hitler's Germany. [10]

Émigré statements that the future would no longer belong to the Junkers and generals, but to Socialist progress, had already preceded the assassination attempt.[11] At that time Weinert had tried to tone them down by pointing to their unofficial nature. Now, after the suppression of the July revolt, any such indications were belied by the Russian reaction, which reflected the general situation so accurately that it served as a reminder of the actual distribution of power within the groups of the National Committee.

In the military field the Soviets' great concern about future losses paled beside the expectation of being able to advance all the way into the heart of Germany under the impetus of their operations.[12] Outstanding victories inspired the Red Army. Concentric Soviet summer offensives in White Russia had almost annihilated Army Group Center. Twenty-eight German divisions had fallen under their onslaught, victims of Hitler's obstinate prestige "strategy."[13] The triumph surpassed even that of Stalingrad. And in the north and south of this vast theater of war, further diastrous losses threatened the Wehrmacht.[14] The battle front approached eastern Prussia and Roumania; the latter's desertion had to be reckoned with. In the west, Great Britain and the United States had kept their promise in the early dawn of June 6, when their invasion forces landed on the coast of Normandy.[15] The attempts to stop them and throw them back into the sea failed mainly because of the unassailable superiority of the Allied air forces, which overwhelmed the German defender's front lines, his communications zones, and his home country with paralyzing blows. Inexorably the decisive breakthrough of the British and American forces into the heart of France drew closer. For Hitler and his High Command there no longer existed any opportunity for a meaningful operational decision; the fortunes of war had finally left them forever.

This hopeless military situation did away with Germany's nearly last political chances; there were no successful conspirators to try them out. The motives which had inspired the attempted *coup*

*d'état* of Stauffenberg and Beck on July 20, 1944, must at that time
have appeared as anything but desirable to the Soviet Union. The
Kremlin wanted total victory now. An anti-National Socialist power
asking for an armistice and possessing a Wehrmacht which tied
down the Red Army in eastern Poland would have become an obstacle. After a campaign whose end now seemed to be in sight,
Soviet divisions were to move into areas which Moscow would be
able to transform according to its ideological concepts. Even a successful *Putsch* might not have prevented the occupation of the
Reich that had been decided upon; but a German about-face in
July 1944 must have been a threat rather than a blessing to Bolshevist Russia.

Under these circumstances, was there any influence which National Committee and League of German Officers could still bring
to bear? Their political significance had disappeared, if it ever had
existed at all. And what about the front propaganda, whose slogans
could now no longer be made difficult by skeptical objections? They
were, it is true, still accepted in the hope that at least in the final
stages of the war the appeals and leaflets might finally have an
effect on the fighting soldier.[16] It is also a fact that subversive units
that the Red Army had formed out of POWs continued to operate,
even daring to appear at the front and behind the German lines in
the name of the Free Germany organization.[17] But from now on the
Soviets curtailed all kinds of work at the fronts, just as the propaganda activities could only serve to underscore the logical development of military operations. The numbers of delegations, especially
of the officers' union, were henceforth drastically reduced,[18] and
the legendary "Seydlitz Army," surrounded by rumors, never did
make its appearance. It had been planned as a modest German
legion but had never grown beyond the stage of a rejected suggestion in the fall of 1943.[19] A single alternative was left: making
one's own arrangement with tomorrow's victors. Only joining their
camp would give the kind of confidence that seemed to be needed
for public co-operation.

The Communist émigrés did not have to meet the demands of
the hour. On the contrary; always eager to do Moscow's bidding
without criticism, they once again felt firm ideological ground under
their feet, which, to their bewilderment, had been pulled out from

under them occasionally in the past. Some of the arguments they used to "justify" the loss of German territories may have been hard for them to express even now. But if these were depressing thoughts at all, they were now supplanted by an exciting prospect. From now on there was a chance to realize the ideological tenets of faith on which the Communist Party had brought up its disciples. It was up to the generals and officers now to recognize that the radical elements were in the driver's seat and that these radical elements would demand their acceptance of that fact and their subordination.

The failure of the July plot had also killed any hopes the officers' union might still have clung to.[20] The extermination of the conspirators' opposition in the Reich left them only the conclusion that chaos had now become perfected. This should have suggested that they ought to reconsider their more sanguine hopes and become used to the omnipotence of the Communist groups upon whom the Soviets manifestly began to concentrate their interest from now on.[21] But Seydlitz and the majority of the League of German Officers were unable to take up new positions.[22] On the one hand, this would have gone against their principles; on the other hand, they remained convinced, despite many indications to the contrary, that the original goals had by no means been invalidated by events. Ever since the officers' union had joined the National Committee, it had only one "ideology"—that of saving Germany.[23] After the abyss of Stalingrad, Hitler was, to them, the corrupter of the German nation. The war was lost and could not be brought to an end by Hitler's criminal régime. Its chief representative had to fall if the people and Reich were to be spared the fate of the Sixth Army, a fate that had manifest the amorality of a system oriented exclusively toward power politics. Amidst all the changes of the propaganda line, it had remained their primary goal to make men conscious of this necessity and to lead them to this realization. All other plans were secondary to these considerations, if only because they could not be realized until Hitler had been overthrown. But even the best kind of propaganda could, of course, not exempt them from asking questions about the shape a future Germany was to take. From the beginning, the League of German Officers had been united in the demand that the dictatorship of National Socialism would have to make way for a democratic, constitutional state.[24] In the light of

World War II it seemed to have a fair chance. It could best be supported by a united front extending from Marxists all the way to Conservatives; a front which had already developed in the Free Germany movement.

That such aims were not altogether utopian had been shown by the Communist émigrés themselves.[25] In 1941–1942 they had pursued a repulsive kind of inflammatory propaganda, but after the founding of the officers' union they had changed into partners who were actively trying to establish the appearance of bourgeois provenance. They affirmed, on the one hand, a democratic objective with the passionate confession that their own narrow party-oriented way of thinking would only be overcome within a united front of all anti-fascist forces.[26] On the other hand, they tried to identify themselves as Germans with a sense of nationality by rejecting any thoughts of class warfare. The common goal of a parliamentary republic was supposed to unite them. It can therefore hardly be surprising that the League of German Officers, thus confirmed in its goals, began to see the Communist world in a new light. National Socialist propaganda had prepared this development to a considerable extent. Its statements about "Bolshevist subhumanity" had been too undifferentiated and slogan-bound to help anyone in orienting himself in a reality it obviously had misrepresented. And now the émigrés even showed an attitude which obviously obeyed not some narrow-minded dogmatism but an enlightened acceptance of necessities.[27] This was to stimulate unexpected theses. While there were some who celebrated Stalinist Russia as a democratic state,[28] Seydlitz argued in radio appeals against the assumption that Bolshevism was to be imposed upon other peoples.[29] The tone characteristic of the officers is an excellent reflection of the atmosphere which had been very adroitly created. Not only did the officers continually point out the parallels to Yorck's action at Taurogen;[30] they also repeatedly recalled the Rapallo agreement and the secret pact between the Reichswehr and the Red Army, for these were treaties which could substantiate Moscow's loyalty and good faith as an ally and were the links in a tradition of Soviet-German rapprochement. But whatever the arguments used to underpin their own political position, there remained a decided coolness against the theoretical foundations of Marxism. There certainly existed a willingness to come to terms with these foundations and to appreciate the critical truth of certain aspects. Thus Arnold, Varga, and Lukács had more than once found attentive listeners in the officers' union with their lectures on politics, economics, and literary history.[31] The officers' union also comprised many ideological nuances; they could be demonstrated only by a detailed analysis which at present is still impossible.

But the independent officer was incapable of opting for Communism, just as the presentations of well-known scholars and functionaries had provoked active objections because of their overworked deductions.[32] No one paid homage to the doctrinaire ideology of Communism, nor did anyone propagate the ideas of a social revolution which might, at best, have associated them with some kind of "National Bolshevism."[33] As a result, the development after July 20 passed over the head of the League of German Officers. In the Soviets' view it had not only become stagnant politically; from their point of view it must have had eliminated itself by then.

The Russians now quite consistently tackled the last task for which the Free Germany movement suggested itself to them apart from continued propaganda missions. The movement now supplemented the Communist émigrés as one of the germinal cells of a future German régime by supplying those officers and soldiers who were willing to join.

The path to joining led via the Antifa School at Krasnogorsk.[34] At Lunyovo participation in its courses was not mandatory, but the graduates of Krasnogorsk were distinctly supported and singled out.[35] From now on Moscow relied exclusively on the clearly defined cadres of these graduates. The lectures and seminars of this reorientation school comprised fields of astonishing variety.[36] Selected *politruks,* of whom Zaisser was an outstanding example, taught dialectical and historical materialism, economics, imperialism, and the history of the proletarian movement. Their teachings were immune to any objections; training and discipline were subject to draconic rules. Repetition, self-criticism, and absolute loyalty to an absolute party were the only things tolerated. With a final oath replete with ritualistic threats, the Communist Party's disciples graduated from the school.

The success of the Antifa School at Krasnogorsk was considerable.[37] Hundreds of POWs were trained there and were pledged to the theses of Stalinism. It was only at the end of 1944 that two generals set out from Lunyovo to participate in the school's course of instruction. But several members of the committee had attended it before July 20 with the result that they returned as obedient Communists.[38] The motives behind these conversions remain uncertain; Count Einsiedel was not the only case of a conversion that bridged enormous ideological chasms. It is certain that the political mentality of the officers' union had no longer been able to satisfy the more prominent members of the National Committee.[39] A fertile imagination could hardly be captured by the goals of the League anyway. But here and there more than a merely external reorientation was desired. Here and there fundamental questions regarding the incredible struggle of the peoples had become pressing, questions to which only fascinating Marxism seemed to know the answers. Did its closed system not provide more intellectual support than the insufficient ideology of National Socialism, which had betrayed them and which had left behind a perplexing emptiness? Did Marxism not order a world full of internal contradictions with penetrating rationality; did it not everywhere point to the tasks which deserved a solution above all others with impressive lucidity? And finally, did it not remove the fear of that inability to believe, which, after all the chaos of the present, only a strong and disciplined collective could overcome? These elements counted all the more heavily where a lack of intellectual independence or, in the case of those thinking for themselves, mere passivity, favored the attraction of Communism. Undeniable as these factors may be, they cannot obscure the symptoms of opportunism. Soviet support of the committee's left wing had become forcefully apparent. Newly converted and convinced, the latest Marxists increased its weight by striving from now on to serve the most promising forces and ideas.

July 20 had shown the Free Germany movement isolated even from the forces of resistance within Germany. But did they at least coincide in their plans? And had not the conspiracy in the Reich tried to establish a loose connection with the committee and the officers' union?

The skepticism with which the German soldier had greeted the

Free Germany organization from its inception was shared by the German opposition to Hitler around Beck, Goerdeler, and Moltke.[40] In their circle doubts about the authenticity of the Russian reports dominated at first; then the idea that tried and proved generals and officers of the German army called for the overthrow of Hitler from inside Russia seemed completely without base in reality, and absurd. Similar uncertainties and reservations continued to remain alive in the men of July 20. Many refused to believe that, in particular, General von Seydlitz's opposition to Hitler was based on his own free decision.[41] But their skepticism was to be shaken quickly and thoroughly. Once the Wehrmacht High Command had reached the conclusion that the propaganda of the committee and the officers' union was no fiction, specific details revealed to the conspirators the mistakenness of their original judgment.[42] Letters written in a personal style which reached higher commanders at the front dispelled many doubts and reservations because of their knowledge of certain details. Then there were also certain turns of phrase in some appeals, leaflets, and newspaper articles which were reminiscent of the hand of well-known fellow officers and which could hardly be forged. The greatest initial doubts began to disappear. Gradually a certain open-mindedness *vis-à-vis* the Free Germany movement began to stir; its activities were now being observed with interest by the opposition inside the Reich even in areas where the opposition from the very start denied that the movement could achieve any palpable results.[43]

In part this reaction was born out of a belief in the activities of the committee and the officers' union; in part it was suggested by the development of the resistance within Germany up to that time.[44] For a long time the German resistance had firmly believed that Hitler, criminal in both his plans and his rule of terror, had led Germany into ruin and had to be eliminated. With great devotion the men of the resistance had constantly tried to improve the efficiency of the opposition against Hitler with the aim of stopping, by a *coup d'état*, a development which threatened to lead all of Europe into an abyss of terror. So far the conspirators had been denied any visible success. On the one hand, there were the dazzling triumphs of the German dictator, which gave him the faithful support of the majority of the people and the Wehrmacht; on the other hand, there was the lack of a military lever ready to touch off the revolution. But since the beginning of the war an "increasing disposition" to thoughts of opposition had slowly developed. The need for an uprising had become apparent; such an uprising could only become more problematical the longer the opposition hesitated.[45] The organized mass murders of thousands upon thousands of Jews in Poland and especially in the Soviet Union had been a shock; these murders, the Commissar Order, and the order concerning martial law raised the burning question whether one could continue to serve a régime capable of committing such crimes.[46] And these extreme ethical provocations were not the only ones. Hitler had no qualms about brutally offending the conscience of his professional military men by his foolish and contemptuous methods of leadership. All of this made apparent and intolerably heightened the essential traits of a political system whose moral responsibility was at best rooted in unbounded autocracy. The opening was provided by the crisis during the winter of 1941–1942, when inflexible holding actions were the one true panacea in the eyes of the Supreme Commander. At Stalingrad warfare that was based only on a megalomaniac's regard for prestige and not on strategy reached its climax. Ruthlessly hundreds of thousands were sent to a meaningless sacrificial death. The conspirators girded their loins. With burning indignation they had hoped for a courageous act on part of General Paulus and when the flaming accusation had failed to come forth from the encirclement at the banks of the Volga, they were determined to take the final step themselves.[47] The period of conspiratorial talks and more or less legal memoranda was over. On March 13, 1943, the group of officers around Major General Henning von Tresckow had already ventured a bombing plot against Hitler that was intended to start the *coup d'état*, which was still insufficiently prepared at that time.[48] They had drawn radical conclusions from Germany's situation by attempting this plot, which failed, however. But it is evidence for the determination of the officers' conspiracy that from now on they strove in attempt after attempt for that "initial explosion" which alone could create the situation "free of the obligations imposed by the oath of allegiance."[49]

Had von Tresckow's assassination attempt succeeded in spring of 1943, it would certainly have presented the opposition within Germany with a *fait accompli*; they would have been dragged along by it instead of accepting it spontaneously and utilizing it. Despite their conviction that under Hitler's leadership the people and the Reich were heading straight to ruin, they still discussed deliberately killing the tyrant as though they were talking of a despicable murder. Goerdeler hesitated to suppress in himself weighty elements of legalism and a rational optimism, which caused him to argue against the plot.[50] Moltke and his circle of friends rejected it out of hand. They were of the opinion that this catastrophe had to end in a complete collapse in order to impress Hitler's guilt upon all of Germany and to make possible a new beginning not burdened by any legends about a stab in the back.[51]

The aims of the committee and the officers' union corresponded to the intentions of the most active conspirators; they reinforced the impulses that favored the act of liberation. Lunyovo could hardly go beyond the insights and experiences which had formed widespread opposition within the state and the Wehrmacht. But even a part of these experiences had to be sufficient to highlight the uniquely exceptional situation that they all had drifted into and which could stir up opposition even outside one's own nation.

Basically, the Free Germany movement stated things which could not be contested. Having gone through hell, the men of Stalingrad spoke for their dead comrades whose horrible death was to be given a profoundly historical meaning.[52] They deplored Germany's hopeless position and with the voice of unbroken patriotism they called upon commanders, generals, and officers to act decisively. The men of Stalingrad reminded them that only an immediate about-face could save Germany from the kind of total destruction which National Socialism was sure to bring about, since it would never be prepared "to open up the path which alone can lead to peace." Subordinated to this appeal was an equally determined propagandistic conception. Up to the beginning of 1944, leaflets and radio appeals generally demanded the orderly withdrawal of German troops from the Soviet Union; with this they demanded a decision now which any new political power would have to reach anyway after the armistice which had now become a pressing necessity. That this demand took shape as a propaganda slogan behind the lines of the Russian enemy should also serve to point out the opportunities which a régime without Hitler still had in the east.

By 1943 the committee and the officers' union agreed in principle with numerous conspirators within the area controlled by German power that Hitler and his régime of insanity and shame had to be removed by an organized revolution. There are reports that many of the officers who helped to support the *coup d'état* on July 20, 1944, were not without sympathies for the National Committee for a Free Germany after Stalingrad.[53] Beck, as the head of the opposition, did not accept Seydlitz, since he worried about the danger that the latter's activities might commit Germany too much to Russian interests.[54] But Goerdeler came out against this cautious interpretation. When asked by the son of General von Hammerstein, he said in the course of a conversation: "Seydlitz does not commit us; we would always be able to correct it if he did, and the fact that he comes out publicly against Hitler must be welcomed."[55] Around the middle of August 1943 the career diplomat Ulrich von Hassell, trying to evaluate the National Committee as a foreign policy factor, viewed it more soberly. Hassell thought that Stalin had begun to move away more and more from the American line.[56] "His German liberation committee, meaningless in itself, is, however, important as a symptom." This was not only aimed at that "intellectual confusion created by Hitler" which von Hassell stressed in his diary during the National Committee's propaganda missions at the Cherkassy pocket;[57] it was directed even more at the political opportunities indicated by Lunyovo. According to Hassell, these opportunities had to be taken up by a decent and politically responsible Germany, if only because the evil of a Hitler-Stalin rapprochement remained intolerable to him.[58] The last German ambassador at Moscow, Werner Count von der Schulenburg, was moved by similar considerations, as was that upright conservative of the resistance, Ewald von Kleist-Schmenzin.[59] As far as Schulenburg was concerned, the committee and the officers' union had the task of encouraging the forces of opposition in the Reich to turn toward the east. Kleist-Schmenzin had welcomed the Free Germany movement from the start as an auxiliary instrument for the revolutionary overthrow of Hitler, which he worked for so passionately.

To him the committee and the officers' union suggested the possibility of a solution in the east; when all hopes had been extinguished in the west, he resolutely supported such a solution.

But these reactions were not characteristic. The Kreisau circle, for instance, rejected any idea of a *Putsch* as well as any tactical maneuvering. But even after Stauffenberg had become the center of the conspiracy, an increasing inner reserve against the Free Germany organization continued to be felt.[60] No unambiguous statements are extant even from the younger staff officers for whom Major General von Tresckow at the front and the Bendler-Strass group in Berlin were the catalysts. Even before the July plot, Colonel Mertz von Quirnheim, of the General Staff, a brother-in-law of Major General Korfes then in the presidium of the officers' union, had hinted at the possibility of a genuine collaboration between the Soviets and the Seydlitz group.[61] But the overwhelming majority came around to Stauffenberg's point of view as time went by. There is some evidence that testifies to his brusque rejection of the National Committee and that substantiates his saying that he had a low opinion of proclamations from behind barbed wire.[62]

At the beginning of 1944 convictions of this sort increased, although this did not influence certain basic tendencies which continued to inspire both the committee and the officers' union and the conspiratorial groups within Germany. When the manifesto on a new Germany had demanded a democracy which should no longer have anything in common with the weakness of the Weimar government,[63] its motto had also reflected the goals of the conspirators. Whether it was Hassell drafting a provisional basic law,[64] Goerdeler framing a detailed constitution,[65] or the Kreisau group developing a state organized around an emphasis on federative principles[66]— they all had in common the idea that the future fate of people and nation had to be determined only by the people and the nation themselves. There was also increasing support for a renewal attempt, "which was to reach spheres of existence quite different from those reached in the 'revolutions' of 1918 and 1933."[67] Another analogy was the argument of unity of the Left and the Right, which Reichwein tried to secure when he attempted to win over groups of the illegal Communist party for the imminent *Putsch* in early July 1944.[68] Beck stressed the necessity for such unity by saying that after the expected final catastrophe an anti-Nazi united party would have to be founded which extended from the extreme Right all the way to the Communists, for he had experienced in Upper Silesia that the Communists were reliable when it came to basic national questions.[69] Even with regard to economic organization, Lunyovo partially agreed with the resistance in Germany. In the manifesto, formulations like the "restoration and expansion of the political rights and social achievements of the workers" and the "freedom of economy, commerce, and trade" may have come out a bit vague,[70] but they did not exclude an occasional correspondence of intentions between the German opposition to Hitler in Germany and that in the Soviet Union. The conceptions developed by the men of July 20 showed an intellectual scope and force which also informed and reflected some of the National Committee's goals. Even if Goerdeler's ideas had not turned out to be convincing—he had assigned an important position to workers and trade unions in the new state —the plans of the Kreisau group should still have held considerable attraction.[71] Rejection of any form of capitalism was an important point of their program; it might have won the applause of even those émigrés and anti-fascists who stood for extreme Marxism.

But the attitude of the conspirators toward the National Committee and the League was not determined by considerations of the future at this time. They now saw above all the differences of opinion between themselves and the Germans in Russia, which manifested themselves more and more forcefully in the methods used by the Free Germany movement. Problems of legality, conceptions of foreign policy, and the practice of subversion created a disparity which led to disparate basic positions; they were regarded as fundamental and displaced any intensive discussion.

Both organizations at Lunyovo were left with the political instrument of open rebellion; under the given circumstances it was inevitable. Appeals and leaflets were offered as the only way to inform the Wehrmacht and the German people of the driving force behind this resistance. This procedure had been approved in principle.[72] In no way did the committee and the officers' union believe that the motives for their actions could be misconstrued. Experience and judgment had created the absolute determination which they tended to generalize and to ascribe above all to the fighting men at the front. To them the accusation of aiding and abetting the enemy and of betraying one's country seemed, therefore, baseless. The National Committee and the League of German Officers thus frankly pleaded guilty to the charge of high treason, for the codified law of a demonic dictatorship forced every opposition into illegality. The fight against Hitler, which was meant to prevent the destruction of Germany, was subject to the dictates of conscience. Their sole justification had to be their striving for ethical goals, unless their personal engagement, which in 1943 was a risk for the soldiers, can be seen as a partial justification.

The activities of the committee and the officers' union were based on premises which the resistance within Germany could not share because it faced a different kind of reality.[73] Contrary to the opinions of Lunyovo, the National Socialist régime was firmly rooted in the majority of the Wehrmacht and the German people. Any attempt to shake their faith by sober reminders of the true situation might well be an advantage to the conspirators, but they misjudged the German mentality and those necessary conditions of a *coup d'état* that the conspirators in the Reich intended to take into account. In Germany, anyone calling for a revolution under the flag of illegality had to expect to be met by the anger of the armed forces. Mutiny and rebellion lay beyond the scope of their professional thinking, which, as a rule, did not even contemplate any abuse of their military virtues. To call for such a revolution from inside the enemy's camp was to put into a questionable light even objectively incontestable statements. The reactions of the troops and the officers' corps to the committee and the officers' union show how unchanged their ethical code had remained. Any public appeal was therefore rejected by the opposition in Germany. Before the completion of a *Putsch* any such version of their resistance suffered from one inherent difficulty. There must not be any dispersed and disconnected actions which the National Socialist state and its organs would be able to fend off without difficulty. Only a *coup d'état*, thoroughly prepared and camouflaged, could succeed in realizing the hope of seizing the régime's power structure. This coup had to be the task of a smoothly functioning minority. This was the intention that was put into action on July 20, 1944;[74] the uprising was to proceed quietly and swiftly in order to prevent chaos and civil war. There was no thought of either a *levée en masse* or of any proclamations to stir the people up aimlessly against the Hitler state. The *Putsch* used the cover of a confidential military document.[75] The conspirators planned to appear in public as the pillars of a new governmental power already constituted only after their triumph.

This technique of a *coup d'état* was in keeping with the sentiments of a still confident people. But there was another reason why the opposition in Germany did not regard outside propaganda support as any help. They had not succeeded in covering the military *Putsch* politically.[76] During the critical hours of the rebellion, the reactions of the enemy powers, which had been approached in vain for some sort of assurance, remained, for the most part, uncertain. It was, therefore, all the more important that the German front lines stood firm for the sake of a well-ordered future. Any influences from the enemy's camp had to be a psychological burden, perhaps even a crushing burden, for the German soldiers. It was sufficient to have a determined opposition that could act without any restrictions, that was ready for the assassination, and that pushed through its political intentions. After that, the interaction between orders and obedience, without which the intentions of the rebellion could never be realized, would, once again, become all-important.

To the very end, the character and goals of the July rebellion also brought with them a special attitude toward other aspects of legality. The conspirators had never tired in their attempts to circumvent, or at least limit, the accusation of treason against the government.[77] All their efforts at legal resistance had failed one by one, yet Goerdeler had undertaken them again and again.[78] Indeed, even July 20 itself was intended to bring about an "orderly legitimate change of government."[79] These tactics were forced upon the conspirators not only by public opinion but also by the inviolability of the legality principle which they accepted as a suprapersonal source of order. But ultimately even the resistance within Germany could not get around the recognition that codified law denied them any mandate for the overthrow of the government, which had finally become necessary. This left them only the moral acceptance of treason against the government: temporal laws gave way to an appeal to higher laws.[80] But in this case the conspirators continued to suffer from problems which the committee and the officers' union had solved long ago.[81] There was also the difficulty that the plans of the opposition had to be restricted to the innermost circle. It alone was thought capable of bearing the responsibility for violations of legality. In an all-important order on July 20 itself, Witzleben and Stauffenberg chose the fiction of an SS-*Putsch* to trigger the *coup d'état* in the Reich and in Paris.[82] There was no promising way in which the opposition could have made public its resistance from the start.

Equally important were the differences of opinion in the conception of foreign policy. The National Committee and the League of German Officers acted from inside the Soviet camp. In their appeals, the demands for a future orientation toward the east had been kept in the background so much that they hardly prejudiced a German conspirary which was supposed, above all, to be encouraged to act.[83] But even if Lunyovo held back on its fundamental readiness for a Soviet-German alliance,[84] its activities already spoke for themselves politically. Up to the beginning of 1944 at least, its propaganda slogans indicated some opportunities concerning the Soviet Union. That is the reason why the resistance within Germany had overwhelmingly identified the National Committee, which they regarded as partially infected by Bolshevism, with the preference for an eastern rapprochement in foreign policy.[85] Precisely that, however, was the opposite of the intentions which moved most of the conspirators.

The opposition within Germany was anti-totalitarian in its thinking and rejected the world of Communism.[86] Its rebellion was intended to revive those ideas of political freedom which alone could assure the dignity of man and which had their roots in the Anglo-Saxon constitutions. It, therefore, felt that a future Germany was obliged to lean toward Great Britain and the United States. Only an alliance with these powers provided security against the threatening Soviet superiority and permitted the retention of the Reich's central position. That such an alliance had a real chance of realization is best testified to by the interests which suggested it. Goerdeler had studied them in detail.[87] By their political structure and as western nations, England and the United States, he reasoned, stood in a kind of natural opposition to Bolshevik Russia, which even temporary alliances would not be able to remove. Incapable of standing their ground in Europe without a continental power morally and militarily intact, they needed an internally revived Germany; all the more so as the Reich in particular was indispensable for the defense against Communism because of its position and its potential. But such a function required an honorable peace. It would have to leave Germany's frontiers and the basis of its economic existence untouched. If the Reich was removed as the frontier bulwark of Europe, then the way would be free for an advance of the Soviet Union, whose stopping point no one could predict.

Almost all the conspirators were moved by similar ideas. What Goerdeler had put down in his plan for peace in the late summer or fall of 1943 is of exemplary importance. Beck's concern about Seydlitz's attitude has already been touched upon. Hassel argued that "visible fairness against England was essential."[88] Indeed, apart from Reichwein, who viewed Russia as the great country of the future which would exert a permanent influence upon any kind of European policy,[89] even the Socialists rejected Bolshevism and its system.[90] Even where they cherished hopes of good neighborly relations with the Soviet Union, they in no way impeded a rapprochement with the western powers, the necessity of which remained indisputable.

Hitler's politics had managed to unite Great Britain and the United States into a coalition with Russia. For them any alternative to the fighting had been eliminated. The demand of unconditional surrender enforced a fixed position and cut off any alternative route. At the conferences of Moscow and Teheran the western powers had entered into obligations concerning the great power of the east which sealed the fate of the Reich. Germany's dismemberment seemed agreed upon and the unity of the wartime alliance seemed consolidated once and for all. Thus all the conspirators' attempts to sound out the attitude of the western powers in case of a *coup d'état* ran into a wall of silence.[91] No supporting word came across the borders, no encouragement helped them move ahead. The opposition group was confronted by only the hate-filled expressions of menace which reflected the official line of self-righteous enemies.

It was only in this desperate situation that the men of July 20 began to raise the question whether an arrangement with the Soviet Union did not offer a better chance for the planned overthrow of government. Hesitatingly they ventured upon a path on which they hardly felt like going. Adam von Trott zu Solz wrote two memoranda, one in January 1943 and the other in April 1944. Addressed to Allen Welsh Dulles in Switzerland, they were intended to point out to Roosevelt's special representative certain similarities in the situations of both Germany and the Soviet Union.[92] Trott was not considered an adherent of the eastern orientation and Dulles, too, could hardly get the impression that he was working toward a convinced rapprochement with Moscow. But the diplomat warned of a social revolution which might well threaten the western world also. For both the German and the Russian peoples had jointly renounced "bourgeois" ideology amidst grave suffering and both of them tended toward a radical solution of their social problems. Trott pointed to the increase of Communist underground activities in Germany and the "constructive ideas and plans" of the East, which the West had not met with any suggestions of its own.[93] But it was their help which the opposition within Germany needed most of all to prevent the masses from going over to Communism, which would deprive the democracies of their victory in peacetime. This moral pressure, which was more like a cry for help, was to be given some weight by a seriously considered opening of talks with Stalin. Hassell confessed that the only move left to the German opposition was "to make it clear either to Russia or to the Anglo-Americans that the preservation of Germany was in their own interest."[94] Personally he preferred to play this game with the West, but if forced to, he would also accept an agreement with Russia. In the fall of 1943, Goerdeler met with Schulenburg and Hassell.[95] The meeting made apparent that Schulenburg considered the chances of reaching an agreement with Stalin surprisingly good. Encouraged by Kleist's contacts with Clauss (which had therefore provided some impulses for the resistance in Germany after all), the former German ambassador thought that the Soviet Union was not yet committed to its allies to an extent which would have eliminated any hope for Germany. Schulenburg offered his services to Goerdeler; for a long time he was prepared to be sent through the German lines in the east.

But Schulenburg's dubious mission never came about. All the plans for an eastern solution remained an episode without results, limited to the circle of the opposition in the Reich. They never came out with a clear declaration that they were willing to found Germany's future, completely or only to a substantial extent, on a pact with the Soviet Union.[96] Even the tactical means of exerting pressure by threatening to switch to the side of the Kremlin lost its attraction as the situation of the Reich continued to deteriorate. In the end the same things applied which had applied from the start: the conspirators did not think that they could establish a permanent collaboration with Bolshevism, nor could they believe that the power of the Soviet Union, having increased to threatening proportions, could be withstood in any way except by establishing close ties with Great Britain and the United States. With this, Germany's path was mapped out most clearly and it meant thinking European. Well into the July uprising, symbolic attempts to open the fronts in the west rather than in the east continued.

All these differences of interpretation were aggravated enormously by the attempts of the Free Germany organization to undermine the coherence of the German armies in the east.[97] Since January 1944, the committee and the officers' union had appealed to the German soldiers to "save themselves by joining the cause of the National Committee." In their view Germany had lost the war it had started. The only hope lay in an attempt to save certain basic elements which had to be snatched from chaos. As far as Lunyovo was concerned, the nation itself was no longer waging war; if it had been, then the call to mutiny now undertaken would have been a crime without parallel. Each additional day of a struggle which had become criminal would simply weaken the base for a new beginning in which the National Committee continued to believe even though it saw that beginning threatened by the heavy hand of the victorious powers. In this self-appraisal and its practical consequences the Free Germany movement had certainly preceded the resistance within Germany. But after a lucid appraisal of the situation, the latter, too, had been tormented for some time by profound doubts as to whether the time for an uprising had not already passed.[98] Immediately before the assassination attempt, Staufenberg raised the pros and cons of this issue to force himself and his fellow conspirators to thoroughly search their consciences once more.[99] There is Tresckow's expressive statement that the blow against Hitler had to be struck no matter what—*coûte que coûte*.[100] "For what counts now is no longer the practical result but the fact that the German resistance movement has risked everything before the world and before history." It is also incontestable that the conspirators in the Reich did not flinch from the path of subversion, and that to an extent even greater than anything risked by the National Committee. They, too, had become victims of a development which had knocked out of their grasp the last military trump cards in the summer of 1944. In the east, Army Group Center had been destroyed; in the west, the invasion had been successful. Now they wanted to give up the western flank of the European theater of war and to call in Anglo-American paratroop and airborne divisions after the coup.[101] Worse still, on July 20 the *coup d'état* was pushed ahead despite the fact that Hitler was still alive. They thus deliberately accepted the risk of civil war and chaos.[102] The only question still relevant was on which side fighting should be stopped. This demonstrates to what extent the peculiar dynamics of an ideological struggle had thrown all concepts into disorder, even in the ranks of the opposition. But these fateful dynamics could hardly be estimated on the day of the revolt. What, in the face of a long overdue act, could at best be conceded to the British and American enemy would have been thought a sacrilege had it been conceded to Russia. In the east any kind of subversion was rejected as intolerable; the *coup d'état* had to be protected from the Red Army as long as possible. In the minds of the conspirators this goal was decisive; it also altered the relative difference of interpretation between the National Committee and the resistance within Germany into an absolute difference.[103] For it was over this political distinction that they divided, and it decided the issue.

The opposition to Hitler in the Reich, therefore, sought no contacts with the committee and the officers' union.[104] No contact was ever established. It would have met with considerable difficulties anyway. And there was no one who knew how to approach the sections at Lunyovo safely. Trott's trips to Sweden were aimed at only general information.[105] Even when Major Joachim Kuhn, who knew of the conspiracy, was captured by the Soviets after July 20,

1944, he found himself put into a regular camp for officers.[106] To the bitter end there remained a mutual isolation that seems to have been intentional on the parts of both Moscow and the German opposition.

But there was no direct communication with the Communist underground in Germany either.[107] The National Committee succeeded in winning the illegal group around Saefkow and Bästlein and other organizations in central Germany for the liberal goal of a united front of all anti-fascist forces.[108] The plans of a coming Socialist Soviet Republic of Germany gave way to a program which tried to follow the example of the manifesto rather closely despite some watering down of its tenets. But at no time did any envoys cross the lines to receive direct instructions for the agitation activities in Germany from Moscow or Lunyovo.[109] As a rule "Radio Free Germany" provided the only link. Where any unity of purpose was manifested inside Germany in the way the National Committee had intended it, it had to operate independently until the arrival of the Red Army according to the general guidelines it had received.

The Free Germany movement had not been able to influence or direct the men of July 20 in the least; but soon after the assassination attempt against Hitler it could at least chalk up a success in its own camp. During the early part of August, Field Marshal Paulus had joined the League of German Officers.[110]

This step by the cautious and hesitant commander in chief had come as a surprise. At Stalingrad Paulus had failed several times to reach the decision which an extraordinary situation had demanded of him. His brilliant military gifts were well known, but he had also shown a fateful weakness of character. As late as September 1943 he had refused to follow the appeal with which Seydlitz had approached him. The League could not win Paulus over. The distinction of his ranks nowhere embellished the appeals, leaflets, and letters which called upon the Wehrmacht's commanders to overthrow Hitler. With dignity and firmness the Field Marshal had refused and had lived in the far distant Generals' Camp 48 since 1943.[111] There, in the circle of the other generals, his position that military imprisonment did not provide any base for a meaningful resistance was accepted. Here the changing situation at the front was measured by the self-satisfied yardstick of the professional soldier and was not yet regarded as hopeless. No one at Lunyovo had, therefore, counted on Paulus any more.[112] And secretly no one wanted to see him make an appearance now. The resentment against this once leading soldier had become too violent among the radical elements for any fruitful collaboration with him.

Paulus joined the Free Germany movement because he had recognized that the situation of the Reich had become hopeless. After the destruction of Army Group Center and the successful invasion by the Allies, the eventual outcome of the war had become clear even to him.[113] He was now deeply influenced by the disclosures of captured German commanding officers about the situation in Germany and inside the Wehrmacht. Reports of atrocities in occupied territories had an especially shocking effect. But it was the participation of well-known generals in the plot of July 20 that convinced the Field Marshal that in the Reich, too, the elimination of Hitler was regarded as the only way out. These events justified his open rebellion. Now Paulus was willing to support the anti-Nazi forces and to help prevent a frightening final catastrophe by his support. On August 8, 1944, the Commander in Chief of the Sixth Army signed an appeal "To the captured German officers and soldiers in the USSR and to the German people."[114] It was a memorable day. While one field marshal of the July rebellion, Erwin von Witzleben, was being strangled to death on a primitive gallows at Berlin, a second field marshal, prisoner of the Soviets, stepped forth with a moving appeal. Restrained in his diction, he endeavored to draw a sober picture of the situation. He tersely pointed to the Russian advance to the borders of eastern Prussia and to the Allied breakthrough in France. A few strokes sketched the impending collapse of Germany. "Despite the heroism of its Wehrmacht and of the whole German people, Germany was led into this situation by Adolf Hitler's leadership of the state and the war. Furthermore, the methods used by some of his representatives against the population in occupied territories must fill every true soldier and every true German with horror and must incur the gravest reproaches of the whole world. The German people will have to bear the full responsibility for these actions unless it rejects them of its own accord. Under these circumstances I regard it as my duty to declare before my fellow soldiers who are prisoners of war and before the whole German nation that Germany must free itself from Adolf Hitler and must give itself a new government that will end the war and bring about conditions which will enable our people to survive and to establish peaceful, or even friendly, relations with our present enemies."

With Paulus, the highest-ranking German officer in Soviet captivity had become a member of the League of German Officers. All reservations notwithstanding, this fact still seemed significant enough to give it some play in propaganda. Seydlitz himself was satisfied, with a profound satisfaction which for the moment even forced back a certain bitterness.[115] But the émigrés swarmed around the Field Marshal with a special attentiveness that concealed their true feelings.[116] Pieck rushed in from Moscow to praise the united front of the National Committee, lauding "Our friend—Herr Paulus." The belated unity was pleasantly celebrated.

But at this time the common front and its unity represented only a façade. Creeping differences of opinion, base informing, and the huge question mark of the political future of the Free Germany organization could no longer be covered up. And although Paulus' joining revived the recruitment drives among the POWs, it could hardly be more than a tarnished symbol. It is true that most of the German soldiers had looked for the signature of Field Marshal Paulus on the leaflets during the first months of the activities of the committee and the officers' union. But his name, which could have served to stimulate thinking about the war, was never on them. For some time to come, that fact condemned the National Committee in the eyes of the soldiers, who met its appeals with silence and rejection. Now Paulus had dared to speak up against Hitler. His decision, like everything emanating from it, had been the result of thorough thinking and soul-searching. But it was as if some permanent evil destiny governed the unhappy Commander in Chief of the betrayed and sacrificed Sixth Army; once more his decision had come too late.

## CHAPTER SEVEN

## Dissolution and End

ALSO TOO LATE came the appeals of those German generals whose divisions had been destroyed in the center and south of the Eastern Front during the summer of 1944. Had they been successful they most certainly could have shortened the final struggle of the National Socialist régime and its Wehrmacht that now began. Faced by Hitler's declared intention to destroy everything, it was still possible to save thousands of German soldiers from a pointless death. It was still possible to spare the Reich some of the devastations which were to ravage it. But it was no longer possible to hold out any political guarantees in the propaganda after the publication of the "Twenty-five Articles for Ending the War," which only formulated general guidelines,[1] nor was the generals' step a decision genuinely based on conscience. It was taken too late to be that. But the captured army commanders' appeals once more stirred the Free Germany movement to frantic activity. They were impelled by a tragedy far surpassing that of Stalingrad. Unless everyone's eyes were opened by this, Germany was really heading toward total collapse.

Indeed, the unfolding and the end of the drama in the center of Germany's Eastern Front had been dictated by a completely demented leadership.[2] This time Hitler had ordered a whole army group to defend a vast bulge that was practically an invitation to the powerful Soviet spearheads. Once again he had rejected as false the warnings about the clearly discernible enemy deployment. The enemy, he announced, would attack Army Group Northern Ukraine in the south of the bulge. Any movements and redeployment of troops were therefore ruled out. The unrealistic order remained one of defense at any price. To underline this decision as the military *ultima ratio*, the threatened armies were deprived of the reserves that alone could have softened their defeat. Thus what the leading soldiers had predicted again and again came about. When four Russian armies attacked successively the great bulge of Army Group Center around Vitebsk, Mogilev, and Bobruisk, on June 22, 1944, the third anniversary of the beginning of Germany's Russian campaign, the thin lines of the German defense were smashed by the concentrated assault.[3] The Soviet offensive developed at breathtaking speed, especially northwest of Vitebsk, where it hit the one cornerstone of the German defense that had been regarded as safe. Penetrations turned into breakthroughs. Senseless orders to stand and defend, which had become meaningless amidst the Red flood, finally forced the German armies, often attacked on three sides simultaneously, into a hopeless position. Although reinforcements were brought in and improvised a closing of the gap, only a few units could fight themselves free of the enemy and thus escape the catastrophe. The bulk of the German troops were crushed by the Russian pressure, which could not be forced open. In numerous pockets the remnants of German strength were used up; complete chaos ruled. By July 8, 1944, twenty-eight German divisions had been destroyed.[4] The losses amounted to more than 350,000 men, not counting an enormous amount of matériel destroyed or lost.

Everywhere in this tragic battle the German soldiers had fought with consummate devotion.[5] Their sense of duty was unbroken; they were determined not to fall into the hands of an enemy whose inhuman cruelty the fighting men knew. Wherever German resistance ceased, it had been overwhelmed by complete exhaustion in a hopeless situation. Nowhere had the National Committee and the League of German Officers influenced the struggle on the field of battle.[6] Wherever individual diversionary acts under Russian direction were successful, they could serve only to hasten the collapse which had been brought about by Germany's leadership.[7]

The end of the Army Group Center had a sequel, nevertheless. Lieutenant General Vinzenz Müller, second in command of the practically annihilated Fourth Army's XII Corps, had at first been captured by the Soviets like many other generals.[8] He, too, had stood his ground to the end and had attempted several times to save his corps, which had been cut off. But now, in Russian captivity, he at once addressed an appeal to the units still in the pockets.[9] "After weeks of heavy fighting our position has become hopeless. . . . Stop the bloodshed! I therefore order you to stop fighting immediately. Under the leadership of officers and veteran noncommissioned officers, groups of one hundred and more are to be formed locally. The wounded are to be collected after that."

An elaborate, detailed appeal quickly followed Müller's brief orders. Whether the Soviets' delighted approval led him to sense a private opportunity that he decided to use without scruple, or whether other commanders, now no longer troubled by any doubts about the outcome of the war, agreed to the necessity of taking steps against Hitler, we cannot say; in either case, the dexterous corps commander, without any contacts with Lunyovo, established a propagandistic united front in which seventeen generals affirmed what would have been unthinkable to them only a short time before.[10] Their document, dated July 22, 1944, was not comparable to a leaflet; it was more like a full-fledged military memorandum. Its scope prevented any sloganlike phrases. As a consequence, it lacked fire, even where all of its arguments were based on the most recent experiences. Unsparingly it worked out the reasons for the catastrophes of the past and for the most recent defeat. It culminated in the demand to now oppose force by force and to end the war by an overthrow of the National Socialist régime. "Do not wait until Hitler has ruined you! To act against Hitler is to act for Germany!"

In the belief that Müller had already become active before he was captured, Seydlitz had emphatically welcomed this general's orders.[11] He could now feel belated satisfaction about this appeal. Not only had it come about independently of the League of German Officers; it had also listed soberly all the arguments with which the soldiers in the Free Germany movement had always operated. Mention was made of the phrase "Victory or death," which was said to prove that Hitler himself no longer believed he could win the war, and of the loss of German initiative since Stalingrad. The inflexible mind of the Supreme Commander was deplored, as was the continuous waste of troops, which had been both psychologically and physically strained beyond endurance. And after dealing in detail with the defeat of Army Group Center, finally there was the reference to the impending collapse of Germany and to loyalty to the perdurable German people, which were said to stand above a "vassal's obligations to a temporal and bankrupt form of government and its supporters." Wisdom after the event? The realization that the total collapse of the Reich had become a bleak reality under Hitler may not have been prophetic any more, but it may have severed the last ties which up to now had still been more or less intact. But the generals' military exposé also revealed a flaw of long standing that could at best be glossed over at the price of a forced and guilt-ridden split personality. It solidly confirmed the ideas that had moved the committee and the officers' union and that had been derided by the front. And it supported impressively the conviction held at Lunyovo that the army would be undermined all the more, the longer it continued to fight.

Only in a limited sense did Müller's united front survive this great appeal to commanders and troops. After signing it once, many generals opted for anonymity. With the end of the war so close, they wanted to avoid the collective imprisonment of their relatives and the ill repute attached to collaboration with the Free Germany organization.[12] The whole thing still resulted in some promising activities. At the beginning of August, six high-ranking commanders joined the officers' union.[13] Together with them and Paulus, the National Committee and the League of German Officers could look back on one year of activities on August 22, 1944.[14] In September, when some more generals of the annihilated Army Group Southern Ukraine fell into Russian hands, the ranks of the officers' union grew after another appeal to end the war.[15] The newspaper *Free Germany* now became an organ for generals to settle accounts with their past in retrospective reviews. But the climax was reached as late as December 8, 1944, when Field Marshal Paulus and forty-nine generals signed an appeal "To the People and the Wehrmacht."[16] This appeal had come about under some difficulties. Many generals, among them the upright Colonel General Strecker, still stood opposed "speechlessly" to those who engaged themselves politically inside the Free Germany movement. But now, the events of July 20 and their consequences had generally provoked grave thoughts.

The threatened Fatherland finally had to be called upon to save itself. The army commanders therefore turned to all Germans, somewhat more urgent in tone but dignified in their adjuration. Deeply moved, they recalled the desperate fighting of a nation mobilized from young boys to old men, and with flaming indignation they took to task a régime which had deceived and misused them, and which was now threatening to destroy both people and Reich. They stressed forcefully that a continuation of the murderous struggle could serve only Hitler and his party; it was, therefore, imperative that Germany rid itself of them since the nation must not perish. The fifty generals did not labor under the delusion of being able to offer assurances to the nation still at war. They depicted a difficult future, talked about the occupation of the Fatherland, and the coming reparations that the enemy would demand. But they also ventured to predict that peace would bring with it a new development toward better things. "In 1918 Hindenburg and Ludendorff demanded that the war be ended when it had become hopeless militarily because of the enemies' superiority. For the same reason we, the generals, together with many hundreds of thousands of soldiers and officers, who have united in the 'free Germany' movement, now call upon you from Russian military confinement: All our feelings and thoughts are dedicated exclusively to the fate of our nation. People of Germany, rise to an act of liberation against Hitler and Himmler, against their pernicious system!"

The appeals of the generals came floating down on the German lines and behind the lines in millions of copies.[17] Their texts were continuously broadcast by the radio station in Moscow. The appeals were even copied, dropped, and distributed in Western Europe. All the front delegations used them as the core of their propaganda missions in order to play the only trump card that the committee and the officers' union still held. The printed and spoken proclamations reached both the troops and the people at home; but neither showed any willingness to heed them.

After July 20, unbridled terror had eliminated all open opposition within the Reich. Now the people at home became ensnared in the artful toils of National Socialist propaganda promising an imminent change for the better.[18] The unscrupulous organizations of Hitler's state had become an unassailable element of everyday life. Everywhere among the populace doubts and lack of faith paralyzed people who were no longer capable of any rebellion because they went in fear of a ubiquitous régime. Again and again there was an upsurge of strong confidence which helped the masses bear the burden of duties which they had been saddled with in the name of total war. A hypnotic state replaced the stirrings of lucidity; many chose the former because it provided a means of escape from rude awakening. The power of an ideology which had once freed people from spiritual and social misery and which had shown them exalted goals joined hands with the unwillingness to bear responsibility. This ideology had always stood in the way of a recognition of the realities of the world: it afforded a chance for such an acceptance of reality only if the system collapsed. Amidst grief and torment, faith and hope, there remained the rule of those who pretended to act in the best interests of Germany. The question remains whether there was some other way out than that of breaking down the destructive intentions of pitiless enemies by the hardest resistance imaginable and whether a decline that would most certainly come about if Germany were left without Hitler was comprehensible and conceivable at all.

But at the front, especially in the east, there still ruled the friend-foe thinking which had become a law unto itself.[19] Even where the generals' appeals were not met by decided disbelief among the troops, they viewed the generals' behavior as opportunism, which filled them with dismay and contempt. To the majority it was incomprehensible how respected commanders could have taken upon themselves the responsibility for the death of many of their fellow soldiers, which they now put down as pointless crime.[20] Whatever did come across the lines from the camp of the National Committee and the League remained without effect; the very struggle of the armies had annulled all the effect of propaganda. Its overwhelming force replaced thinking and forced the soldier onto the path of obedience and devotion as the only way left. The solidarity of all German soldiers was self-evident to them, even where it was not affirmed for the sake of those that had been killed and whose sacrifice bound them together. Driven from one position to the next and from one pocket to the next during the retreat, the German soldier had long ago lost the exhilarating sense of victory of advancing armies. He had become skeptical, tired, and a virtuoso of that undefined situation that he viewed as a reflection of the devouring power of war. But he felt that any success of the agitation had to undermine his own strength, tested every hour as it was, and he discovered ideals he felt bound by even now. As the battles approached the cultural landscape of the West, the German fighting man on the Eastern Front transformed himself into a defender of Germany and Europe. Both had to be defended against the Red Army at all cost.[21] The German fighting man knew the reality of the Soviet Union. He had experienced its bleakest aspects and had suffered from its dreariness. He was firmly determined not to allow Bolshevism to enter the Reich and the ancient continent, and somewhere he counted on the support of the Western Powers in this fight; they might yet show some recognition of the situation at the last minute.[22] No matter what the constellation may have been when the struggle began; it was under way now and threatened the inner core which had to be protected. Whatever the ideas that may have motivated the bulk of the German soldiers at the front, except for the youngest, they had left National Socialism far behind.[23] Its magic was gone. What remained was the "Führer's" charisma. He had once led the army to victories and for this they had remained faithful even in defeat. He now promised them salvation through the imminent use of secret weapons which would decide the war. Would Adolf Hitler continue the war if he were not convinced of a tolerable outcome for Germany?

The period during which such beliefs could still flourish was brief and soon over. The front reached Germany's borders and did not stop there. Had the Red Army now acted like disciplined liberators, the betrayed troops might yet have lent an ear to the proclamations of the committee and the officers' union. But this was the hour of unbridled revenge and thus any propaganda success was not merely made impossible by the end of the war but, as it were, systematically prevented.

On January 12, 13, and 14, 1945, countless Soviet divisions launched an attack from the Baltic Sea to the Carpathian Mountains after an overwhelming artillery barrage.[24] Within a few weeks this tidal wave had crashed across the Wartheland and East and West Prussia. This operation, which brought them close to final military victory, was accompanied by a wave of terrorism which defies the imagination.[25] Another coming of the Hun had beset the ill-fated German provinces of the East. In a paroxysm without parallel, the unleashed and inflamed *soldateska* of the Red Army raged through towns and villages, which were burned down and which rang with the cries of raped women. Rape and violence laid waste the land. Whoever failed to escape to the western parts of the Reich—and many of the civilian population failed to do so since they were being deceived until the end—was crushed, driven back, pillaged, and abducted. But arbitrary murder raged not only through the ranks of the civilians; the lives of prisoners of war and of the wounded were not spared either. There were exceptions in this apocalypse of destruction. All the incomprehensible acts of sadism, killing, and the thirst for destruction repeated themselves as if directed by some satanic power.

Under these conditions, the fighting at the front aroused passions which stifled every reflection and reason. Even where the last hope for a turn of events had disappeared in the horror of the collapse, desperate courage remained as the last way out.[26] As long as the enemy held out death or enslavement, the only meaningful and obvious course to take was that of self-sacrifice, which took a high blood toll from the onrushing Soviets. The events of battle, filled with horror, had already demonstrated that the German soldier was obedient and possessed a sense of duty. He was even more strongly motivated by the desperate plight of the fleeing civilian population that had to be rescued from another Russian blow by a fierce struggle.[27] Now the reason for all the fighting and suffering was to give these columns a head start over the Soviet spearheads and to gain time for the necessary decisions of Germany's leadership. These leaders, it is true, had once more disappointed and embittered the troops by setting goals that they could never attain with their limited resources.[28] But the catastrophe was unable to suppress their hopes for the future; it had, however, eliminated any doubts about the enemy's brutality. The belief that there was something in Goebbels' overwrought propaganda remained a motivating force.[29] There was still the hope that the Western Powers would help; they simply had to recognize the threat to the European continent. The German soldier in the east could not understand the coherence of a coalition which the self-deluded statesman Adolf Hitler had forged together. He had no idea of the full inhumanity of the National Socialist system. He did not realize that he fought for a Germany which had forfeited any right to act as the standard bearer of the Western world.[30] He saw only the dangers of the present, which had to be overcome for the sake of the future. He thus continued to fight to the end in tragic isolation, misled by the most absurd slogans, hopes, and expectations.

The front delegations of the National Committee were now guided by a spirit which often enabled them to interpret every event in the Soviet Union's favor. Discounting the few representatives of the Officers' Union, they were recruited either from Antifa graduates or from aides just won at the front. Their nationalist feelings had in many cases given way to unqualified Marxism.[31] Their missions were being directed openly by forces that did not originate in the House at Lunyovo. They insisted upon a reorientation campaign among the prisoners of war which had the misguided aim of reaching large numbers. They preached hatred against the officers, which made many of the agitators of dubious character fail miserably. But the experiences of the German delegations which followed right on the heels of the Soviet armies were deeply depressing.[32] Their worst fears were being surpassed by far. Any appeal to the German population not to leave their homes out of fear of the Red Army had to be cruel deception from now on.[33] Any appeal to join the cause of the Free Germany movement now turned into an insult to reason. For instead of finding safety, they found torture and death waiting for them at the hands of an enemy whose hate knew no bounds. The committee and the officers' union surely had deserved better; since 1943 they had agitated against Hitler out of conviction. They had never doubted the necessity of their actions despite many disappointments and setbacks. Events had, on the whole, proved them right, and not only in the military field. If any further proof of the viciousness of a régime without conscience had been needed, Steidle's delegation got it when it inspected the concentration camps at Maidanek and Auschwitz, both occupied by the Russians at exactly this time.[34] Furnaces, gas chambers, well-ordered heaps of children's shoes, and jewelry—all bore witness to destructive activity whose systematic nature was deeply shocking and which removed any reservations one might have had about the fight against this kind of inhumanity. But the excesses of revenge and retribution to which Ilya Ehrenburg incited the Soviet armies must have confused every German on both sides of the firing lines. If Germany was to be doomed to ruin anyway, then added adjurations had to be based on a fateful mistake.

The complexity of the situation is shown by the fact that even those who were most open to the charge of having succumbed to "fascist ways of thinking" now dared to come out with public criticism of the Red Army. At the Narev front, Count Einsiedel, who was serving there as a delegate together with Major Bechler, specifically called attention to the disingenuousness of the National Committee's work.[35] In front of a stunned, silent group of front aides, he bravely made public his dismay at the outrages committed by the Red Army. He condemned its atrocities even in cases which he tried to explain with more or less convincing arguments. The result was a certain *succès d'estime*, but also Einsiedel's recall from the front. At Moscow Weinert told him that he had not been up to his task.[36] The shameless opportunism of the National Committee's president was to become symptomatic. The only thing permitted was a kind of subordination that frantically ignored reality and spinelessly bowed to the guidelines of a stern party.

Under these circumstances, work at the front became even more unreal. Wherever it did not wither into a mere routine function, it was burdened with the fulsome reputation associated with spinelessness. But the delegates and their aides had to continue to speak on behalf of goals that had become illusory. Recruitment drives continued among the masses of POWs in the unrealistic hope that it could still influence the course of events. Once more it was believed that some encircled units might be moved to cease resistance. But all these missions ended in dismal failure. It was inevitable, and it did not take a prophet to predict it. The soldiers in the camps were put off by the alternative "For or against Hitler," with which propagandists often extorted pointless telegrams of support to Weinert and Seydlitz.[37] They were unsuccessful in the case of the fortified cities Graudenz and Thorn.[38] Wherever representatives reached the lines of the German defenders with letters or appeals they were either handed over to the military police or shot. Others had already become victims of the minefields and the sniping between the lines. The outflanked troops knew the kind of enemy they faced.[39] Clinging to the hope of relief, they fought fiercely for the breakthrough to the west and they accepted dreaded Soviet imprisonment only when they were completely exhausted.

Graudenz and Thorn were defended by small contingents which held out bravely for a long time. A delegation of the League, headed by Colonel van Hooven, was equally unable to induce the armies in the Kurland pocket to surrender.[40] Although innumerable leaflets guaranteed the soldiers an internment that would keep their units intact, they fought on undaunted until May 1945. No argument could keep them from doing a duty which had become difficult indeed. No appeal, no matter how sober, could shake the firm attitude of their worried commanders. Sinister acts of subversion were now the last thing to change the fate of all the failures of Soviet front propaganda; it was shown by many a shady mission which misappropriated the name of the Free Germany movement. It was especially true in the case of Vieth task force which was made up of Antifa graduates and took part in the fight for Breslau with guns in their hands.[41]

One by one the news of the events at the front reached the House of the committee and the officers' union at Lunyovo. A diversionary act in East Prussia came to their knowledge despite all precautions;[42] but it was Einsiedel's reports which shocked them most thoroughly because they made it clear that even Alexandrov was powerless against Ehrenburg's appeals.[43] At first even some Communists seem to have been genuinely shocked. This grave crisis was sufficient in itself to split the Free Germany movement irreparably. But now the impending annexation of Germany's eastern provinces was brought up for discussion in the name of complete "ideological clarification." Public acceptance of these annexations was demanded, and this was nothing less than an official denial of all patriotic feelings.[44] On this issue the solidarity of the House at Lunyovo was broken; the discrepancy between theory and practice had become too obvious. The right wing around Seydlitz finally withdrew and left the field to the émigrés and recent Marxists.[45]

Now the left wing section ruthlessly established unity in its own ranks. Any resistance to the doctrinaire glorification of the Red Army and the new eastern frontiers of Germany was soon ferreted out by deliberate provocation.[46] All differences of opinion thus elicited were handed on to the NKVD. Once more the informers and listening devices that had poisoned the atmosphere at Lunyovo since its beginning revealed their full despicable nature. The last remnants of solidarity were destroyed. Any attempt undertaken by "centrists" like Lattmann, Korfes, and Steidle to bridge the gap was in vain and wound up being defeated by the now victorious radicalism.[47] Everyone had to take sides. On the one side, the majority of the officers' union, which felt betrayed and which stood aside in the future; on the other side, the Communist cadres, which bragged of the inevitability of their arguments. The only thing still possible was unreservedly changing camps. In the winter of 1944 two generals decided upon this course after they had attended the Antifa school; they were Vinzenz Müller and Arno von Lenski.[48]

Müller had regarded his activities in connection with the appeals of the generals as an opener only.[49] He had hardly returned to Lunyovo when he visibly began to make his mark, although he was a member of neither the committee nor the officers' union. His leading role was accompanied by a change of heart the suddenness of which particularly surprised the left wingers. As late as autumn 1944 he still confessed to a Catholic military chaplain. A short time after that he was already known to be toeing the party line. In contrast to Vinzenz Müller who had embraced the cause of Communism out of calculation, whatever his specific motives may have been, Arno von Lenski had hesitated for quite some time.[50] But now Lenski, too, bowed unconditionally to the demands of his new *Weltanschauung*. Without objecting in any way, he signed a prepared article about the loss of Germany's eastern provinces. Aristocrat and panzer general, Lenski defended this loss with the controversial ideological arguments of a lost war of aggression and of Poland's *raison d'état*.[51]

But the committee and the officers' union were not merely divided among themselves. Both had also lost all significance in relation to the events on the field of battle, since the front propaganda of the delegations, which were allowed to move into Germany together with the Red Army,[52] still remained helpless everywhere in face of the hatred of an embittered enemy. Politically the Crimean Conference confirmed the ideas that the left wing had already been forced to accept unanimously. Its communiqué according to which Stalin, Roosevelt, and Churchill had awarded Poland a "considerable increase in territory in the north and in the west" at Yalta was printed in the *Free Germany* newspaper without any comment.[53] The capitulation of the Reich on May 8, 1945, finally confirmed militarily the failure of all propaganda endeavors. Germany had been defeated and occupied by the victorious coalition of its enemies. It had fought to the last moment and had thus caused widespread destruction which Lunyovo had wanted to avoid.

The balance sheet facing the National Committee and the League of German Officers was depressing. How much good faith had been spent in vain, how many reversals had been suffered in vain. The balance sheet may have looked somewhat less depressing to the Marxists in the committee, who could expect to shape a totally defeated Germany according to their own ideas. But to the officers' union it looked very sad indeed. But even to the officers everything still looked defensible, although it had ultimately become questionable amidst the general chaos which saddled, above all, those German leaders who had fought on pointlessly with ineradicable guilt.[54] Stalingrad and the subsequent all too accurate appraisal of Germany's position had made resistance a necessity as early as 1943. If there remained any satisfaction at all, it lay in the knowledge of having at least tried to do something while the mass of the German people had followed Adolf Hitler into this collapse blindly, submissively, and uncritically. In the eyes of the officers their activities had been "wrong" only because the top echelons of the Wehrmacht had failed to respond and because the Communists had shown that they could not be considered reliable partners in the long run.

In view of the termination of the war, it would have made sense to dissolve the National Committee and the League of German Officers. The two organizations no longer reached any common decisions. By now the work of the editorial offices of the newspaper and the radio station had become routine, although appeals for reparations created the impression that Lunyovo still had some functions to fulfill.[55] But it was especially in its personnel that the Free Germany movement had become a fragmented torso whose continued existence could no longer be justified. As early as April 1945 two selected groups of functionaries had set out to join the armies of Zhukov and Koniev in order to prepare the political "co-ordination" (*Gleichschaltung*) of Germany's Soviet occupied zone immediately after the armistice.[56] In their briefcases they carried with them the guidelines for the future of German schools that two committees of the National Committee had prepared for them.[57] The committee and the officers' union continued to exist as before; no final decision was reached by the Soviets, whose visits to Lunyovo now became more and more infrequent.[58] Ulbricht had already been in Germany for some time now. Pieck took his leave, suggesting the hope of an imminent reunion. Weeks passed in uneasy expectation. Nobody risked any open word any more, since all the inhabitants of the House believed that they would return home soon. They trusted the assurances of the émigrés which, they thought, had been given without guile. They felt their claim to an early repatriation all the more strongly as now confirmed reports began to seep through that relatives of members of the National Committee were being held in concentration camps and prisons. They thought that this persecution must make a difference to the Soviets too.

After the Potsdam Conference a group of the committee and the officers' union approached Weinert with a proposal for a plenary session.[59] Signed by Einsiedel, Fleischer, Gerlach, Hetz, Kayser, and Steidle, the proposal aimed at "comprehensive information of the House about the political situation in Germany and about the Russians' intentions concerning the National Committee." It further suggested that a clearly defined position be expressed concerning the program of the anti-fascist united front in Germany. It also wanted to discuss the opportunities still open to political activity of the National Committee. This was aimed at replenishing the National Committee's ranks with those members who had been delegated to other missions, but it also aimed at establishing contacts with the centers of activity which had already formed in the Eastern Zone of Germany.

Long overdue as this trial balloon may have been, it met with a divided response.[60] Rumors were being spread about a provocation of the Soviet Union reminiscent in its style of the Huber affair. All this made the atmosphere of the House at Lunyovo even more unbearable. Had the Executive Committee not met for a session soon after these events, the position of the six signatories might easily have become very difficult. Based on the memorandum, the group under attack was now able to protest that the accusations were malicious. Thus taken by surprise and forced to react without "directives from above," Weinert decided to welcome the controversial proposal as the "long awaited democratic initiative by members of the National Committee."[61]

But the promised plenary session continued to be put off. It was only on November 2, 1945, that Weinert acted upon the move that he had been forced into praising and which he now dismissed as a desire to dissolve the committee and the officers' union.[62] The assurance, once more confirmed, that the majority of the members still present would be repatriated within the next few days cut off any discussion. The Soviets thus reached a finale without pain or obligation; they could now celebrate the unlamented demise of the Free Germany movement.

The actors took the stage for the last time.[63] The guest stars were Colonel Braginsky; the German Communist Frieda Rubiner, who had also been an active member of the Red Army's Central Political Administration; Kozlov, the director of Institute No. 99, and one of the cadre teachers. The remaining seats in the hall were taken by the remnants of the National Committee and the League of German Officers still at Lunyovo, who listened to their president's rendering of the depressing accounts, which could not be relieved by the rhetorical embellishments he used.

Weinert's report recalled once more the history of the Free Germany movement from its inception to this hour of its dissolution.[64] He recalled those killed in action and stressed, not without dignity, the work of the survivors. The National Committee's lack of unity and its lack of success, however, were toned down. Somewhat forcedly, Weinert praised the co-operation of everyone in the committee and officers' union—which was to serve as an example for the new Germany. He also overstressed some actual achievements of front propaganda whose insignificance only served to highlight the failure of all these endeavors. The discrepancy between the review and the fact that the efforts had failed could not be other than painful.

In contrast to Weinert,[65] Seydlitz felt unable to wax rhapsodical. He looked at reality and tested it in the light of all the bitterness and disappointment which had grown out of all their devotion. As a man of straight thinking, the general had by no means always cut a good figure in circumstances unfamiliar to him. Several times he had met Russian gestures without the skepticism they might, from time to time have deserved. But no one could deny the strength of the convictions with which he had courageously embraced the activists' cause in September 1943 and that now made him unwilling to change his ways, to rethink his position. Now, his obvious isolation made him lucid and he soundly touched upon the foundations of a movement of which Germany, more than anyone else, had become the victim. Seydlitz also stressed gratefully that there had been many common actions within the National Committee. But in the end he saw the collapse of his hopes without that false elation which Weinert had sought refuge in. "What use was the individual's animosity against Hitler if he supported the *Führer* nevertheless? He had more supporters than opponents, but the opponents failed to draw the political conclusions from this fact." "We were also mistaken with regard to the Army leadership's ability to think politically and to take risks."

Both reports had pointed in the direction of dissolving the National Committee and the League of German Officers. Weinert now officially proposed their dissolution. Referring to the proposal of the initiating group of six and speaking on behalf of the Executive Committee, he declared that the continued existence of the Free Germany organization was no longer meaningful.[66] But the plenary assembly pointed out that it lacked a quorum, since some of the émigrés already were in Germany.[67] And so they had to determine whether or not the depleted committee was competent to vote on the motion. Weinert pounced on this and moved that the motion be voted on. With the vote, the end had finally come; there was no further discussion.[68] The National Committee and the League of German Officers had ceased to exist.

Many of the members still had to remain at the House at Lunyovo until May 1946.[69] The only things that concerned them now were questions about their personal future. But if they had believed in the early fulfillment of the repeated assurances, especially after most of the priests in the National Committee had returned home, the last shipment of 1945 had proven them wrong.[70] With the exception of Colonel Luitpold Steidle, it was made up exclusively of Antifa School graduates who had unconditionally embraced Communism and who were now picked to fill positions in party, state, economy, the press, and the radio of the Soviet occupied zone of Germany.[71] Among others, Lieutenant Bernt von Kügelgen, non-commissioned officers Mattheus Klein, Gerhard Klement, Theo Grandi, and of the other lower ranks, Hans Zippel, Leonhard Helmschrott, Dr. Günther Kertzscher, Heinz Kessler, and Otto Sinz all departed.[72] After this group had left Lunyovo, the remnants of the former Free Germany movement were completely isolated inside their camp.[73] All contacts with the outside world were cut off. Not only Seydlitz and the whole presidium of the former officers' union were left behind; the Russians had apparently also forgotten the Antifa graduates Vinzenz Müller and Arno von Lenski, as well as Marxists like Count Einsiedel, Hetz, Homann, and Stösslein. Perhaps their loyalty was not considered genuine enough. Müller and Lenski were told that it was still too early for Communist generals to return.[74] But Einsiedel and the majors of the committee were probably left to ponder about the fact that they had burdened their ideological convictions with too many reservations and acts of independence.[75] The evacuation of the House came in an atmosphere of embittered silence and mutual suspicion.

But once more the hope of returning home was disappointed. Two groups were formed at random which were transferred to Generals' Camp No. 48 and to Camp Susdal.[76] Here the process of splitting them up was continued. Seydlitz, who showed no inclination to serve the cause of Communism as a functionary, was put on trial by a Soviet court.[77] The prosecution dragged in flimsy accusations of war crimes. The general was accused of things which his division's conduct of war had once forced him to do. The building of fortifications with materials taken from Russian buildings was turned into acts of looting, the evacuation of civilians from the zone of battle became a serious crime. Seydlitz had no trouble in rebutting the accusations, although the defense witnesses that he had named were not permitted to appear. Nevertheless, at first the tribunal, under the chairmanship of Major General and Judge Goryatchev, passed the death sentence. The sentence was subsequently changed to twenty-five years' imprisonment. The general's request that he would rather be shot was met by the cynical remark that the only people using this procedure were in the SS. Until his reprieve in the fall of 1955, he had to expiate an imaginary guilt by long years of imprisonment.[78] For quite some time Paulus had lived in renewed separation from those members of the committee and the officers' union who had been left behind. With the help of selected generals, he was allowed to prepare his role as a witness in the Nuremberg Trials as early as 1945; later he was again taken into custody by the Soviet Union.[79] Other members of the former National Committee were distributed over different POW camps until the middle of 1948, when it seemed to the Soviets that the time had arrived to concentrate them in the model quarantine of Krasnogorsk and to win all of them for the Eastern Zone of Germany.[80] There, lectures given by the Antifa School alternated with confidential meetings during which *politruks* of long standing shamelessly coaxed, threatened, and even tried blackmail. Right after the dissolution of the National Committee, the names of some of its members had been used without their consent in the newspaper *News for the German Prisoners of War in the Soviet Union* (*Nachrichten für die deutschen Kriegsgefangenen in der Sowjetunion*).[81] Now unscrupulous pressure was to wear them down once more. Some who had meanwhile become unequivocal Communists succumbed to this insidious kind of recruitment; as functionaries and spies they pledged themselves to the powerful party.[82] But others, even now, showed an independent standpoint in their political views. They fell into disgrace and were handed over to that fatal machinery of condemnation which was an insult to the name of justice and which indiscriminately meted out sentences of forced labor and banishment.[83] Some of these men were fortunate enough to be released to Western Germany during April and May of 1950.[84] But the split within the forces of the committee and the officers' union remained marked, thus inexorably reflecting in its own way the pitiful disunion of the German nation. From now on those who had once believed in fruitful co-operation were to work against each other.[85] But this touches upon our own time. Inscrutable and depressing as it is, it has yet to become history.

## CHAPTER EIGHT

## Summary and Conclusions

THE NATIONAL COMMITTEE and the League of German Officers are among the complex phenomena of Germany's most recent history, which presents many problems. Both organizations are typical of a period of ideological struggle which has brought with it a vast array of so-called positions of treason. It is, therefore, difficult, if not impossible, to understand them dispassionately as complex historical problems. Their actions originated on the territory of the Soviet Union, a country whose politics still evoke violent reactions of antipathy today. This fact alone would impair a sound evaluation that tries to stay aloof from the prejudices of the present. The recognition of this state of affairs simply reflects the almost inevitable limitations of contemporary history. There are, however, two elements which can help to creat the critical distance necessary for some concluding final considerations. On the one hand, there is the awareness that the Free Germany movement was dissolved in November 1945 as a legitimate consequence of its inability to fulfill its original task. On the other hand, there is the conviction that currently accepted categories of judgment are bound to miss the essence and structure of the movement.

It was the intention of the National Committee and the League of German Officers to win Germany's Wehrmacht and people for an overthrow of Hitler and of National Socialism. They also thought of a future German democracy; its constitutionality was to prevent a relapse into the dictatorship of the "Führer." But this aim was subordinated to propaganda, because it could never be realized without previous successful agitation at the front and at home in Germany. Behind barbed wire all activities were necessarily restricted to public appeals; they called for the rescue of a Reich threatened not only by its enemies but also by Adolph Hitler himself. In view of the Red Army's tactics and also of those of the committee itself the initial conception of Lunyovo was not maintained throughout, but the slogan of an orderly withdrawal to the Reich's frontiers was retained until the Teheran Conference. This conception aimed at a *coup d'état* without subsequent chaos. It was based on the hope that those leaders of the Wehrmacht who had been approached would have the courage to eliminate the National Socialist régime. The army's internal structure was to be preserved.

What had begun in the firm expectation of a resistance within Germany was overtaken by the political events at the beginning of 1944. United in their determination and capable of enforcing Germany's unconditional surrender and the capture of the entire Wehrmacht, the Allies had created new premises for the propaganda of the National Committee and the League during their meeting at Teheran. Up to this conference a successful German *Putsch* would have had a chance. A new German government might have hoped to realize its own plans to a certain degree. After Teheran such a change no longer existed; the only thing left then was to save Germany's substance at any price. It no longer mattered which propaganda asked Germany to reconsider. It remained imperative that the Free Germany movement was successful with them; this alone could lessen the impending collapse of the Reich.

The course of this development was too momentous to be passed over lightly. Propaganda has, of course, become a part of modern warfare. But it represented a disconcerting novelty in the history of the German Army. Moreover, the National Committee and the League raised a special problem. Here Germans had united in their resistance to National Socialist leadership; during the war they had met in the camp of one of the Reich's most powerful enemies; civilians and soldiers, they had emerged actively with slogans of agitation. The question of their motives becomes all the more important as only these motives can shed light on the actual course of events.

The motivations of the émigrés and Communists in the committee were predetermined. They were rooted in an ideology raised to the level of an absolute value, which bound them to a ruthless fight against Hitler after June 22, 1941. In their case ideological motives became mingled with nationalist impulses. The soldiers, however, were driven to their extraordinary decisions by the apocalyptic experience of the Battle of Stalingrad. To them this battle became the symbol for an inhuman state which they were duty bound to defend. In the incredible final phases of this sacrificial procession all military values had been violated and suspended. There one could discern the appalling face of a system that rejected all moral ties in favor of naked power politics and that had outraged all the laws of ethical conduct when hundreds of thousands were ordered to die by their Supreme Commander. The inroads of this barbarism, which constituted a cultural relapse without parallel, were first made into the field of military affairs. But there remained the inevitable realization that such a state was capable neither of any ideational conceptions nor of a just and permanent order, unless one was prepared to view the soldier's existence as an isolated end in itself. Dismayed, the survivors of the Sixth Army began to sense the crimes that National Socialism had already, with its contempt for the dignity of man, brought to Germany and Europe. After their experiences, which had turned their world upside down, they felt the necessity to oppose National Socialism for the sake of their own nation, which they now, after the conscious experience of the turning point on the banks of the Volga, saw headed for a still more horrible Stalingrad. Hitler would hardly show the mercy toward the German nation that he had denied even to those of his soldiers who had died a desperate death with their faith buried under the rubble of Stalingrad. Hitler's type of mind must either win or go down to total self-destruction. The impulse to resistance that had thus become possible, therefore, grew out of insights which the historian's analysis has to accept if only because all ensuing consistent actions were inspired by the visionary force of these insights, both politically *and* militarily. Every single analysis tried to show the inexorability of events which could only be averted by a courageous rebellion against an irresponsible régime. Every single leaflet anticipated the agonies of the collapse.

They were politically right because Hitler proved that he was unwilling to make peace. No one else wanted to make peace with him either. Diplomatic attempts at a settlement were truncated and forbidden. Only the instruments of war counted while the last German reserves were insanely used up. If they, too, failed to win the victory that the enemy's coalition of superior strength, created by Hitler, denied him anyway, then people and Reich were to perish. The individual whose role it should have been to open the path to survival to a nation he had shamelessly abused had assumed the role of the destructive martyr. It was blasphemous on his part to identify himself with his nation.

They were militarily right because the course of events reflected most consistently Hitler's fundamental determination. There was no realm of life that was safe from the rising flood of senseless ideology. But events continued to surpass both prediction and imagination. Step by step it became apparent that the Wehrmacht was being crushed by the obstinacy of its Supreme Commander and his spineless generals; that it was destroyed by being bound to orders unrelated to the situation and by being bound to impossible tasks of defense. Against better knowledge, the only thing which Hitler accepted was a pointless military sacrifice that made death at the front even more bitter and that increasingly sapped morale. Helplessly, the soldier was exposed to the crushing weight of forces that crushed his self and his essence as a soldier and that he responded to in part by taking refuge in fighting almost to the end. Actions which followed the traditional soldierly code were now punished by death sentences, demotions, and the arrest of relatives (*Sippenhaftung*). After July 20, 1944, and Himmler's triumph, the last scruples that might have given a semblance of an intact leadership disappeared. The witch hunt which now began destroyed the remaining foundations of tradition; it brought to the top only those soldiers who were submissive, of complete, unquestioning loyalty, and who had become the personification of the smoothly functioning executive. Ambitious cynicism and personal obsession with power finally led to utter destruction. In the end "outmoded ideas about war and fighting" were derided even publicly. Enlisted men turned fanatics sat in judgment over their hesitating or reluctant officers, empowered to do so by the highest authority.

"Werewolf" units, thirsting for action and made up of Hitler

Youth and groups of SS, hanged men of the *Volkssturm* (National Socialism's last military reserves made up of young boys and old men) who were supposed to prolong the catastrophe by a few more days. The end was mercilessly apocalyptic. It pushed people into horror and despair; it left behind a nation torn and a people crowded together who had lost all faith in anything military. No opposition could prevent this political and military development; it could unfold freely, a fact that justified after the event *any* attempt to oppose Hitler. For, in view of the consequences which were to be expected, even the most important moves of an attempted uprising were reduced to insignificance.

The National Committee and the League of German Officers had incessantly stressed the necessity of the liberating action; but this necessity was voiced from inside the camp of that enemy with whom the Wehrmacht was locked in deadly struggle. From the start this fact burdened both organizations with the suspicion of collaboration with the enemy which did indeed become a partial reality later on as the Soviets' power was transformed into an overwhelming omnipotence. The collaboration was obvious and will be condemned especially by those who reject the ideology of Communism. But on this issue every analysis must note and distinguish the considerable differentiations even in the case of the Free Germany movement.

At Lunyovo the life of the German people and the Wehrmacht were the basis of every move. In the form of numerous proclamations this motivation represents an objective constant even where it becomes mixed, subjectively, with more dubious motives. The goal was to spare the nation from the final catastrophe or, worse still, from annihilation. If this necessity was to reach the consciousness of the fighting soldier at the front and of the home front, then the burden of high treason became unavoidable for the committee and the officers' union. The state and the régime had become identical; there no longer existed any legal opportunity to alter the political status quo in the Reich. Any sort of pronounced opposition therefore became a revolutionary act outside the protection of prevailing law. But if this protection had been forfeited, then the ties of all other previously valid obligations were broken also. Thus the path to resistance was opened.

With a few modifications on questions of propaganda, this resistance could even justify its activities behind Russian barbed wire because its motivation had not changed. Thus action was accepted in the conviction that any reservations about acting from the enemy's camp simply missed the point about the essence of the personality of Hitler, who thought only in terms of ruthless alternatives while offering up incense to the idol of his "mission" (*Sendung*). And once more they reminded themselves of what they had already felt at Stalingrad and what the course of the war had proved right: all rules and regulations were suspended. All ties had been broken by their own leaders, who insulted law and morality. Bitter experience served as a reminder that could not be ignored. The German opposition was forced into resistance by the barbarian measures by which the National Socialist régime suppressed and often exterminated as "less valuable" (*minderwertig*) alien nations and races. Thus the evil spirit that they thought they were forced to fight in the Soviet enemy they had arbitrarily challenged raised its head in Germany itself. By its inhumanity this political system had also renounced all dignity to an extent which fully justified the declaration of total war on these destroyers of the Reich. That such a decision might well appear in an ambiguous light if viewed formalistically was strongly felt at Lunyovo, where it lead to fierce conflicts of conscience. It was beyond the soldiers especially to recognize immediately all the viciousness of Hitler and his state. But whereever insight and imagination were sufficient to visualize the goals of National Socialism, there no reservations could reduce the resistance for which officers and soldiers felt themselves chosen. In this context the phrase about collaboration with the enemy is inadequate. And it can afford only very few minor insights when it comes to the political aspects of this resistance. There can be no doubt that Communists and the newly converted Marxists had considerable influence, especially in the committee. Their dependence upon Moscow, which in this case also meant subordination without complaints, is beyond any doubt. The fateful pressure with which many prisoners of war were supposed to be won for Stalinism by an obvious fraudulent use of the Free Germany movement's name can be traced back to Soviet directives.

On the part of the soldiers, a surprisingly tolerant Bolshevism had also received misleading interpretations that misunderstood its totalitarian structure and that weakened the moral position of the POW's opposition to the recruitment pressure. This was especially the case concerning the misleading colors of black-white-and-red. But such elements were hardly significant. What was significant above all else was the general war situation in which the Soviets did not hold all the cards. At Lunyovo the officers did not want to be pressured into Communism, nor were these Christians, liberals, German nationalists, and conservatives being pressured, for the Russians could not claim any omnipotence in 1943. The fighting on the fronts had reached a stalemate. The Soviets were no longer threatened by defeat, but their final victory seemed a long and uncertain way off, considering the intact and threatening military power of Germany. Neither the passionately desired Second Front, nor a satisfactory agreement with the partners of the Alliance had materialized as yet. The possibility of a Bolshevik Germany was not yet a lure; it only began to become a possibility in the course of the Soviet operations of the following year. At Teheran, Moscow wanted to see the pressure on Russia relieved, and to achieve a lessening of its isolation—and both of those pressures it hoped to counteract with the help of the Free Germany movement. Had the propaganda of the committee and the officers' union been able, under these circumstances, to induce Wehrmacht and people to overthrow Hitler and to conclude an armistice, the scales would have been weighted in favor of the Reich. In 1943 it still commanded considerable military and political assets despite the reverses suffered in the east, in Africa, and in Italy.

But Lunyovo failed to make its mark. The Teheran Conference testified to the fact that the Free Germany organization had at least lent greater force to the Soviets' political aspirations at Teheran. Many a chance was lost which the German side might have used. But there still remained the task of rescuing from the growing chaos those human lives and material goods which could still be saved from senseless destruction. In this activity the Free Germany movement was no longer moved by any political expectations but merely by a modest goal. Any hesitation on their part had to reduce the chances of the cause of Germany whereas any activity against Hitler and his system was bound to improve them. But the fighting went on beyond the agony of Germany all the way to its collapse. The "Führer" paved the Red Army's way; in May 1945 it occupied the heartland of Europe. The result was the very constellation which Lunyovo had wanted to avoid from the start.

This outcome also removed the significance of the committee and the officers' union, which had diminished little by little since the beginning of 1944. There remains the question of whether this process had been inevitable. It need not have been, had Stalin been politically prepared to reckon in long-range terms and to predispose Germany, which had been disappointed by the Western Powers, in favor of the Soviet Union with the help of a genuine anti-fascist united front. But this path was not being followed. It might have produced a considerable following for Communism. Russia had been pushed off that line by the far-reaching agreement of the Grand Alliance and the stabilization of its spheres of influence. It had also become totally unrealistic after the Red Army's wild excesses and the Soviet plundering on German soil. Thus events passed over the heads of those sections of the Free Germany movement which had merely aimed to overthrow Hitler and bring an early end to the war.

Under these circumstances they would almost certainly have been condemned to political impotence even in a non-totalitarian state. This risk had been there from the start, but it might just as well have become insignificant. If the soldiers had been determined to take their place in the National Committee and the League of German Officers to save the Reich, then they should not have shunned the company even of Communists until the end of the fighting. There was no automatic mechanism that they had to be afraid of or that would confine them to the role of a tool from the start; everything was decided by success or failure. The final steps that the Soviets took in the flush of their triumph were, however, fraught with significance. They led one to assume that Moscow was able to honor coexistence only on the basis of a complete equality of strength. Independent opinions were persecuted as suspicious and were less and less tolerated. Radical partisanship once again became the decisive criterion; it enforced collaboration with more or less subtle pressure. Some accepted collaboration, some rejected it. Those who accommodated themselves out of an impenetrable conglomeration of motives developed a hectic sort of activism; they obediently passed through the Antifa School, and subsequently lived as dependent functionaries in the Soviet occupied zone of Germany. Those who opposed the pressure on their consciences discontinued their co-operation in propaganda in 1945; they were humiliated morally and physically, and as persons convicted in court they frequently returned from prisons and camps only after many long years. The option for or against Communism had split the Free Germany movement; there were no legitimate successors after its liquidation.

At first the slogan "Orderly withdrawal to the frontiers of the Reich" dominated the front propaganda. Its aims could hardly be opposed. It wanted to save the Wehrmacht and merely stated publicly what a successful opposition within Germany would have had to accept anyway. The next slogan read "Save yourself by joining the cause of the National Committee." After the Allied proclamations the Free Germany movement expected that the Reich would inevitably be stripped of all power, that Hitler would fight to the last round of ammunition, and that it was necessary to oppose the insanity of total anarchy with any means available. The danger that the front might be undermined had become irrelevant. But it was hotly debated nevertheless. Two objections were raised in particular during the embittered polemics. The first one claimed that this propaganda line had rendered useless the instrument that an orderly *coup d'état* would have to use in order to reach a tolerable agreement instead of Germany's surrender. The second objection was that this propaganda line had to offer only Soviet imprisonment, where thousands of German soldiers had met their death already, as an alternative to the impending destruction by Hitler.

No final verdict can be reached regarding the point when subversion became justifiable, even if one agrees with the self-image and the motives of the Free Germany movement. It is a question of personal preference whether one is willing to grant the chance of a limited negotiated peace to a non-National Socialist Germany even after the Teheran Conference. In this case all the means of power would indeed have had to be preserved. In the spring of

1944 there was probably still a chance for this solution despite the seriousness of the situation. But the opposition within Germany no longer believed in such a chance when it indicated to the Western Powers at that time that it was willing to allow the landing of Allied troops in the Reich after a *coup d'état*. By July 20 it was too late for any of these considerations. All Germany could still do then was to acknowledge defeat. After the failure of the rebellion, all tactical reservations had become meaningless.

But the appeal to the troops to surrender to the Soviets was a truly tragic one. The threatening annihilation of the troops under Hitler's leadership, which only tried to prolong its own existence with the help of the irresponsible orders for the soldiers to fight on, had a paralyzing and depressing effect on the men of the Free Germany organization. But the alternative of Soviet imprisonment seemed equally depressing, for this frequently could not be regarded as a real alternative. Had it been chosen by many soldiers, the whole Free Germany movement would have had to bear a grave responsibility. That is especially true with regard to the final stages of the fighting when the movement found itself obviously guilty by association because of the Red Army's attitude. But here, too, no all-inclusive accusation can be leveled. It had not been the committee and the officers' union that had brought about the inferno which broke over the eastern provinces of the Reich, and they did not possess the machinery with which they might have reached the numerous POW camps from Lunyovo. Compared to the deliberately intended ruin of the people and the nation, even Russian barbed wire seemed the lesser evil, especially if the soldiers surrendered in orderly fashion and while they still had some strength left. This imprisonment certainly brought with it humiliations and suffering, hunger and despair, sickness and miserable death. The reasons for this are manifold, hard to define in detail, and therefore cannot be reduced to a simple formula. But this imprisonment also offered the chance of some humane security from physical dilapidation, of an overwhelming helpfulness of Russian men and women, and the frequently fulfilled possibility of returning to a changed homeland sooner or later.

Insofar as the front propaganda reflected the desire for a

democratic constitutionality in Germany, it was subject to un-assailable principles. A renewal of the links with law, morality, and the dignity of man suggested themselves as the unavoidable consequence of the realities of National Socialism. In view of this renewal there also seemed to exist a chance of uniting all the opponents of the Nazi régime in the task of reconstruction. This remained above all the conception of the League of German Officers. A detailed analysis of this attitude, however, suffers from a lack of evidence.

On the one hand, the Free Germany movment never developed any concepts which went beyond guidelines couched in very general terms. Clearly recognizing its limitations, it stressed primarily its function as a propaganda vehicle. On the other hand, even the slogan-like points of the manifesto and the "Twenty-five Articles for Ending the War" became all the more invalidated as the united front of Lunyovo, which had been intended to serve as a model, broke up while still in the Soviet Union. In the end there were no more goals that everyone could subscribe to and that would have held them together.

All the slogans of the front propaganda, expressing an unusual will to resist, remained mere theoretical pronouncements. Both the opposition within the Reich and the Wehrmacht had refused to respond with any palpable action.

The opposition within Germany had refused because, much as it regarded it helpful to find confirmation of its own sentiments which were to erupt in a liberating uprising, it was not prepared in the least to turn east politically. The National Committee and the League of German Officers, however, were regarded as ad-vocates of such a way if they were not simply regarded as being infected by Bolshevism anyway. This does not mean that no one within the opposition to Hitler believed in the necessity of Ger-many's reaching some agreement with the Soviet Union in the future. But with great devotion the German opposition worked above all for a rapprochement with the great Anglo-Saxon powers. It was to their free way of life that the men of the opposition felt drawn, a feeling which was complemented by their rejection of Communism. They believed that they would be able to withstand the overpowering force of the Soviets only in league with Great

Britain and the United States. Any other conception seemed absurd to them if only because they always thought of Germany's central geographic position. What at first had remained irrelevant became relevant when Lunyovo began to appeal to the soldiers to join the cause of the National Committee. Now even initially positive reactions were replaced by bitter criticism. If the desperate step of subversion became necessary in a belated uprising against Hitler, then it could be risked only in the west. The Red Army had to be confronted by a Wehrmacht inviolate to the end in its solidarity. These aims were decisive; they pushed into the background all those elements on which the committee, the officers' union, and the resistance within Germany were basically agreed. No connection was sought between them and consequently none was actually established. The conspirators wanted to and could act only as their own men. Appeals written behind Soviet barbed wire appeared to them in a more and more dubious light. The recognition that their resistance was a necessity had ripened by itself in the men most active on July 20. It was to be presented to the people only after a successful *coup d'état.* They accepted the motives which had brought about the founding of the National Committee, but they regarded its methods as wrong. The German opposition in the Reich therefore would have acted and actually did act without the Free Germany movement.

The Wehrmacht fought on to the horrible end; it never understood the National Committee and the League. Both thought they could pass on their enthusiasm to the whole German army in the east, since to both of them the sum total of their motives and the necessity of their actions seemed beyond question. Both failed in their rescue attempt undertaken from the territory of the enemy; in its uniqueness it was untrustworthy and tainted with the negative connotation of treason. The Wehrmacht as a whole was yet to confront its Stalingrad, the bitter experience of which could not be communicated. When it gradually caught up with the Wehrmacht, the hope for a change for the better was gone. Even the bitterest insights of an ever-growing mass of soldiers could no longer be turned into anything fruitful. There always remained some troops that loyally served and supported a leadership unworthy of such loyalty. In millions of German soldiers often dreadful doubts had

arisen, brought about by the crimes of the National Socialist régime that had become known to them. This created many an
opposition of powerless men, it shaped mental reservations, and
not infrequently awakened a certain preparedness to acknowledge
the act of open rebellion as a dignified decision. But their suffering
either remained private or used up its strength in the attempt to
oppose inhumanity by an attitude guided by conscience. The
course of the war was untouched by all this. The fighting followed
its own laws. These laws were all the more readily obeyed in the
east as the friend-foe relationship had found its most merciless
manifestation there. Deliberately, the Soviets had been stamped
as subhuman, which was intended to do away with any reservations. Deliberately, conquered Russia was humiliated as an object
of terrorism and horror. The struggle was regarded as one between
armies *and* ideologies, and it knew no bounds. There was only
victory or death. The Soviet enemy understood what he was
threatened with and he fought with equal fierceness and bitterness.
Both sides had burned all bridges behind them. The German
soldier fought in the conviction that this war must never be lost.
Once unconditional surrender had been demanded by the Allies,
the consequences of defeat for the people and the Reich seemed
inconceivable to him. Any appeal by the committee and the officers'
union was therefore rejected by him as despicable enemy propaganda. It would have been rejected even if the unquestioning
obedience of the Wehrmacht had not condemned to failure all
the exhortations of the Free Germany organization. For in the
tense atmosphere of the Russian campaign, alternatives other
than those of brutality had become unthinkable and impossible.
Thus the troops despised the obvious abuse of the black-white-red
colors by a Communist minority and they refused to respond in
any way to the contradictory slogans of the committee, the officers' union, and the Red Army. They questioned the chances
of a political arrangement after an overthrow of Hitler, and they
did not view Soviet imprisonment as their salvation. To the
soldier tied to his immediate tasks the cruel realities of the battlefield spoke loud enough, while the questions of moral responsibility
had become irrelevant. If they did not suppress their harrowing

reflections themselves, they at least remained unwilling to believe the enemy and his aides.

This attitude remained unshaken even by the increasing gloom gathering about Germany. Nascent doubts were now smothered not merely by confidence in a leadership which had created an almost inexhaustible fund of good faith for itself with its previous triumphs. Since this leadership was also thought to be incapable of demanding the devotion of the front without good reason, the carefully spread rumors about an imminent change in events by a new secret weapon also fell on fertile ground. Tied to their sections of the front and without any knowledge of the general situation, the troops longed for a ray of hope. And finally they were convinced that Germany fought for Europe and that it would ultimately receive help from the Western Powers in its fight against Bolshevism. Ideas of this kind were utopian, but they showed them once more a task beyond the now dead faith in the ideas of National Socialism, which seemed to oblige the soldiers to hold out some more. Only when even this task was seen to have been deceptive too and after the soldiers had provided thousands of German refugees a head start over the Red Army, only then were all the excuses exhausted which had given meaning to their fighting. The Wehrmacht had ceased to exist; its world had collapsed from within.

The considerations which, in the final result, justify and affirm the National Committee and the League of German Officers did not annul the decision to fight to the bitter end. Frequently its necessity was accepted and confirmed by the unassailable act of self-sacrifice. Thus it cannot be our task even today to think little of it or to defame it. But just as this attitude cannot command absolute validity—which would also mean accepting the incredible ruin of all values during the agony of Germany—it becomes necessary once more, in conclusion, to stress the justice of acting against orders and against the demands for obedience. The whole of Germany was threatened then and this fact had created a unique state of emergency. Hitler had undermined all legal and ethical foundations, and he irresponsibly pushed Germany into total ruin. The Free Germany movement and the men of July 20 had clearly recognized this development. The former, like the latter, tried to counteract the impending catastrophe out of a higher responsibility toward their people, spurred on not only by Germany's situation, but also by the hope for Germany's inner renewal. This, perhaps, justified treason against the government, but not treason against one's nation, which would presuppose the intention to endanger the well-being of the Reich. From the point of view of ethics the rebellious uprising remained justified if the supporters of the opposition were willing to pay for it with their own lives. The resistance within Germany did not shrink from this high gamble. The impressive number of those executed speaks for itself, eloquently and convincingly. This test was denied to the National Committee and the League of German Officers. They were not within the grasp of the National Socialist régime they had challenged. This assures our highest respect for the men of July 20, but it in no way diminishes the genuine moral decision whose call the soldiers behind the Russians' barbed wire followed as early as 1943. For once they had decided to fight against Hitler, they could hardly expect to return home again later on. At the time the Free Germany movement was founded this seemed indeed very dubious. Not to return home would have been a fate worse than death for most of them. Their families were threatened as well. They were dispersed and carried off to prisons and concentration camps, detained as hostages guilty by association, being related to the men in Russia. The Supreme Military Court of the Reich had to pass the death sentence against Seydlitz. He was deprived of his rank and all his rights. Defamed and outlawed, his name was to be covered with eternal shame. After the end of the war, when the Soviets tried to enforce unquestioning collaboration, frequently without success, years of humiliation and imprisonment followed for many of the soldiers in the committee. It becomes difficult to impute base motives in these cases or even that they acted against their own nation. These elements have to be stressed as a matter of principle in order to reduce to the appropriate level all the rash accusations of opportunism that here and there may have been justified at a later date.

The men at Lunyovo, too, had suffered all the moral afflictions which had also troubled the conspirators in the Reich. There was no way to guard against the accusation of having stabbed the front line in the back. Successful propaganda did not necessarily, at any time, bring with it personal advantages for the captured soldiers. Every act would much more readily evoke false charges which only added to the pressures and the pain. The resistance of the committee and the officers' union had at least freed them in one respect; now everything was public and they were no longer under the necessity of having to act against better knowledge. The advantages of this position became apparent when it is compared to the dubious opposition of those generals who had fallen into Soviet hands by the dozen in the summer of 1944. Against better knowledge they had ordered their soldiers to fight with devotion to the very end; once captured, they had immediately signed appeals asking for a quick termination of the senseless struggle.

But some problems remain even today that once were the basis for divergent opinions; certain differences of opinion have remained and refuse to be bridged. It would serve nobody to disregard them, because this kind of blindness would only raise higher the barriers between the intellectual camps within Germany. Rebellion against structures that one cannot do without remains a serious problem that is almost insoluble even if one is willing to think it through. The painful question whether and under which circumstances one may refuse an obedience which has been affirmed by an oath will certainly evoke differing answers. There will always be some who are willing to suppress this question, since it seems to threaten certain eternal principles, while others will tend to face it and to think it through. The problems which Hitler raised are still with us; every individual has to face them. The passage of time may bring with it more lucid judgments. But one thing can already be stressed today: *no* act of commission or omission in those days was considered to demonstrate superiority. There was no way to remain free of guilt both along the path of resistance *and* along the path of obedience. All potential signposts had been smashed by a state which had destroyed all values. Only if we acknowledge all this can we seriously hope to understand a period which we understand only imperfectly up to now.

Under the circumstances then prevailing it was imperative for the Free Germany movement to attempt the fight against Hitler while the war was still in progress; but the movement cannot serve as a model today. The National Committee and the League of German Officers made their appearance in an extraordinary situation which is unlikely to repeat itself in the future. But this does not mean that only the historical aspects of these phenomena are significant, all the more so as we now live in an era in which war can hardly be manipulated by politics any more, let alone by propaganda. But prognostications are not part of the historian's task even if some of them have already become reality. What does remain important about this more or less elucidated historical phenomenon is the strong and active appeal it has for the present. In this sense even the former organization of German prisoners of war in the Soviet Union may still carry a message concerning some present-day tasks. Keeping all this in mind, we should re-examine the militarism of National Socialism's political leadership, as we should deal once again with the conclusions which may be derived from this experience of a conscienceless leadership that shamelessly abused a loyalty that was conferred upon it out of a traditional faith in its moral integrity. The result of these re-examinations might well be a state based on a morality of which the soldier's existence, too, is a part and in which it is based on firm ethical foundations. Such a state remains a most pressing need, as this study has shown. We may judge the committee and the officers' union whichever way we like or are capable of; the legacy of the Free Germany movement will have become superfluous and meaningless only if the struggle for such a state is given up. It serves as a reminder to all of us to strive for a kind of political reality which will render the desperate resistance of yesterday unnecessary in the future.

## *Appendix: Documents*

## I

## TO THE GERMAN PEOPLE AND
## THE GERMAN WEHRMACHT!

Alarming news is pouring in from Germany and from the fronts.

Events fully confirm the predictions made a month ago in the manifesto of the National Committee for a Free Germany. Hitler's summer offensive has been drowned in a sea of blood. In its place the Russians have now started a devastating offensive. Orel, the most important base of the Eastern Front and the most advantageous for all kinds of offensive operations, is in Russian hands. The Byelgorod sector has been smashed on a broad front. The issue of taking Kharkov, the second capital of the Ukraine, has already been decided. The front extending from Kharkov to Taganrog is threatened from the flanks. The road to the Dnieper is wide open.

And it is still the middle of summer. What, then, will winter bring?

Italy has collapsed militarily. Mussolini's régime, which was ten years older than Hitler's, has been swept away. The Berlin-Rome Axis has been smashed. How will Germany replace the missing thirty-six Italian divisions to protect the Balkans, France, and the Brenner from the invading Anglo-American troops? As in 1918, Germany stands alone once more against the rest of the world and with less hope than in 1918.

At home decay and panic rule supreme. Especially in the ranks of the rulers who are responsible for the misery of our people. Hitler is finished as a statesman and as a commander in chief. His cronies, headed by Göring, are already beginning to make their own private arrangements out of fear and helplessness, and they are trying to secure for themselves asylum in neutral countries. But our people cannot run away. Together with the Wehrmacht they will be left behind to hold the bag for all the crimes of the Hitler régime. Hamburg has already paid with the destruction of the city. The next blow will hit Berlin. The population is terrified and leaving the big cities.

That is where the National Socialists have led our Fatherland!

The continuation of the war is tantamount to the suicide of the nation and of the Wehrmacht. Day by day the situation becomes more hopeless, day by day Germany becomes more helpless, day by day the conditions for peace must grow worse. Every additional day that the German armies spend on Russian soil increases the anger of their most powerful enemy, the Russian people. Only the overthrow of the Hitler régime, the immediate cessation of all fighting, and the simultaneous beginning of a withdrawal from the Eastern territories, *i.e.*, the visible renunciation of all imperialist conquests, can make up for the crime of June 22, 1941, and gain us once more the trust of the Russian people and of all democratic forces. This is the only way for Germany to come out of this war honorably.

In this hour of danger the National Committee once more and with greater emphasis renews its appeal:

Put an end to the war immediately!

The whole strength of the people against Hitler's war régime and for the saving of our nation from the impending catastrophe!

Fight for a truly national government which will secure for our country liberty and peace!

NATIONAL COMMITTEE FOR A FREE GERMANY

The President: Erich Weinert

1st Vice-President: Major Karl Hetz

2nd Vice-President: Second Lieutenant Count von Einsiedel

August 1943

*(Free Germany, No. 4, August 13, 1943)*

II

PROCLAMATION

To the German Generals and Officers!
To the People and the Wehrmacht!

We, the surviving fighters of the Sixth Army, of the Army of Stalingrad, its generals, officers, and men, turn to you at the start of this fifth year of the war, to show our country and our people a way to save themselves.

All Germany knows what Stalingrad means.

We went through hell.

We were pronounced dead and have risen to a new life.

We can remain silent no longer!

We, like no one else, have the right to speak up, not just for ourselves, but for our dead fellow soldiers, for all the victims of Stalingrad.

That is our right and our duty!

The serious military defeats suffered since the beginning of this year and the increasing deterioration of the German economy force us to recognize the hopelessness of Germany's position. Stalingrad was a turning-point. After that came the Caucasus and the Kuban area, Africa and Sicily, the collapse of Italy—blow by blow. The German Wehrmacht's summer offensive has failed. The Red Army has recaptured Orel and Byelgorod, Kharkov, Taganrog, and the Donetz basin, and is now advancing toward the Dnieper. The home front is being shaken by massive aerial attacks. The war on two fronts is imminent and inevitable. The overthrow of Mussolini, the disbanding of the Fascist Party, Italy's withdrawal from the war, the almost certain defection of Finland, Hungary, and Roumania are the stations on the way toward a complete isolation of Germany even more disastrous than in 1918.

Every thinking German officer knows that Germany has lost the war. The whole populace senses it. It is also known to the ruling group that has brought about the disaster.

Before history, Hitler and his régime will have to bear the full, undivided responsibility for the disastrous errors of judgment which are leading Germany into ruin unless the people and the Wehrmacht forcibly and quickly bring about a change.

As a statesman, Hitler has welded together the most powerful states in the world into an overwhelming coalition against Germany. As commander in chief, Hitler has led the German Wehrmacht to its gravest defeats. Without the necessary equipment he rushed the German soldier into the winter campaign of 1941–1942. With incorrigible obstinacy he conceived and directed the perilous campaign against Stalingrad and the Caucasus. At Stalingrad and in Africa, he sacrificed Germany's crack armies for his own prestige.

Now is the time to save all Germany from the same fate. The war is continued exclusively for the sake of Hitler and his régime, without any consideration for the people and the Fatherland. The continuation of the senseless and hopeless war may bring about a national catastrophe any day. It is a moral necessity and the patriotic duty of every responsible German to prevent this.

We, the generals and officers of the Sixth Army, are determined to give a profound historical meaning to the hitherto senseless deaths of our fellow soldiers, who sacrificed their lives. They must not have died in vain! The bitter experience of Stalingrad must give rise to an act of redemption. We therefore appeal to the *PEOPLE* and the *WEHRMACHT*. We appeal particularly *to the commanding officers, the generals, and the officers* of the *Wehrmacht*.

A great decision is in your hands!

Germany expects you to have the courage to recognize the truth and to act bravely and immediately in accord with it.

*Do what is necessary,* lest it happen without or even against you!

The National Socialist régime will never open the path which alone can lead to peace.

This fact demands that you begin the fight against that corrupting régime and work for the creation of a government which is supported by the confidence of the people. Such a government alone can create the conditions for an honorable conclusion of this war by our Fatherland and can assure a peace which does not bring with it the misery of Germany and the seed of future wars.

Do not refuse your historic mission! Take the initiative into your own hands! The Wehrmacht and the people will support you. *Demand the immediate resignation of Hitler and his government!* Fight side by side with the people in order to remove Hitler and his régime and to save Germany from chaos and ruin!

The fighters of the Sixth Army, the Army of Stalingrad, and all German soldiers and officers captured in Russia raise their voices in the knowledge that they are thus fulfilling their most sacred duty to the nation.

*Long live a free, peaceful, and independent Germany!*

> Walther von Seydlitz, . . . [This proclamation was signed also by Daniels, Hooven, Steidle, and some ninety other officers.]

*(Free Germany, No. 8/9, September 15, 1943)*


## III

### TO THE GERMAN WEHRMACHT

> The following appeal to the German Wehrmacht was accepted unanimously by the plenary session of the National Committee for a Free Germany on September 24, 1943. President Weinert read it to the assembly; Major General Martin Lattmann explained the meaning and the importance of its arguments.

The National Committee for a Free Germany wants to direct the attention of the fighting men to the following facts:

The front line, reached after two years of war in the east, has begun to retreat continuously. Stretched out over more than 650 miles, the units of the German armies in the east are withdrawing after lost battles and under enemy pressure. They are threatened by outflanking maneuvers on a grand scale.

In the south a wide breach has been opened up in "Fortress

Europe" because of Allied policy of unconditional surrender. British and American troops are advancing north from southern Italy. Italian and French troops are mopping up isolated German units on the islands of the Mediterranean. All the Balkan States are in ferment and threaten to become another battle area.

Air war is laying waste the cities of our country.

Hitler has lost the battle of the Atlantic.

The situation is obvious. Equally obvious are the necessary consequences that derive from it. The National Committee therefore declares: Germany is threatened by a total defeat of the German armies and by war on its own territory. The existence of our Wehrmacht and our Reich are in jeopardy. There is no Reich without an army, no army without a Reich!

What is to be done now to save the still combat-ready core of the army and the lives of millions of Germans from total destruction? There is only *one* way out and that is to let responsible commanders withdraw the German army to the frontiers of the Reich, irrespective of Hitler's orders.

Why does the National Committee consider the withdrawal of the troops as the only way out? For the following cogent reasons:

1. The continuation of fighting and any further sacrifices are pointless, since Hitler's war is lost, and the occupied Russian territories can no longer be maintained.

2. Hitler continues to lay waste foreign countries while the Reich is threatened by ruin. The other peoples will present our people with a bill of horrors. Everything must be done that can prevent it from growing even more horrible and that may save our children and their children from suffering under its weight.

3. It is only autumn now. To continue the fighting is to drag on the war into winter. During the winter of 1941 and 1942 the army escaped a catastrophe only by the greatest exertions. How is it to survive the coming winter now, weakened by the defeats of this summer? The troops are faced with disorganization, decay, and ruin in the vast snowfields *during* winter unless an organized withdrawal is begun *before* winter starts.

4. Unless the army's bleeding to death is stopped immediately, it will no longer be ready at the decisive moment, when the issue will no longer be the Ukraine, Poland, the Balkans, or France, but *Germany herself*, and it will then no longer be in a position to prevent the occupation of German territory.

For these incontestable reasons the National Committee considers the immediate orderly withdrawal of the army to the frontiers of the Reich as the sole action capable of saving our Fatherland. This withdrawal will take place without risk as soon as the clear intention of German commanders to cease all hostilities has become visible.

No one should be misled by the "argument" that it is risky to begin the withdrawal without previous "guarantees"!

If the German army does not withdraw in orderly fashion, there will be no other guarantee than that of total annihilation.

*Genuine* guarantees can be found *only* in carrying out an orderly withdrawal without hostilities. Only in this way will the vital forces of the German army and therefore the military strength of the German people remain intact.

If the army does retreat in an orderly fashion it will thereby *prove by action* that it does not agree with Hitler's policy of conquest, but that it is prepared to seek the path toward peaceful co-operation with other peoples.

No longer commanded by Hitler, under a new commander in chief, and withdrawing from Russia in order and of its own free will, the German army will create a new situation for all countries, a situation which our opponents, too, will be unable to disregard.

The National Committee has reached the following conclusions:

The army can only be saved by an orderly withdrawal to the frontiers of the Reich. No such orderly withdrawal will be possible until Hitler has been removed as Supreme Commander.

The Wehrmacht went to war as Hitler's army. It will either return without or against Hitler or it will not return at all.

The leadership of the National Committee for a Free Germany therefore appeals *to the generals:* Demand and proclaim the removal of Hitler from the Supreme Command! He is the corrupter of Reich and *Wehrmacht!* Lead back the troops in an orderly fashion! Anticipate the danger of your soldiers' running away for home on their own and demoralized in the near future!

*To the officers and men:* Demand immediate withdrawal of the army! Remember that you will be the arms bearers of the liberty of our new Germany.

NATIONAL COMMITTEE FOR A FREE GERMANY
The President: Erich Weinert
The Vice-Presidents: General of the Artillery von Seydlitz
Lieutenant General Edler von
Daniels
Major Karl Hetz
Second Lieutenant Heinrich
Count von Einsiedel
Pfc. Emendörfer

(*Free Germany*, No. 11, September 26, 1943)

IV

Open letter from General of the Artillery Walther von Seydlitz

## TO THE COMMANDER IN CHIEF OF THE NINTH ARMY, COLONEL GENERAL MODEL

Dear General Model,

As commander in chief of the Ninth Army you tried in your order of September 16, 1943, to explain the retreat of the eastern armies and to present future objectives. However, the contradictions in your presentation are so obvious that I cannot help feeling that you had to argue someone else's opinion against your own better judgment, for your reasoning contradicts your oft-proved ability to view things lucidly and without self-deception. The few weeks which have passed since the writing of your order have, moreover, clearly demonstrated that your argumentation is untenable.

In this war, as so often in the history of war, a decision of the supreme command based on an erroneous evaluation of the situation is being paid for with the blood of many German men. This is shown by Stalingrad, the Don, the Caucasus, Africa, the failure of this year's summer offensive, and above all by the large-scale Russian offensive. Now the supreme command has even managed to place the very life of the German people in jeopardy.

This has caused me to comment on your order.

You assert that time is working for Germany. It is easy to disprove this opinion. Our enemies have more time than we do. It is a fact that in the course of the past year our enemies have become disproportionately stronger, while we have become disproportionately weaker. In the case of Stalingrad, it may still have been possible to believe that it represented one of those setbacks which happen in any war; the events of the past year, however, have shown that Germany's fortunes are declining steadily on all fronts. The unbroken chain of defeats is no mere accident. It is the result of the increasingly dangerous exhaustion of Germany's strength, while the reserves of our enemies are by no means exhausted. You know yourself what the latest reserves that the Hitler régime has squeezed out of our people in the course of its mobilization for total war look like. The Red Army, on the other hand, has been so little weakened by its "flexible defense" that it can now continue its offensive with increased force.

It is equally easy to disprove your claim that the advantages of open spaces are working in Germany's favor. No one will be convinced by the assertion that during the first years the Wehrmacht had conquered the vast Russian spaces at an incredible cost of lives and matériel only to create the space for its retreat. The most significant advantage of open space is, moreover, lost if one does not command sufficient reserves.

In your statement that the retreat of the eastern armies had become necessary because of the threat of an invasion by American and British troops, *i.e.*, before a second front had even been established, you admit yourself how hopeless the situation has become for Germany. And what is to happen once the war on many fronts has become a reality?

It is true that the path to the Reich will demand sacrifices from the Russian army. But the German armies in the east will suffer even heavier losses. The Russians can make up their losses with relative ease; we cannot. There is the danger that the war will make its way to the Reich. The German Wehrmacht can eliminate that danger, not by continuing a war which has become hopeless and senseless, but by refusing to obey Adolf Hitler.

Confidence in the present German political and military leadership has already been shaken severely; we are convinced, General, your confidence has been shaken too. All hopes in Adolf Hitler's infallibility will be horribly disappointed. Germany's future is bleak and desperate if the Wehrmacht continues to uphold him.

After the experiences of the last two months it has become highly doubtful whether the Wehrmacht is capable of bringing the front to halt at any time, as you assert. Already the Russians have crossed the Dnieper in several places. There are no reserves behind the German armies in the east which could alter the situation significantly. But before them there lies a threatening winter and the danger that the matériel and vital strength of the troops will be destroyed.

Germany owes the catastrophic development of its political and military situation exclusively to Adolf Hitler's megalomania and amateurish leadership. It is too much of an imposition to ask the German soldier to have faith in this kind of "wise" leadership. You have often shown your talent for clearly recognizing the reality of things. I am convinced that you have also realized that Adolf Hitler can no longer win this war and that he only prolongs it pointlessly because he is afraid of the end. He remains apparently unimpressed by the fact that week by week Germany experiences increasing horrors and that human beings are being sacrificed.

Therefore, General, do what you think is right. Like all commanders of the German Wehrmacht, you must bear responsibility for the fate of Germany to the full. Force Adolf Hitler to step down! Withdraw from Russian soil and lead the eastern army back to the German borders. This decision will create the political conditions for an honorable peace that will help the German people regain the rights of a free nation. Such an action will be of decisive importance for the ending of the war and the shaping of Germany's fate.

But everything will be lost and every hope shattered if Adolf Hitler is enabled to continue the war with your help and if he drags the German people down with him into certain ruin.

> signed: v. Seydlitz, General of the Artillery,
> President of the League of German
> Officers

*Free Germany, No. 14, October 17, 1943*

## V

### National Committee for a Free Germany

### OFFICERS AND SOLDIERS IN MELITOPOL!

Hitler has ordered you to hold Melitopol at any price. He gave the same order at Stalingrad, Kharkov, Vyazma, Bryansk, and Smolensk.

All these cities were taken by storm by the Red Army anyway. And Hitler's order disappeared like a mere shadow in a sea of German blood!

COMRADES!

You know yourselves that your leaders have already thrown their last hastily mustered reserves into this slaughterhouse of Melitopol, among them Construction Battalion 64, old men without combat training. The 111th and the 336th Infantry divisions, almost wiped out on the Myus front, the 370th and 73rd Infantry divisions, smashed at the Kuban, and the 97th Mountaineer Division were immediately returned into combat. Why?

Because all German reserves have been used up in the great battles of the summer.

COMRADES OF MELITOPOL!

You are defending a lost cause!

All the other German troops have already been pulled back behind the Dnieper. What are you doing at Melitopol while your mothers, wives, and children are waiting for you in Germany and are dying with fear and worry! What is that political impostor Hitler to you who are to sacrifice your lives and the happiness of your families for his short reprieve!

COMRADES!

Do you all really want to die in this third Russian winter? There is only one way out: ask those courageous and responsible commanders among you who can still feel for their men to begin an immediate and orderly withdrawal to the frontiers of the Reich!

Comrade!

Listen, the wind already through the steppes does roam
Listen. Mother, wife, and children weep at home.
Say, who loves you more: your mother
Or Hitler who needs you for cannon fodder?

Heinrich Count von Einsiedel
Second Lieutenant of the IIIrd Fighter Squadron
"Udet," No. 3
Vice-President of the National Committee for a Free Germany
Dr. Friedrich Wolf
Member of the National Committee for a Free Germany


VI

*Generals, officers, and soldiers of the German Army East!*

For months we have warned you and predicted what is now facing you more and more clearly every day, more and more threateningly, and more and more finally: the winter catastrophe of the German Army East.

Hitler's megalomaniac war policy is about to collapse completely!

He is now about to add the full burden of shame of the serious and disastrous defeat of the German Army East to all the misery, all the unlimited, inexpressible grief, and to the most monstrously senseless sacrifice of lives that has ever been suffered by a people.

The 18th Army of Army Group North has been smashed completely. Its remnants are fleeing, disorganized and broken up, through the wintry forests and swamps of the Baltic States, fleeing to the west and southwest beyond Lake Peypus.

To the south the 16th Army faces the same fate, now that it has been deprived of all cover on its northern flank and in its rear.

Army Group Center and its completely exhausted troops will soon be engaged in heavy fighting once more.

Its communications already severed completely, Army Group Manstein every day succumbs more and more to the vastly superior Russian attacks, which, contrary to expectations, are increasing in strength. Its catastrophic position is clearly shown by the encirclement of ten German divisions in the area west of Cherkassy.

We honestly wish that the German people might be spared this catastrophe.

But it is the pure, unadulterated truth. The images of horror connected with Napoleon's retreat of 1812 keep appearing before our eyes.

In this hopeless situation we have appealed to the troops of German Army East for months:

Stop all hostilities!

Stop the completely senseless sacrifice of the lives of many more hundreds of thousands!

Join the cause of the National Committee for a Free Germany!

So far our appeal has been heeded only in individual cases and by small units. In the pocket at Kirovograd, the bulk of five German divisions perished pointlessly because they still believed in Hitler and followed his insane orders. Near Leningrad, thousands of the 18th Army could have been saved from death if they had listened to our appeals and had followed our warnings, which we repeated again and again.

How long is all this to continue? Does the German Army East have to bleed to death first, does it have to fall prey to total ruin in the snow and ice of the Russian winter before you will start to think and to accept what we are saying?

Can you not yet see where Hitler is leading you? Do you still believe that this is "only a test," these "couple of miles or couple of hundred miles," as Hitler still jeered as late as November 9, 1943, which have been given up and paid for with the lives of millions of German sons?

We tell you this only out of our deep concern for the German people! We do not want to subvert the German Army East. But even less than that do we want it to melt away and be destroyed because of Hitler's defeats, which is what is happening now.

We want your lives for the fight against the misleader of Germany. We need you to rebuild Germany! We need you to save Germany before Hitler can destroy it completely.

> General of the Artillery Walther von Seydlitz
> Commanding General, LI. Army Corps
>
> Lieutenant General Alexander Edler von Daniels
> Commander, 376th Inf. Div.
>
> Lieutenant General Helmut Schlömer
> Commander, 3rd Inf. Div. (mot.)
>
> • Major General Martin Lattmann
> Commander, 14th Panzer Div.

(*Free Germany, No. 6, February 5, 1944*)

## VII

### LIEUTENANT GENERAL EDLER VON DANIELS,
Vice-President of the National Committee for a Free Germany and Member of the Presidium of the League of German Officers

#### TO FIELD MARSHAL VON MANSTEIN

My Dear Field Marshal,

The encirclement and the destruction, at present under way, of ten divisions of your army group one year after the catastrophe of Stalingrad is not only a military defeat, it is also an incomprehensible and irresponsible sacrifice of an irreplaceable part of our people. I know, my dear Field Marshal, that you are not a faithful National Socialist. You are also not one of the so-called "Party Generals." All the service positions you have filled during the war you received on the basis of your military abilities. And that is also the reason why you must surely see the over-all military picture for what it is—hopeless!

Even before this latest catastrophe you must have known that the arc of the Dnieper front was untenable, jutting out as it does—and you did know it. But you nevertheless bowed to Hitler's orders, the predictable results of which were the senseless slaughter of tens of thousands of German soldiers.

Why did you do it? Why do you continue to throw your divisions into this hopeless battle? How long do you intend to aid in the destruction of the German army that is being carried out by Hitler?

You may reply: I have presented my reservations, my criticisms, but they were not accepted. Is your conscience that easily silenced? Does it satisfy your sense of responsibility and your idea of an officer to obey formalistically that one man, Hitler, whose orders, as you know very well, are irresponsible and criminal?

The German people do not ask their military commanders to continue a hopeless fight against their better knowledge simply because an adventurer wants them to. The German people expect and demand that the military commanders—and that also includes you, my dear Field Marshal—have the courage and determination to act according to their best knowledge and conviction.

And consider one more thing. In the course of the past year the front has been pushed westward by about a thousand miles. Today it runs only about 300 miles east of the borders of the province of Silesia. You, my dear Field Marshal, know only too well that the terms "tactical retreat" and "straightening out of the front" are nothing but a mockery, considering the defeat Germany has, in fact, suffered. It was at the end of last year, moreover, that a decisive sector of the front—precisely the one that you command—was turned into a grotesque east-west axis, away from the north-south direction which alone can be justified strategically. It now runs over a front of 450 miles, from Nikopol to Luzk, and is a veritable invitation for fragmentation and the formation of pockets. You, my dear Field Marshal, must surely realize and feel that it is a disgrace for German generals to "lead" their troops in such a way. What is the explanation for this declaration of bankruptcy on the part of the German generals? When did this sudden decline in their professional abilities take place? The military bankruptcy of the German generals is the natural result of decades of political and moral failure. Let us face the truth: for a mess of pottage, called rearmament, we sold our birthright to a régime inimical to the people, a régime *incapable* of winning the war and *certain* to subvert the generals, professionally and morally. Now the day of reckoning has come. The German generals who remain chained to a régime that works against the people have finished playing any role in the framework of the nation. With every passing day the people view them more and more as the accomplices of the corrupter, as the gravediggers of the nation. After Hitler's overthrow, the people will undoubtedly take every German general to task for his behavior during these fateful times. Do you believe the people will ask you then whether you have directed this or that individual military operation well? No! It will ask you: Field Marshal, did you know that the war was lost? Yes or no! And you will have to answer this question in the affirmative!

The people will ask you further: And although you knew that everything was pointless, you could still lead your armies into battle, into ruin, and bring down immeasurable, preventable misery upon the German people.

My dear Field Marshal, there is a limit beyond which obedience of orders has to be called a crime against the people. Do you want to bring this kind of historical verdict upon yourself?

I hope you will not have to. But you will not be able to avoid this fate unless you rescue at least the remnants of your men from being ruined by Hitler and unless you lead them against Hitler—for Germany!

You must be clear on one point, my dear Field Marshal: if *you* do not act, your *soldiers* will, and soon. And no one will have to ask the soldiers to act. The German people, however, will then stand united on *this* side and it will pronounce its harsh but just verdict against all those who failed: guilty!

(*Free Germany, No. 7, February 12, 1944*)

## VIII

### National Committee for a Free Germany

#### German Generals, Officers, and Soldiers!

At Hitler's orders, German soldiers destroy and ravage Russian cities and villages in the course of evacuating them; the population is being robbed and forcibly abducted to Germany. In all this, units of the SS and Special Commandos excel.

We can tell you as German patriots and men: Our people will have to pay dearly for these crimes!

Everyone knows today that Hitler's war is lost.

Such destruction can, therefore, no longer be justified by military necessity. It can serve only one purpose: to increase the hatred of the Russian people.

But it will not be Hitler who will have to rebuild everything that has been destroyed, but the German people.

What is Hitler's purpose for these orders? Nothing less than to direct the hatred of the people he attacked away from himself and onto our *Wehrmacht* and our people, to make them associates of his crimes and to make peaceful understanding all the more difficult.

Those guilty will be held responsible. Anyone who does not wish to be guilty also and who is willing to save our people from shame should refuse to carry out these criminal orders.

We know instances where German officers refused to obey immoral orders of the Führer.

Today we expect this attitude from every member of the Wehrmacht, general or private, if he cares about the honor and the reputation of his Fatherland.

The day Hitler's power collapses, only *he* and his accomplices should appear before the tribunal of history as the accused, not our German people.

Whoever does not prevent the carrying out of these orders by Adolf Hitler acts as an enemy of the German nation!

> The League of German Officers
> V. Seydlitz, General of Artillery
> [This manifesto bore the signatures of twenty-eight others, among whom were Daniels, Korfes, Lattmann, Hooven, Steidle, and Bredt.]

## IX

The National Committee to the People and the Wehrmacht

*Twenty-five Articles for Ending the War*

Today every German heart is moved by *one* question: How can we get out of this war? "The continuation of a senseless war would mean the end of the nation." That is what we stated in our manifesto of July 1943. Were we right then? Yes! Never before has every German, no matter where he is today, seen imminent danger so clearly before him.

Hitler has brought untold misery on the German people. We have to lead them out of that misery again. At this moment every German should know what he must do, for every one is needed. And every single one will have to render account for this moment, to his people, to his family, and to himself.

Remember that you were born as Germans, not as National Socialists. Then you will see the way before you. The Hitlers disappear, but the people remain.

These are the twenty-five articles for the termination of the war.

## Article 1

This war is Germany's greatest misfortune.

It was not the German people who wanted it. For thirty years political and economic speculators have pushed Germany along a path to suicide: 1914–1918, 1933, 1939–1944. This clique used Hitler to persuade the German people that they are a "master race" and that they need the "living space" of the "auxiliary peoples." By this "teaching" he pushed our hard-working people into a war of conquest against free peoples without parallel in history, and with cold calculation, he prevented them from setting their own house in order. And the German people in their simplicity provoked the anger of the entire world for the sake of the egoistical interests of their own parasites. For other people love freedom just as much as we do. For this reason they united and they are now smashing Hitler's régime and everything allied with it.

## Article 2

"If only Hitler had never led us against Russia!"

The German people sensed danger the moment it moved against Russia in 1941. It feared Russia's superiority. Yes, Russia is stronger than Germany. With powerful blows it throws the German armies westward, smashes them, encircles and annihilates their units. And its strength is growing irresistibly. "But that is impossible!" the officers shout, and then they perish. Anyone clinging to Russian soil will perish. And that *is* possible! For Russia is the largest country in the world, and its industry is more powerful than the industry of the entire European continent.

## Article 3

"If only Hitler had never tried to raze the British cities!"

By his blasphemous threat, Hitler has brought down on Germany the greatest air war in history. Our cities are turning into rubble, millions are wandering around without shelter. With every week the Anglo-American air forces' reign over German air space is becoming more complete and more devastating. The submarine war has failed too. The troops of the Allies have landed in the south and additional superior forces are assembling in the west ready for devastating blows. The Second Front is imminent and with it the rising of the peoples against Hitler's tyranny.

## Article 4

Reserves, too, are running short.

There are shortages of everything. There are shortages at the front. And shortages at home. The last men are being thrown into the jaws of war, and now even women and children. The last shreds of prosperity are transformed into tanks and guns. But still it is not enough. The peoples of the world that Hitler provoked are stronger, and they are getting stronger every day. Today Hitler's statement sounds like a mockery. "The possession of the Ukraine, the Donetz basin, and the Kuban will decide the outcome of the war." Germany was defeated when it still possessed those areas. How much faster will it meet its end now that it has lost them?

## Article 5

The truth is: the war is lost.

Gone forever are the millions of German men who expected a meaningful life for themselves; the millions of once happy families, dozens of once flourishing cities, Germany's strength and reputation. Who is responsible for this national tragedy? Did not the German officers and soldiers give everything they had to give? They are not the ones responsible; they are the victims. The guilty men are Hitler and Göring, criminals in political affairs, amateurs in military affairs.

## Article 6

To continue this lost war is a crime against the nation.

Its continuation pointlessly ruins the few things which still remain and thereby the potential for reconstruction. Everyone should therefore realize: anyone still standing on foreign soil is not defending Germany, but aiding in its complete destruction; anyone still supporting Hitler helps to weaken completely our Fatherland and to bring the horrors of war to Germany, into his own living room. He can no longer win the lost war—but in his blindness he can squander what might still be saved, his own life and the foundations of tomorrow. Soldiers of the Wehrmacht! The lost war is not your fault. But if you continue this lost war, you, too, will become guilty of ruining Germany.

## Article 7

Who needs the war to continue?

Only Hitler and his sponsors and cronies, with whom no one will conclude peace. They have forfeited their lives. That is why they want to fight until the last human beings and values are gone. "Until 5 minutes past 12," as they say. And because with all their instincts the people fight against dying with them, they attempt in every way, with terror and with deception, to force the people to die with them.

## Article 8

All the talk about disunity among the Allies is deception.

Month after month simpletons are waiting for a split in the Allies that never materializes. In its place there came the increasingly powerful blows of their increasingly greater unity. For months simpletons have been waiting for a compromise. But none was forthcoming nor will it be forthcoming. Hitler has not only provoked the governments but the peoples themselves. Peoples and governments are waging their war against him in close co-operation. The peoples shall not rest until the man who robbed them of their peace and liberty has been destroyed. The more he rages, the more unified and powerfully they will strike him down. Peace—with Hitler? Breathing space for the destroyer of peace? Now, of all times, when he is about to collapse? To raise the hope of disunity among the Allied powers is a deception deliberately fostered by Hitler.

## Article 9

All the talk about secret weapons is deception.

How often has Hitler already counted on the short memories of the soldiers? Where were the promised secret weapons at Stalingrad and on the Dnieper? They did not appear because they could not appear. There is no secret weapon and there never will be. The enemy has countered every German weapon with a more powerful counter-weapon. And *he* has the potential to mass-produce them. Hitler himself admits: "The scales are dipping in favor of our enemies." To promise secret weapons when the troops cannot even be sufficiently supplied with normal weapons is blatant and systematic fraud.

## Article 10

Hitler has led our people into a blind alley.

Some stand around helplessly. Others see the way out, but dare not speak up. In the meantime fate takes its course. The people are bleeding to death. Things are coming to an end. . . . Great German People! Are you really already too weak to get rid of a couple of Hitlers? Is there really no one to show you the way out of the misery and to lead you out?

## Article 11

There is such a force: the National Committee.

The National Committee accepts the legacy no matter how difficult it may be. It accepts the legacy with a proud sense of duty. For *that* is a truly national task. The committee assumes it, fully convinced that it will be successful. For it believes in the strength of our people. Contemptible are the pusillanimous souls who show by their inactivity that they no longer believe in their people. We realize that the people want life, peace, reconstruction, happiness. We realize that millions are prepared to end this lost war immediately if they are shown the force that will lead them out of it. To them we appeal: Forward! Germany is not lost unless *we* give it up for lost ourselves—provided we have the courage to liberate it from Hitler. To those who oppose us we say: You should be glad that there is a force which will accept the legacy of your wretchedness.

## Article 12

The National Committee's supreme guiding concept is to speak the truth!

Always and under all circumstances, be it pleasant or bitter. Only in this way can our deeply disappointed people regain the confidence that it will not be lied to again. What the National Committee has said yesterday was the truth. Events prove it. What the National Committee says today is the truth and it will be proved right tomorrow.

## Article 13

The National Committee does not promise an easy future.

There can be no easy future after this war. There will be mountains of rubble and mountains of work. And many things to renounce. And austerity for everyone, and iron controls. But also the joy of reconstruction. And joy in one's own, honest work. And joy in children who will be able to live. And joy in a dearly bought peace that we will never permit any warmonger to snatch from us again!

## Article 14

"Will the National Committee be strong enough?"

The National Committee is strong. And it grows stronger every day. For the will of the National Committee is the will of the people. Is there even one man in your unit who would seriously dare to gainsay the truth of our words? Are you not convinced yourself that the whole people will march with us once it knows about our existence and our intentions? The National Committee is strong—but it can never be too strong! Everyone who does not support us hurts us.

## Article 15

"Will there not be unemployment again after the war?"

You can answer yourself. Will there be a shortage or a surplus of men after the war? Will there be a shortage or a surplus of housing and goods? There will be no unemployment, but an enormous shortage of labor instead. The people whom the economy will then serve need every able hand. They will take good care of their specialists. They will educate the soldiers and officers whom Hitler left without an education and will direct them into new occupations. But they will remove from their corporations all the armament plutocrats, who are good for nothing except the bringing about of wars.

## Article 16

"Will there not be another, worse Versailles after the overthrow of Hitler?"

The decision still lies in the hands of the German people. There is a real danger that Germany will be dismembered and disenfranchised, and it is growing worse every day. The conditions of the peace will depend on *when* this war will be finished and by *whom*. The longer the German people obey Hitler and the German soldier clings to foreign soil, the harsher the conditions will be. The faster the German people rids itself of Hitler and the more powerfully it creates its own order, the more lenient the conditions will be. The fight against Hitler is, therefore, the fight against a harsh peace. The more energetically the German people create a new order in Germany, the less the foreign nations will interfere. Just imagine that the German people rose today in rebellion against Hitler. What would the nations say? Speechless at first, they would applaud the German people in its fight for liberty, would support it against the common enemy. A Versailles after that? One does not have to fear a Versailles from allies. People who continue to support Hitler, however, have to expect the worst.

### Article 17

"Will not all of us be held responsible?"

No one who has not become guilty will be held responsible. And even those who are guilty still hold their fate in their own hands. They can still prove, by action in the fight against Hitler, that they have changed. They can still gain the confidence of peace-loving nations, who will measure their guilt by the extent of their acts against Hitler.

### Article 18

"Will we be turned into Bolsheviks by Russia?"

Bolshevism is the reigning political system in the Soviet Union— not a bad one, apparently, or else it could not have turned backward Russia into the most powerful nation in the world. It is one of the basic principles of Bolshevism that Bolshevism cannot and must not be forced upon people who do not want it. Following this principle, the Soviet Union has never fought a war of aggression. It has concentrated its strength on internal affairs and has thus achieved its present power. The Soviet Union's leaders want the German people, too, to shape their destiny with their own abilities and in accord with their specific conditions.

### Article 19

"Will private property be abolished in Germany after the overthrow of Hitler?"

Legally acquired property will not be abolished after Hitler's overthrow; it will be restored. "Securing legally acquired property, restoring the possessions robbed by the National Socialist dictators to the rightful owners, confiscating the fortunes of those responsible for the war and of war profiteers," that is the way it reads in the National Committee's manifesto.

The expropriation you are worrying about so much is taking place on Hitler's orders today. The régime steals your property, closes the shops, demolishes the rest of your belongings by the bombings which it has provoked. Hitler's lie of the "threatening expropriation" is supposed to deceive you about the fact that he has already expropriated you and it is intended to prepare you for further sacrifices.

### Article 20

You ask: *"What can I do?"*

You understand the necessity of our fight? You want to take part in saving our Fatherland? We clasp your hand, as we accept everybody's who is honest and willing. We make a covenant with you for the fight against that criminal and enemy of the German people, Adolf Hitler. We will tell you what is to be done.

### Article 21

First objective: terminate the war.

An end to the great bleeding to death, the immediate termination of the war, is the precondition for everything else. Every German has to contribute to the termination of the war by actions. Workers, employees, employers—Hitler needs your work for his war. Farmers—Hitler uses up the remnants of your goods and chattels for his war. Wrest from his hands the means of continuing his war! Even the Gestapo is powerless against your solidarity. There is no spot from which Hitler's corrupting régime could not be unhinged. Soldiers, officers, generals—carry the spirit of our movement for liberty into your units. Unite under the flag of the National Committee for the fight against Hitler! We Germans have always excelled in discipline. If the people and the Wehrmacht unite for a disciplined fight against Germany's corrupter, Hitler and his die-hards will remain a tiny, isolated clique. To act against Hitler today is the only way to act patriotically. Tomorrow it will be the yardstick by which everything is measured. Now is the time to act intelligently without shrinking from danger.

### Article 22

The end of the war—the end of thirty unhappy years.

The war should bring about at least one good thing: an end to the past, an end to the eternally war-thirsty German attitude! Never again will it be allowed to survive the death of a faithful German youth. The returning soldiers and the people at home will start cleaning the German house without compromises. Warmongers, war profiteers, and incorrigible Hitlerites will receive no quarter! Away with every sort of accomplice and speculator! May the healthy strength of the German people finally uncoil itself! We are sick and tired of being the scapegoat among the nations for the sake of a few great capitalists!

### Article 23

The power to the people!

Let us put an end to the fear of the people, an end to the neglect of the people! There is no legislative power outside the people itself. They will order their ranks, their economy, their state, and they will spot with an infallible eye all the rotten elements, if nobody stops them from doing so. In truly free elections the people will elect their best men as their representatives. They will pass the constitution useful for them and will protect their well-being from the machinations of dethroned reaction with laws and the sword. The weakness of the Weimar Republic will not be repeated! The rule of the people is the rule of the individual willing to accept responsibility. Untrammeled in his development, his opinions, and their representation, he subordinates himself, of his own free will, to the higher will of the community. He learns from society, society learns from him. Only a people of free, disciplined human beings is the guarantor of the existence and the honor of the nation.

### Article 24

Back into the community of nations!

No people can live by itself. Woe to the nation which does not respect other nations. Woe to those Germans who still do not realize that the community of peace-loving nations is the mightiest organism on earth. Hitler has led us out of the community of nations. We allowed him to misuse us as a battering ram against that community of nations. For this we are being punished today, from every corner of the earth, by hate, contempt, destruction. The old Germany is perishing because of its own arrogance. Let us do away with that inbred, suicidal German arrogance! There is much we have to make up for. Let us draw some conclusions. Let us pave the way to a return into the family of peace-loving nations by honest work, orderliness, and justice. The nations will not deny their respect to a new Germany which respects other nations.

### Article 25

And now on to reconstruction!

How much strength and good faith have the German people now spent and lost on the worst cause on earth! What would Germany look like today if we had used this effort *for* Germany *in* Germany! Hitler will no longer be around, but a vast field of rubble will still be around. Is there any German who is not eager to rebuild his country? And why should the German people not be able to create for themselves a Fatherland worth living in? The world has seen us destroy. May it also see us rebuild!

These twenty-five articles appeal to every patriotic German. To you, German worker. To you, German farmer. To you, German soldier. To you, German scholar, artist, engineer, physician, and clergyman. To you, German official and employee. To you, German of the middle class whom Hitler has plunged into ruin. To you, German employer, whose business has been ruined by Hitler's insatiable wire-pullers. To you, unbowed Germans, who have always fought against Hitler. To you, former National Socialists, who have learned to know and to hate Hitler.

Germans of all ranks of society, you have to unite, as we are united in the National Committee for a Free Germany, united by *one* will—against Hitler, Hitler's clique, and Hitler's war!

Save Germany! Long live Germany! Action is everything! Contemptible is he who hesitates! Hitler must fall—that Germany may live!

*(Free Germany, No. 10, March 5, 1944)*

## X

## TO ALL CHRISTIANS AT THE FRONT AND AT HOME

Appeal of the Clergymen in the Free Germany Movement

We, the priests and officials of the Catholic and Protestant Churches and of the Free Churches of Germany, unanimously united in the determination to serve in faithful obedience our Lord, Jesus Christ, and His Church, and to help our people in active loyalty, have decided, after serious discussion, by free decision, and on our own responsibility, to direct the following appeal to all Christians of the Catholic and Protestant Churches at the front and at home:

With ardent care we sympathize with the fate of our nation. The bloody final battles of this war are now raging on all fronts. At home the atmosphere of decline and the mental agonies are increasing to the point of despair. The present situation is the result of a disastrously wrong political path which Germany has followed under Hitler's leadership. Millions are taking their refuge in the faith of the Lord while their confidence in the military and political leadership of Hitler is breaking down. The Church owes pastoral consolation and the showing of a clear way to these millions in this present hour. We, the servants of the Church, want to fulfill this task in obedience to the word of the Lord and His law, out of our special recognition of the situation. In this we are certain that our bishops, as well as our colleagues at home and at the front, recognize fully the extent of their present responsibility and that they will act in their positions as we are acting here. The Church can take upon itself this duty with a clean conscience, all the more so as it has boldly opposed the unbounded megalomania of the National Socialist leaders in a grave struggle over more than ten years and since it has warned about the coming catastrophe.

In unbridled arrogance Hitler has lit the firebrands of this war. With frivolous candor he has propagated as his war aims the conquest and rape of foreign countries. For the sake of these corrupt goals— without any moral justification and only to prolong his tyranny—he makes millions of German men bleed to death at the front, and at home he exposes flourishing cities, indeed even women and children, to the destruction of aerial warfare. He brings shame upon the honor of Germany's name by unheard-of atrocities in the occupied countries and by bloody terrorism against his own people. These are the products of an ideology which has deified Hitler and blasphemed the Lord, worshipped race and blood and mocked Christ, glorified force and broken the law, persecuted the faith and outlawed love.

In a mighty judgment of the Lord the truth of the biblical saying becomes clear today: "Be not deceived; God is not mocked; for whatsoever a man soweth, that shall he also reap." (Gal. 6:7.)

You can no longer remain silent to all this! For to remain silent is to become guilty, too, and to betray the commandment of Christ to His Church. It is the duty of every Christian to be a witness of God's judgment and God's commandments to the deceivers and the deceived. It is the duty of every Christian in obedience to the Lord's commands to do penance, to keep his conscience clean and his honor unsoiled. But no German and no Christian can achieve that by passively waiting for a miracle! Ward off the feelings of ruin and of passive despair out of the strength of our Christian faith; fight with a praying heart, with candid words and determined action, for immediate peace and for the liberty and salvation of our people. It is up to you to prevent the world's judgment on Hitler from becoming simultaneously its verdict on the German people. By overthrowing Hitler you must pave the way for the German nation into a new future. Join therefore, like us, the struggle of the German liberation movement! Join in the fighting and work of the people's committees of the Free Germany movement! They are the pillars of the liberation and renewal of Germany! No oath can block the path to this fight, for your oath, sworn before the Lord, only obliges you to serve our people. The fight for the existence of our nation will be decided in the everyday affairs at the front and at home. Therefore: Oppose National Socialism, that antichrist and corrupter of the people, with the life of an active Christian confessor!

National Socialism blocks the German people's path to a reasonable peace by fantastic lies about the intentions the enemy powers supposedly have of destroying Germany. Opposing this, it is your duty as Christians to bear witness to truth everywhere and at any time, according to the word of the Gospel: "Wherefore putting away lying, speak every man truth with his neighbor . . ." (Eph. 4:25.)

National Socialism demands that you hate and contemn the upright brethren of our own people, the freedom-loving citizens of the occupied countries, and the foreign and captured workers in German factories and on German farms. It is your Christian duty, in opposition to this demand, to practice love everywhere and at all times and to help those who are oppressed, for the Gospel warns us: "For he shall have judgment without mercy, that hath shewed no mercy; . . ." (James 2:13.)

At the front and at home, National Socialism expects crimes and acts of brutality from German men. It is your Christian duty, in opposition to this expectation, to refuse to obey everywhere and at all times, for the Gospel commands that: "We ought to obey God rather than men." (Acts 5:29.)

National Socialism persecutes Christian faith and freedom of conscience. It is your Christian duty, in opposition to this, to bear witness to your Christian faith everywhere and at all times, and to preserve your liberty of conscience, for Christ said: "Whosoever therefore shall confess me before men, him will I confess also before my Father which is in heaven. But whosoever shall deny me before men, him will I also deny before my Father which is in heaven." (Matt. 10:32–33.) Only in this way can you fulfill your Christian duty today, bound by the holy commandments of the Lord!

Do not fear danger, adversity or death! Germany is at stake! We are certain of victory! Our strength be the prayer:

My shield and my faith are you, O God and Lord!
In you alone I will trust; do never leave me alone
So that I may remain faithful, your servant at all times,
And banish that tyranny which has wounded my heart!

[This appeal was signed by twenty-five Catholic and Protestant clergymen, identified by both military rank and ecclesiastical connection.]

(Free Germany II, No. 29, July 16, 1944)

## XI

*We, the generals and commanders of the former Army Group Center, united by long military service and by our participation in two great wars, appeal to you at a fateful hour for the German people. Our recent battles and especially the defeat of Army Group Center, which has finally decided the war, have led us to the firm conviction of the hopelessness of further fighting and, therefore, to this appeal.*

### THE TRUTH ABOUT THE SITUATION ON THE EASTERN FRONT

The German people, remembering the tested policies of Bismarck, heaved a sigh of relief when the pact of nonaggression and friendship with the Soviet Union was signed in late August and early September 1939. The German attack in the summer of 1941 was chiefly justified by the claim that the Red Army posed a threat. This version is disproved by the fact that the Soviet Union completed its total mobilization only by winter of 1941. It is refuted even further by the utterances of German propaganda during the early fall of 1942, at the height of our alleged successes. It was candidly stated there that the German campaign in the east was fought for German economic goals.

At any rate: the beginning of the war against Soviet Russia by our leaders was the beginning of our decline.

We had some sorry achievements by bluff, like the *Anschluss* of Austria and the Sudeten area, the occupation of Czechoslovakia. After quick victories we occupied Poland, Denmark, Norway, the Netherlands, Belgium, and France.

But we learned the true harshness of war only in Russia. The costly victories of summer and fall 1941 had been only phantom victories against border troops and the first line of the Red Army, which protected the mobilization of the Soviet Union's manpower and material resources. The vast Russian spaces also became our enemy as we advanced.

And then, with the winter of 1941–1942, the *visible* decline began. It is marked, in an order of increasing significance and in general outline, by the following battles and defeats:

a) Winter 1941–1942. Rostov, Moscow, Tikvin.

The reasons: Only now did the first significant reserves of Russia's total mobilization see combat. But in spring 1942 we were told that the Red Army had bled itself to death during the winter battles.

b) Winter 1942–1943. The catastrophe of Stalingrad and the collapse of the whole Caucasus and Don front.

The reasons: Despite the expected additional increases in strength of the Red Army, the German Supreme Command had launched an eccentric attack on the oil fields of the Caucasus and against the lower Volga River during the summer of 1942. It had thus split its forces. The assignment to cover the deep, threatened flank near the Don River had been entrusted mainly to its allies—without any reserves worth mentioning—whose inferior fighting strength and, particularly, inferior equipment was known.

c) Summer 1943. Failure of the German offensive against the bulge at Kursk-Orel with heavy losses and the subsequent decisive Russian offensive all the way to the Dnieper River.

The reasons: The German attack was directed against massed Russian forces preparing their own offensive. Thus our best divisions, which should have served as reserves for the defense against the Russian offensive, were smashed before they could be used in defense.

d) Winter 1943–1944. Smashing of the German front in the south, loss of the Dnieper line, the pockets at Cherkassy, Kirovograd, Nikopol, Uman, Tarnopol, the loss of the Crimea.

The reasons: We no longer had a stable front. The German forces were always outflanked, encircled, and defeated as isolated units.

e) Russian summer offensive of 1944 against Army Group Center leading to the annihilation of thirty divisions, *i.e.*, of almost the whole army group (the entire Fourth Army, the bulk of the Ninth Army, and the Third Armored [Panzer] Army). During these unequal battles, twenty-one generals, including ourselves, were captured by the Russians; more than ten were killed in action.

The reasons for this new defeat: Erroneous estimates of the enemy's operational potential and intentions. Front position menaced from the flanks since winter, lack of reserves and air support. In short, Army Group Center became the victim of a hazardous gamble of our leaders.

At the time of this writing, Russian armies are approaching the Reich's frontiers through a breach of more than 300 miles. They are standing at Dünaburg, at Kaunas, in Grodno, and at Brest.

They have now also launched an attack farther south, have crossed the Polish river Bug on a front of considerable extensions, and are now located close to Lemberg after trapping several divisions. This is the beginning of the inevitable collapse of the southern sector of the eastern front, too.

Army Group North is still holding its positions, where it is not also feeling the Russian attack on Dünaburg, and is in danger of being cut off.

The German Supreme Command has not breathed a word as yet to the German people about the annihilation of Army Group Center. The OKW and other reports have, until now, mentioned only individual localities, moving ever closer to the Reich's frontiers, straightening out of front lines, retreats according to plan, and troops that are fighting their way back, trying to establish contacts westward. But in fact, these troops, insofar as they are former units of Army Group Cented, have long since been trapped, destroyed, or captured. The Führer and German propaganda, however, are trying to conceal the true situation on the eastern front from the German people, to keep them pliable to their attempts to continue the war.

The latest radio news about the assassination attempt against Hitler proves that the military crisis has already developed into a political crisis and that Germany does have men in this situation who are capable and determined to eliminate Hitler from the position of leadership.

## THE REASONS FOR THESE DEFEATS

They are essentially rooted in the adventuristic political and strategic leadership of Adolf Hitler.

a) Hitler misjudged the Soviet Union's power from the start. Caught up in this prejudice, he fell prey to this error again and again. He therefore declared, on several occasions in 1941 and 1942, that victory in the east had already been won and, later, that the offensive strength of the Red Army had now been smashed. This evaluation of enemy strength deceived the people and the army again and again.

b) The expected *lightning* victory over Russia failed to materialize and the subsequent German defeats, becoming more and more momentous in their consequences, gave the Allied enemies so much time that by now, in addition to the air war on Germany, the Second Front in France and Italy has become a reality. Hitler has thus maneuvered Germany into a two-front war that must lead to the inevitable defeat of the Reich.

c) As of late fall 1942, the Red Army had wrested the initiative from the hands of the German High Command for good. From now on the German command limited itself to an attitude of wait and see and to an attempt to defend inflexibly every inch of ground, even without reserves worth mentioning, to delay the impending catastrophe. Experienced and meritorious generals, who were incapable of reconciling the erroneous and inflexible methods of leadership with their consciences, were sent home.

d) Because of these methods of leadership, the best German forces were being squandered beyond repair. There was and is no relief and no rest. The troops are constantly overtaxed psychologically and physically. Thus a Germany filled with horror finds itself at the edge of the abyss, today, because of the political and military guidance of Adolf Hitler and his immediate entourage. They have promised certain victory to the German people again and again. They are deceiving the German people by concealing from it the truth and reality which they dare not admit in order to conceal their errors and crimes.

## WHAT IS THE WAY OUT?

1. Adolf Hitler and his closest accomplices want to continue the war according to the slogan "Victory or Death." This slogan, especially stressed most recently, shows that they themselves no longer believe in victory. The present situation on the eastern front and its imminent final collapse can no longer be altered. This will have its effects on the future battles in the west, where the British and the Americans are going to use additional new forces and equipment.

Under these conditions the continuation of the war means further pointless sacrifices and losses, that the war will end on German soil, and, therefore, that the German people and their means of existence will be destroyed.

2. The only alternative for any general and officer aware of his responsibility to the people must be the quick termination of the war.

The captured soldiers of Army Group Center are of the same opinion. In a speech of July 20, after the assassination attempt against him, Hitler spoke of a "stab in the back" comparable to 1918. The reference to 1918 does not, however, hold water. *Then* our rear in the east was not threatened. The Western Powers were themselves on the brink of exhaustion. But *today* our situation is much worse. Superior forces are advancing against us on all fronts.

Even 1918 had at least left us with the chance for a rebirth which has been destroyed completely by the increasing lack of moderation in National Socialist politics.

There is still a chance now to end the war before it engulfs and destroys Germany. The stab in the German nation's back was struck long ago by the political and military leadership of Adolf Hitler and his closest collaborators, who have led us into this catastrophe and have thus betrayed us.

The whole German people must not, therefore, be sacrificed to the illusion that our leaders must be allowed an honorable exit. Loyalty to the "eternal nation" must rank above the vassal's obligations to a temporal and bankrupt form of government and its supporters.

For these reasons every German general and officer has the following obligations:

a) To divorce himself completely from Hitler and his clique.

b) To refuse to carry out orders by Hitler and his representatives.

c) To cease immediately all hostilities and senseless bloodshed.

These tasks must be courageously explained to the soldiers.

The honest German soldier in the fighting line, together with his officers, has had to bear bravely the consequences of this insolent leadership. Together we shall also remain loyal to the German people.

Today Hitler has strengthened the position of Himmler and his SS and Gestapo even more. But for the sake of the German people this must not deter anyone from pursuing the goals named above.

One always had to assume that the present leaders would not give up their place willingly. But the future course of the war will soon bring Germany's internal problems to a head.

All generals and officers who accept their responsibility are now confronted by the alternative of *either waiting* until Hitler has ruined them and the German Wehrmacht and has pulled the entire German nation into his grave with him, *or* of answering force with force, of opposing Hitler, of refusing obedience to his orders, of putting an end to Hitler's régime, and thus to the war.

Do not wait until Hitler has ruined you!

To stand up against Hitler is to stand up for Germany!

VÖLCKERS, General of the Infantry and Commanding General of the XXVIIth Army Corps

FREIHERR VON LÜTZOW, Lieutenant General, in charge of command of the XXXVth Army Corps

MÜLLER, Lieutenant General and Second in Command of the XIIth Army Corps

BAMLER, Lieutenant General and Commander of the 12th Infantry Division

GOLLWITZER, General of the Inf. and Comm. Gen. of the LIIIrd Army Corps

TRAUT, Lieut. Gen. and Cdr. of the 78th Assault Division

KLAMMT, Major Gen. and Cdr. of the 260th Inf. Div.

GOTTFRIED VON ERDMANNSDORFF, Major Gen. and Cdr. of Fortress Mogilev

CONRADY, Major Gen. and Cdr. of the 36th Inf. Div.

ENGEL, Major Gen. and Cdr. of the 45th Inf. Div.

TROWITZ, Major Gen. and Cdr. of the 57th Inf. Div.

MICHAELIS, Major Gen. and Cdr. of the 95th Inf. Div.

SCHMIDT, Major Gen. and Army Pioneer Commander 9

MÜLLER-BÜLOW, Major Gen. and Cdr. of the 246th Inf. Div.

VON STEINKELLER, Major Gen. Cdr. of the "Feldherrnhalle"

GIHR, Major Gen. and Cdr. of the 707th Inf. Div.

I have personally copied the proclamation on behalf of those generals who have signed it in person.

July 22, 1944            Bamler
                 Lieutenant General and Cdr.
                 of the 12th Inf. Div.

*(Free Germany, No. 31, July 30, 1944)*

## XII

### National Committee for a Free Germany
### To Army Group Narva

*Generals and Officers of Army Group Narva!*

Show the courage and the honesty of this decisive hour by telling your officers and soldiers the truth and leading them onto the path to safety, the path against Hitler.

Our German nation will thank you for it one day.

Army Group Center has been crushed. The Russians have smashed their way through to the borders of East Prussia. Army Group North is cut off. It is threatened by total encirclement.

A new front has sprung up on your right flank, twice the length of the old one, without any prepared positions, without sufficient troops. The position of Army Group North is untenable.

Hitler no longer has any reserves. Recklessly your front line divisions were thrown everywhere: to the open flank, to the central sector, and to the Finnish front, which has been battered no less than your own. Insufficient forces have been dissipated.

The radio general, Dittmar, is already talking openly about a shortening of the front. But it is no longer possible today to lead you out of this gigantic pocket. Where to? Into the great pocket of Germany? Hitler has already written off your units along the Narva River.

Remember Stalingrad, Korsun, Cherkassy, and the Crimea, where Hitler has led armies and divisions into positions as untenable as your own. With deceptive promises he put them off until they were sacrificed completely. To continue to follow Hitler is to give up oneself and Germany.

What is to be done?

You have already waited too long. The only thing left to you now is to save your lives for the Fatherland by joining the cause of the National Committee for a Free Germany against Hitler's orders to die.

Do not hesitate. It is too late if you recognize the senselessness of continued fighting only on the point of death. Enlighten your fellow soldiers now. Listen to, read, and spread the broadcasts of Radio Free Germany, the newspaper of the National Committee for a Free Germany, its leaflets and its loudspeaker appeals on the main fighting line. Make contact with me through your representatives. All necessary precautions for their safety have been arranged with the Red Army.

None of you must die in senseless combat from now on. Defect to the field posts of the National Committee for a Free Germany before the devastating attack starts. Save what is left of matériel and blood and German honor. Do not carry out Hitler's orders, make the continuation of his war impossible and thereby the continuation of the sacrifices. You have a daily opportunity to do so.

Unite into Wehrmacht Free Germany groups in your own units together with active fellow soldiers. These groups will take over the leadership of your units and will silence Hitlerite officers and soldiers.

Do not wait to be helped by others. You yourself must act to save yourself. Down with Hitler! Down with the pointless continuation of a lost war. For safety and peace. For a free, independent Germany!

Front delegate of the National Committee for a Free Germany

Second Lieutenant E. Kehler

## XIII

*To the German people in arms and at home!*

We, the generals and commanders of the former Army Group Southern Ukraine, who have done our duty as soldiers toward our men and the German people until the end, now take the opportunity to candidly utter our thoughts, as prisoners of war, about the present hopeless military situation of Germany, and we appeal below to the German nation in arms and at home.

We are some of the accidentally surviving eyewitnesses of the latest and most grievous defeat suffered by the German Wehrmacht on the eastern front's southern wing in Roumania. After smashing Army Group Center and cutting off Army Group North, the Russian army completely crushed Army Group Southern Ukraine within ten days at the end of August 1944 and destroyed the Sixth and Eighth Armies. This means a loss of twenty divisions. The political and military situation in the Balkans has been fundamentally altered by this defeat. Roumania and Bulgaria, our allies up to now, have turned into enemies and are now fighting against us. We have lost the last strong points on the Black Sea, together with the fleet, as well as the oil fields and the food supplies of Roumania. A new, strong front of states has formed itself in the southeast which has now entered the war against Germany.

Together with them, the people of Yugoslavia and Slovakia, who have risen up in rebellion, are fighting against us.

In the north, Finland has surrendered.

We have lost occupied France and Belgium.

The Anglo-American armies have reached German soil.

In the east, too, fighting is already in progress on German territory.

Even now Germany has already completely lost the war. Its continuation has become pointless for Germany and must lead to its ruin.

We have read the appeal of seventeen generals of Army Group Center of July 22, 1944, addressed to the generals and officers of the German Wehrmacht. We think their conclusions are accurate, since we have been convinced by the same painful experiences that they had.

The activities of Hitler and his collaborators have led to a complete catastrophe for the German Wehrmacht and for Germany as a country. Hitler and his supporters will lead Germany into chaos unless they are eliminated immediately.

There is only one obstacle between the German people and peace: Hitler and his supporters. German people and fellow soldiers of the

Wehrmacht! Decide Germany's fate yourself, before it is too late!

Do not carry out any orders by Hitler and his supporters!

Eliminate Hitler and his régime by force of arms!

Terminate the war as quickly as possible so that Germany and the German people may be saved!

Direct all arms against Hitler!

> POSTEL, Lt. Gen. and Command. Gen. XXXth Army Corps
>
> WEINKNECHT, Lt. Gen. Cdr. of the 79th Inf. Div.
>
> GEBB, Major Gen. and Cdr. of the 9th Inf. Div.
>
> COUNT V. HÜLSEN, Major Gen. and Cdr. of the 370th Inf. Div.
>
> V. BOGEN, Major Gen. and Cdr. of the 302nd Inf. Div.
>
> STINGLE, Major Gen. and Cdr. of Jassy
>
> V. BISSING, Colonel and head of the 76th Inf. Div.
>
> RINGENBERG, Colonel and head of the 106th Inf. Div.
>
> BURCKHARDT, Lt. Gen. and Commandant of Communications Zone Sixth Army
>
> SCHWARZ, Lt. Gen. and Cdr. of the 376th Div.
>
> FRENKING, Major Gen. Cdr. of the 282nd Inf. Div.
>
> TRONNIER, Major Gen. Cdr. of the K.A.F.
>
> V. DEWITZ-KREBS, Major Gen., Commandant of Kishinev
>
> HIELSCHER, Colonel and head of the 258th Inf. Div.
>
> SIMON, Colonel and Cdr. of the 15th Flak Div.

The proclamation has been copied by me personally on behalf of the generals and troop commanders who have signed it in person.

> COUNT VON HÜLSEN
> Major Gen. and Cdr. of the 370th Inf. Div.

(Free Germany, No. 40, October 1, 1944)

## XIV

National Committee for a Free Germany and League of German Officers

Make up your minds!
Smash the terror of the Party!
Only this way will peace come!

Front line soldiers!

The Allies' guns are already roaring at Cologne, at Trier, on the lower Rhine, and under the gates of the Saarpfalz! Russian troops have already reached East Prussia and are within reach of Upper Silesia.

Desperately the population is fleeing for the center of the Reich from all its borders.

Helplessly our whole country lies open before the concentric Allied attacks on land and from the air.

In this final phase of the war the decision rests solely in the hands of the Wehrmacht.

How long do you intend to continue this pointless, already lost war for Hitler?

Are millions of Germans, and you yourself, too, to be driven to their deaths?

You alone can in fact decide this question!

Every day you hesitate about reaching a decision means another day of war on German soil from now on.

Fellow soldiers!

Think of your families, your mothers, wives, and children!

It is truly a matter of life and death!

Therefore your decision can only be one: End the war!

Organize against Hitler! Stop it all at the front! Use your arms to chase the pestilence of Hitler from our country! Eliminate by force that whole parasitic brood: the Gauleiter, the Kreisleiter, the SS, the Gestapo, and all the hyenas of the party, for they alone are interested in continuing the war.

Unite with all truly patriotic men and women, democrats and antifascists! Fight with us, with every weapon, in the great *mass movement* for a Free Germany against Hitler and for freedom and a true democracy!

Only this way will peace come!

STEIDLE, Colonel and Regimental Cdr., Grenadier Reg. 767 of the 376th Inf. Div.
Delegate of the National Committee for a Free Germany and Vice-President of the League of German Officers

The representatives of the National Committee for a Free Germany

ULLRICH, Sec. Lt. . . .

LOSCHE, Sec. Lt. and Company Cdr. . . .

*National Committee 121 October '44*

XV

## TO THE PEOPLE AND THE WEHRMACHT

Moscow, December 8, 1944

*Germans!*

Filled with deep concern about the future of our people, our dearly beloved country, and the continued existence of Germany we, the German generals, together with many hundreds of thousands of soldiers and officers captured in Russia, appeal to you, men and women of Germany, at this late hour.

You have our most sincerely felt sympathy in your desperate efforts amidst incredibly costly defensive battles, in your superhuman efforts, and in your increasing deprivations. Our whole population, without exception, has now been cast into the devastating struggle: on all fronts men are dying, from old men to boys, at home women and children are suffering from tough labor assignments and the increasing force of enemy air attacks. Never before has a war brought such unspeakable misery to our Fatherland! The hour of the collapse under the overwhelming superiority of the united enemies is drawing closer and closer.

Adolf Hitler has led Germany into this situation!

He has deceived our people with nationalistic and social promise. He eliminated unemployment only by enormous armament production, while we saw in it a general economic boom. Even then we put up with the atrocities committed against our own people, the elimination of law and order, the arrogance of racism, the fight against religion, and the corruption among the party leaders.

In the flush of the early successes we did not recognize the grave dangers of Hitler's immoderate plans, which have led us into this terrible war. We have been deceived and abused. We were his blind tools and have finally become his victims.

Hitler the politician has created an unchecked tyranny at home. He has broken all treaties concluded with other nations and has used the German Wehrmacht, relying on its obedient loyalty, for his plans of conquest and for the suppression of other nations. On his orders Himmler's henchmen have committed inhuman atrocities in the occupied countries and have thus covered with shame the honor of Germany's name in the eyes of the world.

This policy of broken treaties and crass violations of international law has finally united all the nations of the world in the war against Germany. After the elimination of our experienced military commanders and Hitler's complete taking over of the supreme command, defeat has followed defeat ever since Stalingrad.

There is no longer any hope for a change in the situation! No power in the world will negotiate with Hitler any more!

The war is lost!

For Germany the results of Adolf Hitler's political and military leadership are millions dead, crippled, and without shelter! Families have been separated; hunger and starvation, cold and sickness approach threateningly.

Hitler nevertheless wants to continue the war. Himmler and Goebbels are painting vivid pictures of terror and fear of enemies' revenge, of the alleged Bolshevik terror, and of the slavery of our whole people in a bleak future. They are appealing to feelings of patriotism, to love of one's country and of the Fatherland, and are thus whipping the German nation into a fight of desperation to the point of self-sacrifice.

This suicidal continuation of a war that has become pointless can only help save Hitler and his party's leaders. That is why SS and party have usurped all important positions of leadership.

But our people must not perish! This war must, therefore, be terminated immediately! You ask: but what comes after it?

Our Fatherland will indeed be occupied by the enemy, but the pointless dying at the front and at home will be stopped and our homes and places of work, which have still remained, will be saved!

The victors will indeed demand reparations for the injustices done to their peoples but only those who have been guilty of crimes against the laws of civilization and humanity will face trial!

Our future will be difficult, of course; we shall have to work, to rebuild, but there will also be a path leading upward again.

Instead of terror, tyranny, and racism, law, order, and humanity will rule.

Instead of misery and horror without end, there will be peace. Step by step our hard work and honest goodwill will bring us closer to the day on which the German people will once again take their free and equal place among the other nations.

In 1918 Hindenburg and Ludendorff demanded an end to the war when it had become militarily hopeless because of the enemy's superiority. For the same reason we, the generals captured by the Russians, together with many hundreds of thousands of soldiers and officers who have united in the Free Germany movement, call upon you: All our thoughts and emotions are directed only toward the fate of the German people!

GERMAN PEOPLE! RISE UP TO THE SAVING ACT against Hitler and Himmler, against their system, which has brought evil!

United in all your ranks you have strength! You also have the arms necessary to act!

LIBERATE YOURSELF from this irresponsible and criminal government which is leading Germany into certain ruin!

END THE WAR before the united attack of the Allied enemies

destroys the Wehrmacht and the rest of whatever has remained intact at home.

There are no miracles that can help us now.

Germans! Restore the honor of Germany's name before the world by an act of courage and THUS TAKE THE FIRST STEP INTO A BETTER FUTURE!

> PAULUS, Field Marshal General and former Commander in Chief Sixth Army (Stalingrad)
>
> V. SEYDLITZ, Gen. of the Art. and LIst Army Corps (Stalingrad); President of the League of German Officers; Vice-President of the National Committee for a Free Germany
>
> STRECKER, Colonel Gen. and former Cdr. Gen. XIth Army Corps (Stalingrad)
>
> HELL, Gen. of the Art. and former Cdr. Gen. VIIth Army Corps
>
> VÖLCKERS, Gen. of the Inf. and former Cdr. Gen. XXVIIth Army Corps
>
> GOLLWITZER, Gen. of the Inf., former Cdr. Gen. LIIIrd Army Corps
>
> SCHLÖMER, Lt. Gen. and former head XIVth Panzer Corps (Stalingrad)
>
> POSTEL, Lt. Gen. and former Cdr. Gen. XXXth Army Corps
>
> MÜLLER (Vinzenz), Lt. Gen. and former head XIIth Army Corps
>
> HOFFMEISTER, Lt. Gen. and former head XXXXIst Panzer Corps
>
> FRHR. VON LÜTZOW, Lt. Gen. and former head XXXVth Army Corps
>
> EDLER VON DANIELS, Lt. Gen. and Cdr. 376th Inf. Div. (Stalingrad)
>
> MÜLLER, Ludwig, General of the Inf. and former Cdr. Gen. XXXXIVth Army Corps
>
> BAYER, Lt. Gen. and former Cdr. 153rd *Feldausbildungsdivision*
>
> HITTER, Lt. Gen. and former Cdr. 206th Inf. Div.
>
> BUSCHENHAGEN, Gen. of the Inf. and former Cdr. Gen. LIInd Army Corps

BÖHME, Lt. Gen. and former Cdr. 73rd Inf. Div.

VON KUROWSKI, Lt. Gen. and former Cdr. 110th Inf. Div.

ARNO VON LENSKI, Major Gen. and former Cdr. 24th Panzer Division (Stalingrad)

LEYSER, Major Gen. and former Cdr. 29th Inf. Div. (mot.) (Stalingrad)

[The names of thirty more officers were appended to this document.]

(*Free Germany*, *No. 50, December 10, 1944*)

# Notes

## CHAPTER ONE: *Stalingrad*

[1] That events and experiences of Stalingrad were of decisive importance for the National Committee and the League of German Officers was attested by W. v. Seydlitz, H. Abel, H. Gerlach, Schlömer, W. Frhr. v. Senfft-Pilsach, A. Bredt, J. Wieder, and I. v. Knobelsdorff-Brendenhoff, among others. Cf. also Otto Korfes, "Zur Geschichte des National-komitees 'Freies Deutschland,'" in: *Zeitschrift für Geschichtswissenschaft*, 6 (1958), 1287, 1290. This article is almost completely based on Weinert's book on the National Committee (cf. the list of sources and secondary material). It follows partisan doctrines with noticeable timidity. The emotionalism of the presentation renders it almost useless, and it is further impaired by biased judgments. But since Korfes was a member of the presidium of the League of German Officers his statements have to be used at least where he recalls personal experiences.

[2] Hitler seemed to believe that Reichenau and his Sixth Army could conquer heaven itself (Poltava 1941). Heinz Schröter, *Stalingrad*, Osnabrück, n.d., p. 13.

[3] Cf. especially Kurt v. Tippelskirch, *Geschichte des Zweiten Weltkriegs*, Bonn 1951, pp. 81f., 87, 95, 100, 102, 211, 218ff., 231ff., 278ff.; Walter Görlitz, *Der Zweite Weltkrieg*, Stuttgart 1951, I, pp. 119ff.; Schröter, *op. cit.*, pp. 9ff., 14ff., 255ff., 335ff.

[4] V. Tippelskirch, *op. cit.*, p. 281.

[5] Herbert Selle, *Die Tragödie von Stalingrad*, Hannover 1948, p. 3; Walther von Seydlitz, *Wer ist schuld an Deutschlands Unglück?* (1945), p. 4.

[6] Selle, *op. cit.*; Joachim Wieder, *Die Tragödie von Stalingrad*, Deggendorf 1955, p. 17.

[7] Selle, *op. cit.*; Wieder, *op. cit.*

[8] V. Seydlitz, *op. cit.*, p. 4.

[9] V. Tippelskirch, *op. cit.*, p. 287; v. Seydlitz, *op. cit.*, p. 5; Selle, *op. cit.*, p. 3; Wieder, *op. cit.*, p. 19.

[10] V. Tippelskirch, *op. cit.*; in greater detail: v. Seydlitz, *op. cit.*, pp. 4f.

[11] V. Seydlitz, *op. cit.*, p. 5; cf. also v. Tippelskirch, *op. cit.*, p. 287 and Selle, *op. cit.*, p. 3.

[12] V. Tippelskirch, *op. cit.*; Günter Toepke, *Stalingrad—wie es wirklich war*, Stade 1949, p. 31; cf.

also Clemens Podewils, *Don und Wolga,* Munich 1952, pp. 124ff., 131ff., 164ff.

13 Personal communication of W. v. Seydlitz.

14 V. Seydlitz, *Wer ist* . . . . , p. 7.

15 Wieder, *op. cit.,* pp. 19f.; Selle, *op. cit.,* p. 4; v. Seydlitz, *op. cit.,* p. 8.

16 Cf. footnote 15. This aspect is also stressed in an exposé on the Battle of Stalingrad by Field Marshal Paulus. I am indebted to Herr Ernst Alexander Paulus, who communicated to me some facts taken from his father's description at my request. The materials from the estate of the Sixth Army's commander were not available for this study. Information supplied by E.A. Paulus is cited below as: Communications from the materials of the estate of Field Marshal Paulus: E.A. Paulus, except in those cases where I used the notes of personal recollections of Ernst Alexander Paulus. For the second edition of this book the materials from the estate of Field Marshal Paulus which had been published in the meantime were checked and used. They corroborate on all points the communications of E.A. Paulus. A summary reference may thereon suffice: Paulus, *Ich stehe hier auf Befehl!,* Frankfurt a. M. 1960.

17 V. Seydlitz, *op. cit.,* p. 6; also v. Tippelskirch, *op. cit.,* pp. 287f.

18 V. Seydlitz, *op. cit.,* pp. 6f.

19 *Op. cit.,* p. 7; v. Tippelskirch, *op. cit.,* p. 288.

20 Cf. v. Tippelskirch, *op. cit.,* p. 311.

21 Cf. Kurt v. Tippelskirch, "Operative Führungsentschlüsse im Höhepunkten des Landkrieges," in: *Bilanz des Zweiten Weltkrieges,* Oldenburg/Hamburg 1953, pp.

56ff; Erich v. Manstein, *Verlorene Siege,* pp. 322ff.

22 V. Tippelskirch, *Geschichte* . . . , p. 312; Görlitz, *op. cit.,* pp. 395ff.; Selle, *op. cit.,* p. 6; Selle, *Stalingrad damals—und heute* (1949), p. 1; Wieder, *op. cit.,* p. 15.

23 At this time the Sixth Army had not yet been cut off as virtually all the literature on Stalingrad insists, dramatizing events. It is correct that General Paulus himself reported over the radio on the evening of November 22 that the army had been cut off (cf. Schröter, *op. cit.,* p. 81). This statement itself is, however, not accurate. Personal communication of W. v. Seydlitz; Communications from the materials of the estate of Field Marshal Paulus: E.A. Paulus.

24 This is the text of the radio message according to Schröter, *op. cit.,* p. 68. No date is given; the actual date is November 22. This is stated accurately only on p. 86.

25 Personal communication of W. v. Seydlitz; Wieder, *op. cit.,* p. 24; Communications from the materials of the estate of Field Marshal Paulus: E.A. Paulus. Concerning the strength of the Sixth Army: its equipment was exceptionally heavy because of the special Stalingrad mission; it comprised four corps headquarters, seventeen divisions at combat strength, and one artillery division. To this were added as of November 19–20, 1942: one corps headquarters of the Fourth Panzer Army, with four divisions at fighting strength, including the Roumanian 20th Infantry Division, *i.e.,* the entire left wing of Hoth's Army; plus the First Roumanian Cavalry division of the Third Roumanian Army stationed near

Kletskaya which was pushed into the pocket. The Sixth Army therefore possessed the quite unusual strength of five corps headquarters, twenty-two divisions of combat strength, and ten to twelve divisions. Cf. also v. Manstein, *op. cit.*, p. 520: four Armies equal fifty-two divisions, an average of 13 divisions per Army. The Sixth Army was twenty-two divisions of combat strength! Cf. also below, footnote 116 of this chapter.

26 The text of this radio message to Hitler can be found in Schröter, *op. cit.*, pp. 86f. The date, November 24, is incorrect. General Paulus sent off the telegram on the evening of November 22, after consultations with Major General Schmidt, General v. Seydlitz, and Colonel Clausius, of the General Staff. The radio message reproduced by Schröter on pp. 81f. shows the normal situation of the Sixth Army that evening. Personal communication of W. v. Seydlitz.

27 Communications from the materials of the estate of Field Marshal Paulus: E.A. Paulus; personal communication by W. v. Seydlitz. According to this evidence the briefing session by the commanding generals of November 22 described by Schröter (*op. cit.*, p. 85) must be called a pure figment of the imagination. This session could not possibly have taken place because generals Strecker and Hube, mentioned by Schröter, were west of the Don on November 22 and could therefore not have been at Gumrak on the same day. The elaborately described discussion of the situation after Hitler's order to stand and fight never took place either (cf. *op. cit.*, pp.92f.). The state-

ments ascribed to General von Seydlitz on this occasion are complete fiction. All of this makes necessary a thorough revision of notions held up to now, which, unfortunately, have dominated almost all of the literature on Stalingrad. Schröter's book contains, on the whole, accurately reproduced documents, provided one is willing to overlook his frequently shoddy and even incorrect dating. But the rest of this publication, which offers fragments of historical events and unverifiable reports of private experiences, suggests considerable caution concerning its use.

28 Personal communication of W. v. Seydlitz, H. Gerlach; cf. also Wieder, *op. cit.*, pp. 23f.

29 Cf. Schröter, *op. cit.*, p. 87.

30 *Op. cit.*, pp. 87f., 90; cf. also v. Tippelskirch, *op. cit.*, pp. 313f.

31 Cf. footnote 30; Wieder, *op. cit.*, p. 33; Toepke, *op. cit.*, pp. 49f.

32 The text can be found in Schröter, *op. cit.*, p. 89.

33 Personal communication of W. v. Seydlitz; cf. also v. Manstein, *op. cit.*, pp. 345, 649ff.

34 Walther v. Seydlitz, *Die Beurteilung der Lage der 6. Armee im Kessel von Stalingrad* (Memorandum of November 25, 1942), pp. 1ff. This document can be found in the first supplementary volume of the *War Diary of the Army Group Don*, Section Ia, available at Washington, D. C.; I used a certified copy, of January 23, 1954, written by Dr. Friedrich-Christian Stahl. The original has apparently been destroyed.

35 *Op. cit.*, p. 5.

36 *Loc. cit.*

37 Personal communication of W. v. Seydlitz; cf. also Wieder, *op. cit.*, p. 27.

38 On the personality of Paulus and his decisions: Kunrat Freiherr von Hammerstein, "Manstein," in: *Frankfurter Hefte*, 11 (1956), p. 452; v. Manstein, *op. cit.*, p. 365; v. Tippelskirch, *op. cit.*, pp. 314–316; Toepke, *op. cit.*, p. 73; personal communications of H. Foertsch, G. Blumentritt; Communications from materials of the estate of Field Marshal Paulus: E.A. Paulus; personal recollections of E.A. Paulus.

39 That the attitude of the Sixth Army's leadership at that time can be characterized in these terms is substantiated by the personal communications of W. v. Seydlitz. For a later date (December 1942), von Manstein also mentions its apparently fundamental character, *op. cit.* pp. 364f.

40 Personal communication of W. v. Seydlitz; Wieder, *op. cit.*, p. 24.

41 Wieder, *op. cit.*, pp. 29, 31f.; also v. Manstein, *op. cit.*, p. 354.

42 Pers. commun. of W. v. Seydlitz; cf. also Wieder, *op. cit.*, p. 32.

43 V. Seydlitz, *Wer ist . . .*, p. 17; Wieder, *op. cit.*, p. 34; Toepke, *op. cit.*, pp. 49f. (an average of 60–100 tons!); cf. also Hans-Detlef Herhudt v. Rohden, *Die Luftwaffe ringt um Stalingrad*, Wiesbaden 1950, p. 87.

44 V. Seydlitz, *op. cit.*, pp. 17f.; Wieder, *op. cit.;* Commun. of materials from the estate of Field Marshal Paulus: E.A. Paulus.

45 V. Manstein, *op. cit.*, pp. 355f.; v. Tippelskirch, *op. cit.*, p. 314.

46 On the operation "Winter Gale" see especially v. Manstein, *op. cit.*, pp. 360ff.; v. Tippelskirch, *op. cit.*, p. 315. An excellent description can be found in Hans Doerr, *Der Feldzug nach Stalingrad*, Darmstadt 1955, pp. 84ff. Cf. also the impressive account of Frido von Senger und Etterlin, *Krieg in Europa*, Cologne/Berlin 1960, pp. 74–92.

47 V. Manstein, *op. cit.*, p. 363.

48 *Loc. cit.*

49 *Op. cit.*, pp. 363ff. *Mission Eismann* (Operation Iceman).

50 *Op. cit.*, pp. 364f.

51 *Op. cit.*, p. 366.

52 *Op. cit.*, p. 367.

53 *Op. cit.*, p. 369; Commun. of materials from the estate of Field Marshal Paulus: E.A. Paulus; personal notes of E.A. Paulus. It is significant for Manstein's strange lapses of memory that he never mentions the code word "Thunderclap," which was never communicated anywhere in his memoirs. Had he sufficiently clarified this point, an entirely different evaluation of Paulus' decisions in December 1942 would now be current.

54 V. Manstein, *op. cit.*, p. 370; Commun. of materials from the estate of Field Marshal Paulus: E.A. Paulus.

55 V. Manstein, *op. cit.*, p. 371.

56 *Op. cit.*, pp. 373ff. This is not the place to enter into the problem of whether there had been any other opportunities for liberating the Sixth Army. In theory this question will probably have to be answered in the affirmative, especially if one is to believe Manstein (*op. cit.*, p. 378) that in the view of his army group the forces, which would have had to be deployed in massive concentration east of the Don, could have been ready within six days. The only thing certain is the fact that these forces would have had to come out of the armies stationed near the Caucasus and they were tied to their operational space by Hitler as rigorously as the twenty-

two divisions were bound at
Stalingrad.

[57] Cf., for instance, v. Manstein, *op. cit.*, p. 393, especially from the point of view of timing.

[58] V. Seydlitz, *Die Beurteilung . . .* , pp. 2f.

[59] Pers. commun. of W. v. Seydlitz; Wieder, *op. cit.*, p. 50.

[60] Cf. footnote 59.

[61] Wieder, *op. cit.*, p. 51.

[62] *Loc. cit.*

[63] *Loc. cit.*; cf. also Selle, *Die Tragödie . . .* , p. 8.

[64] Pers. commun. of W. v. Seydlitz, H. Gerlach; Wieder, *op. cit.*, pp. 40ff.; Toepke, *op. cit.*, pp. 54, 57f., 62, 64.

[65] Schröter, *op. cit.*, p. 103; cf. also Wieder, *op. cit.*, p. 42; Toepke, *op. cit.*, p. 64.

[66] Pers. commun. of W. v. Seydlitz, H. Gerlach; Wieder, *op. cit.*, pp. 45f.; Commun. of materials from the estate of Field Marshal Paulus: E.A. Paulus.

[67] Selle, *op. cit.*, p. 8; Wieder, *op. cit.*, p. 51.

[68] Cf. v. Manstein, *op. cit.*, pp. 326ff., 397ff.

[69] The text can be found in Schröter, *op. cit.*, pp. 153f., and in the document collection *Stalingrad*, Zurich 1945, pp. 132ff.; Wieder, *op. cit.*, p. 53. Von Manstein's statement (*op. cit.*, p. 383) that the Russian ultimatum was presented to the Sixth Army on January 9, 1943, is in error. The correct date is January 8.

[70] V. Seydlitz, *Wer ist . . .* , pp. 19f.; Wieder, *op. cit.*, pp. 51f. This is brought out even more clearly in the excellent and profound article by Joachim Wieder, *Welches Gesetz befahl den deutschen Soldaten, an der Wolga zu sterben?*, in: *Frankfurter Hefte*, 11 (1956), p. 315; Communication of ma-

terials from the estate of Field Marshal Paulus: E.A. Paulus.

[71] Wieder, *op. cit.*; Toepke, *op. cit.*, p. 83.

[72] Wieder, *op. cit.*; cf. also Toepke, *op. cit.*, pp. 49f., 67.

[73] Cf. Wieder, *Die Tragödie . . .* , p. 54.

[74] Schröter, *op. cit.*, p. 154; Wieder, *op. cit.*, p. 55.

[75] Schröter, *op. cit.*, pp. 154f.

[76] *Op. cit.* p. 155; Wieder, *op. cit.*, pp. 55f.; Communication of materials from the estate of Field Marshal Paulus: E.A. Paulus.

[77] Schröter, *op. cit.*, p. 156; undated: v. Tippelskirch, *op. cit.*, p. 319; v. Manstein, *op. cit.*, p. 385.

[78] Wieder, *Welches Gesetz . . .* , p. 317.

[79] *Op. cit.*, p. 315.

[80] *Op. cit.*; Communication of materials from the estate of Field Marshal Paulus: E.A. Paulus.

[81] Wieder, *op. cit.*, p. 316.

[82] *Op. cit.*; a more thorough treatment in Wieder, *Die Tragödie . . .* , pp. 56ff.

[83] Wieder, *Welches Gesetz . . .* , p. 325.

[84] *Op. cit.*; pers. commun. of W. v. Seydlitz.

[85] Cf. *Letzte Briefe aus Stalingrad*, Frankfurt a. M./Heidelberg 1950. The fate of these letters, intercepted in January 1943 and redirected to the OKW (German Armed Forces High Command) is explained in an afterword. An exhaustive analysis of the psychological situation of the fighters in Stalingrad is very difficult, as numerous attitudes would have to be taken into account. But a summary statistical evaluation provides a reliable survey in this case too.

[86] Pers. commun. of W. v. Seydlitz; Wieder, *op. cit.*, p. 324.

87 Pers. commun. of W. v. Seydlitz; W. Frhr. v. Senfft-Pilsach.
88 Pers. commun. of W. v. Seydlitz, H. Gerlach. In this context Heinrich Gerlach, *Die verratene Armee* (Munich, 1957), which gives several instances of this kind of reaction, remains valuable. Although this book is a novel about Stalingrad and can, therefore, not be used as a historical source, it nevertheless provides numerous insights because of its closeness to the actual events. These insights are so fundamental that any future study of the inscrutable problem of Stalingrad might at least use it for inspiration. Cf. finally Jesco v. Puttkamer, *Irrtum und Schuld*, Neuwied/Berlin 1948, p. 7.
89 Cf. Selle, *op. cit.*, pp. 9, 11; pers. commun. of W. v. Seydlitz.
90 Schröter, *op. cit.*, pp. 150ff.; v. Manstein, *op. cit.*, pp. 383, 387; Toepke, *op. cit.*, pp. 71, 85ff., 116ff.
91 Selle, *op. cit.*, p. 12.
92 Schröter, *op. cit.*, 152; Toepke, *op. cit.*, pp. 121, 124.
93 Pers. commun. of W. v. Seydlitz; Commun. of materials from the estate of Field Marshal Paulus: E.A. Paulus.
94 Cf. Wieder, *op. cit.*, pp. 315, 317; Wieder, *Die Tragödie* . . . , pp. 56ff., 6off.; Commun. of materials from the estate of Field Marshal General Paulus: E.A. Paulus.
95 It remains an open question how many enemy forces the Sixth Army did tie down for any length of time. Von Manstein (*op. cit.*, p. 384) states that the number of large enemy units engaged by the Sixth Army during January 1943 (!) amounted to ninety, while one gets the impression from Helmuth Greiner, *Die oberste Wehrmachtführung 1939 bis 1943*, Wiesbaden 1951, p. 436, that the Stalingrad front had held up 107 Russian units (of what strengths?) and thirteen Infantry Tank Regiments. Von Manstein's all too summary statement has been challenged by Wieder (*Welches Gesetz* . . . , pp. 316f.) rather convincingly. Basically one can probably say that the exhausted Sixth Army was at that time no longer in a position to hold any considerable enemy forces. Quite apart from any strategic aspects, which are highly dubious in this context anyway, this seems to be especially true if one approaches the question from the point of view of the sacrifice ordered by Hitler.
96 Schröter, *op. cit.*, p. 201. The date, January 24, is wrong. It was actually January 20. Pers. commun. of W. v. Seydlitz; commun. of materials from the estate of Field Marshal Paulus: E.A. Paulus.
97 V. Manstein, *op. cit.*, p. 390 (the date, according to Manstein: January 22, 1943).
98 Schröter, *op. cit.*, p. 203; Adolf Heusinger, *Befehl im Widerstreit*, Tübingen/Stuttgart 1950, pp. 223 f. According to Heusinger, Hitler felt that to retreat from Stalingrad was incompatible with the honor of the German Army (!).
99 Pers. commun. of W. v. Seydlitz; H. Gerlach, W. Frhr. v. Senfft-Pilsach.
100 Pers. commun. of W. v. Seydlitz; cf. also Wieder, *op. cit.*, p. 324.
101 Wieder, *op. cit.*, p. 316. Cf. also the moving account of Kurt J. Fischer, *Der Gefangene von Stalingrad*, Willsbach (Württ.) 1948, p. 7.
102 Pers. commun. of W. v. Seydlitz, H. Gerlach.

[103] Cf. footnote 102. Wieder, *Die Tragödie* . . . , pp. 94f.

[104] Wieder, *Welches Gesetz* . . . , pp. 324f. Later on suicide was no longer regarded honorable; it was prohibited.

[105] Pers. commun. of W. v. Seydlitz. According to the same source, the conference of the commanding generals and the divisional commanders of the southern front sector described by Schröter (*op. cit.*, p. 209), without any date, which Schröter probably assumes took place at about the same time, must once again be called pure fiction.

[106] Pers. commun. of W. v. Seydlitz. Philipp Humbert ("Ich bitte erschossen zu werden," in: *Der Spiegel*, III, 1949, 5, pp. 15, 17) asserts that another revolt of the generals had been attempted and failed on January 26, 1943. According to W. v. Seydlitz's evidence this affair, too, has to be considered an imaginative invention. Humbert had neither been von Seydlitz's adjutant nor did the commanding general of the LI Corps see the commanding general of the Sixth Army again after January 25, 1943. In his situation report of November 25, 1942 (cf. footnotes 34–36 of this chapter), General von Seydlitz had, furthermore, demanded that action had to be taken, if need be, exclusively out of an obligation toward the army and the German people. This statement had, however, already anticipated that "high treason," which the same general was supposed to have protested against now, at the end of the catastrophe he had predicted. It is necessary at this point to stress the weaknesses in form and content of Humbert's account; there will be occasion to return to it again.

[107] Pers. commun. of W. v. Seydlitz; Schröter, *op. cit.*, p. 196.

[108] Schröter, *op. cit.*, pp. 223, 226; Wieder, *Die Tragödie* . . . , pp. 87ff.

[109] Pers. commun. of W. v. Seydlitz, H. Gerlach; Wieder, *op. cit.*, pp. 89f.; v. Puttkamer, *op. cit.*, p. 10.

[110] Schröter, *op. cit.*, pp. 226ff.; v. Tippelskirch, *op. cit.*, p. 319. The date of January 30 is wrong in these accounts. It was January 31.

[111] Cf. Heusinger, *op. cit.*, p. 235.

[112] Pers. commun. of W. v. Seydlitz, H. Gerlach; Schröter, *op. cit.*, p. 228; Wieder, *op. cit.*, pp. 91f.

[113] Pers. commun. of H. Gerlach; cf. also Wieder, *op. cit.*, pp. 92, 95.

[114] Schröter, *op. cit.*, pp. 231f.; cf. also v. Puttkamer, *op. cit.*, pp. 10f.

[115] Wieder, *op. cit.*, pp. 107f.

[116] Cf. Schröter, *op. cit.*, pp. 80f.; Wieder, *op. cit.*, p. 16; Wieder, *Welches Gesetz* . . . , p. 323. According to W. v. Seydlitz, based on notes: destroyed one army staff, five corps staffs, twenty-two divisions (among them the 20th Roumanian Inf. Div. and the 1st Roumanian Cavalry Div.) plus one flak division. Von Tippelskirch's figures (*op. cit.*, p. 320) are correct but incomplete.

[117] The correct number is probably 270,000 as stated by Toepke, *op. cit.*, pp. 42, 52; Herhudt v. Rohden, *op. cit.*, p. 35; the number of those killed in action and of those taken prisoner are quoted from *Stalingrad*, p. 65. These last figures are reliable if one considers that more than 30,000 wounded and sick were flown out of the pocket in the course of the fighting. Cf. further Schröter, *op. cit.*, pp. 185f.; Selle, *Stalingrad*

..., p. 2. Von Manstein's warning (*op. cit.*, p. 328) that the oft-cited figure of 300,000 soldiers in the Stalingrad pocket is exaggerated, is no doubt correct. His assertion, however, that only 200 to 220 thousand men were trapped in November 1942, despite the large attachments of field artillery and pioneers, cannot be maintained after a check of the data available.

[118] Pers. commun. of W. v. Seydlitz, H. Gerlach, W. Frhr. v. Senfft-Pilsach; Wieder, *op. cit.*, pp. 315, 323ff.

[119] Pers. commun. of W. v. Seydlitz; Wieder, *Die Tragödie . . .* , p. 97.

[120] Cf. v. Manstein, *op. cit.*, pp. 397 ff.

[121] Pers. commun. of W. v. Seydlitz, H. Gerlach.

[122] Selle, *Die Tragödie . . .* , p. 11.

CHAPTER TWO: *The Founding of the National Committee and the League of German Officers*

[1] Pers. commun. of Th. Plievier, W. Leonhard, F. Löwenthal, H. Count v. Einsiedel. Cf. also Wolfgang Leonhard, *Die Revolution entlässt ihre Kinder*, Cologne/Berlin 1955, pp. 120f., 158, 297; also v. Puttkamer, *op. cit.*, pp. 35f.

[2] Cf. footnote 1.

[3] Pers. commun. of Th. Plievier; Leonhard, *op. cit.*, pp. 38ff., 81; an accurate description can be found also in Count v. Einsiedel, *Tagebuch der Versuchung*, Berlin /Stuttgart 1950, p. 214.

[4] Testimony of numerous officers and soldiers. Cf. also Werner Picht, "Der deutsche Soldat," in: *Bilanz des Zweiten Weltkrieges*, Oldenburg/Hamburg 1953, especially pp. 43f.

[5] Testimony of numerous officers and soldiers. Pers. commun. of H. Count v. Einsiedel. Also v. Puttkamer, *op. cit.*, p. 36; Leonhard, *op. cit.*, pp. 120f.; Jürgen Kuczynski, *Freie Deutsche—Damals und heute*, London 1943, p. 13; Wilhelm Florin, *Warum kämpft Hitler gegen die Sowjetunion?*, Moscow 1942, p. 31: "It is even more evident in this war than in

others that the German soldiers are literally fighting to enable the Krupps, Siemenses, and Pönsgens to tie the rope around their [the soldiers'] necks even more tightly." Similar evidence in: *Sie kämpften für Deutschland (Zur Geschichte des Kampfes der Bewegung "Freies Deutschland" bei der 1. Ukrainischen Front der Sowjetarmee)*, Berlin 1959, pp. 129ff., 135. In the personal accounts this book shows the usual colorations, but it is impressive in its full documentation. Cf. finally Jochen Klepper, *Überwindung*, Stuttgart 1958, p. 100. Here, concerning the propaganda asking German soldiers to defect and a poem by Erich Weinert, we read: "What a misunderstanding of German mentality." And pp. 114f.: "Everywhere in the town there is the paper evidence of loudmouthed, weak Soviet propaganda. Such foolish leaflets in German language." (Southern part of the Eastern Front, July 1941.)

[6] Testimony of numerous officers and soldiers. Podewils, *op. cit.*, p. 161. Cf. also Curt Hohoff,

264 / FREE GERMANY

*Woina-Woina,* Düsseldorf/Cologne 1951, p. 348.

7 Testimony of numerous officers and soldiers. Podewils, *loc. cit.;* Paul Hausser, *Waffen-SS im Einsatz,* Göttingen 1953, p. 264; pers. commun. of K. v. Tippelskirch. A typical example is the leaflet "Soldiers of the 9th Army!" dropped by Soviet planes. (The original dates from April 1942.)

In the literature about the war one finds numerous bits of evidence concerning Soviet atrocities against German prisoners of war. Horrifying examples are given, to pick only one title at random, in the sober book by J. W. Oechelhaeuser, *Wir zogen in das Feld,* Boppard a. Rhein 1960, pp. 76, 102, 131f., 159.

8 Testimony of numerous officers and soldiers. Picht, *op. cit.,* pp. 43f.

9 V. Einsiedel, *op. cit.,* pp. 28 ff.; v. Puttkamer, *op. cit.,* p. 37. Cf. also Kurt Langmaack, *Stacheldraht statt Sozialismus,* Hamburg 1952, pp. 22f. Although Langmaack's report has only modest literary qualities, he manages to depict very accurately the actual situation in the POW camps. Erich Weinert (*Das Nationalkomitee "Freies Deutschland" 1943–1945,* Berlin 1957, pp. 11f.), on the other hand, is incapable of suggesting even the rudiments of an accurate description of the bleak atmosphere in which the first actions of political recruitment were supposed to flourish. Valuable hints about a much later period are now provided by the excellent book of Helmut Gollwitzer, *. . . und führen, wohin du nicht willst,* Munich 1951, p. 102.

10 V. Einsiedel, *loc. cit.;* v. Puttkamer, *loc. cit.*

11 Pers. commun. of H. Abel, H. Gerlach, W. Frhr. v. Senfft-Pilsach, J. Wieder, A. Greifenhagen, H. Count v. Einsiedel, J. v. Puttkamer; testimony of German prisoners of war from Camp Yelabuga.

12 Cf. footnote 11.

13 On Wagner cf. especially v. Einsiedel, *op. cit.,* pp. 31–35; Langmaack, *op. cit.,* pp. 22f.; pers. commun. of H.Z.

14 *Free Germany. Research and Analysis Branch,* U. S. Dept. of State, Nov. 26, 1943, pp. 1f. (Library of Congress); Leonhard, *op. cit.,* p. 158; Weinert, *op. cit.,* p. 11; *Sie kämpften . . . ,* pp. 114ff. The full text is published there.

15 Cf. v. Einsiedel, *op. cit.,* p. 35.

16 V. Einsiedel, *op. cit.,* pp. 37ff.; v. Puttkamer, *op. cit.,* p. 37; cf. also pers. commun. of H. Count v. Einsiedel, J. v. Puttkamer.

17 Cf. Ernst Hadermann, *Wie ist der Krieg zu beenden? Ein Manneswort eines deutschen Hauptmanns* (Vorrede: Erich Weinert), Moscow 1942.

18 V. Einsiedel, *op. cit.,* p. 37; typical of a later state (middle of 1943) is the pers. commun. of C.F.: "It created quite a stir when I was seen walking with Hadermann in the street of the camp."

19 Of general significance: Erich Weinert, *Memento Stalingrad,* Berlin 1951; additional information: Weinert, *Das Nationalkomitee . . . ,* p. 13; texts of leaflets: *Sie kämpften . . . ,* pp. 122f., 124f., 126, 127ff. (especially on the 1st Ukrainian Front). Cf. also: *Zur Geschichte der deutschen antifaschistischen Widerstandsbewegung 1933–1945. Materialien, Berichte, Dokumente.* Berlin 1958, p. 203.

20 Pers. commun. of W. v. Seydlitz, H. Schlömer.

21 Pers. commun. of W. v. Seydlitz, Von Puttkamer's description (*op. cit.*, p. 42), according to this evidence, stands in need of considerable correction, since it exaggerates to achieve heightened effects. It was simply a train of normal Russian second class carriages without any service. Nevertheless, it was an enormous contrast to everything the bulk of the prisoners had to endure. A more sober description is provided by Rolf Grams, *Die 14. Panzer-Division 1940–1945*, Bad Nauheim 1957, p. 102.

22 Pers. commun. of H. Abel, H. Gerlach, W. Frhr. v. Senfft-Pilsach, I. v. Knobelsdorff Brenkenhoff, J. Wieder, A. Greifenhagen, H. Count v. Einsiedel; testimony of German prisoners of war from the Camps Yelabuga, Susdal, and Oranky. Cf. also Fischer, *op. cit.*, pp. 11–68, 78, 113, 115.

23, 24, 25 *Loc. cit.*

26 Pers. commun. of H.Z.; some hints in Leonhard, *op. cit.*, pp. 279f.; v. Puttkamer, *op. cit.*, p. 41. Weinert's presentation (*op. cit.*, p. 17), according to which the steering committee had asked the Soviet Union to grant permision for the formation of a National Committee in the USSR, attempts to give the erroneous impression that the Germans had made an important contribution to the decision on their own initiative.

27 Weinert, *op. cit.*, pp. 14, 15ff.; also v. Einsiedel, *op. cit.*, p. 49; v. Puttkamer, *op. cit.*, p. 42.

28 Weinert, *op. cit.*, p. 15.

29 Pers. commun. of H. Count v. Einsiedel. Even Weinert (*op. cit.*, p. 16) states summarily: "The assembly proposed the formation of a committee . . . ."

30 Pers. commun. of H. Abel, H. Gerlach, W. Frhr. v. Senfft-Pilsach, I. v. Knobelsdorff-Brenkenhoff, J. Wieder, A. Greifenhagen, J. Kayser, A. Ludwig; v. Einsiedel, *op. cit.*, p. 51; v. Puttkamer, *op. cit.*, pp. 42f.

31 Cf. footnote 30.

32 Pers. commun. of H. Abel, H. Gerlach, C. F., J. Wieder, A. Greifenhagen, I. v. Knobelsdorff-Brenkenhoff.

33 *Loc. cit.*

34 *Loc. cit.* It remains insignificant in this context that the émigrés and *politruks* specifically mentioned here would for the most part have to be described negatively according to the documents and biographies that have become available since then. What does remain significant is the fact that in the beginning they appeared as reasonable partners to those officers they tried to establish contact with.

35 *Loc. cit.*

36 Pers. commun. of A. Bredt, H. Abel, H. Gerlach, C.F.

37 Pers. commun. of C.F., H. Abel, H. Gerlach.

38 Pers. commun. of A. Bredt, C.F., H. Abel, H. Gerlach, W. Frhr. v. Senfft-Pilsach. Cf. also v. Puttkamer, *op. cit.*, pp. 41ff. It has to be emphasized that Karl O. Paetel ("Das Nationalkomitee 'Freies Deutschland,'" in: *Politische Studien* 6, 1956, 69, particularly p. 10) from the outset overrationalizes the motives of the officers who later founded the League of German Officers into an ideology of, among other things, an "eastward orientation." According to most of the available evidence, what actually moved them

at first were much more sober and concrete considerations. It was "simply" the worry about Germany which, it was feared, would perish in an even more terrible Stalingrad. Cf., also, footnote 90 of this chapter.

39 Friedrich Paulus, *Nach der Schlacht*. These notes by Field Marshal Paulus, unpublished to date, were written while he was still prisoner of war of the Soviets. Pers. commun. of E.A. Paulus. H. Gerlach, C.F., F. Löwenthal.

40 Pers. commun. of A. Bredt, H. Abel.

41 *Loc. cit.*; cf. also v. Puttkamer, *op. cit.*, p. 43.

42 Pers. commun. of A. Bredt, H. Abel, H. Gerlach, C.F.

43 Cf. footnote 42.

44 Weinert, *op. cit.*, pp. 15ff. A facsimile of this newspaper can be found in: *Zur Geschichte . . .* , between pp. 272 and 273.

45 *Loc. cit.*, p. 17.

46 Pers. commun. of W. Leonhard, H.Z.; cf. also Leonhard, *op. cit.*, pp. 279f.

47 Cf. footnote 46.

48 Leonhard, *op. cit.*, pp. 247f. Another significant example can be found on p. 280.

49 V. Puttkamer, *op. cit.*, p. 42; v. Einsiedel, *op. cit.*, pp. 53f.; pers. commun. of A. Bredt, C.F.

50 Pers. commun. of C.F., A. Bredt.

51 Pers. commun. of C.F.; cf. also v. Einsiedel, *op. cit.*, p. 54.

52 *Loc. cit.*

53 *Loc. cit.*

54 *Freies Deutschland* (*Organ des Nationalkomitees Freies Deutschland*, cited below as: FD), I/1, July 19, 1943; v. Einsiedel, *op. cit.*, pp. 55ff.; v. Puttkamer's description (*op. cit.*, pp. 43ff.) is accurate on the whole, but secondhand. Weinert (*op. cit.*, pp. 19ff.)

limits himself to a few remarks, but he offers an excerpt of *Pravda's* report on the founding of the National Committee.

55 Pers. commun. of C.F., A. Bredt, H. Count v. Einsiedel.

56 FD, I/1, July 19, 1943.

57 *Loc. cit.* Cf. also: *Zur Geschichte. . .* , p. 215.

58 FD, I/1, July 19, 1943; *Zur Geschichte . . .* , pp. 212ff.; cf. also v. Einsiedel, *op. cit.*, p. 60.

59 FD, I/1, July 19, 1943.

60 *Loc. cit.*

61 *Loc. cit.*; cf. also Leonhard, *op. cit.*, p. 274.

62 Weinert gave the keynote paper. Published unabridged in: FD, I/1, July 19, 1943.

63, 64 *Loc. cit.*

65 *Loc. cit.*; v. Einsiedel, *op. cit.*, pp. 6of. The name is misspelled here, which happens frequently in this book.

66 Pers. commun. of A. Bredt, C.F., H. Count v. Einsiedel.

67 FD, I/1, July 19, 1943; v. Einsiedel, *op. cit.*, p. 62.

68 FD, I/1, July 19, 1943; cf. also v. Einsiedel, *op. cit.*, pp. 56ff.; v. Puttkamer, *op. cit.*, pp. 44ff. (a reproduction of the document of September 1943 with the signatures of the officers in the League of German Officers, which had been founded in the meantime); Weinert, *op. cit.*, pp. 19ff. A reproduction of the manifesto and numerous other documents can also be found in Peter Strassner, *Verräter—Das Nationalkomitee "Freies Deutschland"—Keimzelle der sogenannten DDR*, Munich 1960. Strassner's publication, which was published after my book, is useless for historical scholarship. The author himself admits that he is not a historian and he merely demonstrates de-

liberate prejudices. The meager use made of the few sources to which he sticks renders superfluous any serious discussion of his book.

69 *Loc. cit.*

70 The Russians had emphatically refused to incorporate in the program certain socialist points that had been requested by a number of POWs. Pers. commun. of C.F., H. Gerlach.

71 Pers. commun. of A. Bredt, C.F., H. Abel, H. Gerlach, J. Wieder, A. Greifenhagen, W. Frhr. v. Senfft-Pilsach, I. v. Knobelsdorff-Brenkenhoff; testimony of German prisoners of war from the camps at Yelabuga, Susdal, and Oranky.

72 FD I/1, July 19, 1943; some details in v. Einsiedel, *op. cit.*, pp. 53f.

73 Cf. footnote 71.

74 Stösslein's speech at the founding assembly of the National Committee can be found in: FD I/1, July 19, 1943.

75 Cf. footnote 71; Korfes, *op. cit.*, col. 1289; pers. commun. of H. Count v. Einsiedel.

76 Pers. commun. of A. Bredt, H. Abel, H. Gerlach, J. Wieder, A. Greifenhagen, J. v. Puttkamer, J. Kayser, A. Ludwig; testimony of German prisoners of war from the camps at Yelabuga, Susdal, and Oranky.

77 Pers. commun. of H. Abel, H. Gerlach.

78 Pers. commun. of A. Bredt, C.F.

79 *Loc. cit.*; cf. also v. Einsiedel, *op. cit.*, p. 56; v. Puttkamer, *op. cit.*, pp. 48f.

80 Cf. footnote 79.

81 V. Puttkamer, *op. cit.*, p. 49; pers. commun. of A. Bredt.

82 Pers. commun. of A. Bredt, H. Gerlach.

83, 84 *Loc. cit.*

85 Alfred Bredt, *Die Entstehung des Bundes Deutscher Offiziere in der Gefangenschaft.* Pers. commun. of A. Bredt, C.F., H. Gerlach.

86 Pers. commun. of A. Bredt, C.F., H. Abel, H. Gerlach, A. Greifenhagen, I. v. Knobelsdorff-Brenkenhoff.

87 *Loc. cit.*

88 *Loc. cit.*; a few details can also be found in v. Puttkamer, *op. cit.*, pp. 48f.; v. Einsiedel, *op. cit.*, p. 75.

89 Pers. commun. of A. Bredt, H. Abel, H. Gerlach, A. Greifenhagen, I. v. Knobelsdorff-Brenkenhoff. A more detailed study of the question of social provenance could not be undertaken on the basis of the material available. The documentary sources were either too insufficient or too biased. Cf. also p. 165.

90 At this point the profound experience of Stalingrad, which I tried to describe in the first chapter, has to be stressed once again as the decisive motivating factor, if only because Hermann Graml presents some questionable theories on this subject in his poorly documented article "Das Nationalkomitee 'Freies Deutschland,'" in: *Neues Abendland VII*, 1952, pp. 676ff. Graml says (on pp. 667f.) that, in its fight against Hitler, the conservative group in particular (by which he seems to refer to the League of German Officers) did not fight against power as such, but against its abuse, and not against the authoritarian system as such, but only against *this* specific authoritarian system. He misses the fact that to the survivors of the Sixth Army, Stalingrad had unmasked a state which treated the soldiers in such inhuman fashion precisely because

of its totalitarianism, which was unwilling to respect any moral bounds. After their bitter experiences they, therefore, rejected *any* kind of totalitarianism in Germany, for it now appeared to them as the source of all errors. No less nonsensical is the defamatory argument that Hitler's failures had become the stumbling block for the nationalist wing in the National Committee. The fact that resistance showed itself only in view of the impending ruin of the German people and the nation is bound to raise the cry of opportunism. But where this resistance was coupled with the individual decision to act, the attempt to save the Reich should unquestionably be accorded an ethical value of its own. This is especially the case if this attempt was risked as early as 1943.

91 Pers. commun. of A. Bredt, H. Gerlach, A. Greifenhagen, I. v. Knobelsdorff-Brenkenhoff. Additional evidence in H. Gerlach, *Die Werbung der Generale*, p. 1.

92 *Loc. cit.*

93 *Loc. cit.*; cf. also Korfes, *op. cit.*, col. 1290.

94 H. Gerlach, *loc. cit.*; cf. also—despite some gaudy details—v. Einsiedel, *op. cit.*, p. 73, and finally Grams, *op. cit.*, pp. 104f.

95 Pers. commun. of A. Bredt, H. Abel, H. Gerlach, J. Wieder, A. Greifenhagen, I. v. Knobelsdorff-Brenkenhoff, W. Frhr. v. Senfft-Pilsach.

96 Pers. commun. of H. Abel; testimony of German prisoners of war from camp Yelabuga.

97 Pers. commun. of H. Gerlach; Gerlach, *Die Werbung* . . . ; Korfes' presentation on this point is biased (*op. cit.*, col. 1289).

98 H. Gerlach, *Die Haltung der Kom-munisten im NK und BdO*, p. 1. Certain reservations against the Wehrmacht's higher ranks remained virulent among the émigrés despite their subsequent experiences with the officers' union. Cf. Weinert, *op. cit.*, p. 88; Leonhard, *op. cit.*, pp. 297f.; as well as pers. commun. of W. v. Seydlitz.

99 Pers. commun. of A. Bredt, A. Greifenhagen, I. v. Knobelsdorff-Brenkenhoff, H. Gerlach; also Gerlach, *Die Werbung* . . .

100 Cf. footnote 99.

101 H. Gerlach, *Die Werbung* . . . ; pers. commun. of A. Bredt, A. Greifenhagen, I. v. Knobelsdorff-Brenkenhoff. Von Puttkamer's description (*op. cit.*, pp. 49f.) is correct in its general outline, but it remains too vague; v. Einsiedel (*op. cit.*, pp. 75f.), finally, can offer only a few details; he could not directly observe the activities of the initiating group of the officers' union, since he was a member of the National Committee—which characterizes the whole situation.

102 to 106 *Loc. cit.*

107 Individual details: pers. commun. of W. v. Seydlitz, H. Gerlach, J. Wieder, A. Greifenhagen, A. Ludwig. Additional details: v. Puttkamer, *op. cit.*, p. 51; also Heusinger, *op. cit.*, p. 177; finally, if a bit too personal in one passage, Hermann Teske, *Die silbernen Spiegel*, Heidelberg 1952, pp. 68f.

108 Pers. commun. of W. v. Seydlitz; H. Gerlach, *Die Werbung* . . .

109 Cf. preceding footnote.

110 Pers. commun. of W. v. Seydlitz; once again overstated, but corroborating: v. Einsiedel, *op. cit.*, p. 77; v. Puttkamer, *op. cit.*, p. 52. Cf. also: *Die Front war überall*, Berlin 1958, pp. 43ff.

111 Pers. commun. of W. v. Seydlitz, A. Greifenhagen; H. Gerlach, *Die Werbung* . . .

112, 113, 114 *Loc. cit.*

115 Pers. commun. of W. v. Seydlitz; also v. Seydlitz, *Gründe für meinen Eintritt in den "Bund Deutscher Offiziere" und das "Nationalkomitee Freies Deutschland"* (Dec. 14, 1955). The decisive effect of Melnikov's assurances (Minutes: Daniels, October 4, 1943) is also attested by the evidence of A. Greifenhagen. Dr. Greifenhagen, Second Lieutenant of the 297th Inf. Div. (Stalingrad), had had a talk with Seydlitz on the previous day in the course of which the general inquired about the younger officers' evaluation of the situation. But he came to no decision despite emphatic encouragement.

116 Pers. commun. of W. v. Seydlitz; H. Gerlach, *Die Werbung* . . .

117 *Loc. cit.*

118 *Loc. cit.*; pers. commun. of Schlömer. Von Puttkamer's presentation (*op. cit.*, p. 53), according to which Seydlitz was supposed to have approached Field Marshal Paulus and the rest of the generals of Stalingrad only after the founding of the League of German Officers, is absurd. Cf. also v. Einsiedel, *op. cit.*, p. 78. Here the recruitment procedure is, however, described too one-sidedly and too emotionally on the basis of only one eyewitness account.

119 Pers. commun. of W. v. Seydlitz; H. Gerlach, *Die Werbung* . . . ; v. Puttkamer, *op. cit.*, pp. 53f.; Friedrich Paulus, *Gründung des "Bundes Deutscher Offiziere."*

120 Pers. commun. of W. v. Seydlitz; v. Puttkamer, *loc. cit.*

121 Pers. commun. of W. v. Seydlitz;

v. Puttkamer, *op. cit.*, p. 50; Paulus, *Nach der Schlacht.*

122 Paulus, *op. cit.*

123 Pers. commun. of W. v. Seydlitz; Paulus, *Gründung* . . .

124 *Loc. cit.*; cf. also v. Puttkamer, *op. cit.*, p. 54.

125 Pers. commun. of W. v. Seydlitz; Paulus, *loc. cit.* According to this evidence, von Puttkamer's (*loc. cit.*) reproduction of Paulus' arguments is incorrect. More accurate: v. Einsiedel, *op. cit.*, p. 78.

126 FD I/8/9, Sept. 15, 1943; *Die Gründung des Bundes Deutscher Offiziere* (minutes of the founding assembly), September 1943. Sporadic data: v. Puttkamer, *op. cit.*, pp. 52f.; Weiner *op. cit.*, pp. 32ff.; in greater detail: v. Einsiedel, *op. cit.*, pp. 78ff.

127 *Loc. cit.*; pers. commun. of A. Bredt, H. Abel, H. Gerlach, J. Wieder, A. Greifenhagen, I. v. Knobelsdorff-Brenkenhoff, W.W. v. Wildemann. Cf. also: *Sie kämpften* . . . , p. 159.

128 FD I/8/9, Sept. 15, 1943; *Die Gründung* . . . , pp. 20–98.

129 *Die Gründung* . . . , pp. 22ff.

130 *Op. cit.*, p. 23.

131 *Op. cit.*, pp. 23ff., pp. 29ff.

132 *Op. cit.*, p. 35.

133 *Op. cit.*, p. 38.

134 *Op. cit.*, p. 44.

135 *Op. cit.*, pp. 45ff., 66ff.

136 *Op. cit.*, pp. 66ff.; reprinted in part in v. Einsiedel, *op. cit.*, pp. 83ff.

137 *Die Gründung* . . . , pp. 68–70. After these binding assurances it would have been suggested to discard the national emblems; that, however, occurred only late in autumn when the German retreat had made manifest "senseless and militarily unjustified destruction and crimes." Cf. FD I/18, Nov. 14, 1943.

138 *Die Gründung* . . . , pp. 52ff., 93ff.
139 *Op. cit.*, pp. 53, 55.
140 *Op. cit.*, pp. 58f.
141 *Op. cit.*, p. 59.
142 *Op. cit.*, p. 59.
143 H. Gerlach, *Die Werbung* . . .
144 *Die Gründung* . . . , pp. 5–19; the signatures: pp. 8–11; facsimile of the text: pp. 12–16.
145 *Loc. cit.* Cf. Appendix II.
146 Pers. commun. of W. v. Seydlitz, A. Bredt, H. Gerlach.
147 Pers. commun. of W. v. Seydlitz, A. Bredt, H. Gerlach.
148 This is corroborated by the bulk of the available leaflets up to January 1944. Cf. also: *Sie kämpften* . . . , pp. 189, 190, 200, 206, 214f.
149 Pers. commun. of W. v. Seydlitz, H. Gerlach; cf. also Weinert, *op. cit.*, p. 88; *Sie kämpften* . . . , pp. 194, 196f., 201f.
150 *Die Gründung* . . . , pp. 61ff., 64f.
151 *Op. cit.*, p. 77.
152 Pers. commun. of A. Bredt, H. Abel, H. Gerlach, J. Wieder, A. Greifenhagen, I. v. Knobelsdorff-Brenkenhoff.
153 Pers. commun. of W. v. Seydlitz. Helmut Bohn ("Die patriotische Karte in der sowjetischen Deutschlandpolitik," in: *Ost-Probleme* VI/No. 38, p. 4) oversimplifies by saying that the primary motivation for the activities of the officers' union was that it did not want to leave the struggle and the fruits of the fighting "for an independent and free Germany" to the Communists.
154 Pers. commun. of W. v. Seydlitz, H. Abel, H. Gerlach, J. Wieder, A. Greifenhagen, I. v. Knobelsdorff-Brenkenhoff; cf. also H. Gerlach, *Die Haltung* . . .
155 *Die Gründung* . . . , pp. 96ff.
156 V. Puttkamer, *op. cit.*, pp. 46f.

157 W.S. Churchill (German language edition), *Der Zweite Weltkrieg. III, Die Grosse Allianz, Zweites Buch: Amerika im Krieg*, Bern 1950, pp. 294f.; Cordell Hull, *The Memoirs*, London 1948, vol. II, pp. 1165–1170.
158 Churchill, *op. cit.*, pp. 295, 367.
159 Hull, *op. cit.*, pp. 1171f.
160 Hull, *op. cit.*, pp. 1172–1174; I. Ciechanowski, *Defeat in Victory*, New York 1947, pp. 104–108.
161 Ciechanowski, *loc. cit.*
162 That this was a development which had started as early as 1940 is shown in the *Journal of Central European Affairs I*, 1941–1942, pp. 96ff. Cf. further: Boris Meissner, *Russland, die Westmächte und Deutschland*, Hamburg 1954, p. 12.
163 Cf. especially I. Deutscher (German language edition), *Stalin*, Stuttgart 1951, pp. 525ff.
164 J. Stalin (German language edition), *Über den Grossen Vaterländischen Krieg der Sowjetunion*, Moscow 1946, pp. 49f.; Leonhard, *op. cit.*, pp. 247f., 259f.
165 Stalin, *loc. cit.*
166 Cf. Peter Kleist, *Zwischen Hitler und Stalin*, Bonn 1950, pp. 235–284.
167 Cf. Meissner, *op. cit.*, p. 13; Bohn, *op. cit.*, p. 3; and also A.F. Lowenfeld, "The Free Germany Committee," in: *Review of Politics* 14, 1952, pp. 344–352. But the most impressive account is Leonhard's, *op. cit.*, pp. 293ff.: "The withdrawn offer of an armistice." Leonhard's description hardly leaves room for any further doubts about the seriousness of the Soviets' intentions at Stockholm. But he, too, has to acknowledge that the contacts in the Swedish capital were doomed to fail because of Hitler's attitude. It seems,

therefore, pointless to ask whether the delay of the founding of the League of German Officers should be traced back to the September contacts of Clauss and Kleist for the result of which Moscow had decided to wait (*op. cit.*, p. 295).
168 Kleist, *op. cit.*, p. 284.
169 Cf. also Schulenburg's reaction in Kleist, *op. cit.*, pp. 242f.
170 *Op. cit.*, p. 273. Cf. also Ulrich v. Hassell, *Vom andern Deutschland*, Zurich/Freiburg i. Br., n. d., p. 298.

171 Kleist, *op. cit.*, pp. 255, 260f. Cf. also Heinrich Fraenkel/Roger Manvell, *Goebbels*, Cologne/Berlin 1960, pp. 287f.
172 Kleist, *op. cit.*, p. 266.
173 *Op. cit.*, pp. 242f.
174 Meissner, *op. cit.*, pp. 11ff.; cf. especially on this problem: Ernst Deuerlein, *Die Einheit Deutschlands*, Frankfurt a.M./Berlin 1957, whose well-documented book continually stresses this aspect.
175 Kleist, *op. cit.*, pp. 235ff.; cf. also footnote 115 of this chapter.

CHAPTER THREE: *Allied and German Reactions*

1 Erich H. Boehm, "The 'Free Germans' in Soviet Political Warfare," in: *The Public Opinion Quarterly* 14/II, 1950, p. 293. Cf. also the *New York Times* of July 29, 1943.
2 *New York Times*, July 23, 1943. No commentary was forthcoming at a later date either.
3 *The London Times*, Parliamentary Report, July 29, 1943. "His Majesty's Government were not informed in advance of the establishment of this committee. They do not propose to recognize any similar committee in this country." This renders irrelevant, indeed, v. Puttkamer's contention (*op. cit.*, p. 43): "Later [after the founding of the National Committee on July 12, 1943] rumors were heard that the Russian government had received reports that similar ideas [of forming a committee] existed in the Western world. This they meant to anticipate at any price."
4 *New York Herald Tribune*, July 23, 1943; cf. also Weinert, *op. cit.*, p. 107.
5 *New York Times*, July 23, 1943.
6 *Op. cit.*, September 2, 1943.

7 *New Statesman and Nation*, July 26, 1943.
8 Thus the Stockholm correspondent of the *New York Times* reported, for instance, on January 28, 1945, that now (!) Seydlitz would become the new German chief of state.
9 *Neue Zürcher Zeitung*, July 22, 1943.
10 *Basler Nachrichten*, August 6, 1943.
11 *Neue Zürcher Zeitung*, July 26, 1943.
12 Radio Rome: Disunited Nations (July 26, 1943), quoted from Boehm, *op. cit.*, p. 294.
13 Tokyo's *Domei* news broadcast (July 24, 1943), quoted from Boehm, *loc. cit.*
14 Joseph Goebbels, *Tagebücher 1942 bis 1943* (German ed.), ed. by Louis P. Lochner, Zurich 1948, pp. 450, 482.
15 *Op. cit.*, p. 482.
16 Siegbert Kahn, *The Nationalcommittee Free Germany*, London 1943, p. 3.
17 V. Manstein, *op. cit.*, p. 395.
18 Felix Gilbert, *Hitler directs his war*, New York 1950; I used the

German version of the briefing in the Führer's headquarters of February 1, 1943, as printed in: *Die Welt als Geschichte* X/4, 1950, pp. 276ff.

19 *Op. cit.*, pp. 279f., 281.

20 *Op. cit.*, p. 282.

21 Pers. commun. of W. Scheidt. Dr. Scheidt was a member of the Commission of Military History of the OKW (German Armed Forces High Command) from Feb. 1, 1941 until the end of the war.

22 Jürgen Thorwald, *Es begann an der Weichsel*, Stuttgart 1951, p. 171.

23 Lothar Rendulic, *Gekämpft, gesiegt, geschlagen*, Heidelberg 1952, p. 338. It may be worth mentioning in this context that Matern bid farewell to everyone in the National Committee's House after a Christmas party, saying: "Be prepared for Königsberg!" Pers. commun. of H. Gerlach.

24 Gilbert, *op. cit.*, pp. 117f.

25 Pers. commun. of G. Engel, Lieutenant General, retired, who was an Army aide-de-camp to Hitler.

26 Cf. footnote 25.

27 Pers. commun. of W. v. Seydlitz, based on documentary material that I was permitted to consult.

28 Pers. commun. of W. v. Seydlitz, H. Gerlach. Cf. also Isa Vermehren, *Reise durch den letzten Akt*, Hamburg 1947, pp. 153f. The statement contained in this book that the wife of Pastor Schröder had been interned at Buchenwald "because her husband held the Lutheran service of Radio Moscow every two weeks for the troops (?) of the Free Germany movement," is only partially correct. On February 5, 1945, Keitel, the chief of the OKW (German Armed Forces High Command) issued a general order concerning measures to be taken against all members of the armed forces who committed acts of high treason while prisoners of war. The order, which went out on the radio, gave as "the Führer's orders":

"1. The families of members of the German Armed Forces who commit high treason while prisoners of war and who are legally sentenced to death for this crime are held responsible for them with their property, liberty, and life. The extent of this family-liability is determined by the Reichsführer SS and Chief of the German Police in every individual case.

"2. This order is to be immediately communicated orally to the troops and it is to serve at every opportunity as the object of intensive instruction in conjunction with the relevant decrees on high treason. This order is not to be communicated in writing beyond the staffs of divisions, etc."

Reproduction of a photocopy in Erich Kuby (ed.), *Das Ende des Schreckens*, Munich, n.d., pp. 46f.

29 Pers. commun. of W. v. Seydlitz.

30 Available documents on which the following description is based are:

I. German Armed Forces High Command (OKW). Communications for the Officers Corps. October 1943 (Special edition: *Moskauer Komitee Freies Deutschland*), Library of Congress.

II. *Was will das Nationalkomitee Freies Deutschland?* Ed. by the Army High Command (*Armeeoberkommando*). Probable date: October 1943.

III. *Nationalkomitee Freies Deutschland. An NSFO Ostheer und Ostluftwaffe.*

IV. *Soldaten der Ostfront.* Proclamation by Colonel General Guderian. Date: after July 20, 1944.
II, III, and IV at Yiddish Scientific Institute, New York.
V. *Verfügungen/Anordnungen/ Bekanntgaben.* Ed. by the *Parteikanzlei*, vol. 7, Part 2, 1944.
VI. *Politischer Dienst für SS und Polizei.* Ed.: *Der Reichsführer SS, SS-Hauptamt*, 1. Folge, 1944. V and VI at the *Institut für Zeitgeschichte*, Munich.
VII. German *Truppenmitteilungen* 1944 on Paulus and the National Committee, private papers of E.A. Paulus.

31 *Soldaten der Ostfront* (Soldiers of the Russian Front). Proclamation by Colonel General Guderian.

32 *Was will das Nationalkomitee Freies Deutschland?* (What are the goals of the National Committee for a Free Germany?), p. 2.

33 *Mitteilungen für das Offizierskorps* (Communications for the Officers Corps), p. 1.

34 *Was will . . .* , pp. 1f.

35 *Soldaten der Ostfront . . .*

36 Pers. commun. of H. v. Wedel (Chief of the Wehrmacht propaganda units), W. Scheidt, G. Engel, P.E. Schramm, A. Heusinger.

37 Pers. commun. of G. Engel, K. v. Tippelskirch.

38 V. Manstein, *op. cit.*, p. 602.

39 *Völkischer Beobachter,* October 18, 1944.

40 There is no mention of the numerous generals who signed various proclamations during 1944 in any of the German propaganda material available. The only name always mentioned is that of General von Seydlitz.

41 Cf. footnote 40.

42 *Reichssender* (official German radio station), October 15, 1944; *Völkischer Beobachter,* October 18, 1944; *Front und Heimat,* No. 38, September 1944.

43 *Front und Heimat . . .*

44 Pers. commun. of P. Schmidt, E. Kordt.

45 Pers. commun. of G. Hilger, v. Herwarth. Cf. also Karl Michel, *Ost und West—Der Ruf Stauffenbergs,* Zurich 1947, p. 191.

46 Cf. preceding footnote.

47 FD I/3, August 6, 1943.

48 *Sozialistische Mitteilungen,* Nos. 53/54 (1943), September–October, p. 12.

49 *Op. cit.*, Nos. 70/71 (Jan.–Feb. 1945), pp. 2f. Here Koenen is mentioned as a member of the KPD's (German Communist Party) Central Committee.

50 *Op. cit.*, pp. 3f.

CHAPTER FOUR: *The Organization, Front and Camp Propaganda of the National Committee and the League of German Officers*

1 Pers. commun. of W. v. Seydlitz, A. Bredt, H. Abel, H. Gerlach, W. Frhr. v. Senfft-Pilsach, I. v. Knobelsdorff-Brenkenhoff, J. Wieder, A. Greifenhagen, H.Z. Cf. also: *Die Gründung des Bundes Deutscher Offiziere* (Minutes of the founding session), September 1943, p. 53; Weinert *op. cit.*, pp. 29f.

2 Pers. commun. of W. v. Seydlitz, A. Bredt, H. Abel, H. Gerlach.

3 *Die Gründung . . .*

4 Pers. commun. of W. v. Seydlitz,

A. Bredt, H. Abel H. Gerlach; Weinert, *op. cit.*, p. 26.

5, 6 *Loc. cit.*

7 *Loc. cit.;* Weinert, *op. cit.*, p. 26f.

8 Weinert, *op. cit.*, p. 27. In 1944 an important memorandum of the generals referred to this "super democratization." Cf. footnotes 103–105 of Chapter Five.

9 Pers. commun. of W. v. Seydlitz, A. Bredt, H. Abel, H. Gerlach, I. v. Knobelsdorff-Brenkenhoff.

10 Cf. footnote 9.

11 Pers. commun. of H. Gerlach.

12 Pers. commun. of W. v. Seydlitz, H. Abel, H. Gerlach; cf. also v. Puttkamer, *op. cit.*, pp. 68f.; v. Einsiedel, *op. cit.*, p. 75.

13 Pers. commun. of W. v. Seydlitz; v. Puttkamer, *op. cit.*, p. 69.

14 Cf. preceding footnote.

15 Pers. commun. of H. Gerlach, J. v. Puttkamer.

16 Pers. commun. of W. v. Seydlitz, H. Abel, H. Gerlach, I. v. Knobelsdorff-Brenkenhoff; v. Puttkamer, *loc. cit.*

17 Pers. commun. of W. v. Seydlitz, H. Abel, H. Gerlach, J. v. Puttkamer.

18 *Loc. cit.*

19 *Loc. cit.;* cf. also Leonhard, *op. cit.*, p. 285.

20 Leonhard, *op. cit.*, pp. 282, 284f.

21 Pers. commun. of W. Leonhard.

22 Leonhard, *op. cit.*, p. 285.

23 Leonhard, *op. cit.*, p. 284.

24 Leonhard, *op. cit.*, pp. 285ff.

25 Pers. commun. of W. v. Seydlitz, H. Abel, H. Gerlach, I. v. Knobelsdorff-Brenkenhoff; cf. also Leonhard, *op. cit.*, p. 289.

26 Leonhard, *op. cit.*, p. 290.

27 Leonhard, *op. cit.*, pp. 289 and 274; pers. commun. of W. v. Seydlitz.

28 Pers. commun. of W. v. Seydlitz, H. Abel, H. Gerlach, J. Wieder, A. Greifenhagen, I. v. Knobels-dorff-Brenkenhoff. Cf. also v. Puttkamer, *op. cit.*, p. 74.

29 Pers. commun. of W. v. Seydlitz, H. Abel, H. Gerlach; Leonhard, *op. cit.*, pp. 290f., 309.

30 Pers. commun. of W. v. Seydlitz, H. Abel, H. Gerlach, W.W. v. Wildemann. Cf. also footnote 51 in Chapter Seven.

31 Leonhard, *op. cit.*, pp. 286ff.

32 *Loc. cit.*, p. 286.

33 Pers. commun. of H. Abel, H. Gerlach, I. v. Knobelsdorff-Brenkenhoff.

34 Cf. footnote 33.

35 Leonhard, *op. cit.*, pp. 300ff., 305 ff.

36 *Loc. cit.*, p. 305f.

37 *Loc. cit.*, 306ff.

38 Pers. commun. of W. v. Seydlitz, H. Abel, H. Gerlach; v. Puttkamer, *op. cit.*

39 Leonhard, *op. cit.*, p. 308; pers. commun. of W. v. Seydlitz.

40 Pers. commun. of W. v. Seydlitz, H. Abel, H. Gerlach, I. v. Knobelsdorff-Brenkenhoff.

41 Leonhard, *op. cit.*, pp. 290f.

42 *Op. cit.*, pp. 297, 309.

43 *Op. cit.*, p. 309.

44 *Op. cit.*, p. 292.

45 *Op. cit.*, p. 293.

46 *Op. cit.*, pp. 302ff.; pers. commun. of W. Leonhard.

47 Leonhard, *op. cit.*, pp. 307f.; pers. commun. of W. v. Seydlitz, H. Abel, H. Gerlach.

48 Seehaus, Sonderdienst: Funk-Abhörberichte 1943–1945; British Broadcasting Corporation (BBC) Monitoring Service: Daily Digest World Broadcasts, 1943–1945. Both series are available at the Library of Congress and at the Hoover Library, Stanford, California.

49 *Loc. cit.;* Leonhard, *op. cit.*, p. 308.

50 Seehaus; BBC; especially for the

period September 1943 to June 1944.

51 *Loc. cit.*

52 Pers. commun. of W. v. Seydlitz, H. Abel, H. Gerlach; cf. also Heinrich Count v. Einsiedel, *Das Nationalkomitee und seine Verantwortung für die Kriegsgefangenen* (The National Committee and its responsibility for the Prisoners of War).

53 FD I/1, July 19, 1943.

54 Pers. commun. of W. v. Seydlitz, H. Abel, H. Gerlach, I. v. Knobelsdorff-Brenkenhoff, J. Wieder, A. Greifenhagen.

55 *Loc. cit.;* cf. also Weinert, *op. cit.*, p. 88.

56 V. Puttkamer, *op. cit.*, pp. 44ff.

57 Pers. commun. of W. v. Seydlitz, H. Abel, H. Gerlach, I. v. Knobelsdorff-Brenkenhoff.

58 *Loc. cit.*

59 *Loc. cit.;* also FD I/19, November 21, 1953. As one outstanding example among others, this issue of *Freies Deutschland* reproduces the text of a leaflet in which the appeal to establish contacts with the National Committee merely suggests talks about conspiratory steps. No intention of undermining the front by isolated action can be read into the document either. Any such ambitions, which the Communists may have continued to harbor secretly, remained subordinated officially to the conception of the officers' union until the turn of 1943 to 1944. The articles and proclamations by Ulbricht (FD I/12, Oct. 3, 1943) and Weinert (FD I/16, Oct. 31, 1943) offer additional proof for this attitude. Cf. also: *Zur Geschichte* . . . , p. 210.

60 Cf. v. Tippelskirch, *Operative Führungsentschlüsse*, pp. 58ff.; v. Tippelskirch, *Geschichte* . . . , pp.

378ff.; v. Manstein *op. cit.*, pp. 474ff.

61 Pers. commun. of W. v. Seydlitz, H. Abel, H. Gerlach, W. Leonhard; cf. also Weinert, *op. cit.*, pp. 28f., 42. Von Puttkamer's statements (*op. cit.*, pp. 75f) are too vague and faulty.

62 Pers. commun. of W. v. Seydlitz, H. Abel, H. Gerlach, I. v. Knobelsdorff-Brenkenhoff; Weinert, *op. cit.*, p. 41.

63 Pers. commun. of W. v. Seydlitz, H. Abel, H. Gerlach.

64 *Loc. cit.* Not even a detailed talk delivered at the National Committee's fifth plenary session on November 19, 1943, supplied accurate figures. It continued to mention individual brigades of aides, although it spoke of twelve permanent delegates and about 120 representatives at the front at that time. Cf. Weinert, *op. cit.*, p. 89, and finally: *Zur Geschichte* . . . , p. 267.

65 Pers. commun. of W. v. Seydlitz, H. Abel; cf. Weinert, *op. cit.*, p. 28.

66 Pers. commun. of W. v. Seydlitz, H. Abel, H. Gerlach, I. v. Knobelsdorff-Brenkenhoff. I also consulted more than fifty different copies of leaflets, proclamations and handouts for the period from September to December of 1943.

67 Pers. commun. of W. v. Seydlitz, H. Abel, H. Gerlach, I. v. Knobelsdorff-Brenkenhoff, J. Wieder, A. Greifenhagen. Cf. also Leonhard, *op. cit.*, 297; v. Einsiedel, *Tagebuch* . . . , pp. 87, 105.

68 One such ID card without any date, but obviously dating from the year 1943, was available to the author.

69 Pers. commun. of H. Abel; cf. also v. Einsiedel, *op. cit.*, pp. 87ff., 150.

70 Pers. commun. of H. Count v. Einsiedel, H. Abel; v. Einsiedel, *op. cit.*, pp. 87, 155; *Die Front war überall*, pp. 22ff.; *Sie kämpften . . .* , pp. 56f., 60; cf. further Helmut Bohn, *Vor den Toren des Lebens*, Überlingen 1949, pp. 25ff.

71 Weinert, *op. cit.*, p. 42; cf. also: *Zur Geschichte . . .* , p. 232.

72 Pers. commun. of H. Count v. Einsiedel, H. Abel; *Die Front war überall*, pp. 22ff.; Weinert, *op. cit.*, p. 54.

73 Pers. commun. of W. v. Seydlitz, A. Bredt, H. Abel, H. Gerlach, I. v. Knobelsdorff-Brenkenhoff.

74 *Loc. cit.*

75 *Loc. cit.;* cf. also v. Einsiedel, *op. cit.*, pp. 87, 149; Wienert, *op. cit.*, pp. 55ff. *"Zentrale Flugblätter"* ("Crucial Leaflets") in: *Sie kämpften . . .* , pp. 165–184.

76 Pers. commun. of H. Count v. Einsiedel, H. Abel; testimony of numerous officers and soldiers; cf. Weinert, *op. cit.*, p. 58.

77 *Loc. cit.;* Weinert, *op. cit.*, p. 49.

78 V. Einsiedel, *op. cit.*, p. 96. According to the testimony of numerous officers and soldiers the example here cited is pretty typical. Occasionally the delegates would also be announced by leaflets. Cf. *Sie kämpften . . .* , pp. 188, 191, 309.

79 V. Einsiedel, *loc. cit.*

80 *Op. cit.*, pp. 96, 98.

81 *Op. cit.*, p. 98.

82 Pers. commun. of W. v. Seydlitz, H. Abel, H. Gerlach, H. Count v. Einsiedel; Weinert, *op. cit.*, p. 55; FD I/12, Oct. 3, 1943 and I/16, Oct. 31, 1943; cf. also appendices III, IV, and V. According to Weinert (*loc. cit.*), a total of eight million copies of the manifesto were printed; special leaflets were intended as a commentary for it,

e.g.: *Welche Ziele stellen sich das Nationalkomitee "Freies Deutschland" und der Bund Deutscher Offiziere?* Date: Autumn 1943.

83 V. Einsiedel, *op. cit.*, p. 98; Weinert, *op cit.*, p. 43; *Die Front war überall*, p. 42; testimony of numerous officers and soldiers.

84 Not all of Weinert's statements (*op. cit.*, pp. 44ff., 135ff.) can, of course, be challenged, but they are full of contradictions and their general significance is so poor that they corroborate indirectly what they seek to conceal even in retrospect.

85 Testimony of numerous officers and soldiers; cf. once more Picht, *op. cit.*, pp. 40ff., 44; Oechelhaeuser, *op. cit.*, pp. 170, 193f., 205; Richard Scheringer, *Das grosse Los*, Hamburg 1959, pp. 406ff.

86 Testimony of numerous officers and soldiers; cf. also Rendulic, *op. cit.*, p. 42; Klepper, *op. cit.*, p. 50; also Erich Kern, *Der grosse Rausche*, Waiblingen 1950, pp. 8f.

87 Testimony of numerous officers and soldiers; Kern, *op. cit.*, p. 111; Peter Bamm, *Die unsichtbare Flagge*, Munich 1952, pp. 174f.; Richard Hasemann, *Gejagt*, Stuttgart 1953, p. 68.

88 Testimony of numerous officers and soldiers; Bamm, *op. cit.*, p. 200; less superficially: Teske, *op. cit.*, p. 226.

89 Testimony of numerous officers and soldiers; Bamm, *op. cit.*, p. 153; Teske, *loc. cit.*

90 Testimony of numerous officers and soldiers; pers. commun. of H. Foertsch, K. v. Tippelskirch.

91 Testimony of numerous officers and soldiers; Kern, *op. cit.*, pp. 127f.; pers. commun. of E. Deth-

leffsen, H. Foertsch, M. Fretter Pico, H. Friessner, F. Hossbach, E. v. Manstein, K. v. Tippelskirch. There is also evidence available that leaflets of the National Committee were read, handed on, and discussed. But it has to be stressed that such reactions remained isolated. Any significant success had to be denied these actions as long as the initiative of the army commanders remained decisive according to the original propaganda line of the National Committee and the League. The generals, however, refused to co-operate.

92 FD I/14, Oct. 17, 1943; II/7, Feb. 12, 1944; cf. also appendices IV and VII. It is significant that Daniels' letter is still based on the idea of an orderly change of government at a time when the National Committee already propagated that salvation lay only in joining its cause. For Daniels the only thing which matters is German initiative—in this case that of Field Marshal von Manstein. There is no mention of any retreat to the Reich's frontiers, nor of the crucial argument of the second propaganda conception which the entire Free Germany organization had had to accept in early January 1944. Von Seydlitz's letters to Busch, Küchler, and Holidt, written in 1943 *and* 1944 and also available as leaflets, also show unmistakably a certain tactical continuity in the propaganda of the League. All of them stress primarily the need for independent action from the German side. Cf. also footnote 25 of Chapter Five.

93 The most convincing account is v. Manstein's, *op. cit.,* pp. 303ff., chapters 12–15; cf. also v. Tippelskirch, *op. cit.,* pp. 383ff.,

392ff.; Görlitz, *op. cit.,* II, pp. 217ff. and generally Hans Friessner, *Verratene Schlachten,* Hamburg 1956.

94 V. Manstein, *op. cit.,* pp. 308ff., 507ff.; v. Tippelskirch, *loc. cit.;* Görlitz, *loc. cit.*

95 Pers. commun. of E. Dethleffsen, H. Foertsch, M. Fretter Pico, H. Friessner, F. Hossbach, E. v. Manstein, K. v. Tippelskirch, E.B., and Frhr. v. L. Cf. also v. Manstein, *op. cit.,* p. 602. Especially useful: v. Senger und Etterlin, *op. cit.,* p. 69.

96 Pers. commun. of E. Dethleffsen, H. Foertsch, M. Fretter Pico, F. Hossbach, K. v. Tippelskirch.

97 Cf. footnote 96.

98 Pers. commun. of H. v. Wedel, E. Dethleffsen, M. Fretter Pico, F. Hossbach, K. v. Tippelskirch.

99 Cf. preceding note.

100 Pers. commun. of A. Bredt. As a member of the presidium of the League of German Officers, Bredt had to keep the membership lists; he carefully registered every member's joining and leaving and was able to show an average membership of forty percent in the officers' camps as early as the beginning of 1944.

101 Pers. commun. of W. v. Seydlitz, A. Bredt, H. Abel, H. Gerlach; cf. also v. Einsiedel, *op. cit.,* p. 38.

102 Pers. commun. of W. v. Seydlitz, A. Bredt, H. Abel, H. Gerlach, I. v. Knobelsdorff-Brenkenhoff, H. Count v. Einsiedel.

103 *Loc. cit.*

104 *Loc. cit.;* testimony and reports of numerous German prisoners of war, officers and soldiers, quoted below as: *AuB* (*Aussagen und Berichte*).

105 *AuB;* this is confirmed, for a later period, by Gollwitzer, *op. cit.,*

especially pp. 57ff.; Weinert (*op. cit.*, pp. 62ff.) is useless on the whole, despite some concrete data.

106 *AuB;* cf. also Gollwitzer, *op. cit.*, pp. 66, 102f., 138ff., 152ff., 177ff.

107 *AuB;* report of K.H.F.

108 *AuB;* cf. also Gollwitzer, *op. cit.*, p. 181.

109 *AuB;* Gollwitzer, *op. cit.*, especially pp. 147ff.

110 *AuB.*

111 *Loc. cit.;* report by K.H.F.; Gollwitzer, *op. cit.*, p. 133.

112 *AuB;* report by K.H.F.; Gollwitzer, *op. cit.*, pp. 57ff., 131ff., 172, 186, 208ff.; cf. also Franz F. Wurm, *Schuld und Niederlage der Antifa,* in: *Neues Abendland VII* (1952), pp. 404f., 407ff. The enforced isolation of Lunyovo is shown by the fact that General von Seydlitz needed special permission to visit an otherwise inaccessible camp; appalled by conditions there he called it a red Maidanek. Pers. commun. of W. v. Seydlitz, confirmed by H. Gerlach.

113 *AuB;* Gollwitzer, *op. cit.*, p. 186. Cf. also Grams, *op. cit.*, p. 106.

114 *AuB;* report by K.H.F.; Golwitzer, *op. cit.*, pp. 227f. Cf. also Ingbert Franz, *Licht im Osten,* Eichstätt/Wien/Düdingen 1952, p. 92. That National Socialism itself had already given rise to heated discussions is confirmed by v. Senger und Etterlin (*op. cit.*, p. 448) for a British camp in 1946 (!).

115 *AuB;* report by K.H.F.; Gollwitzer, *op. cit.* p. 133; Grams, *loc. cit.* An impression of the implacable opposition between the camps is offered by Assi Hahn (*Ich spreche die Wahrheit!*, Esslingen 1951, pp. 35ff.), although his definition of the terms "anti-fascist" and "fascist" remains superficial and indebted to propaganda terminology.

116 *AuB;* cf. also Gollwitzer, *op. cit.*, pp. 90, 92ff.

117 Cf. Weinert, *op. cit.*, pp. 62ff. There is no point in emphasizing in detail the available data on the propaganda successes of the National Committee; they cannot be verified and are, to anyone familiar with the conditions, for the most part without any value.

118 *AuB;* Grams, *op. cit.*, pp. 106f.; Hahn, *op. cit.*, pp. 147ff., 155ff., 165ff.; Humbert, *op. cit.*, No. 8, pp. 15f.; No. 9, pp. 14ff.; No. 10, pp. 16f. Hahn and Humbert are so reckless about many facts that a detailed analysis would unearth numerous half-truths and errors. Frequently personal opinions are presented as general statements of fact and mere rumors become incontestable truths. Numerous arrogant value judgments without any actual base in fact have to be met with a consciously critical attitude and marked skepticism. But in their own way both reports also speak the truth. Unmitigated by any reflection, they represent the attitudes of the opposition to a National Committee behind barbed wire and remain, therefore, indispensable. It is only in this sense that they can and should be used as sources.

119 Cf. Hahn, *op. cit.*, pp. 7ff. and pp. 114ff.

120 *Op. cit.*, pp. 147ff., 155ff. (especially p. 157, on Colonel von Hanstein, "who drove the Russians to a frenzy by his provocations"), 165ff.; Humbert, *loc. cit.* Paulus' alleged secret message to Block VI (Hahn, *op. cit.*, p. 160) must be regarded as highly improbable.

121 Hahn, *op. cit.*, pp. 83ff., 130ff.

122 Hahn, *op. cit.*, pp. 153, 156; *AuB;* report by K.H.F.

[123] Hahn, *op. cit.*, p. 154; report by K.H.F.

[124] Hahn, *loc. cit.*

[125] *Loc. cit.*

[126] Hahn, *op. cit.*, p. 153.

[127] Humbert, *op. cit.*, Heft 9, p. 14.

[128] *AuB;* report by K.H.F.; cf. also Weinert, *op. cit.*, p. 64.

[129] *AuB;* report by K.H.F.

[130] *Loc. cit.;* Hahn, *op. cit.*, pp. 127ff.; Humbert, *op. cit.*, No. 10, p. 17. And this remained unchanged although the number of crimes reported in the newspaper *Free Germany* and evoking helpless bitterness at Lunyovo became almost overwhelming and incredible. On the Kharkov trials: FD I/24, Dec. 27, 1944; on the massacre at Kiev (Babi Yar): FD II/2, Jan. 9, 1944; II/10, March 5, 1944; on Osaritchi: II/20, May 14, 1944.

[131] *AuB;* report by K.H.F.; pers. commun. of J. Kayser, Schlömer.

[132, 133] *Loc. cit.*

[134] *Loc. cit.;* pers. commun. by W. v. Seydlitz, A. Bredt, H. Burmeister; cf. also Weinert, *op. cit.*, p. 65. The figures mentioned here are confirmed by A. Bredt.

[135] Pers. commun. of A. Bredt.

[136] *AuB;* report by K.H.F.

[137] *AuB;* pers. commun. of W. Frhr. v. Senfft-Pilsach.

[138] *AuB;* pers. commun. of A. Bredt, H. Abel, H. Gerlach.

[139] Pers. commun. of W. v. Seydlitz, A. Bredt, H. Abel, H. Gerlach; cf. also Weinert, *op. cit.*, pp. 62ff.

[140] Pers. commun. of W. v. Seydlitz, A. Bredt, H. Abel, H. Gerlach, I. v. Knobelsdorff-Brenkenhoff.

[141] *AuB;* report by K.H.F.

[142] *Loc. cit.;* pers. commun. of A. Bredt.

[143] Pers. commun. of F.W.K., J. Schröder, H. Hennersdorf, J. Kayser, A. Ludwig.

[144] Pers. commun. of J. Schröder.

[145] Pers. commun. of F.W.K., J. Schröder, A. Ludwig.

[146] Pers. commun. of F.W.K., J. Schröder.

[147] Pers. commun. of J. Schröder, A. Ludwig.

[148] Pers. commun. of F.W.K., J. Schröder, H. Hennersdorf, J. Kayser, A. Ludwig.

[149] *Loc. cit.*

[150] *Loc. cit.* This consideration played a significant role, as some of the priests who were captured by the Soviets during 1943 had themselves seen the mass graves of the SD's victims, *e.g.*, F.W.K. in Kiev.

[151] *Loc. cit.*

[152] Pers. commun. of H. Hennersdorf, A. Ludwig.

[153] *Christen für ein neues Deutschland,* private ed., 1945, p. 40; parts of the relevant paper are also printed in Weinert, *op. cit.*, pp. 37f.

[154] Pers. commun. of F.W.K., J. Schröder, A. Ludwig. It is typical that the bulk of the priests felt that after the German capitulation of May 1945, the conditions for continued active participation in the National Committee no longer existed. The challenge of the exceptional situation existed only for the duration of the war, which had to be terminated as soon as possible for Germany's sake.

[155] Pers. commun. of F.W.K., J. Schröder, J. Kayser, A. Ludwig.

[156] *Loc. cit.;* cf. also Gollwitzer, *op. cit.*, pp. 129f.

[157] Pers. commun. of F.W.K., J. Schröder, H. Hennersdorf, J. Kayser, A. Ludwig.

[158] Pers. commun. of J. Schröder, J. Kayser.

[159] Pers. commun. of F.W.K., J. Schröder.

160 Pers. commun. of F.W.K., J. Schröder, H. Hennersdorf, A. Ludwig.

161 *Loc. cit.*; cf. also Georg v. Rauch, *Geschichte des bolschwistischen Russland*, Wiesbaden 1955, pp. 442f.

162 *Christen für . . .* , p. 41. Despite many cuts, which impair its value as a source, this brochure gives a good impression of the scope of the intellectual attempt to come to terms with the anti-Christian elements in National Socialism. Cf. also: FD II/26, June 25, 1944, II/27, July 2, 1944.

163 *Christen für . . .*

164 Pers. commun. of F.W.K., J. Schröder, J. Kayser, A. Ludwig. *Loc. cit.* The Church Committee (*Kirchenkreis*) nominated all the colleagues captured by the Soviets who could be contacted for pastoral service in the camps. But not all would agree to the Russians' condition of rejecting the National Socialist régime. Those priests who did join the National Committee were vouched for by a pledge provided by the Church committee.

165 *Loc. cit.*; cf. also Seehaus; BBC, especially the 1944 series.

166 Pers. commun. of F.W.K., J. Schröder, J. Kayser, A. Ludwig.

167 *Loc. cit.* The demands of the Catholic priests in the National Committee can no longer be reconstructed in detail. They did, at any rate, present the Catholic concept of the state and demanded denominational schools and a party of their own.

168 *Loc. cit.*

CHAPTER FIVE: *From Teheran to Cherkassy*

1 Pers. commun. of W. v. Seydlitz, A. Bredt, H. Abel, H. Gerlach, I. v. Knobelsdorff-Brenkenhoff, J. Wieder, A. Greifenhagen, Th. Plievier, H. Count v. Einsiedel. Cf. also v. Einsiedel, *op. cit.*, pp. 103, 104f.; Leonhard, *op. cit.*, p. 297.

2 Testimony of numerous officers and soldiers; cf. also Gollwitzer, *op. cit.*, pp. 43f., 159f. Scheringer, *op. cit.*, p. 453 (the date for this, however, is 1945).

3 Testimony of numerous officers and soldiers; cf. also the realistic appraisal of any such chances in v. Einsiedel, *op. cit.*, p. 88.

4 This cannot be denied, despite Weinert, *op. cit.*, pp. 44ff., 135ff.

5 The most important of these leaflets is: *Antwort an das OKW.* Cf. the appendix of illustrations in Weinert, *op. cit.*, pp. 167ff.; FD II/1, Jan. 3, 1944. It was signed for the National Committee by Weinert as its president, for the League of German Officers by Colonel General Bredt as the chief of the personnel section. The bottom part of this leaflet was intended to serve as legitimation for establishing contacts with the National Committee delegates. It was in this way, according to Weinert (*op. cit.*, p. 90), that the troops could find out about the true situation themselves.

6 Pers. commun. of W. v. Seydlitz, A. Bredt, H. Abel, H. Gerlach, Th. Plievier, H. Count v. Einsiedel.

7 Cf. Seehaus; BBC; for October to December 1943.

8 Weinert, *op. cit.*, p. 88.

9 FD I/16, October 31, 1943.

10 Leonhard, *op. cit.*

11 Pers. commun. of W. v. Seydlitz, H. Abel, H. Gerlach; cf. also v. Einsiedel, *op. cit.*, p. 106.

12 V. Einsiedel, *op. cit.*, pp. 105ff.; pers. commun. of H. Abel, H. Gerlach.

13 V. Einsiedel, *op. cit.*, pp. 86ff.; pers. commun. of H. Count v. Einsiedel, H. Abel, H. Gerlach. Cf. also in this context: *Sie kämpften* . . . , p. 35.

14 V. Einsiedel, *op. cit.*, pp. 106f., as well as pers. commun. of H. Count v. Einsiedel, H. Abel, H. Gerlach.

15 V. Einsiedel, *op. cit.*, p. 106; pers. commun. of W. v. Seydlitz, A. Bredt, H. Abel, H. Gerlach, I. v. Knobelsdorff-Brenkenhoff, J. Wieder, A. Greifenhagen. Cf. also Weinert, *op. cit.*, p. 90.

16 I used a leaflet of autumn 1943.

17 Weinert, *op. cit.*, p. 51.

18 This is again shown by the bulk of the available propaganda material for the period of September to December 1943.

19 On the details of this: pers. commun. of W. v. Seydlitz, A. Bredt, H. Abel, H. Gerlach, I. v. Knobelsdorff-Brenkenhoff, J. Wieder, A. Greifenhagen, W. Frhr. v. Senfft-Pilsach. Cf. also: Wieder, *Die Tragödie* . . . , p. 112; and generally Hans Dibold, *Arzt in Stalingrad*, Salzburg 1949.

20 On the Teheran Conference cf. Meissner, *op. cit.*, pp. 27ff.; Deuerlain, *op. cit.*, pp. 36ff.; W. S. Churchill, *The Second World War*, Vol. V: *Closing the Ring*, London 1952, pp. 302–360; R. Sherwood (German tr.), *Roosevelt und Hopkins*, Hamburg 1950, pp. 632–655; W. D. Leahy, *I Was There*, London 1950, pp. 239–251.

21 FD I/21, Dec. 5, 1943; I/22, Dec. 12, 1943.

22 That these commentaries decided the issue is confirmed by W. v. Seydlitz, A. Bredt, H. Abel, H. Gerlach, I. v. Knobelsdorff-Brenkenhoff.

23 *Loc. cit.*; cf. also, despite his overstatements: v. Einsiedel, *op. cit.*, p. 107.

24 Pers. commun. of W. v. Seydlitz, Schlömer, H. Gerlach.

25 Weinert, *op. cit.*, p. 90; Leonhard, *op. cit.*, pp. 297f.; FD II/2, Jan. 9, 1944, II/14, April 2, 1944, II/17, April 23, 1944; cf. also Appendices VI, IX, XII, and XIV. Copious material on the second propaganda line in: *Sie Kämpften* . . . , pp. 220–224, 235, 299, 311–324, 327–331, 335–338, 356f., 360ff. All these sources and documents are unambiguous. The argument "Save yourself by joining the cause of the National Committee" was used from now on not only for trapped units but for the German front as a whole. This presents a clear situation to historical analysis and evaluation, for it remained constitutive both in intention and reality. It has to be stressed, nevertheless, that the important appeals of the generals of 1944 (cf. Appendices XI, XIII, and XV) avoided any appeal to subversion which would have occurred if the second propagandistic program of the National Committee for a Free Germany had proven itself effective. The fact that the captured generals simply called in general terms for the overthrow of Hitler and the termination of the war after July 20, 1944, should not be overestimated. Tactical considerations about the most effective propaganda line had become illusory in view of Germany's political situation. The existence of divergent approaches side by side

even within the committee and the officers' union could hardly have been helpful. But the generals' appeals also show the renewed breakthrough of ideas which the Communist section could smother only after a tough struggle at the beginning of January 1944.

26 Pers. commun. of W. v. Seydlitz, A. Bredt, H. Abel, H. Gerlach, I. v. Knobelsdorff-Brenkenhoff, J. Wieder, A. Greifenhagen. On the following cf. also: Leonhard, *op. cit.*, p. 298.

27 Cf. v. Tippelskirch, *Operative Führungsentschlüsse* . . . , pp. 58ff.; v. Tippelskirch, *Geschichte* . . . , pp. 378–402; v. Manstein, *op. cit.*, pp. 473ff., 507ff.

28 Particularly v. Tippelskirch, *Operative Führungsentschlüsse* . . . , p. 60.

29 Cf. footnote 27.

30 Pers. commun. of W. v. Seydlitz, Schlömer, A. Bredt, H. Gerlach.

31 Meissner, *op. cit.*, pp. 21ff.; Deuerlein, *op. cit.*, pp. 35f.; Churchill, *op. cit.*, pp. 247–266; Hull, *op. cit.*, pp. 1274–1315; I. R. Deane, *Ein seltsames Bundnis* (German tr.), Vienna, n.d., pp. 17–29.

32 *Loc. cit.*

33 Hull, *op. cit.*, pp. 1285, 1304.

34 Hull, *op. cit.*, p. 1287; FD II/2, January 9, 1944; Weinert, *op. cit.*, pp. 90f.; *Zur Geschichte* . . . , p. 263.

35 Hull, *loc. cit.*

36 This has been shown very impressively by Meissner, *op. cit.*

37 Free Germany. Research and Analysis Branch (US Dept. of State, Nov. 26, 1943), Library of Congress, Washington, D.C., p. 6: "In the first place, the possibility of using the Free German committee as the contact point for sep-

arate peace negotiations, if it ever existed in force, has by now been eliminated by the Moscow agreements."

38 Cf. footnote 31.

39 Hull, *op. cit.*, pp. 1298f.

40 Kleist, *op. cit.*, pp. 280ff.

41 Pers. commun. of W. v. Seydlitz; cf. also v. Einsiedel, *op. cit.*, p. 106; Leonhard, *op. cit.*, p. 297.

42 Kleist, *op. cit.*, p. 280.

43 Kleist, *op. cit.*, p. 255.

44 Cf. footnote 20 of this chapter and especially Meissner, *op. cit.*, pp. 27ff.

45 Kleist, *op. cit.*, p. 281.

46 Meissner, *op. cit.*; Deuerlein, *op. cit.*, pp. 36ff.; Churchill, *op. cit.*, pp. 302–360; Sherwood, *loc. cit.*; Leahy, *loc. cit.*

47 Churchill, *op. cit.*, pp. 319f., 349ff., 356f.; Leahy, *op. cit.*, p. 249.

48 Churchill, *op. cit.*, p. 354; Sherwood, *op. cit.*, p. 651; Leahy, *loc. cit.*; cf. also Deuerlein, *op. cit.*, pp. 40f.

49 Kleist, *op. cit.*, pp. 280f.

50 Pers. commun. of W. v. Seydlitz, A. Bredt, H. Abel, H. Gerlach, I. v. Knobelsdorff-Brenkenhoff, J. Wieder, A. Greifenhagen, W. Frhr. v. Senfft-Pilsach. Cf. also Weinert, *op. cit.*, pp. 99f.

51 Pers. commun. of W. v. Seydlitz, A. Bredt, H. Abel, H. Gerlach, Th. Plievier, H. Count v. Einsiedel.

52 FD I/21, December 5, 1943; I/22, December 12, 1943.

53 V. Tippelskirch, *Geschichte* . . . , pp. 428ff.; Görlitz, *op. cit.*, II, pp. 241ff. (but he is misleading concerning the "ideology" of the National Committee for a Free Germany); v. Manstein, *op. cit.*, pp. 582ff.; Hausser, *op. cit.*, pp. 116ff. All of these books present, more or less satisfactorily, military details. The best general study is

that of Nikolaus v. Vormann, *Tscherkassy,* Heidelberg 1954; cf. pp. 62, 68. On the preceding operations: pp. 11ff., 16ff., 25ff., 57ff. The book (vol. 3 of the series *Die Wehrmacht im Kampf*) also provides valuable insights into the psychological situation of the German troops at the front in 1944. Von Einsiedel (*op. cit.,* pp. 111ff.) and Leonhard (*op. cit.,* pp. 298f.) are of practically no use on Cherkassy. Both rely on Soviet data that are demonstrably untenable as v. Vormann (*op. cit.,* p. 112) has convincingly shown. Maps on the Cherkassy operations can be found in v. Vormann and v. Tippelskirch.

54 Cf. v. Manstein, *op. cit.,* p. 586 footnote.

55 V. Manstein, *op. cit.,* pp. 582f.; v. Tippelskirch, *op. cit.,* pp. 428f.; v. Vormann, *op. cit.,* pp. 25ff.

56 V. Tippelskirch, *op. cit.,* p. 429; v. Manstein, *op. cit.,* p. 583; v. Vormann, *op. cit.,* pp. 62, 96.

57 V. Tippelskirch, *loc. cit.;* v. Manstein, *loc. cit.;* v. Vormann, *op. cit.,* pp. 67ff., 71ff., 78ff., 83ff.

58 V. Tippelskirch, *loc. cit.;* v. Manstein, *op. cit.,* pp. 584f.; v. Vormann, *op. cit.,* pp. 72ff., 78ff., 82ff.

59 V. Vormann, *op. cit.,* pp. 95ff., 109.

60 Pers. commun. of W. v. Seydlitz.

61 *Loc. cit.* Von Puttkamer's statements (*op. cit.,* p. 72) are erroneous and beside the point, according to the evidence of General v. Seydlitz, who must be regarded as authoritative on this particular issue. That goes especially for the alleged hint by Shcherbakov "that Stalin himself had voiced the wish that Seydlitz should undertake this trip."

62 FD II/6, Feb. 5, 1944.

63 *Loc. cit.*

64 *Loc. cit.,* pers. commun. of W. v. Seydlitz, H. Gerlach; *Zur Geschichte* . . . , p. 274.

65 *Loc. cit.*

66 V. Vormann, *op. cit.,* p. 105. The text of the Russian ultimatum, without signature: pp. 106ff.

67 Pers. commun. of W. v. Seydlitz, H. Abel; also in FD II/8, Feb. 21, 1944; v. Puttkamer, *op. cit.,* p. 73; v. Vormann, *op. cit.,* p. 112; *Sie kämpften* . . . , pp. 230–234, 237–245.

68 Pers. commun. of W. v. Seydlitz, H. Abel; v. Puttkamer, *loc. cit.;* *Sie kämpften* . . . , p. 52.

69 *Loc. cit.*

70 *Loc. cit.;* v. Vormann, *op. cit.,* p. 113.

71 Pers. commun. of W. v. Seydlitz, H. Abel, Lieb; v. Puttkamer, *op. cit.;* v. Vormann, *op. cit.,* p. 114. The texts of the letters (Seydlitz to Lieb, Mattenklott, and Fouquet; Korfes to Gille) can be found in FD II/9, Feb. 27, 1944. Cf. also: *25 Artikel zur Beendigung des Krieges,* Stockholm 1944, pp. 21ff.; Weinert, *op. cit.,* pp. 52f.; *Sie kämpften* . . . , pp. 51, 246–250; *Zur Geschichte* . . . , pp. 272–275.

72 Pers. commun. of Lieb, W. v. Seydlitz, H. Abel; *Sie kämpften* . . . , pp. 51f.

73 Pers. commun. of Lieb; cf. also v. Vormann, *op. cit.,* pp. 112ff.

74 Pers. commun. of Lieb.

75 *Loc. cit.*

76 *Loc. cit.*

77 V. Vormann, *op. cit.,* pp. 96ff. Von Vormann mentions the figure of 50,000 men for the time immediately preceding the breakthrough. Considering the losses they had already suffered up to that time (cf. *op. cit.,* p. 109), this figure is probably too high,

rather than too low. It does, at
any rate, accurately reflect the
strength of the trapped German
units. Cf. also footnote 54 of this
chapter.

78 Pers. commun. of Lieb; v. Tippelskirch, *op. cit.*, pp. 378–402,
427ff.; v. Manstein, *op. cit.*, pp.
397ff., 473ff., 507ff.; v. Vormann,
*op. cit.*, pp. 11, 21; cf. also Kern,
*op. cit.*, pp. 121f.

79 V. Vormann, *op. cit.*, pp. 12, 25ff.,
46f; cf. also Kern, *op. cit.*, pp.
118ff.; Albert Benary, *Die Berliner
Bären-Division*, Bad Nauheim
1955, p. 144.

80 Pers. commun. of Lieb; v. Vormann, *op. cit.*, pp. 46f.

81 Pers. commun. of Lieb, A. Count
Schenk v. Stauffenberg, testimony
of German soldiers and officers
trapped at Cherkassy; v. Vormann,
*op. cit.*, p. 47. Von Vormann also
concedes the great psychological
pressure exerted by the activities
of the committee and the officers'
union: "The German side clearly
recognized the great dangers inherent in this kind of propaganda
at that time. In practice, and considering the unfortunate situation
on all fronts, nothing could be
mustered against it except the
appeal to the German military
traditions." The whole ambiguity
of the situation (*op. cit.*, p. 52)
becomes obvious in the passage:
"Even where their faith in the
Führer was shaken, they [the
German soldiers] continued to
believe staunchly in their people
and in their Germany. They believed that loyalty demanded
loyalty in turn. Until *their* world
collapsed in May 1945."

82 Pers. commun. of Lieb; testimony
of German officers and soldiers
trapped at Cherkassy.

83 *Loc. cit.*

84 *Loc. cit.*

85 Pers. commun. of W. v. Seydlitz,
Lieb.

86 Pers. commun. of Lieb; testimony
of German officers and soldiers
trapped in the Cherkassy pocket.
Cf. also v. Vormann, *op. cit.*, p.
114.

87 FD II/9, February 27, 1944.

88 Pers. commun. of Lieb; v. Vormann, *op. cit.*, pp. 115ff.; v. Puttkamer, *loc. cit.*

89 V. Vormann, *op. cit.*, pp. 121ff.

90 *Loc. cit.* especially p. 123. The
number of prisoners stated here
represents a cautious estimate
based on the figures offered by v.
Manstein and v. Vormann; it may
actually have been even higher.

91 Pers. commun. of W. v. Seydlitz,
H. Abel; Leonhard, *op. cit.*, p.
299. In contrast to this evidence
Weinert (*op. cit.*, p. 91) believes,
with an abnormal falsification of
reality, that the 18,000 soldiers
and officers who did surrender had
joined the cause of the National
Committee.

92 Pers. commun. of W. v. Seydlitz,
H. Abel. Von Vormann (*op. cit.*,
p. 113) overstates his case when
he contends that the failure of this
first large-scale mission had sealed
the National Committee's fate.
Stalin by no means cast aside the
instrument "which he himself had
created for the subversion of the
German Wehrmacht."

93 *Loc. cit.*; v. Puttkamer, *op. cit.*

94 Pers. commun. of W. v. Seydlitz,
H. Abel, H. Gerlach.

95 FD II/7, Feb. 12, 1944; Weinert,
*op. cit.*

96 FD II/9, Feb. 27, 1944.

97 Testimony of numerous officers
and soldiers. Cf. also v. Vormann,
*op. cit.*, pp. 50f.

98 V. Einsiedel, *op. cit.*, pp. 114ff.

99 *Loc. cit.*, p. 115; pers. commun.

of W. v. Seydlitz, A. Bredt, H. Abel, H. Gerlach, I. v. Knobelsdorff-Brenkenhoff.
100 *Loc. cit.*
101 Pers. commun. of W. v. Seydlitz, H. Abel, H. Gerlach.
102 *Loc. cit.;* v. Einsiedel, *op. cit.,* pp. 115f.
103 Pers. commun. of W. v. Seydlitz, A. Bredt, H. Abel, H. Gerlach.
104 Pers. commun. of W. v. Seydlitz; cf. also, despite exaggerated and incorrect statements, v. Einsiedel, *op. cit.,* pp. 116f.
105 Pers. commun. of W. v. Seydlitz.
106, 107 *Loc. cit.*
108 *Loc. cit.;* cf. also v. Einsiedel, *op. cit.,* p. 117.
109 H. Gerlach, *Der Fall Huber,* p. 1; cf. also v. Einsiedel, *op. cit.,* pp. 116, 118. Von Puttkamer (*op. cit.,* pp. 65ff.) cannot be used in this case as he gets Huber and Stolz mixed up and, again, accepts second-hand reports.
110 H. Gerlach, *loc. cit.*
111 *Loc. cit.*
112, 113, 114 *Loc. cit.*

115 Pers. commun. of W. v. Seydlitz.
116 V. Einsiedel, *op. cit.,* p. 116; H. Gerlach, *loc. cit.*
117 Pers. commun. of W. v. Seydlitz; H. Gerlach, *loc. cit.*
118 H. Gerlach, *loc. cit.*
119 *Loc. cit.*
120 *Loc. cit.;* pers. commun. of W. v. Seydlitz.
121 H. Gerlach, *loc. cit.;* pers. commun. of O. Jahn.
122 H. Gerlach, *op. cit.;* cf. v. Einsiedel, *op. cit.,* p. 118. Captain Stolz did not return to Lunyovo from his mission at the front. His further fate remains unknown. Pers. commun. of W. v. Seydlitz, H. Gerlach.
123 H. Gerlach, *op. cit.*
124 *Loc. cit.;* pers. commun. of J. Wieder, A. Greifenhagen. Thus Dr. Wieder, for example, once dared to challenge a dogmatic historical talk given by the Communist émigré Edwin Hörnle.
125 Pers. commun. of W. v. Seydlitz, A. Bredt, H. Abel; H. Gerlach, *loc. cit.*

CHAPTER SIX: *July 20, 1944, and the Free Germany Movement*

1 Pers. commun. of W. v. Seydlitz, A. Bredt, H. Abel, H. Gerlach, I. v. Knobelsdorff-Brenkenhoff. Cf. also v. Einsiedel, *op. cit.,* p. 127; Leonhard, *op. cit.,* pp. 315f.
2 Pers. commun. of W. v. Seydlitz, A. Bredt, H. Gerlach, Th. Plievier, H. Count v. Einsiedel. Cf. also footnote 5 of this chapter.
3 Pers. commun. of W. v. Seydlitz, A. Bredt, H. Abel, H. Gerlach, I. v. Knobelsdorff-Brenkenhoff, W. Frhr. v. Senfft-Pilsach, J. v. Puttkamer.
4 Pers. commun. of W. v. Seydlitz, H. Count v. Einsiedel.
5 BBC, I, 832, July 23, 1944.
6 Pers. commun. of W. v. Seydlitz,

A. Bredt, H. Abel, H. Gerlach, I. v. Knobelsdorff-Brenkenhoff, J. v. Puttkamer. Cf. also v. Einsiedel, *loc. cit.;* Leonhard, *op. cit.*
7 Pers. commun. of W. v. Seydlitz, A. Bredt, H. Abel, H. Gerlach, W. Frhr. v. Senfft-Pilsach.
8 *Loc. cit.;* Leonhard, *op. cit.,* pp. 316f.; cf. also Dieter Ehlers, *Die Methoden der Beck/Goerdeler-Verschwörung,* Bonn, n.d., pp. 60ff.
9 V. Einsiedel, *op. cit.,* pp. 127f.; cf. also v. Puttkamer, *op. cit.,* pp. 83f.
10 Pers. commun. of W. v. Seydlitz, A. Bredt, H. Abel, W. Frhr. v. Senfft-Pilsach.

11 Cf. preceding note.
12 Cf. v. Tippelskirch, *Operative Führungsentschlüsse*..., pp. 61f.
13 V. Tippelskirch, *Geschichte* ..., pp. 530ff.; Hermann Gackenholz, "Zum Zusammenbruch der Heeresgruppe Mitte im Sommer 1944," in: *Vierteljahreshefte für Zeitgeschichte* 3 (1955), pp. 317 ff.; Teske, *op. cit.*, pp. 208ff.
14 V. Tippelskirch, *op. cit.*, pp. 541ff., 556ff.
15 *Loc. cit.*, pp. 466ff. (The invasion of 1944.)
16 Pers. commun. of W. v. Seydlitz, H. Abel, H. Gerlach, I. v. Knobelsdorff-Brenkenhoff, W. Frhr. v. Senfft-Pilsach, H. Count v. Einsiedel.
17 Pers. commun. of W. v. Seydlitz, A. Bredt, H. Abel, H. Gerlach. Cf. also, once more: *Die Front war überall*, pp. 22ff., 30ff., 50ff., 62ff. The reports referred to here are contradictory, tendentious, and not verifiable as to details, but they show more than the mere intention of a subversive activity.
18 Pers. commun. of W. v. Seydlitz, A. Bredt, H. Abel, H. Gerlach.
19 Pers. commun. of W. v. Seydlitz, J. v. Puttkamer. It was impossible to reconstruct specific figures on this, since the evidence is too divergent; their mere reproduction would be without value, since it would necessitate too many qualifications.
20 Pers. commun. of W. v. Seydlitz, A. Bredt, H. Abel, H. Gerlach, I. v. Knobelsdorff-Brenkenhoff, W. Frhr. v. Senfft-Pilsach.
21 *Loc. cit.*; v. Puttkamer, *op. cit.*, pp. 81.
22 Pers. commun. of W. v. Seydlitz, A. Bredt, H. Abel, H. Gerlach, Th. Plievier, H. Count v. Einsiedel.
23 *Loc. cit.*
24 *Loc. cit.*; v. Seydlitz, *Gründe* ..., p. 2; cf. also Korfes, *op. cit.*, cols. 1293f.
25 Pers. commun. of W. v. Seydlitz, A. Bredt, H. Abel, H. Gerlach, I. v. Knobelsdorff-Brenkenhoff, J. Wieder, A. Greifenhagen; H. Herlch, *Die Haltung*. . .
26, 27 *Loc. cit.*
28 FD II/13, March 26, 1944, II/18, April 30, 1944.
29 *Seehaus* . . . , October 29, 1944.
30 Pers. commun. of W. v. Seydlitz, A. Bredt, H. Abel, H. Gerlach, I. v. Knobelsdorff-Brenkenhoff, W. Frhr. v. Senfft-Pilsach, J. v. Puttkamer. They knew too well that these were merely historical examples. Cf. also: *Die Gründung* . . . , p. 56.
31 Pers. commun. of W. v. Seydlitz, A. Bredt, H. Abel, H. Gerlach, I. v. Knobelsdorff-Brenkenhoff, J. Wieder, A. Greifenhagen, W. Frhr. v. Senfft-Pilsach. Weinert (*op. cit.*, pp. 99ff.) only offers summary remarks.
32 Pers. commun. of W. v. Seydlitz, A. Bredt, H. Gerlach, J. Wieder, W. Frhr. v. Senfft-Pilsach.
33 *Loc. cit.* I have to refer once more to Paetel's misleading presentation (*op. cit.*, p. 10).
34 V. Einsiedel, *op. cit.*, pp. 119ff.; 130ff.; v. Puttkamer, *op. cit.*, pp. 37ff.; Fritz Löwenthal, *Der neue Geist von Potsdam,* Hamburg 1948, pp. 240f.
35 Pers commun. of W. v. Seydlitz, A. Bredt, H. Abel, H. Gerlach, I. v. Knobelsdorff-Brenkenhoff, W. Frhr. v. Senfft-Pilsach; v. Puttkamer, *op. cit.*, pp. 81f.
36 V. Einsiedel, *op. cit.*, p. 126; Löwenthal, *loc. cit.*
37 V. Einsiedel, *loc. cit.*
38 V. Einsiedel, *op. cit.*, p. 119; pers. commun. of W. v. Seydlitz, H. Abel, H. Gerlach, Th. Plievier, H.Z.

39 Pers. commun. of H. Count v. Einsiedel; v. Einsiedel, *op. cit.*, pp. 119, 232.

40 Pers. commun. of Frhr. v. Gersdorff, P. van Husen, J. Kaiser, A. Leber, F. v. Schlabrendorff, Th. Steltzer, K. Strölin. Korfes (*op. cit.*, p. 1296) offers only polemics or misleading utterances on the reaction of the resistance within Germany.

41 Cf. footnote 40.

42 V. Hassell, *op. cit.*, p. 341. "There are some doubts about the authenticity [of the letter], but Daniels has made a personal reference to a former company leader of his battalion at Rastenburg, who is now commander of a division. You can't simply invent something like that." Pers. commun. of Frhr. v. Gersdorff, R. Pechel, F. v. Schlabrendorff, W. Frhr. v. Senfft-Pilsach. F. v. Schlabrendorff and W. Frhr. v. Senfft-Pilsach belonged to the circle of friends around Ewald v. Kleist-Schmenzin. Decisively shaped by his mind, v. Schlabrendorff recognized the "School of Schmenzin" in many a turn of phrase of v. Senfft-Pilsach's FD articles.

43 Pers. commun. of Frhr. v. Gersdorff, J. Kaiser, A. Leber, R. Pechel.

44 Eberhard Zeller, *Geist der Freiheit—Der Zwanzigste Juli*, Munich, n.d.; Gerhard Ritter, *Carl Goerdeler und die deutsche Widerstandsbewegung*, Stuttgart 1954, especially Book Three; Ehlers, *op. cit.*, vols. I and II; v. Hassel, *op. cit.*, pp. 200ff.

45 V. Hassell, *op. cit.*, pp. 231.

46 V. Hassell, *op. cit.*, pp. 200, 209; Zeller, *op. cit.*, pp. 127ff., 134; Fabian v. Schlabrendorff, *Offiziere gegen Hitler*, Zurich/Vienna/Konstanz 1946, pp. 33, 53f.; Alexander Dallin (German tr.) *Deutsche Herrschaft in Russland 1941–1945*, Düsseldorf 1958, pp. 42ff.

47 Cf. v. Hassell, *op. cit.*, p. 291; Ritter, *op. cit.*, pp. 344ff.

48 V. Schlabrendorff, *op. cit.*, pp. 109ff.

49 Zeller, *op. cit.*, pp. 185ff.; Ritter, *loc. cit.*; v. Schlabrendorff, *op. cit.*, pp. 123f.

50 Ehlers, *op. cit.*, pp. 50ff.; Ritter, *op. cit.*, p. 358.

51 Zeller, *op. cit.*, p. 88; cf. also Helmuth James Count v. Moltke, "Einer vom deutschen Widerstand. Die letzten Briefe des Grafen Moltke," in: *Neue Auslese* 2 (1947), I.

52 Proclamation: *To the German Generals and Officers! To the German People and the Wehrmacht!* Reproduced in: *Die Gründung* . . . , p. 7. Cf. also Appendix II.

53 Kunrat Frhr. v. Hammerstein, "Schleicher, Hammerstein und die Machtübernahme 1933," in: *Frankfurter Hefte* 11 (1956), I, p. 14. Pers. commun. of R. Pechel.

54 V. Hammerstein, *loc. cit.*

55 *Loc. cit.*

56 V. Hassell, *op. cit.*, p. 321.

57 *Op. cit.*, p. 341.

58 *Op. cit.*, p. 321.

59 Michel, *op. cit.*, p. 191; Kleist, *op. cit.*, pp. 242f. Pers. commun. of H. J. v. Kleist-Retzow.

60 Pers. commun. of Frhr. v. Gersdorff, P. van Husen, J. Kaiser, F. v. Schlabrendorff, Th. Steltzer. The decisive aspect remained that of the subversion of the German armies in the east, which was the heart of the National Committee's second propaganda program. In the testimony and statements this element is dominant to such an extent that one sometimes gets the impression that the first program

of Lunyovo had never been no-
ticed by the resistance circles in
Germany.

61 *Kaltenbrunner reports* (Nov. 29,
1944), series in the War Dept.,
Departmental Records Branch,
Alexandria, Va.
62 Pers. commun. of A. Count
Schenk v. Stauffenberg; *Kaltenbrunner reports* (Nov. 29, 1944).
They seriously challenge the all
too vague description given by v.
Puttkamer, *op. cit.*, p. 83.
63 FD I/1, July 19, 1943.
64 V. Hassell, *op. cit.*, pp. 376ff.
65 Ritter, *op. cit.*, pp. 208–289.
66 Zeller, *op. cit.*, pp. 70ff., 82ff., 85.
67 *Op. cit.*, p. 158.
68 *Op. cit.*, p. 209.
69 Friedrich Meinecke, *Die deutsche
Katastrophe*, Wiesbaden 1949, p.
150.
70 FD I/1, July 19, 1943.
71 Ritter, *loc. cit.*
72 Pers. commun. of W. v. Seydlitz,
A. Bredt, H. Abel, H. Gerlach, Th.
Plievier, H. Count v. Einsiedel.
73 Ehlers, *op. cit.*, pp. 50ff.
74 *Op. cit.*, pp. 60ff.
75 *Loc. cit.*
76 *Op. cit.*, pp. 54f., 62.
77 *Op. cit.*, pp. 40ff., 50.
78 Cf. generally Ritter, *op. cit.*
79 Ehlers, *op. cit.*, p. 50.
80 *Loc. cit.*, p. 51f.; cf. also v.
Schlabrendorff, *op. cit.*, p. 103.
81 Pers. commun. of W. v. Seydlitz,
A. Bredt, H. Abel, H. Gerlach. Cf.
also the excerpts of Steidle's talk
in Chapter Two.
82 Ehlers, *op. cit.*, pp. 52, 70.
83 The propaganda material available
for the period of September 1943
to December 1945 does not offer
any clues regarding an eastern
orientation.
84 Pers. commun. of W. v. Seydlitz,
A. Bredt, H. Abel, H. Gerlach, H.
Count v. Einsiedel.
85 Pers. commun. of Frhr. v. Gersdorff, H.B. Gisevius, P. van Husen,
F. v. Schlabrendorff.
86 Cf. on this especially v. Schlabrendorff, *op. cit.*, pp. 102ff. and footnotes 64–66.
87 Ritter, *op. cit.*, pp. 570ff.; Zeller,
*op. cit.*, p. 202.
88 V. Hassell, *op. cit.*, p. 332.
89 Ritter, *op. cit.*, p. 334.
90 *Op. cit.*, pp. 334f.
91 Cf. especially Ritter, *op. cit.*, pp.
368ff. and also Zeller, *loc. cit.*
92 Allen W. Dulles (German tr.),
*Verschwörung in Deutschland*,
Kassel 1949, pp. 131f.
93 *Loc. cit.*
94 V. Hassell, *op. cit.*, p. 321; additional information can be found
on pp. 241, 315, 327, 352.
95 Ritter, *op. cit.*, pp. 379f.
96 *Kaltenbrunner reports* of August
8 and 28, November 21 and 29,
1944; cf. also Ritter, *op. cit.*, p.
381.
97 Pers. commun. of Frhr. v. Gersdorff, P. van Husen, J. Kaiser, F.
v. Schlabrendorff, Th. Steltzer;
Ehlers, *op. cit.*, pp. 55, 62; Zeller,
*op. cit.*, p. 203.
98 Zeller, *op. cit.*, pp. 208f.
99 *Loc. cit.*
100 V. Schlabrendorff, *op. cit.*, p. 175.
101 Dulles, *op. cit.*, p. 171.
102 Zeller, *op. cit.*, pp. 223f., 238ff.
103 Pers. commun. of Frhr. v. Gersdorff, P. van Husen, J. Kaiser, F.
v. Schlabrendorff; Ehlers, *op. cit.*,
p. 55; Zeller, *op. cit.*, p. 203.
104 Pers. commun. of Frhr. v. Gersdorff, E. Gerstenmaier, H.B.
Gisevius, P. van Husen, J. Kaiser,
A. Leber, F. v. Schlabrendorff, Th.
Steltzer, K. Strölin. On the Western Front: G. Blumentritt, E.
Jünger, H. Speidel, F. v. Teuchert.
On another resistance group: F.
Hielscher.
105 Pers. commun. of P. van Husen,

Th. Steltzer. Dulles' description (*op. cit.*, p. 172), according to which Trott had tried to establish contacts with the Seydlitz Committee via Stockholm shortly before July 20, 1944, is misleading.

106 Pers. commun. of J. Kuhn.

107 Cf. Werner Plesse, "Zum antifaschistischen Widerstandskampf in Mitteldeutschland (1939–1945)," in: *Zeitschrift für Geschichtswissenschaft*, 2 (1954), No. 6, pp. 823–834. This strictly partisan article is reliable only on some concrete data. Also: Gertrud Glondajewski/Heinz Schumann, *Die Neubauer–Poser–Gruppe;* Gerhard Nitzsche, *Die Saefkow–Jacob–Bästlein–Gruppe.* Both Berlin 1957.

108 Plesse, *op cit.*, pp. 825ff., 828ff.

109 Pers. commun. of W. v. Seydlitz, H. Gerlach, Th. Plievier, W. Leonhard, H. Count v. Einsiedel.

110 Weinert, *op. cit.*, p. 95; v. Puttkamer, *op. cit.*, pp. 77; Leonhard, *op. cit.*, p. 320; Friedrich Paulus, *Mein Beitritt zur Bewegung "Freies Deutschland."*

111 Pers. commun. of W. v. Seydlitz; v. Puttkamer, p. 79.

112 Pers. commun. of W. v. Seydlitz, A. Bredt, H. Abel, H. Gerlach, J. v. Puttkamer, H. Count v. Einsiedel.

113 Paulus, *op. cit.*

114 FD II/34, August 20, 1944; Leonhard, *op. cit.*, pp. 320f. The appeal must have been drafted before the day of the signing. The date, "8," was inserted by hand in the text written on a typewriter.

115 Pers. commun. of W. v. Seydlitz.

116 Pers. commun. of W. v. Seydlitz, A. Bredt, H. Abel, H. Gerlach; v. Puttkamer, *op. cit.*, p. 80; cf. also the appendix of illustrations in Weinert, *op. cit.*, pp. 167ff.

CHAPTER SEVEN: *Dissolution and End*

1 Twenty-five Articles for Ending the War, FD II/10, March 5, 1944. This proclamation was edited by Herrnstadt. Cf. Appendix IX.

2 V. Tippelskirch, *op. cit.*, pp. 530ff.; Gackenholz, *op. cit.*, pp. 317 ff.; Teske, *op. cit.*, pp. 208ff. Maps showing the collapse of the Army Group Center can be found in v. Tippelskirch and Gackenholz.

3 Gackenholz, *op. cit.*, pp. 323ff.

4 *Op. cit.*, p. 317.

5 *Op. cit.*, p. 318. It remained up to Heinrich Himmler ("Rede vor den Gauleitern am 3. August 1944," in: *Vierteljahreshefte für Zeitgeschichte* 1 (1953), 4, p. 377) to attest for the troops that they had "become absolutely unstable internally by the spreading custom or ill custom of surrendering and playing at generals with Herr Seydlitz and the Russians." Theodor Eschenburg, the editor of this highly suggestive document, has already pointed out that this was intended to divert attention from the actual causes of the collapse of the Army Group Center.

6 Gackenholz, *loc. cit.*

7 *Loc. cit.*

8 Leonhard, *op. cit.*, pp. 318f.; v. Einsiedel, *op. cit.*, p. 143.

9 FD II/29, July 16, 1944; Leonhard, *op. cit.*, p. 318.

10 FD II/31, July 30, 1944; pers. commun. of W. v. Seydlitz, A.

Bredt, H. Gerlach. Cf. also Appendix XI.

[11] Pers. commun. of W. v. Seydlitz; Leonhard, *op. cit.*, pp. 318f.; FD II/29, July 16, 1944.

[12] Pers. commun. of W. v. Seydlitz, Schlömer, H. Gerlach, J. v. Puttkamer; v. Puttkamer, *op. cit.*, p. 78; v. Einsiedel (*op. cit.*, p. 143) only offers a highly emotional description.

[13] FD II/32, Aug. 6, 1944; II/33, Aug. 13, 1944; cf. also Leonhard, *op. cit.*, p. 319; Weinert's data (*op. cit.*, p. 95) are inaccurate.

[14] Weinert, *op. cit.*; pers. commun. of W. v. Seydlitz, H. Gerlach.

[15] FD II/40, Oct. 1, 1944; Leonhard, *op. cit.*, p. 321. Cf. Appendix XIII. Kurt Schiebold, *Opfergang in Rumänien*, Tübingen 1952, conveys a harrowing impression of the sequel of the collapse of the German Army Group Southern Ukraine.

[16] FD II/50, Dec. 10, 1944; Leonhard, *op. cit.*, p. 322f.; Weinert, *op. cit.*, p. 96. Cf. Appendix XV. The appeal with which Vinzenz Müller approached the generals at first threatened to *miscarry* because of one sentence which the generals wished to see deleted. It was impossible to ascertain what the wording of the contested sentence was. It was, at any rate, eliminated by the personal intercession of General von Seydlitz, and Müller finally managed to push through his appeal. During the signing only General Heine refused to put his name to the document, which several generals had drafted, among them Paulus, Strecker, Seydlitz, Korfes, and Lattmann. Heine was neither threatened nor pressured. In October 1955 he returned home to Germany as one of the first of the prisoners of war who had been freed by Chancellor Adenauer's visit to Moscow. Pers. commun. of W. v. Seydlitz. Also: Paulus, *Mein Beitritt. . .*

[17] Pers. commun. of W. v. Seydlitz, Schlömer, A. Bredt, H. Gerlach; cf. also v. Einsiedel, *op. cit.*, p. 149.

[18] Zeller, *op. cit.*, pp. 270ff.; v. Tippelskirch, *op. cit.*, pp. 497ff.; Picht, *op. cit.*, pp. 44f.; Ehlers, *op. cit.*, p. 61; v. Senger und Etterlin, *op. cit.*, pp. 349f.; cf. also on general aspects: Jürgen Thorwald, *Es begann an der Weichsel*, Stuttgart 1951; by the same author: *Ende an der Elbe*, Stuttgart 1950.

[19] Testimony of numerous officers and soldiers; Picht, *loc. cit.*; Kern, *op. cit.*, pp. 85, 127, 155ff.; Reinhard Hauschild, *Plus–Minus–Null*, Darmstadt 1952, pp. 40, 163; Joachim Günther, *Das letzte Jahr*, Hamburg 1948, p. 265.

[20] Testimony of numerous officers and soldiers.

[21] *Loc. cit.*; Picht, *loc. cit.*; v. Tippelskirch, *op. cit.*, p. 625; Wurm, *op. cit.*, p. 405; Bamm, *op. cit.*; Oechelhaeuser, *op. cit.*, pp. 204, 221, 299; Andreas Engermann, *Einen Bessern findst Du nicht*, Bad Wörishofen 1952, p. 437; Dietrich v. Choltitz, *Soldat unter Soldaten*, Konstanz/Zurich 1951, pp. 130f.

[22] Testimony of numerous officers and soldiers; v. Tippelskirch, *loc. cit.*; Wurm, *loc. cit.*; Bamm, *op. cit.*, p. 273.

[23] Testimony of numerous officers and soldiers; Picht, *op. cit.*, p. 45; Scheringer, *op. cit.*, p. 445.

[24] V. Tippelskirch, *op. cit.*, pp. 611ff.

[25] Testimony of numerous officers and soldiers; Thorwald, *Es be-*

*gann.* . . , pp. 121–126; v. Einsiedel, *op. cit.*, pp. 154f.; Kern, *op. cit.*, pp. 169ff.

26 Testimony of numerous officers and soldiers; v. Tippelskirch, *op. cit.*, pp. 625, 631; on general aspects: Thorwald, *Es begann.* . . , *passim*; Friedrich Hossbach, *Die Schlacht um Ostpreussen*, Überlingen 1951.

27 Testimony of numerous officers and soldiers; v. Tippelskirch, *op. cit.*, p. 625; cf. also Kern, *op. cit.*, p. 177.

28 Cf. v. Tippelskirch, *op. cit.*, pp. 161ff.

29 Testimony of numerous officers and soldiers; Kern, *op. cit.*, p. 152; Hauschild, *op. cit.*, p. 83; Joachim Schultz, *Die letzten dreissig Tage*, Stuttgart 1951, pp. 22, 26f., 55, 62f.; Walter Lüdde-Neurath, *Regierung Dönitz*, Göttingen 1950, pp. 61f.

30 Cf. especially Paul Kluke, "Nationalsozialistische Europaideologie," in: *Vierteljahreshefte für Zeitgeschichte*, 3 (1955), pp. 240ff.

31 Pers. commun. of W. v. Seydlitz, H. Gerlach, H. Count v. Einsiedel; cf. also v. Einsiedel, *op. cit.*, pp. 156, 161ff.; testimony of numerous officers and soldiers.

32 V. Einsiedel, *op. cit*, pp. 154f.

33 Even the priests within the Free Germany organization urged this in a document entitled: "To the Lutheran and Catholic clergy and communities in the Eastern parts of the Reich" (October 27, 1944) and, more fundamentally in: "German priests call the German people" (end of 1944). The second document was formulated only after a tough struggle between the Lutheran and Catholic clergy. The Catholic section has proposed an appeal (according to a note by J. Kayser) which was to contain a more explicit delineation *vis-à-vis* Communism. The second document contained the following passage nevertheless: "On the basis of our own better information about the situation we assure you that even under occupation, especially by the Red Army, no Christian will have to suffer for his faith. As we have done as prisoners of war here in the Soviet Union, so you will be able at home to direct the life of your church with complete liberty of faith and conscience and with a complete clear recognition of the differences in *Weltanschauung*. Therefore all of you Christians, especially you clerics and you leading men in the life of the Churches, have to unite in brotherly and calm prudence and must not be misled into leaving your homes and communities. You must also prevent your native cities and villages from being destroyed by pointless resistance and our people from being finally hurled into the abyss by an insane guerrilla war. You best protect your possessions by staying, by which you will also assure the continuity of church life. To flee, on the other hand, means immense misery, poverty, hunger, and exposure!"

34 Pers. commun. of W. v. Seydlitz, H. Gerlach; also FD II/42, Oct. 15, 1944, II/20, May 16, 1945. Steidle suffered a nervous breakdown and was hardly able, because of his shock, to report his experiences even after his return to Lunyovo.

35 V. Einsiedel, *op. cit.*

36 *Op. cit.*, p. 163; cf. also v. Puttkamer, *op. cit.*, p. 83.
37 Testimony of numerous German
prisoners of war.
38 *Loc. cit.*, v. Einsiedel, *op. cit.*, pp.
158f.; FD III/13, March 28, 1945.
The report of Bechler, delegate at
the front near Graudenz, is useless; it merely substantiates that
the National Committee was active near that fortress.
39 Thorwald, *op. cit.*, pp. 323ff.
40 Pers. commun. of W. v. Seydlitz,
H. Gerlach. As early as August
1944, Field Marshal Paulus had,
with the Soviets' permission, sent
the draft of an honorable surrender to the German army group
in the Kurland pocket and a personal letter to its commander in
chief, Colonel General Schörner.
Both documents remained unanswered. Paulus, *Mein Beitritt. . .*;
cf. further: *Zur Geschichte . . .*,
pp. 304f.; Werner Haupt, *Kurland*,
Bad Nauheim 1960, especially p.
116; Hans Breithaupt, *Die Geschichte der 30. Infanterie-Division*,
Bad Nauheim 1955, p. 278;
Werner Buxa, *Weg und Schicksal
der 11. Infanterie-Division*, Kiel
1952, p. 63.
41 *Sie kämpften. . .*, pp. 105ff.; *Zur
Geschichte . . .*, pp. 309ff.; cf.
further: Paul Klatt, *3. Gebirgs-
jägerdivision 1939–1945*, Bad
Nauheim 1958, p. 322.
42 *Loc. cit.* It was an act of diversion
near Tannenwald in East Prussia.
A combat mission is described in:
*Sie kämpften. . .*, pp. 105.
43 *Loc. cit.* (Alexandrov wrote in
*Pravda*: Comrade Ehrenburg over-
simplified!)
44 *Loc. cit.* How absolute this resistance was is shown by Walther
v. Seydlitz, *Stellungnahme 1944*
(December 1944). He analyzes
public statements by Weinert and

Ackermann and emphasizes the
German character of the three
eastern provinces chosen to be
annexed. He also argues for
reparations to Poland. But he is
convinced that an Oder-Neisse line
must make impossible any fruitful
Polish-German rapprochement.
45 Pers. commun. of W. v. Seydlitz,
A. Bredt, H. Abel, H. Gerlach.
46 V. Einsiedel, *op. cit.*, pp. 167f.;
pers. commun. of W. v. Seydlitz,
H. Gerlach.
47 Pers. commun. of W. v. Seydlitz,
A. Bredt, H. Abel, H. Gerlach;
v. Einsiedel, *op. cit.*, p. 171.
48 V. Einsiedel, *op. cit.*, p. 168;
Leonhard, *op. cit.*, p. 319.
49 Leonhard, *loc. cit.*; v. Einsiedel,
*op. cit.*, p. 170.
50 V. Einsiedel, *op. cit.*, pp. 170f.
51 FD III/33, August 16, 1945; pers.
commun. of H. Gerlach.
52 Cf. v. Puttkamer, *op. cit.*, p. 83.
53 FD III/9, February 25, 1945.
54 Pers. commun. of W. v. Seydlitz,
A. Bredt, H. Abel, H. Gerlach, I.
v. Knobelsdorff-Brenkenhoff, W.
Frhr. v. Senfft-Pilsach.
55 *Loc. cit.*; v. Einsiedel, *op. cit.*,
p. 172; cf. also FD III/May
through October, 1945. The number of proclamations, articles, and
resolutions on the question of
reparations alone increased so
much during this period that individual references had to be
abandoned. That was easily possible, as the tenor of the printed
documents remained the same
throughout.
56 Leonhard, *op. cit.*, pp. 329, 334ff.
57 Pers. commun. of W. v. Seydlitz,
H. Abel, H. Gerlach, v. Puttkamer,
*op. cit.*, p. 85. The statement in
v. Puttkamer that Ulbricht was
still in the Soviet Union in the
Fall of 1945 is, however, incorrect.

58 Pers. commun. of W. v. Seydlitz, H. Abel, H. Gerlach; v. Einsiedel, *loc. cit.*

59 V. Einsiedel, *op. cit.*, pp. 172f.; pers. commun. of H. Gerlach.

60 V. Einsiedel, *op. cit.*, p. 174; pers. commun. of H. Gerlach.

61 V. Einsiedel, *op. cit.*, pp. 174f.

62 *Loc. cit.*; FD III/44, November 3, 1945; Weinert, *op. cit.*, pp. 130ff.; v. Puttkamer, *op. cit.*, p. 86.

63 Minutes of the Final Session of the National Committee for a Free Germany at Lunyovo, November 2, 1945 (unpublished copy), p. 1.

64 *Loc. cit.*, pp. 1ff.

65 *Loc. cit.*, pp. 10ff.

66 *Loc. cit.*, p. 14.

67 *Loc. cit.*

68 *Loc. cit.*

69 Pers. commun. of W. v. Seydlitz, A. Bredt, H. Abel, H. Gerlach, v. Einsiedel, *op. cit.*, p. 177.

70 V. Einsiedel, *op. cit.*, p. 176; v. Puttkamer, *op. cit.*, p. 87.

71 Cf. v. Puttkamer, *op. cit.*, pp. 88ff. It would be pointless to attempt anything like a complete listing of the functions carried out by individual members of the National Committee after the war. What applied in 1945 and after does not necessarily apply any more today. The general references in the text may therefore take the place of fragmentary and dubious information.

72 Cf. v. Puttkamer, *op. cit.*, p. 87.

73 Pers. commun. of W. v. Seydlitz, H. Abel, H. Gerlach; v. Puttkamer, *loc. cit.*

74 V. Puttkamer, *op. cit.*, p. 88.

75 Cf. v. Einsiedel, *op. cit.*, pp. 175f.

76 Pers. commun. of W. v. Seydlitz, H. Gerlach; v. Einsiedel, *op. cit.*, p. 177; v. Puttkamer, *loc. cit.*, the last one giving a wrong date for the evacuation of the House at Lunyovo.

77, 78 Pers. commun. of W. v. Seydlitz.

79 V. Einsiedel, *op. cit.*, p. 181.

80 Pers. commun. of H. Abel, H. Gerlach, J. Wieder; cf. also Gollwitzer, *op. cit.*, pp. 223ff.

81 Pers. commun. of H. Abel, H. Gerlach, J. Wieder.

82, 83, 84 *Loc. cit.*

85 Pers. commun. of W. v. Seydlitz, H. Abel, H. Gerlach, J. Wieder.

## Sources and Additions

THE SOURCES on which a history of the Free Germany movement has to be based are particularly ambiguous and varied in their importance. The committee and the officers' union were passionately attacked from the moment they were founded, which has prevented any fruitful and unbiased investigation to this day. Instead of sober reports we find one-sided apologies; instead of elucidating information, mutual accusations. Witnesses who have returned home after years as prisoners of war either decided to remain silent or to make statements dictated by the moment and its requirements. Serious discussion seemed to have become inconceivable; only a few emphasized what can claim attention as historical truth. It took several years before this state of affairs was ended. Only after a certain amount of documents and primary sources had become available was the historian able to move participants to objective statements in personal interviews. He was aided in his task by the growing distance in time. Now the description of an unusual organization behind barbed wire has become possible.

The Free Germany movement in its final shape of September 1943 cannot be understood without considering Stalingrad. The catastrophe on the banks of the Volga, therefore, had to be described in its psychological effects to make sufficiently clear in which ways it served as the precondition for the events which were to spring from it. The military events had to be touched upon where they explained the intellectual and psychological position of the soldiers.

The literature on the Battle of Stalingrad is abundant and rewarding. The necessity of coming to terms with one of the greatest defeats of the German Army has produced considerable results. On this subject Puttkamer, Rohden, Selle, Toepke, Wieder, and Schröter were used, among others. Schröter's book contains exceptionally rich documentary material, while most of the others provide valuable insights, enriched by personal recollections. Schröter's documents are, unfortunately, the only merit of this book, which has often been mentioned as a model of how not to write history. What is lacking in Schröter was therefore taken from Tippelskirch. In his *History of the Second World War* he was the first to treat the Battle of Stalingrad in its totality, despite the sometimes too general survey he prefers. Manstein's memoirs are the last military word on the battle between Don and Volga. It is, of course, doubtful that the former commander of an army group always recalls his feelings and thoughts accurately. There is a considerable body of documentary evidence that emphatically questions his volume *Lost Victories*. There is also Wieder's profound article, which came out subsequently and which contains telling criticisms of several passages of Manstein's account. But all this does not invalidate what the general has to say with his great authority on the destruction of the Sixth Army. He remains a master of strategy.

On the history of the Free Germany movement one has to name first of all the books by Einsiedel and Puttkamer. Written after their return from Soviet prison camps, they reflect the situation mentioned above; both try to justify and explain their own positions. This results in peculiarly strange aspects and distorting points of view but also in disclosures and truths that must not be overlooked. The importance of these works is, therefore, undeniable even where their errors had to be pointed out. The same thing holds true of their opponents Hahn and Humbert. Their publications are still redolent of the hatred, at times quite impossible, which they felt toward the National Committee and the League. But they also provide a clear description of those groups which strictly opposed any "collaboration" behind barbed wire.

After the use of these publications there still remained serious information gaps which could be closed only by interviews and written inquiries. The problems of this method, which had to be developed by scholars working in contemporary history, are obvious.

Impaired memories and the fear of provoking undesirable consequences by being candid acted as serious impairments. But on the whole the results of these labors turned out quite satisfactorily. Personal contacts opened up unexpected avenues of external criticism. It was only through several pieces of oral evidence that the variegated picture of the Free Germany movement came to life, not to mention the written evidence which was supplied willingly. It was neither avoidable nor need it be undesirable in all cases that such men as Seydlitz, Abel, Gerlach, Einsiedel, Puttkamer, Bredt, Schlömer, Senfft-Pilsach, Knobelsdorff-Brenkenhoff, Wieder, and Plievier spoke mainly for and about themselves, for innumerable opposing voices filled with resentment were and still are being heard.

So much for personal memories. By way of documentary material there was available: the newspaper *Free Germany, radio broadcasts* monitored in Germany and Great Britain, and finally numerous propaganda *leaflets, handouts,* and written *appeals.* Critical doubts had to be entertained only with regard to the *Free Germany* paper. But there was a distinct line separating the useful from the impossible. There was, on the one hand, the blatant bias fostered by the Communist editor in chief, which was easily eliminated. On the other hand, the weekly newspaper did offer appeals, articles, reports, and excerpts from minutes which were genuine and simply had to be taken into account. The same holds true for the documentary volumes *They Fought for Germany* and *On the History of the German Anti-Fascist Resistance Movement 1933–1945.* The documents, frequently reproduced in facsimile, remained eloquent, although every single personal report in these volumes had been altered.

This useful material and the newspaper *Free Germany* are thoroughly corroborated by Leonhard's brilliant book, while Weinert's published memoirs about the committee and officers' union turned out to be useless. The miserable publication raises the question to what extent it represents the personal hand of the late president of the National Committee. Weinert also shows only too often a kind of Marxist partisanship which does not recoil from contradictions and which distorts many relationships. The Free Germany movement, for instance, achieved great successes if one believed this book blindly. Only a few of its data are therefore reliable. They concern the by-laws, the structure, and some of the plenary sessions of the two organizations at Lunyovo.

The committee and the officers' union would hardly take on a recognizable shape were one to disregard Allied and German reactions to them. *Radio broadcasts*, as well as American and British reflections, can be found in the *New York Times, New York Herald Tribune, New Statesman and Nation, Neue Züricher Zeitung*, and the *Basler Nachrichten*. It is hardly surprising that Hitler viewed the Free Germany movement with implacable hatred. He had to view the organization of German prisoners of war in the Soviet Union as the incarnation of blackest treason. Wherever, therefore, hate-filled accusations by Hitler are mentioned in Gilbert and in the *Official Publications* they can be accepted as authentic with some confidence. The same attitude can be taken regarding the communications of Heusinger, Engel, Scheidt, Wedel, and Schramm, who testify to the total rejection of the committee and the officers' union on the basis of their various functions. The only thing left for an analysis, therefore, was to elucidate the arguments used by the leadership of the National Socialist state in pronouncing their anathema.

The attitude of the resistance within Germany toward the Free Germany movement is barely mentioned in the relevant literature. Some publications which mention in passing the committee and the officers' union have to be contested on this point; even the excellent study by Ehlers provides only limited information here. In addition to the *Kaltenbrunner Reports* the survivors of the July 20 plot had to be interviewed in person on this issue. Although the statements by Schlabrendorff, Gerstenmaier, Kaiser, and A. Count Schenk von Stauffenberg, among others, were not always unambiguous on this point, they at least hinted at some hitherto unknown attitudes.

Equally difficult was the question of the attitudes which dominated the German soldiers and prisoners of war in the east; *i.e.*, those masses whose feelings and convictions had to be studied in order to explain the success or failure of propaganda under the colors of black-white-and-red. Quality and quantity had to be combined in this case to achieve an adequate picture. Only thousands can express, normally, what thousands are moved by. It was therefore necessary to approach them. This task, practically insoluble for an individual, could be handled only by using representative sampling. Fortunately this worked out well. The attitudes toward the committee and the officers' union were overwhelmingly uniform; several hundreds of *Statements* produced, on the whole, the same elements. The sum of these statements supplemented the literature that had proved useful. Examples of the latter are Bamm, Hauschild, Hasemann, Hohoff, and Gollwitzer. Among these Gollwitzer's book deserves a special ranking, since it also evaluates the committee and the officers' union according to their actual importance within a circumspect general description.

Where the political background of the Free Germany movement had to be studied, the basic texts of Churchill, Sherwood, Leahy, Hull, Deane, Deuerlein, and Kleist were used. They cannot, of course, take the place of the missing Russian documents, for which the historian will probably have to wait for some time to come. This meant that the delineation of the Soviet Union's intentions could be substantiated only tentatively rather than conclusively in every instance. But just as we have to accept the existence of witnesses condemned to silence or determined to remain in seclusion, we will also have to bear with this kind of shortcoming. It is somewhat reduced by the studies on Soviet foreign policy between 1943 and 1945 which have appeared in the meantime and are here taken into account. Its general lines have been established by scholarship to an extent which permits an evaluation of the significance of the National Committee and the League of German Officers in this context too.

# Bibliography

LIST OF SOURCES AND SECONDARY MATERIAL

## Documents, unpublished reports, and other sources

[In this part of the bibliography titles have been translated where it was meaningful to do so, since they normally designate the contents of the documents and reports. They are not necessarily, however, available in English translations under these titles.–*Tr. note*]

Bredt, Alfred. *The Origins of the League of German Officers in Captivity*
BBC Monitoring service. *Daily Digest World Broadcasts,* 1943–1945
Daniels, Alexander Edler v. Minutes of October 4, 1943
Einsiedel, Heinrich Graf v. *The National Committee and its Responsibilities for the Prisoners of War*
*Free Germany. Research and Analysis Branch* (U.S. Dept. of State, November 26, 1943)
*Freies Deutschland.* Official organ of the National Committee Free Germany
    Vol. I (1943), Nos. 1–24
    Vol. II (1944), Nos. 1–52
    Vol. III (1945), Nos. 1–44
Appeals, leaflets, and handouts (1943–1945), material on organizational matters (1943)
Minutes on: (a) the founding of the League of German Officers
    (b) the final session of the National Committee for a Free Germany at Camp Lunyovo, November 2, 1945 (unpublished copy)
*Twenty-five Articles for Ending the War,* Stockholm 1944
*Christians for a New Germany,* privately printed, 1945
Gerlach, Heinrich. *The Recruiting of the Generals; The Attitude of the Communists in the National Committee and the League of German Officers; The Huber Case*
German Communications to the Troops, 1944: on Paulus and the National Committee

Hadermann, Ernst. *How Can We End the War? The Honest Word of a German Captain.* Moscow 1942

*Kaltenbrunner reports* (on the investigations relating to the plot of July 20, 1944)

National Committee for a Free Germany. *To NSFO* (National Socialist Political Officers) *of the German Army and Air Force in the East*

Paulus, Friedrich. *After the Battle; The Founding of the "League of German Officers"; My joining of the "Free Germany" movement*

*Political Service of SS and Police.* Ed. by Der Reichsführer SS, SS-Hauptamt (Central Office), Series 1, 1944

Radio Reich (*Reichssender*) (1944)

Report by K.H.F.

*Seehaus, Special Service: Radio Monitoring Reports,* 1943–1945

Selle, Herbert. *Stalingrad Then—and Now* (1949)

Seydlitz, Walther v. *Evaluation of the Sixth Army's Position in the Stalingrad Pocket* (Memorandum of Nov. 25, 1942); *Commentary 1944* (December 1944); *Who Is Responsible for Germany's Misery?* (1945); *The Reasons for my Joining the "League of German Officers" and the "National Committee for a Free Germany"* (December 14, 1955)

*Soldiers of the Eastern Front.* Proclamation by Colonel General Guderian.

*Socialist Communications.* London 1943, September-October; 1945, January-February

*Stalingrad,* Zurich 1945

*Verfügungen/Anordnungen/Bekanntgaben.* Ed. by the Central Office of the NSDAP (*Parteikanzlei*), Vol. 7, Part 2, 1944

Wehrmacht High Command. Communications to the Officers Corps. October 1943 (Special edition: The Moscow Committee Free Germany)

*What Are the Aims of the National Committee for a Free Germany?* Ed. by the German Army High Command

Newspapers used: *New York Times* (1943, 1945), *New York Herald Tribune* (1943), London *Times* (1943), *New Statesman and Nation* (1943), *Neue Zürcher Zeitung* (1943), *Basler Nachrichten* (1943), *Völkischer Beobachter* (1944), and *Front und Heimat* (1944).

## Oral and written testimony:

1 *On the National Committee and the League of German Officers:*

| | |
|---|---|
| H. Abel | H. Graf v. Einsiedel |
| A. Bredt | C.F. |
| H. Burmeister | H. Gerlach |

A. Greifenhagen
H. Hennersdorf
O. Jahn
J. Kayser
I. v. Knobelsdorff-Brenkenhoff
F.W.K.
W. Leonhard
F. Löwenthal
A. Ludwig

Th. Plievier
J. v. Puttkamer
H. Schlömer
J. Schröder
W. Frhr. v. Senfft-Pilsach
W. v. Seydlitz
J. Wieder
W.W. v. Wildemann
H.Z.

2 Communications of materials from the estate of Field Marshal General Paulus and notes of personal recollections by his son, E.A. Paulus.

3 *On the generals:*

G. Blumentritt
E.B.
E. Dethleffsen
H. Foertsch
M. Fretter Pico
H. Friessner

F. Hossbach
Lieb
Frhr. v. L.
E. v. Manstein
K. v. Tippelskirch

4 *On diplomacy:*

v. Herwarth
G. Hilger

E. Kordt
P. Schmidt

5 *On the Führer's Headquarters:*

G. Engel
A. Heusinger
W. Scheidt

P.E. Schramm
H. v. Wedel

6 *On the resistance circles:*

Frhr. v. Gersdorff
E. Gerstenmaier
H. B. Gisevius
F. Hielscher
P. van Husen
E. Jünger
J. Kaiser
H.-J. v. Kleist-Retzow
J. Kuhn

A. Leber
R. Pechel
F. v. Schlabrendorff
H. Speidel
A. Graf Schenk v. Stauffenberg
Th. Steltzer
K. Strölin
F. v. Teuchert

There were additional witnesses who did not wish to be named. They were used for general references, as was the evidence given by numerous German officers and soldiers. To mention them all by name would have made this list completely unreadable.

## Printed sources and secondary materials:

Bamm, Peter. *Die unsichtbare Flagge,* Munich 1952
Benary, Albert. *Die Berliner Bären–Division,* Bad Nauheim 1955
*Bilanz des Zweiten Weltkrieges,* Oldenburg (Oldbg.)/Hamburg 1953
Boehm, Eric H. "The 'Free Germans' in Soviet Political Warfare," in: *The Public Opinion Quarterly,* 14/II, 1950
Bohn, Helmut. *Vor den Toren des Lebens,* Überlingen 1949; "Die patriotische Karte in der sowjetischen Deutschlandpolitik," in: *Ost-Probleme,* VI/Nr. 38
Breithaupt, Hans. *Die Geschichte der 30. Infanterie-Division 1939–1945,* Bad Nauheim 1955
Buxa, Werner. *Weg und Schicksal der 11. Infanterie-Division,* Kiel 1952
Choltitz, Dietrich v. *Soldat unter Soldaten,* Konstanz/Zurich 1951
Churchill, Winston S. *Der Zweite Weltkrieg,* III, *Die Grosse Allianz,* Zweites Buch: "Amerika im Krieg," Bern 1950; *The Second World War,* Vol. V, "Closing the Ring," London 1952
Ciechanowski, I. *Defeat in Victory,* New York 1947
Dallin, Alexander. *Deutsche Herrschaft in Russland 1941–1945,* Düsseldorf 1958
Deane, I. R. *Ein seltsames Bündnis,* Vienna, n.d.
Deuerlein, Ernst. *Die Einheit Deutschlands,* Frankfurt a. M./Berlin 1957
Deutscher, I. *Stalin,* Stuttgart 1951
Dibold, Hans. *Arzt in Stalingrad,* Salzburg 1949
*Die Front war überall,* Berlin 1958
Doerr, Hans. *Der Feldzug nach Stalingrad,* Darmstadt 1955
Dulles, Allen Welsh. *Verschwörung in Deutschland,* Kassel 1949
Ehlers, Dieter. *Die Methoden der Beck/Goerdeler-Verschwörung,* Bonn, n.d.
Einsiedel, Heinrich Graf v. *Tagebuch der Versuchung,* Berlin/Stuttgart 1950
Engermann, Andreas. *Einen Bessern fundst Du nicht,* Bad Wörishofen 1952
Fischer, Kurt J. *Der Gefangene von Stalingrad,* Willsbach (Württ.) 1948
Florin, Wilhelm. *Warum kämpft Hitler gegen die Sowjetunion?,* Moscow 1942
Fraenkel, Heinrich and Manvell, Roger. *Goebbels,* Cologne/Berlin 1960
Franz, Ingbert. *Licht im Osten,* Eichstätt/Vienna/Düdingen 1952
Friessner, Hans. *Verratene Schlachten,* Hamburg 1956
Gackenholz, Hermann. "Zum Zusammenbruch der Heeresgruppe Mitte im Sommer 1944" in: *Vierteljahrshefte für Zeitgeschichte,* Vol. III, 1955, 3
Gerlach, Heinrich. *Die verratene Armee,* Munich 1957

Gilbert, Felix. *Hitler Directs His War*, New York 1950

Glonjadewski, Gertrud and Schumann, Heinz. *Die Neubauer-Poser-Gruppe*, Berlin 1957

Goebbels, Joseph. *Tagebücher 1942–1943*; edited by Louis P. Lochner, Zurich 1948

Görlitz, Walter. *Der Zweite Weltkrieg 1939–1945*, 2 vols., Stuttgart 1952/53

Golwitzer, Helmut. *. . . und führen, wohin du nicht willst*, Munich 1951

Graml, Hermann. "Das Nationalkomitee 'Freies Deutschland,'" in: *Neues Abendland*, VII, 1952

Grams, Rolf. *Die 14. Panzer-Division 1940–1945*, Bad Nauheim 1957

Greiner, Helmuth. *Die oberste Wehrmachtführung 1939–1943*, Wiesbaden 1951

Günther, Joachim. *Das letzte Jahr*, Hamburg 1948

Hahn, Assi. *Ich spreche die Wahrheit!*, Esslingen 1951

Hammerstein, Kunrat Freiherr v. "Schleicher, Hammerstein und die Machtübernahme 1933," in: *Frankfurter Hefte*, Vol. XI, 1956, 1; "Manstein," in *Frankfurter Hefte*, Vol. XI, 1956, 7.

Hasemann, Richard. *Gejagt*, Stuttgart 1953

Hassell, Ulrich v. *Vom andern Deutschland*, Zurich/Freiburg im Breisgau, n.d.

Haupt, Werner. *Kurland*, Bad Nauheim 1960

Hauschild, Reinhard. *Plus-Minus-Null*, Darmstadt 1952

Hausser, Paul. *Waffen-SS im Einsatz*, Göttingen 1953

Herhudt v. Rhoden, Hans-Detlef. *Die Luftwaffe ringt um Stalingrad*, Wiesbaden 1950

Heusinger, Adolf. *Befehl im Widerstreit*, Tübingen/Stuttgart 1950

Himmler, Heinrich. "Rede vor den Gauleitern am 3. August 1944," in: *Vierteljahrshefte für Zeitgeschichte*, Vol. I, 1953, 4

Hohoff, Curt. *Woina-Woina*, Düsseldorf/Cologne 1951

Hossbach, Friedrich. *Die Schlacht um Ostpreussen*, Überlingen 1951

Hull, Cordell. *The Memoirs*, London 1948

Humbert, Philipp. "Ich bitte erschossen zu werden," in: *Der Spiegel*, III, 1949, 5–11

*Journal of Central European Affairs*, I/1941–42

Kahn, Siegbert. *The Nationalcommittee Free Germany*, London 1943

Kern, Erich. *Der grosse Rausch*, Waiblingen 1950

Klatt, Paul. *3. Gebirgsdivision 1939–1945*, Bad Nauheim 1958

Kleist, Peter. *Zwischen Hitler und Stalin*, Bonn 1950

Klepper, Jochen. *Überwindung*, Stuttgart 1958

Kluke, Paul. "Nationalsozialistische Europaideologie," in: *Vierteljahrshefte für Zeitgeschichte*, Vol. III, 1955, 3

Korfes, Otto. "Zur Geschichte des Nationalkomitees 'Freies Deutschland,'" in: *Zeitschrifte für Geschichtswissenschaft*, Vol. VI, 1958, 6

Kuby, Erich, ed. *Das Ende des Schreckens*, Munich, n.d.

Kuczynski, Jürgen. *Freie Deutsch—Damals und heute*, London 1943

Langmaack, Kurt. *Stacheldraht statt Sozialismus*, Hamburg 1952

Leahy, W. D. *I Was There*, London 1950

Leonhard, Wolfgang. *Die Revolution entlässt ihre Kinder*, Cologne/Berlin 1955

*Letzte Briefe aus Stalingrad*, Frankfurt am Main/Heidelberg 1950

Löwenthal, Fritz. *Die neue Geist von Potsdam*, Hamburg 1948

Lowenfeld, A. F. "The Free Germany Committee," in: *The Review of Politics*, 14/1952

Lüdde-Neurath, Walter. *Regierung Dönitz*, Göttingen 1950

Manstein, Erich v. *Verlorene Siege*, Bonn 1955

Meinecke, Friedrich. *Die deutsche Katastrophe*, Wiesbaden 1949

Meissner, Boris. *Russland, die Westmächte und Deutschland*, Hamburg 1954

Michel, Karl. *Ost und West—Der Ruf Stauffenbergs*, Zurich 1947

Moltke, Helmuth James Graf v. "Einer vom deutschen Widerstand. Die Letzten Briefe des Grafen Moltke" in *Neue Auslese*, Vol. II, 1947, 1

Nitzsche, Gerhard. *Die Saefkow-Jacob-Bästlein-Gruppe*, Berlin 1957

Oechelhaeuser, Justus W. *Wir zogen in das Feld*, Boppard am Rhein 1960

Paetel, Karl O. "Das Nationalkomitee 'Freies Deutschland,'" in: *Politische Studien*, Vol. VI, 1956, 69

Paulus. *"Ich stehe hier auf Befehl!,"* Frankfurt am Main 1960

Plesse, Werner. "Zum antifaschistischen Widerstandskampf in Mitteldeutschland (1939–1945)," in: *Zeitschrift für Geschichtswissenschaft*, Vol. II, 1954, 6

Podewils, Clemens. *Don und Wolga*, Munich 1952

Puttkamer, Jesco v. *Irrtum und Schuld*, Neuwied/Berlin 1948

Rauch, Georg v. *Geschichte des bolschewistischen Russland*, Wiesbaden 1955

Rendulic, Lothar. *Gekämpft, gesiegt, geschlagen*, Heidelberg 1952

Ritter, Gerhard. *Carl Goerdeler und die deutsche Widerstandsbewegung*, Stuttgart 1954

Scheringer, Richard. *Das grosse Los*, Hamburg 1959

Schiebold, Kurt. *Opfergang in Rumänien*, Tubingen 1952

Schlabrendorff, Fabian v. *Offiziere gegen Hitler*, Zurich/Vienna/Konstanz 1946

Schröter, Heinz. *Stalingrad*, Osnabrück, n.d.

Schultz, Joachim. *Die letzten dreissig Tage*, Stuttgart 1951

Selle, Herbert. *Die Tragödie von Stalingrad*, Hannover 1948

Senger und Etterlin, Frido v. *Krieg in Europa*, Cologne/Berlin 1960

Sherwood, R. *Roosevelt und Hopkins*, Hamburg 1950

*Sie kämpften für Deutschland*, Berlin 1959

Stalin, J. *Über den Grossen Vaterländischen Krieg der Sowjetunion,* Moscow 1946

Teske, Hermann. *Die silbernen Spiegel,* Heidelberg 1952

Thorwald, Jürgen. *Es begann an der Weichsel,* Stuttgart 1951; *Das Ende an der Elbe,* Stuttgart 1950

Tippelskirch, Kurt v. *Geschichte des Zweiten Weltkriegs,* Bonn 1951

Toepke, Günter. *Stalingrad—wie es wirklich war,* Stade 1949

Vermehren, Isa. *Reise durch den letzten Akt,* Hamburg 1947

Vormann, Nikolaus v. *Tscherkassy,* Heidelberg 1954

Weinert, Erich. *Memento Stalingrad,* Berlin 1951; *Das Nationalkomitee "Freies Deutschland" 1943–1945,* Berlin 1957

Wieder, Joachim. *Die Tragödie von Stalingrad,* Deggendorf 1955; "Welches Gesetz befahl den deutschen Soldaten, an der Wolga zu sterben?," in: *Frankfurter Hefte,* Vol. XI, 1956, 5

Wurm, Franz F. "Schuld und Niederlage der Antifa" in: *Neues Abendland,* VII, 1952

Zeller, Eberhard. *Geist der Freiheit—Der zwanzigste Juli,* Munich, n.d.

*Zur Geschichte der deutschen antifaschistischen Widerstandsbewegung 1933–1945. Materialien, Berichte, Dokumente,* Berlin 1958

## Index of Names

308 / FREE GERMANY

# DATE DUE

| 5-20-75 | | | |
|---------|---|---|---|
| | | | |
| | | | |
| | | | |
| | | | |
| | | | |
| | | | |
| | | | |
| | | | |
| | | | |
| | | | |
| | | | |
| | | | |
| | | | |
| | | | |
| | | | |
| | | | |
| | | | |

GAYLORD                                PRINTED IN U.S.A.